Peace at All Costs

Studies in Contemporary European History

Editors:
Konrad Jarausch, University of North Carolina, Chapel Hill
Henry Rousso, Institut d'historie du temps présent, CNRS, Paris

Recent volumes:

Volume 23
Peace at All Costs: Catholic Intellectuals, Journalists, and Media in Postwar Polish–German Reconciliation
 Annika Elisabet Frieberg

Volume 22
From Eastern Bloc to European Union: Comparative Processes of Transformation since 1990
 Edited by Günther Heydemann and Karel Vodička

Volume 21
Migration, Memory, and Diversity: Germany from 1945 to the Present
 Edited by Cornelia Wilhelm

Volume 20
Ambassadors of Realpolitik: Sweden, the CSCE and the Cold War
 Aryo Makko

Volume 19
Wartime Captivity in the 20th Century: Archives, Stories, Memories
 Edited by Anne-Marie Pathé and Fabien Théofilakis

Volume 18
Whose Memory? Which Future? Remembering Ethnic Cleansing and Lost Cultural Diversity in East, Central and Southeastern Europe
 Edited by Barbara Törnquist-Plewa

Volume 17
The Long Aftermath: Cultural Legacies of Europe at War, 1936–2016
 Edited by Manuel Bragança and Peter Tame

Volume 16
Memory and Change in Europe: Eastern Perspectives
 Edited by Małgorzata Pakier and Joanna Wawrzyniak

Volume 15
Tailoring Truth: Politicizing the Past and Negotiating Memory in East Germany, 1945–1990
 Jon Berndt Olsen

Volume 14
Shaping the Transnational Sphere: Experts, Networks and Issues from the 1840s to the 1930s
 Edited by Davide Rodogno, Bernhard Struck, and Jakob Vogel

Volume 13
Samizdat, Tamizdat, and Beyond: Transnational Media during and after Socialism
 Edited by Friederike Kind-Kovács and Jessie Labov

For a full volume listing, please see the series page on our website:
http://berghahnbooks.com/series/contemporary-european-history

Peace at All Costs

Catholic Intellectuals, Journalists, and Media
in Postwar Polish–German Reconciliation

Annika Elisabet Frieberg

berghahn
NEW YORK • OXFORD
www.berghahnbooks.com

First published in 2019 by

Berghahn Books

www.berghahnbooks.com

© 2019, 2024 Annika Elisabet Frieberg
First paperback edition published 2024

All rights reserved.
Except for the quotation of short passages
for the purposes of criticism and review, no part of this book
may be reproduced in any form or by any means, electronic or
mechanical, including photocopying, recording, or any information
storage and retrieval system now known or to be invented,
without written permission of the publisher.

Library of Congress Cataloging-in-Publication Data

Names: Frieberg, Annika Elisabet, author.
Title: Peace at All Costs: Catholic Intellectuals, Journalists, and Media in Postwar Polish–German Reconciliation / Annika Elisabet Frieberg.
Description: New York: Berghahn Books, 2019. | Series: Studies in Contemporary European History; volume 23 | Includes bibliographical references and index.
Identifiers: LCCN 2019011737 (print) | LCCN 2019016145 (ebook) | ISBN 9781789200256 (ebook) | ISBN 9781789200249 (hardback: alk. paper)
Subjects: LCSH: Poland—Relations—Germany (West)—History. | Germany (West)—Relations—Poland—History. | Reconciliation—Political aspects—Poland—History—20th century. | Reconciliation—Political aspects—Germany (West)—History. | Catholics—Political aspects—Poland—History—20th century. | Catholics—Political aspects—Germany (West)—History. | Mass media—Political aspects—Poland—History—20th century. | Mass media—Political aspects—Germany (West)—History.
Classification: LCC DK4185.G3 (ebook) | LCC DK4185.G3 F75 2019 (print) | DDC 303.48/243043809045—dc23
LC record available at https://lccn.loc.gov/2019011737

British Library Cataloguing in Publication Data

A catalogue record for this book is available from the British Library.

ISBN 978-1-78920-024-9 hardback
ISBN 978-1-80539-312-2 paperback
ISBN 978-1-80539-425-9 epub
ISBN 978-1-78920-025-6 web pdf

https://doi.org/10.3167/9781789200249

Contents

Acknowledgments	vi
Introduction	1
Chapter 1. Unexpected Meetings and New Beginnings: Inspirations, Transformations, and Opportunities, 1939–58	24
Chapter 2. Victims, Heroes, and Dark Reflections: Polish Travelers, West German Journalists, and the New Relations, 1958–64	53
Chapter 3. Radio Relations: Klaus von Bismarck, Poland, and the Audiovisual Media Institutes	82
Chapter 4. Televising the Territorial Conflict: Documentary Portrayals of Polish–German Relations	107
Chapter 5. Of Forgiving and Forgetting: The Religious Memoranda and the Media, 1961–68	128
Chapter 6. Brandt-ing Reconciliation: Politics, Media, and New Relations, 1968–72	154
Chapter 7. Remembering and Rewriting Reconciliation: The 1990s	179
Conclusion	201
Bibliography	209
Index	238

Acknowledgments

The road to completing this book project has been a long one. I could not have done it without the generous assistance and support of many institutions, colleagues, and friends during several years, and I am immensely grateful to everyone who enabled me to research, complete, and publish *Peace at All Costs*.

I undertook my research with financial assistance from the Institut für Europäische Geschichte in Mainz and from the German Academic Exchange Service. An earlier summer grant from the International Studies Center of the University of North Carolina–Chapel Hill allowed me to initiate my research in Poland. Finally, a grant from the University of North Carolina–Chapel Hill permitted me to complete my initial research in a timely manner. In a later phase of the project, San Diego State University's College of Arts and Letters awarded me a Critical Thinking Grant, and the history department, especially my department heads Joanne Ferraro and Andrew Wiese, assisted and supported me in securing time to complete the manuscript.

A great number of scholars, librarians, and archivists have helped me find my way in archives across Central Europe, and I wish to thank these people who have generously shared their time and expertise with me. They include Michał Smoczyński at the then Archiwum Jerzego Turowicza in Krakow and the late Ewa Bąkowska at Jagiellonian University Library. I also wish to thank Dr. Birgit Bernard at the Historisches Archiv der WDR in Cologne, the Friedrich-Ebert-Stiftung in Bonn, the Polen-Institut in Darmstadt, and the Norddeutscher Rundfunk for their generous decision to permit me to use the audiovisual sources with Ludwig Zimmerer's radio shows from the 1960s. Others who helped at various stages of my research process included Błażej Kazmierczak at the Karl-Dedecius-Archiv at Collegium Polonicum der Europa-Universität Viadrina, Christoph Rohde at Norddeutscher Rundfunk, and Ulf Bollmann at Staatsarchiv Hamburg. The Indiana University History Department and my colleagues there, including but not limited to Maria Bucur, Christopher Molnar, Michelle Moyd, Julia Roos, and Mark Roseman provided intellectual feedback, encouragement and support along the way. Colleagues in the Working Group on Germany and Poland, organized by David Johnson, provided a stimulating intellectual framework for conversations on postwar Polish–German relations and their future. In equal measure Winson Chu, Andrew Demshuk, Brendan Karch, Piotr Kosicki, and Adam Seipp have supported and provided intellectual feedback for this project. I am grateful to C. K. Martin Chung and Jean-Pierre Cabestan at Hong Kong Baptist University for the opportunity to participate in a comparative, interdisciplinary project in 2014 on the strengths and weaknesses of political reconciliation processes. I also wish to thank Karlheinz Koppe, Klaus Otto Skibowski, Hansjakob Stehle, and Stanisław Stomma, as well as Winfried Lipscher, Joanna Olczak-Ronikier, Gottfried Erb, and Renate Marsch-Potocka, for agreeing to talk to me and to share their memories, reflections, and thoughts on these events.

Konrad Jarausch has of course been integral to the conceptualization of this project, and he has provided continual support, mentoring, and advice. At the University of North Carolina–Chapel Hill, Chad Bryant, Christopher Browning, Karen Hagemann, and Madeline Levine provided mentorship, gave feedback on translations, and assisted this project in its early stages. Benjamin Pearson, Rósa Magnúsdóttir, Jennifer Walcoff-Neuheiser and Bethany Keenan each read parts of it as well. Later on, Peter Polak-Springer and Edward Beasley gave helpful feedback on parts of or the entire manuscript. Padraic Kenney and Frank Biess provided mentorship, advice, and help in its various stages. I also wish to thank Kathryn Epstein for her careful professional editing of the full manuscript. Steven Franklin and Patrice Dabrowski graciously assisted me with translations between Polish, German, and English. Of course, any remaining errors in this regard are entirely mine. Finally, I am very grateful to Chris Chappell, Soyolmaa Lkhagvadorj, and to my anonymous readers at Berghahn Books who provided me with honest, constructive, and clear-sighted reports and thus allowed for the content and argument of *Peace at All Costs* to be greatly improved and strengthened.

Other friends and colleagues in Europe also deserve a heartfelt thank you, including Simone Derix, Thomas Gijswijt, and Eike Eckert, who helped me localize source materials and further my ideas through conversations and feedback in Mainz. The Herder-Institut in Marburg, Hans Henning Hahn and Heidi Hein-Kircher, gave me an opportunity to present and receive feedback on my project in its early stages. The theoretical background of political and national myths, which was the topic of the Summer Academy in Marburg in the summer of 2004, continues to inform my work. Volker, Erika and Julia Keil, and Boris Schymetzko housed me during my time in Berlin and taught me to appreciate and love the city.

The final years of completing this project were quite difficult on a personal level due to health problems, family illness, and loss. For finding the time, resources, energy, and faith to persevere, I must credit family, friends, and my yoga practice. I want to thank Cliff Johnson and Julie Gillen for providing a creative and nurturing studio space for me during the revision at Lola's Fresh Patina in 2017, and my studio mates there for companionship during the revising process. Special thanks to John Metcalf for designing the front cover of this book. My parents and sister traveled halfway across the world to see me when I was unable to go to them. While they did not always understand the nature of my work, they still fully expected me to finish whatever projects I had taken on and trusted in my ability to do so. They also modeled the independence of mind, drive, and perseverance necessary to complete the book. My mother-in-law also unfailingly expressed her support for my plans, projects, and intellectual capacity. She also traveled great distances to see us and kept up my morale with a steady stream of care packages and cards. I am very lucky in my friendships. Edward Beasley must be mentioned again as someone who enabled me, through consistent practical and moral support, and with the help of healthy doses of sarcasm and bad jokes, to balance out a difficult professional and personal equation. Therese Choquette, Bhanu Kapil, Maria Rybakova, and Kristine Vendelsten all provided listening ears, shoulders to cry on, couches to crash on, and, basically, the necessary means to preserve sanity and balance. Finally, I want to thank my husband, Steven Seegel. Without him, this project would quite simply not have been possible. From endless cups of coffee and hot tea to his unwavering confidence in my capacity, the book project, and considerable efforts and sacrifices on my and its behalf, he has been part of it all the whole way. All my love, always.

This book is dedicated to my mother, Christina Frieberg, who waited long for its completion but did not get to see it happen. Only recently, and faced with losing her to cancer, did I understand the true importance of one of the key phrases in this book: "to forgive and ask for forgiveness." Förlåt, mamma . . . och tack!

INTRODUCTION

> War and peace start in the hearts of individuals.
>
> —Pema Chödrön

"For me, it always began with friendship!"[1] This comment by Stanisław Stomma during an interview about Polish–German relations on a rainy October afternoon in Warsaw in 2004 has stayed with me throughout this project. He was ninety-six when we spoke, and ill; he died a few months later. He had welcomed my request for an interview, however, and he seemed excited about the subject. Stomma was born in 1908 in Szacuny near Kėdainiai in today's Lithuania. He experienced the German occupation of Eastern Europe during the First World War as a young boy. His mother, a widow in an unstable region, drew on the support and aid of occupying German soldiers.[2] As a consequence, Stomma forged friendships with Germans, acquired fluency in the German language as well as an admiration for German culture. In the postwar era, he rejected mainstream Polish memories, which demonized all Germans as "Hitlerites."[3] He became an integral conversation partner in the earliest dialogue between Poles and West Germans in the 1950s, only eleven years after the end of the Second World War. Stomma embodied through his personal and public life the winding and complex path of Polish–German relations. As Polish–German relations waxed and waned, his engagement proved that personal backgrounds and individual agency mattered in these public and political developments. It also pointed to the entanglements, on structural and personal levels, that preceded and accompanied the reconciliation process. This book analyzes the role of civil-society groups and media along unconventional channels in Polish–German relations. It interrogates the concept of reconciliation in the Polish–German context as well as comparatively as a concept in international relations, creating an alternative narrative of the long-term challenges and successes in conflict resolution.

Notes for this chapter begin on page 18.

At its heart, this book traces the efforts of a highly influential network of Polish and West German intelligentsia and media personalities to promote and improve a particular version of religious and cultural Polish–German relations, which they termed reconciliation. They initiated dialogues, traveled and met across borders, networked, and struck up personal friendships. They attempted to begin dialogues in the interest of lasting peace. They acted through audiovisual and traditional media to counter prevalent victim-centered and antagonistic understandings of both nations and of Polish–German relations. In the late 1960s and 1970s, and again in the 1990s, their efforts intensified and drew more attention in connection to the interest surrounding Ostpolitik and the 1990 Two Plus Four Agreement, the official peace treaty after the Second World War.[4]

In the 1990s, the Polish Catholic publishers and West German participants in early relations wrote their own stories about Polish–German relations, particularly their religious and cultural dimensions. Together with politicians and scholars, they established the narrative of Polish–German reconciliation, a particular vision of improvement in postwar relations that came to dominate representations throughout the Cold War. This narrative was superimposed onto deeply entangled Central European populations and territories, and it also interacted with the process that Rogers Brubaker and others called the unmixing of Central European populations.[5] From its earliest days, it contained inherent tensions and contradictions, transnational actors insisting on national realities and civil-society pioneers prioritizing state relations. The reconciliation narrative simplified postwar relations into a two-sided ethnonational dialogue. The impact of this narrative on politics and the societies was significant but problematic. The activists contributed in the short term to change the discourse around Polish–German relations, to establish networks and introduce new media approaches to European peace. However, the long-term cost of their insistence on a linear narrative of steady improvements within a postwar national grid became the exclusion of certain segments of their populations, including the voices and alternative histories of surviving Jewish and other ethnic minorities, the voices of the displaced populations in Central Europe and the East Germans. Finally, one must consider to what extent and in which guises understandings of Polish–German relations reached beyond urban elites with already existing ties abroad.

Definitions, Methodology, and Historiography

In considering the reconciliatory aspects of postwar Polish–German relations, this book deals with three separate definitions of reconciliation: reconciliation as traditionally used in Polish–German relations; reconciliation as a framework for post-conflict engagement in international relations and peace studies, and reconciliation as a religious process. In Polish–German relations, reconciliation denoted a success story introduced for political purposes by media, politicians, religious groups, and scholars from the 1960s to the 1990s.[6] "Polish–German reconciliation" included efforts in West Germany and Poland to create closer relations, overcome tensions in the mutual past, and combat stereotypes and unjustified fears domestically vis-à-vis the other country. The efforts also included travels and meetings to build connections, the publication of a series of religious memoranda and statements, and, finally, efforts by public intellectuals and media to publicize and further those memoranda.[7]

Polish–German reconciliation as a media-driven political narrative in West German and Polish public space was a selective narrative. This analysis makes its exclusions as well as its inclusions visible. East Germans were occasionally invited to participate in the process or in meetings. Equally often, they were excluded. Reasons included their perceived loyalty to the East German communist state, a sense of rivalry between West and East Germans concerning positive relations to Poland, and, last but not least, a fear that by including East Germans the West German participants would inadvertently signal an acceptance of the division of Germany to a domestic and international audience. The East German Protestant initiative Aktion Sühnezeichen, a group that traveled into Poland for volunteer work at concentration camps as atonement for German crimes during the war, was fully accepted by and upheld a conversation and contacts with the same Polish groups as the West Germans. However, sources from this era do not indicate meetings and interactions in which all three groups took part. In addition, reconciliation as a narrative did not find its way into East German public space.

On the other hand, "peace" and "world peace" were important signifiers in communist East Germany. They denoted the resistance against a perceived Western military imperialism, including the nuclear threat, and it described socialism as a key aspect of world peace. While some of these notions were propaganda driven, many people in the communist states genuinely supported peace within this framework, and many active peace groups existed.[8] East German communist media described a successful Polish–German friendship as having begun in 1953 as East Germany recognized the Polish–East German postwar border.[9] As a consequence of such dynamics, East Germany and East Germans played a less active role in these emerging conversations about the past and present in the 1950s and 1960s.[10] The 1950s and 1960s dialogue and the resulting narrative also almost entirely excluded Jewish memories and voices. In Polish war memories during the Cold War, victimhood was primarily, if not exclusively, of Polish suffering.[11] In addition, as they considered Polish–German relations a question of national security and order, participants did not think inclusion of Jewish voices was necessary since the Jewish minority remaining in Poland was too small to constitute a substantial political force.

Secondly, definitions of reconciliation as used in peace and conflict-resolution studies, namely the healing of international or interethnic relations in the aftermath of conflict, serve here to pose more in-depth and critical questions about Polish–German relations by adding a theoretical comparative framework. These definitions involve models, roads, methods, and paths to reestablish postwar and postgenocidal intra- and international relations.[12] Peace scholars understand reconciliation as efforts on a collective and social level, such as apologies, reparations, justice, and the work of Truth and Reconciliation commissions, intended to heal damaged relationships and restore relations between ethnic groups, societies, or countries.[13] Thirdly, theological understandings of the term matter, particularly as they inspired many participants within these pages to engage with Polish–German relations. Reconciliation in a Christian context involves penitence, atonement, and, according to one participant in the relations, "the preparedness to carry the consequences of guilt and to offer compensation for injustices committed."[14] In theology, reconciliation is the result of penance and emphasizes inner transformation for the party atoning but also for the recipient of the action, if they are able to move toward forgiveness socially but also in the eyes of God.[15]

For both Polish and German media activists, there was also a sense that the impetus behind reconciliation came from civil society, the communicative space between the individual and the state.[16] Thus, it is also necessary to define civil society and its role in these events. David Ost in *Solidarity and the Politics of Anti-Politics* describes the idea of civil society as having become prominent to Polish opposition in the 1970s. Following earlier writers and philosophers, Ost, by using the term, wishes to highlight the "public role of citizens outside the government."[17] The groups here were civil-society actors in the sense that much of their activity took place outside of and sometimes in challenge to states and organized politics. However, Poland in the late 1950s to early 1970s, as Ost also points out, had a much more limited civil society than it did in the 1980s. Secondly, several of the Polish Catholic intellectuals traced here were indeed political actors, if marginal ones, in the late 1950s to the late 1960s. They had been allowed as a small group of opposition to join the Polish communist parliament, the Sejm. A few of them considered themselves representatives of the state.

On the West German side, while print media journalists were more clearly part of civil society, one must ask whether the radio and television employees were civil-society groups as civil servants, salaried by political entities. They did have considerable independence vis-à-vis organized politics, however, and considered it their role and duty to challenge and question state policy and leaderships. Both the Polish and German side pursued agendas that frequently fell outside of or contradicted state policy. One might argue that they took part in a civil-society dialogue. Religious and church actors fall more easily into the category of civil-society actors. While my intention here is to redirect the focus onto civil-society initiatives as mediated through the public sphere, it is difficult in reality to separate these groups and layers from one another.

The other organizing principle for the 1960s conversations is the notion of a public sphere, in Ost's words a space in which "something approaching public opinion can be formed."[18] The public sphere plays a role as the stage on which Polish–German reconciliation was presented, performed, debated, told, and retold as a positive postwar story. The public sphere was much more limited in Polish society than in the West German one, and this draws attention to the asymmetry of Polish–German relations as well as to the larger numbers of Polish citizens who were neither aware of nor engaged in this particular movement toward improved postwar relations. When we discuss concepts such as a media freedom, public space, and civil society, the differences between communist Poland and the Federal Republic are considerable. These sources nonetheless show surprising parallels between the two societies in that, on the one hand, a limited public sphere existed in Poland in the late 1950s to 1960s and, on the other, the West German state leadership made considerable, and not always constitutional, efforts to control its media and public space. In addition, debates in one state's media was picked up and carried on by other state's media in entangled developments throughout this time period. Ultimately, this argument and approach draws attention to the permeability of the Iron Curtain. It questions an east–west, starkly polarized, and symmetric approach to Polish–German relations.

Polish–German Relations as a Field of Research

Does the study of reconciliation have a place in scholarship today? Polish–German relations trended as a topic in the 1990s when the recently signed Treaty of Good Neighbourship and Friendly Cooperation between noncommunist Poland and united Germany seemed to indicate political success in the efforts to overcome the two countries' troubled past. The drive toward European integration and eastward expansion became a motivating factor in bringing attention and funding to the study of friendlier historical links and connections between the Polish and German peoples and societies. This body of research celebrated Polish–German reconciliation as more or less completed.[19] Finally, scholars of Catholicism in Poland and Europe have inserted the events surrounding Polish–German relations in the 1960s into analyses of the church's importance to postwar politics and of its liberal and illiberal strands of thought.[20] In most of these studies, Polish–German relations, although fraught and plagued by the past, were steadily improving in a linear fashion in the postwar era thanks to efforts of both Poles and Germans to find common ground for dialogue and cooperation. Since then, the optimism of those early postcommunist years has faded. Polish–German relations have faced new challenges, including cooperation within the European Union and other recent political developments, which preoccupy scholars.[21] The narrative of steady progress should be considered within four political objectives: the West German efforts to gain support among West German voters for Ostpolitik in the 1960s, the further efforts to ratify Ostpolitik in West Germany between 1970 and 1972, the elation surrounding the final peace and friendship treaties in 1990 and 1991, and, finally, Polish efforts to join the European Union in the 1990s and 2000s, and the German support for that bid.[22] Nonetheless, while not the fairytale ending many dreamed of in 1989 and 1990, comparative reconciliation studies still indicate the relative success of postwar efforts to improve relations and offset antagonism between Poland and West Germany. The stability and peace accomplished in the wake of the Second World War was a remarkable achievement, and today the task remains to make sure that countries in the region maintain working relations and do not revert back to open or armed hostilities.

Connection to Memory, Nationalism, and Transnationalism Studies

The complex, multinational, and transnational realities of nineteenth- and twentieth-century Central Europe provide another conceptual framework for this book. Significantly, Polish–German relations as a narrative recognized neither existing borderlands identities nor fluid or loosened national identities. It also downplayed ethnic diversity and complexities, such as Jewish, Ukrainian, German, Russian, or Belarussian existence in Polish lands or the roles these minorities played in twentieth-century historical developments. Thus, one must also understand the project of Polish–German reconciliation within the context of its omissions and silences.

The peace process in Europe was very closely linked to continuing efforts of nation-building and the restoration of control and authority to the states. In *Seeking Peace in the Wake of War*, the editors point out in their introduction that postwar European nation-states were "inventing or re-inventing themselves, or indeed being re-invented under pressure from others."[23] The individuals who promoted and worked for improved Polish–German relations continued their efforts to find formulas, acceptable for both sides, for postwar borders and belonging of Polish and German populations. In this sense, the peace process and multilayered dialogues contributed to construct homogeneous nation-states and national identities or, alternatively, to reconstruct the "mental maps" of audiences in the postwar era.[24] International relations scholars Siri Gloppen, Erin Skaar, and Astri Suhrke referenced Benedict Anderson's notion of "imagined communities" in the reconciliatory establishment of a "common narrative of the past and shared vision of the future" between formerly antagonistic groups.[25] In other words, in the discursive construction of peaceful relations, politicians and other participants strove also to reimagine and to reinforce the stable national communities created in 1945 and to downplay competing memories that undermined postwar stability.

Similarly, William J. Long and Peter Brecke established as a goal for one of their models of reconciliation "transcending certain beliefs about oneself and the other, that opens the possibility of new, beneficial relations."[26] In Polish–German relations those beliefs included entangled notions of what it meant to be of Polish or German nationality as defined and contrasted against the other nationality or against injustices suffered historically in the hands of the other nation.[27] Many of the participants themselves in Polish–German dialogue in the 1950s and 1970s had multicultural, multilingual, and, before the war, loosened or alternative national identities.[28] They felt it necessary as participants in the postwar peace process to conform on an individual as well as a national level to more rigid postwar national models. Historian Philip Nord writes that "a number of post-war states made the promotion of a unified, national consciousness a matter of policy-making priority."[29] In promoting European peace and stability, they also strove to suppress, marginalize, neutralize, or silence divisive or ill-fitting minority memories.

Through this case study of reconciliation efforts in Central European borderlands, I am contributing to understandings of conflict resolution from a historical perspective, illustrating how a peace process might work longitudinally and in areas with fluid national categories and tenuous state control. The approach of focusing on civil-society participation and developments in Polish–German relations brings attention to the interplay between current state structures, historic memories, and broader societal groups. In peace studies, Polish–German reconciliation has frequently been cited as a model for conflict resolution.[30] Such analysis must be mindful of the illusion of stable nation-states superimposed onto the shifting demography, geography, and ever-present violence of postwar Europe. International relations scholars must consider the wide and varied groups and stories that had to be excluded to make the optimistic narrative of progress and peace possible.[31]

This study has particularly drawn on models and understandings of reconciliation developed by international relations scholars William J. Long and Peter Brecke, and on Yinan He's understanding of "deep intrastate reconciliation."[32] Drawing on theories of evolutionary psychology, Long and Brecke described a "signaling model" of reconciliation in which a leading representative for one side performs a "costly signal that the other side is likely to interpret as a genuine offer to improve relations."[33] Meanwhile, their forgiveness model indicates "a process of forgiveness, transformation of certain emotions and transcending certain beliefs about oneself and the other, that opens the possibility of new beneficial relations."[34] While both of these models are helpful in understanding Polish–German relations, they are primarily applicable to communities whose ethnic or national belongings are clear and unquestioned. He posited that deep reconciliation, beyond addressing normalization and shared security or economic needs, must also be founded in a shared understanding between participating societies that "war is unthinkable and [that they] must hold generally amicable feelings toward one another."[35] She emphasized national mythmaking by elites as playing a central role in creating deep reconciliation.[36] Her model addressed the role and efforts by media and civil-society actors in preceding, complementing, and reinforcing peace efforts by states but once more paid scant attention to fluid national belongings or multiethnic historical memories.

Polish–German relations show the importance of considering initiatives toward and effects of peace processes beyond existing state frameworks. They also caution about the risks of focusing on short-term political success, stability, and especially marketing relations as successful for political purposes. Short-term gains might hamper long-term and genuine open-ended dialogue or alienate nonstate participants, in this case the growing Polish opposition, who later move into leading political roles.

Background: The Imperial and Interwar Era

The demography and borders as well as political systems in Poland and Germany shifted multiple times during the first half of the twentieth century. The oldest participants in the postwar dialogue, like Stomma, were born in the Russian and German empires. During the First World War, parts of Poland were occupied by Germany under the leadership of German military Ober-Ost. The Soviet Union followed Russia and the Weimar Republic followed the German Empire in 1917 and 1918. The third empire that had controlled Polish territory, Austria-Hungary, became multiple new states.[37] The 1919 Versailles Treaty ceded western Prussia and Silesia from Germany to Poland, and the interwar period saw territorial disputes in the east between Poland and the Soviet Union. The Polish-Soviet War, 1919–20, ended in the Treaty of Riga and a border agreement that left neither side completely satisfied. Poland gained control over parts of Ukraine, Lithuania, and Belarus, but the border treaty also meant that a large number of Poles became minorities in the Soviet territories.

Poland became an authoritarian state in 1926 when Józef Piłsudski led the military coup that installed *Sanacja*. Hitler assumed the role of chancellor of Germany in 1933, the end of the Weimar Republic. By 1939, Poland had lost its independence during the joint German-Soviet invasion and become occupied territory once more. In the ensuing six years, German occupying forces displaced 1.65 million Polish citizens and sent two million to Germany into forced labor. Five to six million Poles perished at the hands of German invading forces.[38] Fifty percent of those killed, that is to say ninety percent of Poland's Jewish population, perished in the Holocaust, in concentration camps, labor camps, ghettos, or during transportation to the camps. In the aftermath of the Second World War, Poland's western border was moved to the rivers Oder and Neisse, while its eastern border was redrawn to the Curzon Line.[39] The ten to thirteen million ethnic Germans who lived east of the Oder-Neisse Line became part of the diminished German lands and later of the four occupation zones that emerged as the two Cold War German states.[40] The Soviet Union also displaced 1.5 million ethnic Poles from the lands east of the Curzon Line westward. The cities of Lviv/Lwów, Vilnius/Wilno, and Hrodna/Grodno, which had been centers of Polish cultural life, now belonged to the Soviet republics of Ukraine, Lithuania, and Belarus. In 1946, after Nazi Germany's defeat, the communist Polish People's Republic followed.

The Participants—An Overview and Background

The lay Catholic Poles who worked toward reconciliation were born in the 1910s and 1920s. During the 1950s and 1960s, when most media was state controlled, they wrote for the semi-independent Catholic journals *Znak*, *Więź*, and *Tygodnik Powszechny*. Several of them were also members of a small Catholic group, the Znak Circle, who held seats in communist leader Władysław Gomułka's reconstituted parliament (the Sejm) after

1956. Leading figures included Stanisław Stomma; Jerzy Turowicz, the editor of *Tygodnik Powszechny*; Stefan Kisielewski, composer and writer for *Tygodnik Powszechny* and for the Parisian exile-journal *Kultura*; historian and Auschwitz survivor Władysław Bartoszewski; *Tygodnik Powszechny* writer Mieczysław Pszon; *Więź* editor Tadeusz Mazowiecki; and Znak Circle member Jerzy Zawieyski, a poet and an old friend of Polish party leader Władysław Gomułka.[41] Between the 1950s and the 1970s, these members of the Catholic intelligentsia and writers for the Catholic journals engaged with West German media personalities and travelers. Members of church hierarchy who supported the lay groups and, to an extent, the West German dialogue included Cardinal Karol Wojtyła of Cracow (later Pope John Paul II) as well as Bolesław Kominek, the archbishop of Wrocław.

In the Federal Republic, the participants belonged to several groups. One group consisted of religious activists. They included the Bensberger Circle in the late 1960s, an interest group of a hundred-some left-wing Catholics who wished to improve Polish–German relations and oppose West German nuclear rearmament.[42] In the Protestant Church, Polish–German activism emerged in the early 1960s among groups of lay Protestants. Over the next few years, groups within the Protestant Church leadership called for a new Eastern Policy and acceptance of the territorial losses in the east.[43] Their activity culminated in 1965 in a famous statement, the Protestant Expellee Memorandum. Under the aegis of the group Aktion Sühnezeichen, a group of East German Protestants also made efforts toward reconciliation through traveling to Poland, visiting concentration camps, and performing service there—demonstrations of penance on behalf of the German nation.

Another group consisted of media personalities, reporters, and journalists working for elite journals and newspapers, such as *Die Frankfurter Allgemeine Zeitung*, *Die Zeit*, *Der Spiegel*, and *Stern*, and for the audiovisual media, in particular the Cologne-based Westdeutscher Rundfunk (WDR) and Hamburg-based Norddeutscher Rundfunk (NDR). The editor of *Die Zeit*, the Countess Marion Dönhoff, the editor of *Stern*, Henri Nannen, and the director general of WDR, Klaus von Bismarck, great nephew of Germany's "Iron Chancellor" Otto von Bismarck and former Wehrmacht officer and Prussian landowner, provided some of the structural frameworks for writing and broadcasting on Polish–German relations. This group, beyond merely reporting on developments, made concerted efforts to establish connections in Poland with communists and noncommunists, and to reform the image of Poland in West German public space.[44]

Many of those involved in Polish–German relations came from an international, borderlands, or bilingual background. They had received their education in multiple countries, and their upbringing in multicultural regions and contexts influenced them through coexisting and competing regional, national, and supranational loyalties. Several of the contributors to *Tygodnik Powszechny* originally came from the Polish-Lithuanian borderlands and had attended gymnasium and university in Wilno, as the city of Vilnius was named in Polish at the time. The Lithuanian Poles' national identities and historical experiences, particularly during the First and Second World Wars, differed from other Poles.[45] Vilnius/Wilno was particularly diverse before the Second World War, consisting of equal numbers of Poles and Jews, as well as Russians, Belarussians, Lithuanians, Germans, and others.[46]

During the interwar era, these groups also spent extended times abroad. Stomma and Kisielewski lived at times in France in the late 1930s.[47] Jerzy Zawieyski lived in France between 1929 and 1933.[48] Jerzy Turowicz studied Maritain's texts, spoke fluent French, and was engaged through the university and through Catholic organizations in international congresses that took him to Vienna as well as Luxembourg.[49] Bishop Kominek studied at German schools in his youth, which enabled him to cultivate German connections then and later.[50] Both Stomma and Bishop Kominek spoke fluent German from childhood, facilitating their participation in Polish–German relations. Similarly, among German participants, Bensberger Circle member Winfried Lipscher spoke fluent Polish. He came from a German-speaking home but went to Polish gymnasium in the early postwar era before leaving for the Federal Republic.[51]

Many Germans involved in Polish–German relations and West German media concerned with Poland came from the eastern borderlands that the Allies transferred to Poland in 1945. They originated from Prussia, Silesia, Pomerania, Masuria, and from some of the cities that formerly had a German population, prominently Breslau/Wrocław. In these borderlands, particularly Silesia, religious or regional affiliations had competed with and sometimes superseded national ones.[52] Those with a borderlands background also included Catholic activists connected to the 1960s group that published the Bensberger Memorandum on Polish–German relations and some of the early correspondents working for West German audiovisual media in Poland.

East Prussian Marion Dönhoff and Pomeranian Klaus von Bismarck were members of the Prussian landed aristocracy. They were brought up into a sense of their own centrality as bureaucrats, responsible citizens, soldiers, and leaders. They lost their estates and positions but retained the understanding of themselves as national leaders by natural right and duty even as the nation had to be reconstituted along new, civilian lines. Their childhoods in Prussia in an area with a mixed ethnic population did not offset or weaken their national loyalties, but it did complicate them.

Their class had been integral to Prussia's state-building project since the eighteenth century, and they transferred their loyalty to the postwar West German state as well. However, they also had roots in a pan-European imperial nobility predating the nation-states in Central Europe.[53]

Germans involved in reconciliation also shared the experience of living extensively abroad. Television reporter and documentary maker Jürgen Neven-du Mont belonged to a prominent family associated with publishing house M. DuMont Schauberg in Cologne and Munich. His father was an artist in Munich. His family had branches in the Netherlands, England, and Italy as well as in Germany. Neven-du Mont was bilingual from his childhood schooling in Italy and felt comfortable in multiple countries. Warsaw correspondent for West German radio Ludwig Zimmerer, who became West German radio's earliest and most famous Warsaw correspondent during the Cold War, was born in 1924 in Augsburg. He finished gymnasium in December 1945, then entered the army but never actually saw battle. After Germany's surrender, he became a prisoner of war in France. With an ear for foreign languages, he quickly acquired a high degree of fluency in French. Eastern Europe expert commentator and journalist Hansjakob Stehle was born in 1927 in Ulm, where he finished primary school and gymnasium, but he was partially educated in Italy, spoke Italian, and later learned passable Polish. Overall, the biographies of these individuals speak to the entanglements of prewar European networks and lives.

After the war, in the absence of official diplomatic relations, these Polish and German Catholic organizations, networks, and media had to rely on preexisting connections to revive contacts across borders. The churches in Poland and Germany in the postwar era frequently reinforced ethnonational states, and nationalizing state missions, yet smaller groups within these institutions played key roles in reconciliation.[54] A majority of the participants in the dialogue were connected to such religious networks, and the Catholic and Protestant Churches played prominent roles in their lives and identities. In Poland, the postwar Catholic media, particularly *Tygodnik Powszechny*, was constituted around liberal Polish networks and intellectual schools of thought from the interwar era, particularly the Catholic interwar youth movement Odrodzenie (Rebirth).[55] Jerzy Turowicz and Stanisław Stomma met through Odrodzenie during the interwar era and continued their postwar collaboration in publishing *Tygodnik Powszechny*. The Catholic Church had cultural centers and meeting points, prominently Rome, that facilitated meetings and dialogues between Poles and Germans. As we will see, international Catholic media connections and the Second Vatican Council, 1962–65, would play a role in laying the foundation for new dialogue.[56] While functioning as political commentators, Ludwig Zimmerer and Hansjakob Stehle became engaged with

Polish–German questions specifically because of their interest in the Polish Catholic Church's relationship with the communist state. In West Germany, lay groups within both the Protestant and the Catholic Churches spearheaded powerful initiatives toward dialogue.

Legacies and Lessons from the Prewar Era

Fluidity, fragmentation, and change characterized Central European states in the first half of the twentieth century. In 1919, Poland had six currencies, three legal codes, and four languages of command in the army.[57] Many of the Polish Catholic intellectuals who became advocates for reconciliation were engaged in the strengthening and preservation of the newly founded Polish Second Republic in the interwar era. They sought to unify and modernize the republic while protecting its position in Europe and defining what it meant to be Polish in a post–Treaty of Versailles world. These conversations went beyond divisions in civic and ethnic nationalisms and were further complicated by ethnic, linguistic, and religious diversity as well as the looser connection between the new state and the nation.[58] In terms of national belonging, more open-ended federal state models based on the old Rzeczpospolita and associated with the ideas of Marshal Jozef Piłsudski competed with rigid ethnoreligious "Polak-Katolik" notions.[59] The differences also concerned Polish foreign policy. Roman Dmowski, Piłsudski's great rival, and leader of the Endecja, always considered Germans and Jews the greatest dangers to Polish sovereignty, whereas Piłsudski was more concerned with the Soviet threat. The Poles in Wilno/Vilnius, including Stomma, were generally in favor of the Piłsudskian ideals of Polishness and primarily concerned with the Soviet Union.[60] Jerzy Turowicz, in Cracow, also supported Piłsudski. His wife Anna was a niece of the famous general.[61]

Stefan Kisielewski, on the other hand, opposed Piłsudski and criticized from a left-wing perspective his ideas about a multinational state as well as Piłsudski's later coup d'état in Poland.[62] The members of Odrodzenie also sympathized to some extent with the political left but ultimately distanced themselves from the socialists. Stomma recalled in his memoirs, "The break with the Left was not easy, fundamentally or personally."[63] He stated that he shared with the left an awareness of social injustice and also felt closer to them in terms of the nationalities question. Stomma's reference to "personal" difficulty alludes to his resulting conflict with a friend who took a more radical left-wing turn.

Dmowskian ideas played a powerful role in interwar Poland and would carry over to influence postwar politics, including those of the Polish Catholic intelligentsia. In the prewar era, one of the activists furthest to the right was Mieczysław Pszon, who later wrote for *Tygodnik Powszechny* and became an important contact for East German Aktion Sühnezeichen. Pszon belonged to the far-right (anti-Semitic) spectrum of Polish politics in his youth. He later justified his position, describing himself as a conservative who believed in democracy but who had chosen to support the authoritarian nationalists, the Endecja, over the socialists because he saw them as his best option after democracy failed in Poland.[64] Bolesław Piasecki (1915–79), once the leader of the more extreme, deeply anti-Semitic and proto-fascist interwar movement Obóz Narodowo-Radykalny-Falanga (National-Radical Camp, ONR), founded the Catholic PAX movement after reinventing himself as a communist in 1945. Through PAX, he combined prewar right-wing ideals of ethnic nationalism and anti-Semitism with Catholicism and loyalty to the communist state. A number of members of the Catholic intelligentsia, for example *Więź* editor Tadeusz Mazowiecki, initially joined PAX, only to leave it later on to join other groups.[65]

Among the German advocates for reconciliation, only a few were old enough to be politically active in the interwar era. Walter Dirks, initiator of the Bensberger Circle, was a well-known Catholic socialist and radio personality already in the 1920s. He came from a working- or lower-middle-class background, completed his Abitur in 1920 and began to study theology at the university. His older brother died in combat in the German reoccupation of the Ruhr in 1923. Anchored in multiple civil-society organizations in Weimar Germany from a young age, he had been part of the youth movement Wandervogel (the wandering birds) and a leading member of another youth movement, Quickborn. These organizations were characterized by "pathos for truth and striving for authenticity in pulling bourgeois youth out of the bourgeois world," and such engagement carried over into Dirks's later societal engagement as well.[66] As he grew older, Dirks became engaged with the peace movement. He was the editor of left-wing Catholic *Rheinmainischen Volkszeitung* from 1924. During the Nazi era, Dirks went into internal emigration.[67]

Klaus von Bismarck and Marion Countess Dönhoff were conservative centrists during the interwar era. Neither supported the National Socialists. In his memoirs *Aufbruch aus Pommern*, published in 1996, von Bismarck described himself as having been politically very naive at that time. He had made typical choices of someone from his background, studying agrarian science to be able to assist his widowed mother in managing the family estate and joining the army in 1934.[68] He described himself as apolitical but bound by a duty to the nation, incidentally a common refrain of other officers taking part in the invasion on the eastern front.[69]

Why would a former landowner and officer from the Junker class become a spokesman for reconciliation with Poland? Von Bismarck attempted in his memoirs to trace in his prewar background the reasons that he later came to deviate politically from his compatriots. In part, he credited his political choices to his father who he recalled as a nonconformist, although his brother Philipp, later a prominent expellee politician, disagreed.[70] Although von Bismarck grew up in largely Polish-speaking Pomerania, he did not know many Poles personally.[71] As we will see later, von Bismarck's true engagement seemed to have grown from his religious beliefs, war experiences and his experiences with displacement and loss following the war.

As for participants in the groups from West German print and audiovisual media, they benefitted from what Helmut Kohl once called "the blessings of a late birth," and most were not directly politically involved with either support or resistance to the National Socialists in interwar Germany or the early days of the Third Reich.[72] They traced their earliest memories to the 1930s and the early Nazi era. They came of age, began school, and became highly indoctrinated into the Third Reich but were too young to vote or become party members and were only drafted in the end stages of the war, if at all. As young *Flakhelfer*, some of them participated in the final defense of Germany and later struggled to survive during the first harsh postwar winters in the German occupation zones.[73] They shared in the deep shock and full disillusionment in the Nazi state. The fall of Nazi Germany created in them a deep distrust of propaganda and ideology. They have been called the "skeptical generation."[74] This younger group would rise quickly into prominent positions in the West German media because an older generation of journalists had been decimated in the war or, in some cases, were professionally compromised by working for the Nazi press. From these positions, they became able to create substantial media platforms for the promotion of Poland, Polish–German relations, and reconciliation. Their skepticism toward traditional forms of patriotism and national pride also later colored Polish–German relations and their expressions in the media during the postwar era.

Chapter Breakdown

This book is organized into seven chapters. Chapters 1 and 2 show the motivations behind and practical approaches to peace-building outside of official and state efforts in Polish–German relations. They illustrate the significance of networking and travels in establishing cross-border cooperation in a politically unsupportive climate, and in renegotiating personal and public memories of the past within a mutually acceptable framework.

Chapter 1, "Unexpected Meetings and New Beginnings: Inspirations, Transformations, and Opportunities, 1939–58," describes the war and immediate postwar experiences of participants, outlining how these contributed to their ability and willingness to engage with postwar Polish–German relations and how they shaped participants' political views in profound ways. Chapter 1 also describes the way in which the 1956 Polish October became a turning point in Polish–West German relations.

Chapter 2, "Victims, Heroes, and Dark Reflections: Polish Travelers, West German Journalists, and the New Relations, 1958–64," expands on the role of face-to-face interactions between West German journalists and correspondents and Polish Catholic publishers and intelligentsia in establishing relations. Drawing on their Polish contacts, these journalists modified the prevailing West German anticommunist stereotypes of Poland and offset dominant memories of German victimization during the Second World War while striving to reinforce postwar national boundaries. The chapter also shows how understandings of postwar Poland's need for internal stability and the necessity of reforming communism from the inside informed West German media coverage.

Chapter 3, "Radio Relations: Klaus von Bismarck, Poland, and the Audiovisual Media Institutes," and chapter 4, "Televising the Territorial Conflict: Documentary Portrayals of the Polish–German Relations," describe work in audiovisual media to further disseminate and shape new understandings of Polish–German relations. Public controversies about the expellee question, the Oder-Neisse Line, and Polish–German relations as they played out in audiovisual media functioned as catalysts for reformulating German historical self-perceptions. In addition, the format of radio and television contributed to the nationalizing aspects of the reconciliation narrative, often to the exclusion or marginalization of problematic minority perspectives and voices.

Chapter 5, "Of Forgiving and Forgetting: The Religious Memoranda and the Media, 1961–68," shows the interconnectedness between media and religious reconciliatory statements and memoranda in Polish–German relations. The documents in this dialogue included the Polish bishops' letter of reconciliation to the German Catholic bishops and the Protestant Expellee Memorandum in 1965.[75] Again, the chapter indicates the trend of retrenching postwar national identities further as reconciliation messages were disseminated through media channels and public controversies to broader layers of the population in both societies.

Chapter 6, "Brandt-ing Reconciliation: Politics, Media and New Relations, 1968–72" shows the effects of political lobbying on reconciliation connected to the West German Ostpolitik's effect. The chapter also incorporates a larger context of simultaneous Polish–German–Jewish relations as it related to Polish–German relations, memories of the Second World War, and to participants' engagement with the anti-Zionist campaign by the Gomułka government in 1968. The chapter shows that the efforts to salvage Ostpolitik despite the 1968 purge and the Prague Spring's ending in some ways hampered reconciliation.

Finally, chapter 7, "Remembering and Rewriting Reconciliation: The 1990s," discusses how politicians, civil-society institutions, and the activists themselves remembered, complicated, celebrated, and rewrote the 1960s and 1970s reconciliation project in the early 1990s. The chapter explores the purposes of the reconciliation narrative in the 1990s political landscape, particularly with regards to Poland's ambition to join the North Atlantic Treaty Organization (NATO) and the European Union, and the reunited Germany's ambition to support this project while simultaneously furthering European integration.

Today, Polish–German relations are troubled. The current Polish government is hesitant to support or improve the relationship with Germany and has actively attempted to revive older anti-German sentiments in the population—for example, through the demand for reparations for war damages—for political purposes.[76] It may seem that postwar peace and good relations in Europe were just an illusion or a short-lived experiment. The conversations described here created openings and connections and established common ground for a dialogue, but they also suppressed problematic topics in relations and excluded segments of the German and Polish societies from the conversation, potentially creating divisions and a sense of alienation that could later be used politically to undermine European cooperation and stability.

What then is left of the reconciliation efforts, and what lessons can we take from the developments in the postwar era? First, models of peace-building need to extend beyond state relations into broader layers of societies and into multiple groups within those societies. In attempting to construct durable peace, activists and politicians must count on the possibility that the state with whom they are engaging may not survive long term. Secondly, today as much as in the early postwar era, we need groups and networks of moderates and patient peace-builders engaged in dialogue on our political scenes, domestically and internationally. In Poland a new generation of politicians has at times accused the groups of moderates who built postwar relations of being German lackeys.[77] National paradigms and the defense of national frameworks continue to exist uneasily with multinational or transnational individuals or trends in European history. Nevertheless, such trends and individuals play central roles in troubled relations by forging connections or finding common ground when states are in transition or official relations are locked. The main characters of this analysis had weaknesses and blind spots, and they made mistakes. Their tasks were often difficult and tedious and certainly lacked the glamour of the resistance of 1989, or of those national heroes of old. However, they were to an equal extent patriots and protectors of their country's national interests. Within their understanding of what peace and stability meant and required, they worked actively and sometimes at great personal cost to create a durable peace in Europe.

Notes

1. Stanisław Stomma, interview by author, 7 October 2004.
2. Connections between occupying soldiers and women, often in vulnerable positions, occur frequently during wartime. See several of the essays on gender and occupation in Nancy M. Wingfield and Maria Bucur, eds., *Gender and War in Twentieth Century Eastern Europe* (Bloomington, IN, 2006). See for example Lulu Anne Hansen, "'Youth off the Rails': Teenage Girls and German Soldiers—A Case Study in Denmark 1940–1945," in *Brutality and Desire: War and Sexuality in Europe's 20th Century*, ed. Dagmar Herzog (London, 2009), 135–67.
3. Wolfgang Pailer, *Stanisław Stomma: Nestor der polnisch-deutschen Aussöhnung* (Bonn, 1995), 26. These mainstream Polish memories of the Second World War, cultivated by veteran's organizations, the communist state, and media, are analyzed and outlined in Joanna Wawrzyniak, *Veterans, Victims, and Memory: The Politics of the Second World War in Communist Poland* (Frankfurt/Main, 2015), 25, 95 and throughout the text.
4. See Christoph-Mathias Brandt, *Souveränität für Deutschland: Grundlagen, Entstehungsgeschichte und Bedeutung des Zwei-plus-Vier-Vertrages vom 12. September 1990* (Cologne, 1993).
5. Rogers Brubaker, "Migrations of Ethnic Unmixing in the 'new Europe,'" *International Migration Review* 32, no. 4 (1998): 1047–65.
6. Aspects of Benedict Anderson's famous notion of the imagined nation can be applied in many ways to Polish–German relations, the necessity of reimagining the two nations, the construction of a communicative space, and the close association of nation-building with modernity. Benedict Anderson, *Imagined Communities: Reflections on the Origin and Spread of Nationalism* (London, 1983).
7. Hans-Adolf Jacobsen and Mieczysław Tomala, eds., *Bonn-Warschau 1945–1990: Analyse und Dokumentation* (Cologne, 1992); Mieczysław Tomala, *Patrząc na Niemcy: Od wrogości do porozumienia 1945–1991* (Warsaw, 1997); Anna Wolff-Powęska, ed., *Polacy wobec Niemców: Z dziejów kultury politycznej Polski 1945–1989* (Poznań, 1993). For a discussion of political uses of the concept of Polish–German reconciliation, see Klaus Bachmann, "Die Versöhnung muss von Polen ausgehen," in *Erinnerungskultur und Versöhnungskitsch*, ed. Hans Henning Hahn, Heidi Hein-Kirchner, and Anna Kochanowska-Nieborak (Marburg, 2008), 17–20.
8. Melissa Feinberg, *Curtain of Lies: The Battle over Truth in Stalinist Eastern Europe* (Oxford, 2017), 45–56.
9. Sheldon B. Anderson, *A Cold War in the Soviet Bloc: Polish–German Relations, 1945–1962* (Boulder, 2001). See also David Tomkins, *Composing the Party Line: Music and Politics in Early Cold War Poland* (West Lafayette, IN, 2013).

10. It should be noted that in the late 1970s and 1980s, the East German dissidents had connections with and sometimes modeled themselves on the Polish opposition. See for example Christhardt Henschel, "Aus der Geschichte lernen? Zweiter Weltkrieg, Wiederstand und der Oppositionsbewegungen in der DDR und der Volksrepublik Polen," in *Gegengeschichte: Zweiter Weltkrieg und Holocaust im ostmitteleuropäischen Dissens* (Leipzig, 2015), 57–78.
11. Michael Meng, *Shattered Spaces: Encountering Jewish Ruins in Postwar Poland and Germany* (Cambridge, MA, 2011), 28.
12. For examples of such scholarship, see Bruno Charbonneau and Genevieve Parent, eds., *Peacebuilding, Memory, and Reconciliation: Bridging Top-Down and Bottom-Up Approaches* (New York, 2012); Siri Gloppen, Elin Skaar, and Astri Suhrke, eds., *Roads to Reconciliation* (Lanham, MD, 2005); Yinan He, *The Search for Reconciliation: Sino–Japanese and German–Polish Relations since World War II* (Cambridge, 2009); Birgit Schwelling, ed., *Reconciliation, Civil Society, and the Politics of Memory* (Bielefeld, 2012).
13. Mark Gibney et al., eds., *The Age of Apology: Facing Up to the Past* (Philadelphia, 2009); Colleen Murphy, *A Moral Theory of Political Reconciliation* (Cambridge, 2012).
14. Helmut Hild, "Was hat die Denkschrift der EKD bewirkt?" in *Feinde werden Freunde: Von den Schwierigkeiten der deutsch-polnischen Nachbarschaft*, ed. Friedbert Pflüger and Winfried Lipscher (Bonn, 1993), 90–102. Helmut Hild, 1921–99, was the former president of the Protestant Church in Germany at the time that *Feinde werden Freunde* was published. He led a delegation from the EKD to Poland in 1973, received an honorary doctorate at the Christian Theological Academy in Warsaw in 1974, and was active in the contacts between the German Protestant Church and the Polish Ecumenical Council. Also Robert Żurek and Basil Kerski, "Der Briefwechsel zwischen den polnischen und deutschen Bischöfen von 1965: Entstehungsgeschichte, historischer Kontext und unmittelbare Wirkung," in *"Wir vergeben und bitten um Vergebung": Der Briefwechsel der polnischen und deutschen Bischöfe von 1965 und seine Wirkung*, ed. Basil Kerski, Thomas Kycia, and Robert Żurek (Osnabrück, 2006), 8.
15. Hans Henning Hahn, Heidi Hein-Kirchner, and Anna Kochanowska-Nieborak, "Einleitung: überlegungen zum Verhältnis von Erinnerungskultur, Versöhnung und Versöhnungskitsch," in Hahn, Hein-Kirchner, and Kochanowska-Nieborak, *Erinnerungskultur und Versöhnungskitsch*, 6; Piotr Kosicki, "*Caritas* across the Iron Curtain: Polish–German Reconciliation and the Bishops' Letter of 1965," *East European Politics and Society* 23, no. 2 (Spring 2009): 217–18.
16. Richard von Weizsäcker, "Rede beim Staatsbesuch des Präsidenten der Republik Polen am 30.3.1992," in Pflüger and Lipscher, *Feinde werden Freunde*, 289–93.
17. David Ost, *Solidarity and the Politics of Anti-Politics: Opposition and Reform in Poland since 1968* (Philadelphia, 1990), 19–21. For a discussion of the developments of the term in long-term European politics and history, see Jürgen Kocka, "Zivilgesellschaft als historisches Problem und Versprechen," in *Europäische Zivilgesellschaft in Ost und West. Begriff, Geschichte, Chancen*, ed. Manfred Hildermeier, Jürgen Kocka, and Christoph Conrad (New York, 2000), 13–40.
18. Ost, *Solidarity*, 23.
19. For particular examples see Jacobsen and Tomala, eds., *Bonn-Warschau*; Pflüger and Winfried, eds., *Feinde werden Freunde*; Pailer, *Stanisław Stomma.*; Tomala, *Patrząc na Niemcy*; Eva Rommerskirchen, ed., *Deutsche und Polen: Annäherungen—Zbliżenia, 1945–1995* (Düsseldorf, 1996); Wojciech Pięciak, ed., *Polacy i Niemcy pół wieku później: Księga pamiątkowa dla Mieczysława Pszona* (Cracow, 1996); Ekkehard Buchhofer and Bronisław Kortuś, eds., *Polska i Niemcy: Geografia sąsiedztwa w nowej Europy* (Cracow, 1995); Wolff-Powęska, ed., *Polacy wobec Niemców*.

20. Brian Porter-Szücs, *Faith and Fatherland: Catholicism, Modernity and Poland* (Oxford, 2011); Kosicki, "*Caritas* across the Iron Curtain"; and also Karina Paulina Marczuk, "The Origins of the Polish–German Reconciliation, 1965–1966," *Arhivele Totalitarismului* 1–2 (2017): 171–80.
21. Klaus Bachmann, "Die Versöhnung muss von Polen ausgehen," *Taz*, 5 August 1994.
22. For discussion of the political dimensions of Germany developing a policy of reconciliation, see Lily Gardner Feldman, *Germany's Foreign Policy of Reconciliation: From Enmity to Amity* (Lanham, MD, 2012).
23. Stefan Ludwig Hoffmann, Sandrine Kott, Peter Romijn, and Oliver Wievorka, "Introduction," in *Seeking Peace in the Wake of War: Europe 1942–1947*, ed. Stefan Ludwig Hoffmann, Sandrine Kott, Peter Romijn, and Oliver Wievorka (Amsterdam, 2015), 17.
24. Robert Traba makes the point that it is difficult to define a firm identity of an individual. I agree, particularly given the constant shifts and fluctuations in one's self-perception with regards to region and nations. Robert Traba, "'Region,' 'Regionalismus,' 'Identität,' 'Identifikation': Bemerkungen zur Begrifflichkeit und ihrer wissenschaftlichen Rezeption nach 1989," in *Region, Staat, Europa: Regionale Identitäten von Diktatur und Demokratie in Mittel- und Osteuropa*, ed. Burkhard Olschowsky et al. (Munich, 2014), 36.
25. Siri Gloppen, Elin Skaar, and Astri Suhrke, "Introduction," *Roads to Reconciliation*, 4; Anderson, *Imagined Communities*.
26. William J. Long and Peter Brecke, *War and Reconciliation: Reason and Emotion in Conflict Resolution* (Boston, 2005), 23.
27. The notion of *histoire croisée*, a reaction to comparative history, which was still trapped in the paradigm of the nation, was developed by Michael Werner and Bénédicte Zimmerman. See for example Michael Werner and Bénédicte Zimmerman, "Beyond Comparison: Histoire Croisée and the Challenge of Reflexivity," *History and Theory* 45, no. 1 (February 2006): 30–50. For the Polish–German case, see for example Philipp Ther, "Comparisons, Cultural Transfers and the Study of Networks: Towards a Transnational History of Europe," in *Comparative and Transnational History: Central European Approaches and New Perspectives*, ed. Heinz-Gerhardt Haupt and Jürgen Kocka (New York, 2009).
28. For discussions of such alternative identities in prewar Central European borderlands, see James Bjork, *Neither German nor Pole: Catholicism and National Indifference in a Central European Borderland* (Ann Arbor, 2008); Mark Tilse, *Transnationalism in the Prussian East: From National Conflict to Synthesis, 1871–1914* (New York, 2011); Pieter Judson, *Guardians of the Nation: Activists on the Language Frontiers of Imperial Austria* (Cambridge, MA, 2007).
29. Philip Nord, "Conclusion," in Hoffman et al., *Seeking Peace*, 322.
30. Yinan He uses the case study in this fashion. He, *Search for Reconciliation*. See also older texts, such as Gregory Baum and Harold Wells, eds., *Reconciliation of Peoples: Challenge to the Churches* (New York, 1997) or Long and Brecke, *War and Reconciliation*, 96–100.
31. Among the groups neglected by the narrative of reconciliation were the German expellees from Eastern Europe, the Jewish emigrants and survivors, and other minorities that left or were forced to leave postwar East European nations. A lot of high quality scholarship now exists on these groups; to mention a few works, Andrew Demshuk, *The Lost German East: Forced Migration and the Politics of Memory, 1945–1970* (Cambridge, 2012); Christian Lotz, *Die Deutung des Verlustes: Erinnerungspolitische Kontroversen im geteilten Deutschland um Flucht, Vertreibung und die Ostgebiete, 1945–1970* (Cologne, 2007); or, Monika Adamczyk-Garbowska and Feliks Tych, eds., *Jewish Presence in Absence: The Aftermath of the Holocaust in Poland, 1944–2010* (Jerusalem, 2014).
32. He, *Search for Reconciliation*, 2.
33. Long and Brecke, *War and Reconciliation*, 18.

34. Ibid., 22.
35. He, *Search for Reconciliation*, 2.
36. Ibid., 4.
37. Timothy Snyder, *The Reconstruction of Nations: Poland, Ukraine, Lithuania, Belarus, 1569–1999* (New Haven, CT, 2003); Tomasz Kamusella, *Silesia and Central European Nationalisms: The Emergence of Ethnic Groups in Prussian Silesia and Austrian Silesia 1848–1918* (Purdue, 2006).
38. See Philipp Ther, "A Century of Forced Migration: The Origins and Consequences of "Ethnic Cleansing," in *Redrawing Nations: Ethnic Cleansing in East Central Europe 1944–1948*, ed. Philipp Ther and Ana Siljak (New York, 2001), 50; Marcin Zaremba, "The 'War Syndrome': World War II and Polish Society" in Hoffman et al., *Seeking Peace*, 30.
39. The Curzon Line took its name from a British official from the First World War era, George Curzon. It was an envisioned borderline between Poland and the Soviet Union that became a reality after 1945.
40. A growing literature explores the Polonization of Poland in the 1940s and 1950s: Gregor Thum's *Die fremde Stadt—Breslau 1945* (Munich, 2003); David Curp's *A Clean Sweep? The Politics of Ethnic Cleansing in Western Poland, 1945–1960* (Rochester, NY, 2006). A recent article situating the responsibility for the ethnic cleansing and Polonization of the borderlands with the communist rulers is Hugo Service, "Reinterpreting the Expulsion of Germans from Poland, 1945–9," *Journal of Contemporary History* 27, no. 3 (July 2012): 528–50.
41. Hansjakob Stehle, "Vorwort," in Stefan Kisielewski, *An dieser Stelle Europas* (Munich, 1964), 12. For descriptions of the Znak Circle, see, among others, Andrzej Friszke, *Opozycja polityczna w Polska 1945–1980* (Warsaw, 1994), and Christina Manetti, "Sign of the Times: The Znak Circle and Catholic Intellectual Engagement in Communist Poland, 1945–1976" (PhD diss., University of Washington, 1998).
42. See for example Friedhelm Boll, "Der Bensberger Kreis und sein Polenmemorandum (1968): Vom Zweiten Vatikanischen Konzil zur Unterstutzung sozial-liberaler Entspannungspolitik," in *Versöhnung und Politik: Polnisch-deutsche Versöhnungsinitiativen der 1960er Jahren und die Entspannungspolitik*, ed. Friedhelm Boll et al. (Bonn, 2009), 77–117.
43. For cultural changes in the Protestant Church, see Benjamin Pearson, "Faith and Democracy: Political Transformations at the German Protestant Kirchentag, 1945–1969" (Diss., University of North Carolina–Chapel Hill, 2007). See also Klaus Fitschen et al., eds., *Die Politisierung des Protestantismus: Entwicklungen in der Bundesrepublik Deutschland während der 1960er und 70er Jahre* (Göttingen, 2011), and Nicolai Hannig, *Die Religion der Öffentlichkeit: Medien, Religion und Kirche in der Bundesrepublik 1945–1980* (Göttingen, 2010), and for changes in the Protestant Church directly related to its East European relationships, see Martin Greschat, "Vom Tübingen Memorandum (1961) zur Ratifizierung der Ostverträge (1972): Protestantische Beiträge zur Aussöhnung mit Polen," in Boll et al., *Versöhnung und Poltik*, 29–51.
44. Christina von Hodenberg, *Konsens und Krise: Eine Geschichte der westdeutschen Medienöffentlichkeit, 1945–1973* (Göttingen, 2003), 304.
45. Snyder, *Reconstruction of Nations*, 54; Robert Jarocki, *Czterdzieści pięć lat w opozycji (O ludziach, Tygodnika Powszechnego")* (Cracow, 1990), 28, 30.
46. Snyder, *Reconstruction of Nations*, 54.
47. Stomma, *Pościg za nadzieją*, 76, 83.
48. Andrzej Friszke, "Jerzy Zawieyski, szkic portretu," in Jerzy Zawieyski, *Dzienniki: Tom 1, Wybór z lat 1955–1959* (Warsaw, 2011), 10.
49. Jarocki, *Czterdzieścipięć lat w opozycji*, 19–20.

50. Tomasz Serwatka, *Kardynał Bolesław Kominek (1903–1974): Duszpasterz i polityk, zarys biograficzny* (Wrocław, 2013).
51. Winfried Lipscher, "Rückkehr in die Heimat?" in Pflüger and Lipscher, *Feinde werden Freunde*, 427–32.
52. Bjork, *Neither German nor Pole*; Philipp Ther, "Beyond the Nation: The Relational Basis of a Comparative History of Germany and Europe," *Central European History* 36, no. 1 (March 2003): 45–73; Snyder, *Reconstruction of Nations*; Tilse, *Transnationalism in the Prussian East*; Peter Polak-Springer, *Recovered Territory: A German-Polish Conflict over Land and Culture 1919–1989* (New York, 2015); Beata Halicka, "The Oder-Neisse Line as a Place of Remembrance for Germans and Poles," *Journal of Contemporary History* 41, no. 1 (January 2014): 75–91; Tomasz Kamusella, "The Changing Lattice of Languages, Borders, and Identities in Silesia," in *The Palgrave Handbook of Slavic Languages, Identities and Borders*, ed. Tomasz Kamusella et al. (Basingstoke, 2016), 185–205.
53. Marion Dönhoff, *Kindheit in Ostpreussen* (Berlin, 1988), 8; Klaus von Bismarck, *Aufbruch aus Pommern* (Munich, 1996).
54. Porter-Szücs, *Faith and Fatherland*, and Robert Żurek, *Zwischen Nationalismus und Versöhnung: Die Kirchen und die deutsch-polnische Beziehungen 1945–1956* (Cologne, 2008). See also Piotr Kosicki, "Five—Vatican II and Poland," in *Vatican II behind the Iron Curtain*, ed. Piotr Kosicki (Washington, DC, 2016), 127–98. All three illustrate the tensions between international and nationalizing forces in the German, Polish, and East European Catholic Churches.
55. For a history of this movement, see Konstanty Turowski, *"Odrodzenie": historia Stowarzyszenia Katolickiej Młodzieży Akademickiej* (Warszawa, 1987).
56. Kosicki, "Five—Vatican II and Poland."
57. For a discussion of the notions of the nation in interwar Poland, see Paul Brykczynski, *Primed for Violence: Murder, Antisemitism and Democratic Politics in Interwar Poland* (Madison, 2016), or Porter-Szücs, *Faith and Fatherland*, in particular the chapter "Polak-Katolik," 328–59.
58. Rogers Brubaker, *Citizenship and Nationhood in France and Germany* (Cambridge, 1998).
59. For Polish national models, see Snyder, *Reconstruction of Nations*, 55–60. See also the older essay by Andrzej Walicki, *Trzy patriotyzmy: trzy tradycje polskiego patriotyzmu i ich znaczenie współczesne* (Warsaw, 1991). See also Paul Brykczynski, "Reconsidering 'Piłsudskiite Nationalism,'" *Nationalities Papers* 42, no. 5 (2014): 771–90.
60. Specifically on Polish national thought in Vilnius, see Snyder, *Reconstruction of Nations*, 55–57. See also Zbigniew Kurcz, *Mniejszość polska na Wileńszczyźnie: studium socjologiczne* (Wrocław, 2005).
61. Jarocki, *Czterdzieścipięć lat w opozycji*.
62. Ibid., 66.
63. Stomma, *Pościg za nadzieją*, 26–27.
64. Pszon, "Wspomnienia—1915–1945," in Pięciak, *Polacy i Niemcy*, 479.
65. Mikołaj Stanisław Kunicki, *Between the Brown and the Red: Nationalism, Catholicism, and Communism in Twentieth-Century Poland—The Politics of Bolesław Piasecki* (Athens, OH, 2012), 93.
66. Ulrich Bröckling, *Katholische Intellektuelle in der Weimarer Republik: Zeitkritik und Gesellschaftstheorie bei Walter Dirks, Romano Guardini, Carl Schmitt, Ernst Michael und Heinrich Mertens* (Munich, 1993), 38.
67. Ulrich Bröckling, *Walter Dirks: Bibliographie* (Bonn, 1991), and Bröckling, *Katholische Intellektuelle*.
68. Bismarck, *Aufbruch aus Pommern*, 82.

69. Geoffrey P. Megargee, "A Blind Eye and Dirty Hands: The Wehrmacht's Crimes in the East," in *The Germans and the East*, ed. Charles Ingrao and Franz A. J. Szabo (West Lafayette, IN, 2008), 316.
70. Bismarck, *Aufbruch aus Pommern*, 35. For discussion of Pomerania, see Richard Blanke, *Orphans of Versailles: The Germans in Western Poland, 1918–1939* (Lexington, KY, 1993), but also, for an alternative perspective, essays in *Mazowsze, Pomorze, Prusy, Studia z Dziejów Średniowiecza nr 7*, ed. Blażej Śliwinski (Gdańsk, 2000). Also, Karlheinz Koppe considered his political choices as a continuation of his father's independence of mind. Koppe, *Dreimal getauft und Mensch geblieben* (Berlin, 2004), 62–63. For a description on the DNVP, see Blanke, *Orphans of Versailles*, 55.
71. Klaus von Bismarck, "Ein evangelischer Christ erfährt Polen," in *Ungewöhnliche Normalisierung: Beziehungen der Bundesrepublik Deuschland zu Polen*, ed. Werner Plum (Bonn, 1984), 133
72. Wulf Kansteiner, *In Pursuit of German Memory: History, Television, and Politics after Auschwitz* (Athens, OH, 2006), 252.
73. Ibid., 356.
74. The concept of a skeptical generation dates from sociologist Helmut Schelsky in his book *Die skeptische Generation: Eine Soziologie der deutschen Jugend* (Cologne, Düsseldorf, 1957). On the emergence of a new journalistic elite in West Germany, see Simone Christine Ehmig, *Generationswechsel im deutschen Journalismus: Zum Einfluss historischer Ereignisse auf das journalistische Selbstverständnis* (Munich, 2000), 52–53. For critical perspectives and an emphasis on long-term continuities as well as in elite networks, see Hodenberg, *Konsens und Krise*, and Christina von Hodenberg, "Die Journalisten und der Aufbruch zur kritischen Öffentlichkeit," in *Wandlungsprozesse in Westdeutschland*, ed. Ulrich Herbert (Göttingen, 2002), 278–314
75. Żurek, *Zwischen Nationalismus and Versöhnung*, or the collected essays in Boll et al., *Versöhnung und Politik*.
76. "Gutachten sieht Deutschland zu Reparationen verpflichtet," *Zeit Online*, 11 September 2017, 4:39 P.M., http://www.zeit.de/politik/deutschland/2017-09/polen-gutachten-reparationen-deutschland-zweiter-weltkrieg.
77. Anna Wolff-Powęska, "Zur Aktualität von Dialog und Versöhnung im polnisch-deutschen Verhältnis," in Boll et al., *Versöhnung und Politik*, 396.

Chapter 1

Unexpected Meetings and New Beginnings
Inspirations, Transformations, and Opportunities, 1939–58

In a text he wrote after the war but never published, Jürgen Neven-du Mont, who was a soldier on the eastern front during the Second World War, described himself as only becoming fully aware of the Poles and their situation during the Warsaw Uprising in 1944. Under the title "Why I Love Warsaw," he spoke of visiting the Polish capital just as the uprising broke out. In the story, he sought shelter from bombardments in a basement together with two Polish women belonging to the Home Army. They gave him vodka and confronted him about the German atrocities in the east. He described discovering one of the women dead on a barricade with one arm torn away as he left Warsaw later and running into the other woman when he filmed the fifteenth anniversary of the Warsaw Uprising for West German television in 1959.[1]

It is possible that this is fiction. Neven-du Mont was in Poland in 1944 and had a close friend who did witness the Warsaw Uprising, but their correspondence at the time gives no indication that Neven-du Mont himself was in the city during the course of the Uprising. At any rate, it is interesting that Neven-du Mont situates his coming face to face with Polish perspectives in personal meetings across enemy lines and due to his physical presence in the midst of wartime chaos. During the war, Polish–German relations were at a low point, as violence and distrust dominated most interactions. Yet, total war can function as an entangled event, not only through negative experiences and antagonistic confrontations but also in occasionally breaking down previous paradigms and the boundaries between ethnicities, nations, classes, and sometimes genders.[2] Such breakdowns planted seeds for meetings and closer encounters between Poles and Germans once the war was over. This chapter traces the multi-

---

Notes for this chapter begin on page 47.

ple reasons during the war, the immediate postwar era, and up to the Polish October in 1956 that particular groups and individuals among media representatives, journalists, and Catholic and public intellectuals were inspired and able to play a role in Polish–German relations.

German Reconciliation Participants' War Experiences

Not only Neven-du Mont but also Klaus Otto Skibowski—a Catholic journalist and public relations expert in the 1950s to Konrad Adenauer, the long-time Christian Democratic politician and former mayor of Cologne—and Klaus von Bismarck served as soldiers on the eastern front during the war. When the Third Reich and the Soviet Union invaded Poland in September 1939, Klaus von Bismarck was part of the invading army. Like Neven-du Mont, he claimed to first have become conscious of the culture and history of the Poles and Poland as a Wehrmacht officer during the war. Many years later, he described going to a conquered area in September 1939 and seeing how

> old, haggard women searched for their possessions or for dead relatives in the destroyed houses. Others prayed in a church that had been considerably damaged from bombing and artillery fire. For the first time I saw people who had been hit by war, by us, and for the first time I was confronted with the consequences of the war for the civilian population. These scenes are engrained in my memory. I have never forgotten them.[3]

The Polish population's deep religiosity and their hatred of the Germans struck him and perhaps inspired his will to achieve dialogue and understanding in the postwar era.

In 1939, Germany and the Soviet Union divided Poland between them. The western part became integrated into the Reich, and the occupiers began to remove Polish populations from the western territories. The German-controlled Generalgouvernement ruled the central and southern part. In 1941, Germany attacked the Soviet Union and occupied the rest of Poland. As a senior lance corporal, Jürgen Neven-du Mont participated in Operation Barbarossa in the summer of 1941. During the war, as mentioned, the Germans displaced a total of 1.65 million Polish citizens, sent two million to Germany to become forced labor, and murdered five to six million, including the Polish Jewish population.[4] Germany established over 400 concentration camps on Polish territory. The eastern territories became Reichskommissariat Ostland and Reichskommissariat Ukraine. Neven-du Mont witnessed firsthand SS units' mass executions of Jewish women and children.[5]

Though he described these events in later texts, Neven-du Mont made no mention of it in his carefully worded and censored wartime letters to his family. The letters nonetheless make clear that he was deeply shocked by his experiences. In the only letter from the war years where he addressed his mother "Dear Elisabeth" rather than "Dear Mother," from Bad Schandau on 5 November 1942, he wrote: "I don't know what to tell you. The difference in my worldview from yesterday and today is so great that it is simply impossible to describe it."[6] The letters from 1943 and 1944 gave evidence to a deeply felt crisis. He kept apologizing to his correspondents for long silences and spoke of feeling increasingly alienated from them.[7] He wrote to his mother,

> You were not entirely happy with my letters lately. Please, do not read into them any ungratefulness. I was merely gripped often by lethargy lately that completely immobilized me. But is not lethargy the sickness of a deceived soul? And we are deceived souls today. I have sensed it for a long time and often felt it. One cannot really express these things in letters.[8]

In 1942, Neven-du Mont was injured and spent the rest of the war training recruits in Poland. By this time, his letters also indicated that he had become a relatively unwilling soldier, skeptical of the ideological line and consistently, if not openly, critical of the war.

Ludwig Zimmerer, Hansjakob Stehle, and Klaus Otto Skibowski all shared the experience of being prisoners of war in 1945 as Germany was defeated. Zimmerer spent time in a French camp while von Bismarck, who was fighting on the western front, was captured by the British forces. They held von Bismarck in a POW camp until August 1945, when many other German soldiers were also released. He then traveled to Westphalia in search of his wife and family. He wrote in his memoirs, "For me, the time of being a prisoner of war between May and August 1945 was a necessary time and felt like waking up from a nightmare. I needed this time to breathe mentally and spiritually and to stretch, just as one who has been sick stands up dizzily for the first time and precariously takes the first steps."[9]

When he returned from France, Ludwig Zimmerer became part of a left-wing Catholic circle and began working as a translator from French to German, another indication of the way the war might actually break down national boundaries as well as constructing them. Stehle, a schoolboy who had defended the German home front during the last months of war, also briefly became a prisoner of war. Skibowski served as a soldier on the eastern front at the end of the war.

Karlheinz Koppe, who later became a member of the Bensberger Circle, had been protected from extensive military service through his enrollment in an elite gymnasium during most of the war. He left Breslau (now Wrocław) and Silesia for good in the fall of 1944, traveling west together with his schoolmates.[10] Moving by train and on foot to the southwest of Germany and carrying only a small backpack with his personal belongings, he reached Bavaria and the American sector as the war finally ended. His descriptions of his war experiences were generally full of youthful optimism and the spirit of adventure. He worked for the Americans during the early postwar months. However, he traced the origins of his later pacifism to his experiences during those years, stating, "My father had been right: humans are not suited to war! I made this insight to a tenet to live by for the rest of my life."[11]

In the spring of 1945, Germany had been invaded from the west as well as the east, and many of its cities were in ruins. The German army was retreating on multiple fronts. Following Hitler's suicide and Germany's full surrender in May of 1945, the Allied powers divided Germany into four occupation zones. The Allies at the Yalta and Potsdam meetings drew the postwar borders in Europe and approved the removal of the ten to twelve million Germans living in Eastern Europe in a "humane and orderly fashion."[12] The Soviet Union encouraged German communists who had spent the war years in Soviet exile to set up a new communist state in the so-called Soviet Zone of the German lands, the area that would become the German Democratic Republic. The British, French, and Americans administered the other three zones that became the Federal Republic after 1950.

In the American zone, Neven-du Mont spent the first few postwar years attempting to build a life as a civilian. A letter his father wrote to him in May 1945 pointed out that he had lost a lot of time because of the war and that he must "use every minute and try, despite the shortage of further educational opportunities of an official nature, to educate [him]self."[13] Neven-du Mont struggled with the adjustment to postwar life however. He studied multiple subjects at the university of Munich, all of which he discontinued. He married in 1946, and his son Christian was born soon afterward, but the family had to live separately because of housing shortages and financial difficulties that also made Neven-du Mont reliant on his extended family for support.[14] He finally secured a permanent and full-time position in 1953 or 1954, first publishing a Sunday edition for several newspapers and then becoming a reporter for Bayrischer Rundfunk. Meanwhile, he attempted through writing and documentary production to come to grips with the German nation's past and present, its changing character. In 1946, he started a journal named *die verlorene Generation* (the Lost Generation) together with Nicholas Sombart. In 1956, he published a controversial book, *Denk' ich an Deutschland* (When I Think about Germany) with Michael Mansfeld.[15] The book was a document of fragmented text and images that compared and contrasted East and West Germany, and life in the two states.[16] Neven-du Mont's creative and professional output and correspondences from those years reflected intensity and hard work, but also frustration. His career from this point would be characterized both by great productivity and frequent personal and professional conflicts.

Several million Germans fled or were forced to leave their homes and home areas east of the rivers Oder and Lusatian Neisse that belonged to Poland after 1945. Contrary to descriptions of expellees as forces that always firmly and loudly opposed improved Polish–German relations, many of the leading participants in Polish–German relations in fact originated from the prewar German east. They included von Bismarck, Koppe, Skibowski, and Marion Countess Dönhoff. For all, this was a time of great upheaval as the Third Reich ended and Germany, economically broken and war-torn, became divided by the Allies. During the spring and summer of 1945, Dönhoff put words to the sense of destruction of the very fabric of the nation she had grown up with. She left East Prussia on horseback in January 1945 as the front came closer and a retreat command was issued. She arrived at Vinsebeck in Westphalia in mid-March and made her way to Hamburg, where she joined the newly founded weekly *die Zeit*.[17] In a 1946 article, one of her first, she described her emotions as she moved along the road, permanently leaving her home. She asked, "Is that still Germany, this piece of soil on which the East and the West meet, helpless, without home or goals, driven together like fleeing game into an entrapment? Is this the 'thousand-year Reich': a mountain ridge with a few ragged beggars?"[18] She spoke of the tumbling world and of herself as a member of a generation of "late born" who was now left in the ruins of previous value systems and cultures, and with empty hands. Nevertheless, she felt that it would be futile to attempt to master the current situation with "a knife-sharp intellect and skeptical hearts." Instead, the survivors had to cultivate a new sense of humanity and transform the memory of the dead into a responsibility for the future: "hate into love" and "a new world order in the spirit of brotherhood."[19]

Immediately after the war, the so-called license era began in the occupied territories. Between 1945 and 1950, during the occupation, only journalists and media outlets that had been cleared politically by the occupation powers were allowed to work and operate in the four zones.[20] Since many established journalists who had elected to work for the conservative and National Socialist press during the war years had been banned, and others had died during the war, the license era opened space for more left-wing and newly minted journalists. Walter Dirks was among those who, as a known opponent to National Socialism, could continue working throughout the license era. In 1946, together with Eugen Kogon, who wrote one of the first books on the concentration camps in Germany, Dirks founded the left-wing Catholic journal *Frankfurter Hefte*. *Frankfurter Hefte* was to become an important contact point for the Polish Catholic intellectuals in the Znak Circle in the late 1950s.[21] Hansjakob Stehle also rose unusually quickly to prominent positions in the press because of the space that had opened up in postwar West German journalism. Having studied philosophy, history, and international law at the University in Frankfurt am Main after the war, he earned his PhD in 1950. Immediately, a local newspaper in Wurzburg hired him.[22] Soon thereafter, in 1955, he advanced to the larger and more influential daily *Frankfurter Allgemeine Zeitung*, eventually to move to Warsaw and become its foreign correspondent in Eastern Europe.

The German expellees who would become part of reconciliatory efforts with Poland all eventually relocated to the western, Allied territories. By 1949, the Federal Republic of Germany and the German Democratic Republic, West and East Germany, were established. As the GDR was founded in 1950, it opened relations with Poland by Soviet request, unwillingly recognizing the border on the rivers Oder and Neisse and signing a friendship treaty with its eastern neighbor.[23] Under the leadership of Konrad Adenauer, the Federal Republic recognized neither the existence of the GDR nor the new border, however. The Federal Republic would not sign a final peace treaty until Germany was unified in 1990 and the Soviet Union had withdrawn from its eastern half. Nazi Germany had surrendered unconditionally, but the Federal Republic, its legal heir, never completed the process.

In the absence of a peace treaty, Poland's right to the western territories remained in question. Political interests among the German expellees further complicated the situation, as they argued in the political realm that they had a legal right, *Recht auf Heimat*, to the property and territory they had been forced to abandon. Given the large numbers of expellees, about 16.1 percent of the total population, West German politicians considered these groups an important voting bloc. An active expellee cultural and political sphere existed in West Germany, including regional organizations—the *Landsmannschaften*—and journals, newsletters, and dailies, the expellee press, which became a particular thorn in the side to the media groups promoting improved relations with Poland and the relinquishing of the eastern territory. Outside of official political battle lines, the position of expellees in West German politics was more complicated, neither one of perfect integration nor of hardline, absolute revisionism, as Andrew Demshuk has shown. On local levels, there were ongoing tensions between newer and long-term inhabitants. From the time of the expellees' arrival in the late 1940s, the earlier population tended to accuse the newcomers of being ungrateful, crude, and generally problematic to integrate.[24] While silently prepared to accept the loss of the eastern territories, West German politicians publicly continued to make concessions to the expellees' right to return home, making Polish–German relations difficult to pursue.[25]

The border move meant that Klaus von Bismarck had to abandon his prewar life as landed aristocracy and his longtime family property. Instead, he was able to secure a position as the leader of the Jugendhof Vlotho, an educational facility for young people in Westfalen. He assumed this position despite having almost no background in education. At Vlotho, he became engaged with Protestant youth groups and with efforts toward French–German reconciliation.[26] By 1949, he advanced from his position at Vlotho to become the head of the new Social Office for the Protestant Church in Westfalen. He settled in Villigst bei Schwerte together with his wife and children and lived there until 1951. These years were a time of adjustment for him. He wrote about his life there: "We were like a pile of leaves blown together. People whom the war had spared. The uprooted, the injured, the guilty. (The guilty were perhaps the most important ones.)"[27] He credited a deepening religiosity and moral engagement to his sense of rootlessness and sorrow during these years. At the same time as he was grappling with his own past and present, he extended his political, social, and ecumenical work, and efforts toward peace and dialogue particularly with French–German youth exchanges that he had first initiated in Vlotho. He became very active at the annual Protestant national conventions (*Kirchentage*) and played a role in Protestant factions that would eventually create a shift in the Protestant Church's stance on Polish–German relations.[28]

Von Bismarck's public engagement with Poland began as an extension of his internal struggles to accept the loss of his family lands and prewar life. In 1954, at the German Protestant Convention in Leipzig, he made a public speech about the way his faith prompted him to accept the loss of the former German areas in Poland. He described himself as having become "Bismarck-West" in that process, and said that his former self, "Bismarck-East," "who was active as an agronomist for fifteen years in Pomerania[,] would not have been able to entirely understand" the position he took in 1954.[29] His speech created waves inside and outside of the church. He drew criticism from expellee organizations as well as praise from German and Polish observers. The speech raised his profile in Poland and augmented his engagement with Polish–German relations in the coming years.

Other West German religious activists were also originally engaged in restoring French–German relations. Walter Dirks and Klaus von Bismarck became acquainted with each other in the late 1940s to the early 1950s through ecumenical grassroots activism in French–German relations. In one of their earliest correspondences, von Bismarck pledged the resources of the Jugendhof Vlotho to improving French–German relations, saying that he and his faculty were convinced they were "of crucial importance for the future of Europe."[30] A working group consisting of Protestants from Vlotho and Catholic intellectuals from *Frankfurter Hefte* and the publisher Dokumente, which also published a Catholic journal, possibly together with French members, began to meet to hold conversations about the past and try to understand each other's points of view.

One might argue that Karlheinz Koppe's journey to become involved in peace efforts went through France as well. After the war, his hometown Breslau and Silesia at large had become part of Poland. Koppe finished school in Dessau in the Soviet Zone but ran into problems with the Soviet Military Command and therefore fled to American-controlled West Berlin.[31] He began training as a journalist on lower-level positions in the press, including *Der Tag*, the Berlin daily. Looking for a place of belonging and because he admired its social engagement compared to its Protestant counterpart, he also joined the Catholic Church.[32] He went to Paris to study in 1951 with no concrete plan to ever return to Germany again. He had no particular loyalty or connection to either part of postwar Germany, particularly as his father had passed away in November 1944. In the conservative and Christian Democratic political climate, he doubted his own as well as Germany's future prospects.[33] However, the Catholic Church and the Social Democratic youth movement, which had provided Koppe with a social context in Berlin, continued to do so in Paris. After a few years of studies in France and one year as a volunteer in Algeria, Koppe did return to the Federal Republic in 1953 but denied any strong patriotic attachment to the country, preferring to think of himself as a European. In his memoirs, he described himself as returning "in full confidence of good political and personal prospects."[34] In the Federal Republic, he began a career in public relations and journalism. He first became engaged with Polish–German relations in 1956 and grew more active in the 1960s.

Ludwig Zimmerer never lived in France after his release from the prisoner-of-war camp, but in the early postwar era he supported himself and his first wife, Margaret, by translating French literature into German.[35] The couple belonged to a small subculture of young Catholic socialists and eked out a living by Zimmerer's translation work and by founding a used bookstore in Essen. In 1952, Zimmerer spearheaded the founding of the publication *Glaube und Vernunft* (Faith and Common Sense), a Christian-Marxist publication of the Working Committee for Catholic Youth Against Rearmament Policy. Because of their socialist politics, the Working Committee was barred from the Alliance of Catholic Youth (Bund der Katholischen Jugend) and the publication as well as Zimmerer himself struggled with serious financial difficulties. Zimmerer found a supporter and patron in Walter Dirks, who shared his belief in a Catholic form of socialism, but the cooperation with Dirks's *Frankfurter Hefte* never developed fully, and a financial conflict soured their relationship by the mid-1950s.[36]

While Zimmerer was initially given a publication license, he was in many ways operating on the margins of the increasingly anticommunist culture of West Germany. Meanwhile, more centrist media grew rapidly. Due to a shortage of experienced and politically acceptable journalists, a number of newcomers to media, including Stehle, Dönhoff, and Neven-du Mont, were able to rise to prominent positions in well-established weeklies and dailies by the early to mid-1950s.[37] By the mid-1950s, the growth rate of the media leveled out, and the press was divided into city, regional, and supranational press (which was still generally localized to a particular city, such as *Frankfurter Allgemeine Zeitung* to Frankfurt am Main).

Mainstream West German media's portrayals of Poland at this time were shaped by the emerging Cold War and limited access to information. Much of the press was concentrated around a few powerful publishing houses, most notably Springer Press, which was staunchly anticommunist in its commentary on Eastern Europe and the Soviet Bloc.[38] In the initial postwar period, the late 1940s, West German media published reports about and writings by ethnic Germans in Poland that covered the dismal situation there and the destruction of their former lands. Media coverage was generally sympathetic to the fate of the displaced expellees from Poland and Czechoslovakia.[39] As the Cold War conflict worsened, West German newspapers and western media at large described Poland as a powerless pawn in the hands of an oppressive Soviet Union, drawing on information derived from expellees but also from political refugees and émigrés from the East European countries.[40] West German media used particular terminology when engaging with Eastern Europe, in particular with Poland. It never referred to East Germany, the German Democratic Republic, or the GDR, instead using the term "the Zone" or "the Soviet Zone."[41] It described the new Polish territories as being "under Polish administration" and the newly drawn border between Poland and East Germany as "the Oder-Neisse Line." Outside of reports by expellees and émigrés, media struggled with a lack of updated information about Poland. In the early 1950s, western journalists could not get accreditation to work in Poland, and general travel restrictions were in place. On the other hand, most media outlets saw no great need to report extensively on Poland. This disinterest also contributed to the lack of relations and limited interest before the 1950s.

The era has been called a time of West German consensus journalism, and this was also reflected in discussions about the eastern territories. In the interest of national unity, the mainstream media tended to avoid disagreements, especially with the state, about contentious topics such as German responsibility for war crimes in the east or the future of the eastern territories, now in Poland. The West German government and Konrad Adenauer strove to control media content and to limit the freedom of the media with regards to political reporting in the interest of state security and stability. Most media outlets were happy to comply with the state's agenda.[42]

Polish Reconciliation Participants' War Experiences

The Polish participants' war experiences were also ones of reexamining prewar value systems and beliefs, and of upheaval, loss, and displacement toward the end of the war. Mieczysław Pszon had been firmly anti-German and anti-Semitic in the interwar era, but the Second World War and direct interactions with Jewish people contributed to reverse his position.[43] Pszon himself, in his memoirs, attributed his changed attitude toward the Germans to "getting to know a few Germans during the war" who were "decent."[44] He also described his time in Stalinist prison, 1947 to 1956, as a time of reflection during which he revised his prewar beliefs.

The Polish army had been dissolved after its defeat in 1939. The Polish participants were civilians or part of the resistance during the war years. Jerzy Zawieyski spent the war in Warsaw, engaged with underground culture and theater, after leaving briefly when the Germans invaded the city in the fall of 1939.[45] Stefan Kisielewski and Władysław Bartoszewski also spent the war years in Warsaw, and both participated in the Warsaw Uprising in 1944, during which Kisielewski was injured. He left the city as a civilian, leaving behind his wife and son, with no way to know for months that they were safe. He returned after the defeat and withdrawal of the Germans to find his native city all but obliterated. Many of the Polish cities, including Warsaw and Wrocław were almost entirely destroyed during the final months of the war. Cracow was a notable exception. Jerzy Turowicz and his family spent the war years in the rural areas surrounding Cracow, his home town, and could return there after the war was over.[46]

Stanisław Stomma and other Poles in the Lithuanian lands had a different experience of the war compared to their compatriots in Warsaw or southern Poland. Vilnius had initially become part of the Soviet Union in 1939, to be occupied in 1940. While the Germans slaughtered the Jewish population, they treated the Lithuanian Polish population better on the whole in these areas than in other parts of Poland. Stomma recalled, "The German occupation in the Vilnius area was milder than in the General-gouvernement, not to mention in the lands incorporated into the Reich."[47] The fact that the German occupation succeeded the Soviet one also colored the Vilnius Poles' perceptions. Józefa Hennelowa lacked Stomma's positive childhood experiences with Germans, and she was active in the underground movement. Yet she also described a much more neutral relationship between Poles and Germans in Vilnius.[48]

The Red Army reinvaded Vilnius in 1944. Stomma left the city ahead of the Red Army, since he believed that the Soviet occupation would last much longer this time.[49] He went to Cracow, where he had contacts and friends, and where he eventually founded *Tygodnik Powszechny* together with Jan Piwowarczyk, priest and professor at the Jagiellonian University, and Jerzy Turowicz, whom he knew from the prewar Catholic youth movement Odrodzenie. Hennelowa and her family left Vilnius as "repatriates" in 1947. She wrote, "When we crossed the [postwar border between Lithuania and Poland], I naturally had mixed emotions but, in the end, I told myself: this too is Poland, and perhaps even more so."[50] She described her experiences on the journey through Poland and the impression of the war damages. In Warsaw she saw "a sea of ruins that just went on and on. A shocking feeling. As I looked at it all, I thought to myself: this too is Poland." She and her family continued to Poznań, where the local priest told them that people did not think highly of "easterners." Once in Cracow they were reunited with other acquaintances, including Stanisław and Elwira Stomma. These groups shared the experiences of losing the connection to their own nation, of displacement and having to start over, with the German expellees and refugees.

Polish Participants after the War

In the initial aftermath of the war, Poland had two governments; one government-in-exile in London and, from June 1945, the Provisional Government of National Unity, which the Soviet Union installed in the country. The Allies moved Poland's borders in the east as well as the west. In 1947, fixed elections were held in Poland under Soviet auspices, and the communist Polish People's Party (PPR) assumed power. At this point, Władysław Gomułka assumed a leading role of a dominant group of Polish "national" communists and became a government minister, but he served less than a year. Stalin, who objected to Gomułka's ideological and national position, demoted the Polish leader and placed him under house arrest in the summer of 1948.[51] By this time the Polonization of the territories in the west was complete: the German names of streets, parks, and schools had been replaced, and the use of the German language in schools and churches was banned.[52] However, the process would continue for several more years. The state strove to control the public sphere, not only by erasing the traces of German presence but also by suppressing all political opposition. It tolerated no deviation from the communist party line and attempted to regulate public discourse about the past and present.

At the same time, postwar Poland differed significantly from other communist countries with respect to the strength of its Catholic Church. Over 90 percent of the Polish population was Catholic, following war losses, border changes, genocide, and ethnic cleansing. Further strengthening its position, the church had a reputation as a focal point of spiritual resistance to the Nazi occupation. Almost all other communist leaderships in the Soviet bloc were able to weaken or at least marginalize their churches. By contrast, the Polish communist party leadership needed the Polish Catholic Church's help to rebuild the country and also to integrate the displaced population into new areas. Meanwhile, they also wanted to ensure that the church did not destabilize the new state even further by openly opposing it. Thus, in 1946 and 1947, the Polish cardinal August Hlond and Archbishop Stefan Sapieha in Cracow negotiated a deal of coexistence with the communist leadership. The church agreed not to oppose the communist state and Poland's *raison d'état*. In return, the communists allowed the church's continued existence, its right to have a number of discussion clubs, the Clubs of Catholic Intellectuals (KIK, Klub Inteligencji Katolickiej), an independent press, and its right to religious education in the schools.[53] The semi-independent Catholic press, including the journals *Tygodnik Powszechny* (the Universal Weekly), *Więź* (the Connection, the Link), and *Znak* (the Sign) were founded as a result of this compromise.[54]

In the late 1940s, *Tygodnik Powszechny* could engage in public debates relatively freely. The state censorship at that time focused on suppressing rival political factions rather than on Catholic activity.[55] Some of the earliest debates in *Tygodnik Powszechny* and another Catholic journal at the time, *Tygodnik Warszawski*, concerned the nature and extent of the Catholic Church's involvement in politics. At this point, Stanisław Stomma argued that the Catholic Church had to count on the continued existence of a communist state in Poland, and that the church should not risk its very existence in Polish Catholic society by a provocative political stance. The appropriate course of action for Poland's Catholic Church and communities was to avoid direct confrontations with the communist state by avoiding participation in the political process entirely.[56] As the communists secured their position, and the time of Stalinism began under Bolesław Bierut, censorship also harshened, and the church became increasingly pressured, culminating in 1953 when Cardinal Stefan Wyszyński was placed under house arrest.

Stalin died in 1953, leaving an internal Soviet power struggle in his wake. Under Bierut's rule, the state removed the Catholic journals from their editorial boards' control because they had refused to publish an obituary for Stalin. The PAX movement took over *Tygodnik Powszechny* and *Znak* and refashioned them into party-loyal publications.[57] In a strategic move used by communist parties in multiple countries, PAX functioned as a "national Catholic" movement, trying to undermine the traditional Catholic hierarchy and distance its followers from Rome. PAX, under the leadership of former fascist Bolesław Piasecki, also published a daily newspaper, *Słowo Powszechne* (the Universal Word) and was connected to a weekly, *Dziś i jutro* (Today and Tomorrow), edited by the Social-Christian Institute's Jan Frankowski.[58] These journals would later engage in debates about Polish–German relations with *Znak*, *Więź*, and *Tygodnik Powszechny*.

Nikita Khrushchev became the new leader in the Soviet Union in 1955. In February 1956, attempting to distance his party from Stalinism, Khrushchev held a presentation at the party's twentieth congress, a closed session, which came to be known as "the Secret Speech," a four-hour criticism of Stalin's era and policies. Bolesław Bierut died from unknown causes while attending the congress. The Secret Speech leaked through Polish sources, having appeared in Polish translation first, and then became known to the rest of the world.

Poland at this point faced an economic crisis and, in late June, a challenge to its internal stability. Strikes broke out in Poznań among factory and shipyard workers and threatened to spread countrywide. The summer unrest also contributed to a leadership crisis. In October, Władysław Gomułka became the new leader of the party through deliberations that involved Polish officials as well as delegations from the Soviet Union.[59] His reinstatement was intended to stabilize and calm the society. Stalin's objections to Gomułka became an asset to the Polish leader as he attempted to gain the confidence of the population. He also impressed West German observers, who suddenly felt a sense of hope with regards to Poland's turn toward a more liberal order and greater independence from the Soviet Union. On October 31, 1956, *Der Spiegel* reported that "Poland's will to freedom broke out of the Soviet confinements" "like a tortured bull" with "Władysław Gomułka, who was still ostracized a half year ago" riding on its back.[60] Thus, the Polish October began as a time of optimism, as the reinstalled Gomułka government reversed some of the harsher policies from the Stalinist era, allowed the Polish borders to be partially opened, and permitted, for a few years, the media to write and discuss internal developments more freely. A moment of weakness and transition for the

Polish communist state became a moment of opportunity for journalists and civil-society activists engaged in foreign relations.

Soon after his reinstatement, on October 28, 1956, Gomułka also released Cardinal Wyszyński from house arrest. The cardinal returned to his palace on Miodowa Street in Warsaw, where he appeared before cheering crowds on his balcony. Once more, the communist leadership bargained for the cardinal's and the church's support in calming the widespread protests. In return for such support, the church demanded that the state restore control of their journals to the one-time editors. Gomułka complied and also allowed the representatives from *Znak*, *Więź*, and *Tygodnik Powszechny* to form a small Catholic political group within the reformed parliament, the so-called Znak Circle.[61] As another gesture of goodwill, the state permitted the foundation of Clubs of Catholic Intellectuals in five Polish cities.[62]

The parliamentary Znak Circle prominently featured Stanisław Stomma, Tadeusz Mazowiecki, Jerzy Turowicz, Stefan Kisielewski, Wanda Pieniężna, and Jerzy Zawieyski. Jerzy Zawieyski was an old wartime acquaintance of Władysław Gomułka and in many ways key to these developments. He obtained a chair in the powerful State Council, the higher executive body in the communist regime. From this position he could function personally as a mediator between Cardinal Wyszyński and Gomułka and promote the position of the Polish Catholic intelligentsia.[63]

After Gomułka took control of the government, the writers surrounding *Tygodnik Powszechny* and the Znak Circle believed that working for political change from inside the existing system would finally be possible. Their political outlook built on their previously discussed experiences and understandings of Polish history, their recent Second World War experiences, as well as nineteenth-century and interwar-era debates about Polish nationhood. The Circle partially drew on disagreements between Piłsudski's and Dmowski's political models for Poland's national character and foreign relations in the interwar era. While many of the Catholic intellectuals had been Piłsudskiites in the interwar era, they now distanced themselves from this federal tradition, believing that the war had proven the instability of a multicultural society and that at this point Poland needed internal stability and ethnic homogeneity as well as positive foreign relations to survive. In his writings, Stomma distinguished sharply between prewar multicultural Poland, which he had known, and postwar Poland as a de facto modern ethnic nation-state, which needed to be realistic about its geographically difficult location on the European continent.[64] He cautiously stated that he approved of "a few—I emphasize, a few—of Dmowski's theses."[65] Those of which he approved included Dmowski's assessment of Poland's need to become a modernized nation-state and that it should accept its current borders and maintain friendly alliances with powerful neighboring states in order to secure its survival. Kisielewski stated that after the war "a new, united Poland emerged, which proved to be a viable creation. It was elastic and dynamic, and to a high extent the result of a new geographic and ethnographic situation, new historical situation, and new geopolitics."[66] In other words, the unmixing of the borderlands, while a sad historical event, had strengthened and vitalized Poland. As Marcin Zaremba has shown, Polish political thought drew more broadly between 1956 and 1970 on Dmowski in conceptualizing postwar Poland and its situation within Europe.[67]

The members of the Znak Circle resisted the heroic, martyrdom-centered versions of Polish patriotism on which the episcopate, particularly Cardinal Wyszyński, relied heavily in public rhetoric during the communist era. In a 1957 article, Stomma criticized the actions of those he deemed to be reckless national heroes, such as Tadeusz Kościuszko, and those responsible for the uprisings against the Russians in 1830 and 1863.[68] Stomma said that because the group was too small, their actions could result in "disaster, and only disaster." He added, "Being 'heroic' is good for a soldier but bad for a politician."[69] In a 1959 article titled "Cień Winkelrieda," (In the Shadow of Wienkelried) which responded to accusations in the Vatican newspaper *Osservatore Romano* of Polish collaboration with the communists, Stomma complained about this external pressure on Polish Catholics to fight against, rather than cooperate with, the communist regime.[70]

The Znak Circle labeled the more complex stance they developed to justify their cooperation with the national communists "neopositivism." The term referenced the Cracow school of positivism dating from the late nineteenth century, and the Habsburg possession of Poland that had emerged as a reaction to the failed 1863 uprising against Russia. This school of thought preferred a strategy of reform-oriented opposition over militant or open resistance against foreign occupying powers. Cooperation with the system, the philosophy of "organic work" or moderate change and self-improvement from within, would better serve Poland and contribute to its future strength and independence.[71] Along such lines, the Znak Circle claimed that postwar Poland had too much to lose from open opposition to the communist party—not only the risk of brutal repression internally but also a potential Soviet intervention and the loss of the country's newly acquired sovereignty. Key to this argument was also the understanding that Poland needed to rebuild and modernize to survive in a postwar world.

While the Znak members held no sympathy for communism, they were also not fervently anticommunist. They wanted more democratic freedoms in Poland but considered a stable state an absolute priority, believing in the possibility of changing the communist state from within. Kisielewski once wrote, "Because, after all, I am a person of the state [*państwowiec, Staatsmensch*] and do not like peoples without states—regardless of the system of that state and whatever hesitations I may have against that system."[72] Stomma defined his political program as the acceptance of the existing Marxist *raison d'état* and the alliance with the Soviet Union, preferring political method above political romanticism, promoting compromise, and rejecting risks, violence, and prestige politics.[73] In explaining his participation in communist politics in the late 1950s, Stomma also stated his hope that the new government would begin to "take into account the will of the nation, to take into consideration the nation as it really was and not some hypothetical stereotype" of it.[74]

The Catholic writers also began to revise the image of the Germans and Germany as an aspect of their program for Poland's foreign relations. Memories of the occupation and official memory politics shaped dominant Polish perceptions of Germans. As Joanna Wawrzyniak and others have shown, the Polish communist state cultivated anti-German sentiments and memories in order to unify postwar Poland and argue for the necessity of a close alliance with the Soviet Union.[75] All Polish media was under the control of the Department of Propaganda and Agitation of the Polish Communist Party's Central Committee (Wydział Propagandy i Agitacji Komitetu Centralnego PZPR).[76] The party mainly controlled the press through personnel management in which correspondents, editors, and journalists were selected based on their political profile and loyalty to the communist party. In addition, the state directly censored the press. In a process of self-censorship, journalists learned to avoid topics and statements that they knew might not pass the official censors.[77] The desire to distinguish between the good communist East Germans and the threatening West Germans further complicated the position of the Polish communist state and the communist media on German questions.

The Department of Propaganda and Agitation issued particular guidelines for the media discussions of the two German states. The writings on the GDR should focus on the traditions of mutual revolutionary battle that Poles and East Germans shared, the roles of antifascist or Marxist Germans in the concentration camps, and descriptions of present-day cultural and economic cooperation between the Polish People's Republic and the GDR.[78] Other guidelines involved never referring to Germany or the Germans as one state or one people and using "Berlin" only with reference to the German Democratic Republic. "East Berlin" was not appropriate. The media must refer to the border as "the border on the Oder and the Neisse" or "the border between Poland and the GDR" but never "the Polish–German border." East Germany should only be described in positive terms while the West German state, at least before 1956, should be described wholly negatively, with reference to its fascist past.[79] The position on the German division proved a particular challenge for two reasons: while it was relatively easy to encourage antagonisms toward the Germans in a broader Polish population, it was considerably more difficult to convince the public of the distinction between good East and bad West Germans. Secondly, when the official media fueled the collective memories of the German occupation of Poland, and the German threat to Polish territory in the postwar era, they always risked an anti-Soviet backlash, given the Soviet participation in the occupation, and the Polish loss of territory in the east.

In the late 1950s, the Catholic journals actively challenged the image of the postwar West Germans as a threat to Poland. Contrary to the communist press and official guidelines, they introduced the idea of a postwar emergence of "other Germans" who were different from those who had partitioned, occupied, and killed Poles.[80] In his article "Czy Hitler nie był Prusakiem?" (Was Hitler Not a Prussian?), Stomma distinguished Prussians as different from other German political traditions. He argued that the Prussian tradition in particular was the root of National Socialism, calling it "an idea more political than geographic, more a system than a country."[81] Prussianism (*Preussentum*) was not a nation but a caste of Junkers and a political-administrative order. Stomma also suggested in his writings that the West German Catholic tradition in particular was less anti-Polish and more salvageable for postwar Europe than most Poles believed.[82] Other writers for the weekly also attempted to counter the demonization of Germans in Polish postwar public discourse and media.[83]

The Catholic intellectuals emphasized the stability and protection that the Cold War system afforded Poland. They argued that the protection of the Soviet Union, making a new German invasion all but impossible, improved relations and prompted exploration of mutual interests with the Federal Republic, particularly security on the European continent.[84] Culturally, the Catholic intellectuals always felt that they belonged to "Europe" rather than Eastern Europe or a Slavic realm, and they therefore wanted closer ties to the west. Establishing relations with West Germany was an important aspect of their European agenda. Arguing for a proactive foreign policy stance to secure Poland's position, Stomma stated that "our contribution, thus, will be to move in the direction of bridging the chasm between East and West. Catholics in Poland want to be a link connecting East and West [and] in this way serve [the cause of] peace."[85]

Tygodnik Powszechny and its writers made Polish national interests and the development of closer ties to the West European countries central to their vision of Poland's foreign policy. While arguing that Poland needed the protection of the Soviet Union, they also imagined ties to West Germany as a way of decreasing Poland's security dependence on its powerful eastern neighbor. Their travels and cross-border networking in this era also indicated the significance they assigned to promoting Polish interests in Western Europe. Stomma, Kisielewski, and Turowicz developed a specific political agenda for peace in the 1960s, in which Poland would be able to develop and become stronger and more prominent culturally, politically, and economically. In a 1965 article titled "Pokój i treci świat" (Peace and the Third World), Stomma and Turowicz connected the view on the (geo)political reality of states and lingering conflicts with an agenda for peace. They wrote:

> Conflicts will not suddenly disappear, nor politicians turn into angels. There is no sense in chasing utopias. We must set real goals, express them in real categories. Real is striving to confront the growing feeling of helplessness, and above all to confront the forces of extremism, which consciously or unconsciously impel toward conflict.[86]

The bottom line of this agenda included two important points: first, negotiation and dialogue was always preferable to violent protest, internally as well as internationally; and second, peace in Europe would depend on the existence of the Polish communist state, which they were now attempting to reform from the inside.[87] Turowicz and Stomma prided themselves on a realistic assessment of postwar Poland. Their ideas were founded in Catholic theology but were also based on the modern Polish state's interests. The agenda for peace harmonized well with the neopositivist solution, which they proposed for domestic progress in its emphasis on gradual change and avoidance of open confrontation.

The Polish October in West Germany

Not only Gomułka's ascent but also Cardinal Wyszyński's release and return made headlines in West German newspapers, particularly in the Catholic press, such as conservative *Rheinischer Merkur*, which had closely covered the cardinal's internment and the church's difficulties since 1953. Writers for the *Merkur* were well-informed but tended to frame the state–church relations as a question of Catholic suffering, continuous resistance to communism, and spiritual courage. They downplayed the Polish Church hierarchy's pragmatism and intermittent readiness to seek agreements and compromises with the communist state. In 1954 and 1955, the newspaper wrote about the Polish Catholics' "silent battle" and argued that although small groups in Poland promoted a compromise between the communists and the church, Polish Catholics broadly condemned the idea and felt that it was impossible.[88]

West German media observed the Polish developments with great interest. They had some hope that Gomułka would respect civil society, in the form of the Catholic Church, and would be able to reform and soften communism and distance Poland from Soviet hegemony. In early July, *Der Spiegel* reported that Polish radio was broadcasting about new developments and the unrest in Poznań.[89] *Der Tag* in Berlin compared Gomułka to Yugoslav leader Josip Tito, suggesting that Gomułka might be the first admirable Polish leader in a long time.[90] The lionization of Gomułka also translated into demands in West German newspapers for the ruling Christian Democratic Union (CDU) to revise its Eastern Policy.[91] As for Cardinal Wyszyński, the press described him as "Poland's most powerful man" and emphasized the state's dependence on the church for the preservation of stability in Poland.[92]

The Polish developments in 1956 created an upswing in West German interest in Poland, which brought further career advantages for several leading Poland experts. Hansjakob Stehle became the *FAZ* correspondent in this period while Ludwig Zimmerer became *Die Welt*'s, later Norddeutscher Rundfunk's (NDR), permanent correspondent to Warsaw. As a young Catholic socialist, Zimmerer visited Poland in 1955 through an invitation by the communist-Catholic organization PAX. He expected to find a successful experimental cooperation between the communist state and the Catholic Church, the only one of its kind across the globe, but was soon disappointed.[93] Zimmerer had separated from his wife Margaret by 1956 and had left West Germany permanently as the communist party was banned and the Constitutional Court closed down all or most communist publications. In Poland, once the strikes broke out in 1956, he contacted *Die Welt* and asked whether they were interested in eyewitness reports. He submitted several freelance articles before becoming permanently employed.[94]

Hansjakob Stehle entered Poland for the first time together with Zimmerer in 1956. One of his earliest commentaries on the Polish October, written two days after the return of Cardinal Wyszyński to Warsaw, highlighted the role of Piasecki and PAX as intermediaries in the agreement between Wyszyński and Gomułka. The article mentioned Piasecki's background as the leader for a "short-lived Polish 'Falange'" but also emphasized the importance of PAX in the new developments.[95] In this early article, Stehle was still relatively unfamiliar with the Catholic groups and factions in Poland. He made no mention of the removal and return of the Catholic journals to the original editors or the depth of tensions between the episcopate and the PAX movement. Over time, as he familiarized himself with Poland, he would transfer his hopes for state–church cooperation from PAX to the Znak Circle and the editors of *Znak* and *Tygodnik Powszechny*.

West German liberal and moderate journalists shared the Polish groups' assessment of the importance of the status quo and a stable state even if that state happened to be communist. They found the hardline western anticommunism of early 1950s America and West Germany increasingly problematic. This made them very interested in the Znak Circle's arguments concerning neopositivism, compromise, peace, and stability. It seemed to confirm their own opinions that Cold War Europe sorely needed compromise within the existing system, dialogue across borders, and nonviolent solutions.

Once Gomułka's government allowed western journalists to travel in Poland, West German visitors took advantage of the opening either to see the new Poland or see the places where their families had lived before the expulsions. They visited Warsaw and Wrocław and reported their impressions in the German newspapers, comparing the cities and the countryside to their prewar impressions.[96] They wrote of the economic shortages that still existed and attempted to measure the mood among the population. They faced obstacles in their efforts to gain information about and contacts in Poland: on the one hand, the existing language barriers, and on the other, the Polish state's efforts to limit contacts between its own citizens and foreign visitors through surveillance and pressure on those with western contacts.

The Polish October interested the Adenauer government as well. Unwilling to reverse the Hallstein Doctrine, the policy of refusing diplomatic relations with all countries that recognized East Germany, the Christian Democratic leadership relied on informal or semiofficial visitors such as journalists, business travelers, and writers to gather information in the late 1950s. Polish state-level representatives were aware that some of the western travelers had direct lines of communication to the foreign department and met with them in order to communicate with the West German state. Klaus Otto Skibowski served as such an intermediary, and also became central to the connections between the Znak Circle and West German Catholics in the late 1950s. He traveled to Poland on a state-sponsored reconnaissance mission in 1957. He also became one of Stomma's earliest West German contacts.

Skibowski was born in 1927 in Lyck (later Ełk), Masuria, in postwar Poland. He began his career as a journalist in 1946 after serving on the eastern front. Much later, in 2003, his semiautobiographical novel *Wolken über weitem Land* (Clouds Over a Wide Country), described over multiple generations a family in Masuria expelled at the end of the Second World War. In this novel, Skibowski addressed his family's relocation to and experiences with postwar West Germany. Closely paralleling Skibowski's own career trajectory, the son in the novel, Ottchen, becomes a journalist in West Germany. The novel gives the reader a sense of what it meant to be a Masurian in postwar Europe and postwar West Germany.[97]

Employed by the Catholic News Agency, and occasionally writing for *Rheinischer Merkur*, Skibowski hosted Stanisław Stomma on his earliest visit to the Federal Republic in 1957. In the Adenauer era he worked with developing national representations of West Germany as a civilized, progressive, and European state that would mobilize and unify the population while maintaining a safe distance from the Nazi official aesthetics and public celebrations. He shared with official and semiofficial Polish representatives a concern with the image and reputation of their nations, the importance of appearance abroad. In his 1956 visit to Poland, Skibowski drew on prewar contacts to establish connections in Warsaw. His father was an acquaintance of Cardinal Wyszyński, as they had studied music in Gdańsk together before the war.

Thus, between 19 April and 7 May 1957, Skibowski traveled to Poland at the official invitation of the Polish Church. There, he met with journalists of *Tygodnik Powszechny* through the Cardinal's intervention. He produced a report about his travels for Adenauer and the Foreign Office, as well as an article for *Rheinischer Merkur*.[98] Skibowski reported the changes in Poland, commenting specifically on the Polish curiosity toward West Germans. He established connections to the Catholic circles, particularly to Stanisław Stomma, whom he described in his reports as the political leader of Znak, the spiritual leader of *Tygodnik Powszechny*, and a personal friend of Cardinal Wyszyński. However, Skibowski described Stomma as a communist loyalist. "Stomma does nothing without the government's agreement."[99] His perspective differed from that of Zimmerer and Stehle, who tended to treat the Znak Circle as intellectually autonomous and to assign them greater independent agency and influence on Polish politics.

The version of Skibowski's report that reached the West German Foreign Office emphasized the Polish public's respect for and support of Adenauer. It downplayed the territorial problem, stating that the Poles wanted to build an atmosphere of trust and goodwill and later, presumably after the fall of communism, approach the border issue "in a European spirit." The Foreign Office's reaction to his description of Poland made clear the general West German political climate and dominant political understandings of the Polish October. The Foreign Office representative commented in its notes that Skibowski's report was quite interesting but overly optimistic.[100] A strongly anticommunist stance dominated the ministry's policy toward Poland at the time, evidenced in a preference for ruthless negotiations, distrust, power displays, and political maneuvering. The ministry considered Skibowski's optimism about the vitality and influence of the Catholic Church farfetched.

Karlheinz Koppe took advantage of the opened borders and visited his birthplace of Wrocław in May 1957. He reported that the Poles in Wrocław were friendly toward West Germans and commented on their "preparedness to speak openly and freely about the basic problems in Polish–German relations."[101] He commented particularly on the great economic problems that the Poles still faced. Gomułka's primary problem, in Koppe's opinion, was not ideological but economic.[102]

Another development colored early Polish–German relations during the late 1950s. In 1957, the Polish government attempted to improve its relations with the West European governments and to open diplomatic relations with the Federal Republic of Germany. Its efforts culminated in the Rapacki Plan, named for Polish foreign minister Adam Rapacki, which proposed partial nuclear disarmament, a nuclear-free zone, in Central Europe between the two Germanys, Poland, and Czechoslovakia.[103] Whereas the Soviet Union, after some hesitation, agreed to let the Poles proceed with the plan, the West German government did not take it seriously or respond to the overtures by the Polish government. As a consequence of this fraught interaction, the relations between the Federal Republic and Poland cooled even further by the end of the 1950s. Stehle placed great hope in the Rapacki Plan, and when it became clear that it would not be realized, he harshly criticized this failure of West Germany to capitalize on the Polish overtures. He promoted international cooperation as a key aspect of European stability and peace.[104]

Yet another behind-the-scenes intermediary in unregulated political overtures between Bonn and Warsaw during those years was the businessman Berthold Beitz. Beitz, who like von Bismarck originated from Pomerania, was the CEO of Krupp Industries and had lived in Poland during the Second World War, working as a manager for a gasoline production plant in Poland. He became famous for saving hundreds of Jews and Poles from the concentration camps.[105] Using his goodwill in Poland, he negotiated in 1958 and 1960 with high-level communist leaders about a partial opening of official relations. The Polish communist leadership was generally Polish first and communist second, and they treated Beitz as an honored guest and old friend. The intent of the Beitz mission was to establish economic ties to Poland without tampering with the official policy of the Hallstein Doctrine. Beitz's efforts resulted in the 1963 exchange of trade missions between Bonn and Warsaw, but, according to Stehle, the distrust and unwillingness of the West German and Polish governments to respond to his efforts at diplomacy deeply frustrated Beitz, and in the end the Polish communists never fully accepted the function of the trade mission.[106] The lack of concrete initiatives by the sitting CDU government, the Hallstein Doctrine, and the failure of the Rapacki Plan soured official Polish–German relations further in the late 1950s and early 1960s. Instead, initiatives took an alternative path outside of organized politics, and alliances formed between elite media, left-wing religious groups, and a few political actors in the Federal Republic, and the Catholic intelligentsia in Poland.

Conclusion

Experiences during the war, as chaos ensued, and prewar systems and boundaries broke down, caused many activists to rethink and renegotiate their previously held beliefs about and attitudes toward the other country, people, and society. In addition, for both Polish and German participants in the postwar dialogue, the destruction during the final months of the war inspired and shaped their commitment to stability and peace in Europe. They became motivated to participate in the efforts to renegotiate Polish–German relations based on a variety of personal circumstances, including a geographic or personal connection to the other country, religious motivations, fluency in the other country's language, or through their engagement with questions of peace and pacifism, but equally often for reasons based in their understanding of their own countries' national self-interests in the postwar era. Religious transnational networks and subcultures within both countries provided a foundation for the postwar interest in and effort toward reconciliation in the case of many participants. This did not mean, however, that the mainstream churches as institutions could credit themselves with initiating reconciliatory efforts or dialogue at this point of time.

The year 1956 became an important signpost for early Polish–German relations in several ways. First, it permitted West German correspondents and journalists to enter Poland and the Polish Catholic intellectuals to travel and gain attention in West Germany. Contacts between the Polish intellectuals and their West European Catholic, intellectual, and media conversation partners intensified because of the events in 1956. Second, the high hopes for the Polish October and Gomułka's reforms, despite soon petering out into the so-called "Little Stabilization," drew public attention to Poland and jumpstarted the media careers of many of the West German "Poland experts."[107] The Polish state's temporary weakness in 1956 forced it to negotiate with the Polish Catholic Church for assistance in controlling the population, thus giving the Catholic institutions bargaining power. The lack of official relations allowed journalists and representatives from these civil society groups the freedom to interact across borders, giving them opportunity to assume roles as unofficial cultural diplomats and inspiring them to greater efforts to lobby for political and cultural change.

Notes

1. Jürgen Neven-du Mont, "Warum ich Warschau liebe," unpublished manuscript, BAK NL 1279/137.
2. For such an approach, see Michael David-Fox, "Introduction," in *Fascination and Enmity: Germany and Russia as Entangled Histories, 1914–1945*, ed. Michael David-Fox, Peter Holquist, and Alexander M. Martin (Pittsburgh, 2012), 4–5. Hansen, "Youth off the Rails," 135–67.
3. Bismarck, *Aufbruch aus Pommern*, 123–24.
4. Zaremba, "War Syndrome," 30. Zaremba points out that these numbers exclude Belorussian, German, and Ukrainian citizens of Poland. Mateusz Gniazdowski estimated the numbers, based on recent research, to 1.4 million ethnic Poles killed during German occupation. The German occupation killed a total of 5.2 to 5.3 million Polish citizens. Mateusz Gniazdowski, "Zu den Menschenverlusten, die Polen während des Zweiten Weltkrieges von den Deutschen zugefügt wurden: Eine Geschichte von Forschungen und Schätzungen," in *Historie: Jahrbuch des Zentrums für Historische Forschung Berlin der Polnischen Akademie der Wissenschaften 2007/2008* (Berlin 2008), 88.
5. BAK NL1279/200 Grabrede, BAK.
6. Letter from Jürgen Neven-du Mont to Elisabeth Neven-du Mont, 11 November 1942, BAK NL1279/1.
7. For context see Jochen Hellback, "'The Diaries of Fritzes and the Letters of Gretchens': Personal Writings from the German–Soviet War and Their Readers," in David-Fox, Holquist, and Martin, *Fascination and Enmity*, 123–53. For more context on West German war veterans after the Second World War, see Frank Biess, *Homecomings: Returning POWs and the Legacies of the Defeat in Postwar Germany* (Princeton, 2006).
8. Letter from Jürgen Neven-du Mont to Elisabeth Neven-du Mont, 12 March 1943, BAK NL1279/1.
9. Bismarck, *Aufbruch aus Pommern*, 166.
10. Koppe, *Dreimal getauft*, 74.
11. Ibid., 80.
12. Ingo von Münch, ed., *Dokumente des geteilten Deutschlands* (Stuttgart, 1968), 42–43.
13. BAK NL1279/1b, Letter from Carl August Neven-du Mont to Jürgen Neven-du Mont, 14 May 1945.
14. BAK NL1279/83-84 Lebenslauf.
15. Ibid.
16. Michael Mansfeld and Jürgen Neven-du Mont, *Denk ich an Deutschland: Ein Kommentar in Bild und Wort* (Munich, 1956). The volume was very unfavorably reviewed in *Die Zeit*. "Verzerrte Gedanken über Deutschland," *Die Zeit*, 31 March 1956.
17. Marion Dönhoff, "Ritt gen Westen," *Die Zeit* 5 (21 March 1946): 6.

18. Ibid., 6.
19. Marion Dönhoff, "Totengedenken 1946," *Die Zeit* 4 (21 March 1945): 1.
20. Hodenberg, *Konsens und Krise*, 103.
21. Wilfried Köpke, *Geschäftsführung ohne Auftrag: Das Journalismusverständnis von Walter Dirks* (Munich, 2007). Eugen Kogon (1903–87) was the son of a Russian diplomat and a Russian citizen originally. He had grown up in Germany, spent his childhood at Catholic academies, studied national economy and sociology in Munich, Florence, and Vienna, and received his PhD in 1927. As an opponent of National Socialism, he had been in the Buchenwald concentration camp six years when he was liberated in 1945. Kogon wrote one of the first standard works on Nazi Germany, *Der SS-Staat: Das System der deutschen Konzentrationslager* (The SS-State: The System of the German Concentration Camp) (Frankfurt, 1946). He participated in early debates on the Nazi war crimes and their connection to German society at large. In 1951, Kogon became professor at the Technischen Hochschule in Darmstadt, where he was affiliated until his retirement in 1968.
22. Hansjakob Stehle, "Der Reichsgedanke im politischen Weltbild von Leibniz" (PhD diss., Frankfurt, 1950).
23. Recent literature on Polish–East German relations includes Konstantin Hermann, *Die DDR und die Solidarność : ausgewählte Aspekte einer Beziehung* (Dresden, 2013), and the contributions to the anthology *Zwangsverordnete Freundschaft? Die Beziehungen zwischen der DDR und Polen, 1949–1990*, ed. Basil Kerski, Andrzej Kotula, and Kazimierz Wóycicki (Osnabrück, 2003). For an English-language overview of the official relations between Poland and East Germany, see Anderson, *Cold War in the Soviet Bloc*.
24. Demshuk, *Lost German East*, Robert E. Alvis, "Holy Homeland: The Discourse of Place and Displacement among Silesian Catholics in Postwar West Germany," *Church History* 79, no. 4 (December 2010): 828.
25. Pertti Ahonen, *After the Expulsion: West Germany and Eastern Europe 1945–1990* (Oxford, 2003), 21.
26. Bismarck, *Aufbruch aus Pommern*, 182.
27. Ibid., 217.
28. See Hannig, *Die Religion der Öffentlichkeit*, and Pearson, "Faith and Democracy."
29. Klaus von Bismarck, "Die Freiheit des Christen zum halten und hergeben," 9 July 1954, *Seid fröhlich in Hoffnung: Der sechste Evangelische Kirchentag vom 7. Bis 11. Juli 1954 in Leipzig* (Stuttgart, 1954), 432.
30. Klaus von Bismarck to Walter Dirks, date unknown, Nachlass Walter Dirks, Box 23:3, FES.
31. Koppe, *Dreimal getauft*, 80, 91.
32. Ibid., 92–93.
33. Ibid., 65.
34. Ibid., 130.
35. These facts are taken from a correspondence between Zimmerer and Walter Dirks in which Zimmerer introduced himself and attempted to secure support, financial and otherwise, from Dirks, the well-known media personality. Ludwig Zimmerer to Walter Dirks, 23 September 1949, Nachlass Walter Dirks, Box 47A, FES.
36. Ludwig Zimmerer to Arbeitskreis katholischer Jugend gegen die Wiederaufrüstungspolitik, 27 October 1952, Nachlass Walter Dirks, Box 80A, FES; Ludwig Zimmerer, Ludwig Zimmerer to Walter Dirks, 27 November 1954, Nachlass Walter Dirks, Box 102, FES. For more on the Catholic youth culture and movement in West Germany, see Mark Ruff, *The Wayward Flock: Catholic Youth in Postwar West Germany, 1945–1955* (Chapel Hill, NC, 2005). For the rearmament and nuclear debate in the 1950s, see Susanna Schrafstetter,

"The Long Shadow of the Past: History, Memory and the Debate over West Germany's Nuclear Status, 1954–69," *History and Memory* 16, no. 1 (Spring/Summer 2005): 118–45.
37. Ehmig, *Generationswechsel im deutschen Journalismus*, 52–53. See also Hodenberg, *Konsens und Krise*, 229.
38. For a contextualization of the Springer imperium in emerging German postwar media, see Gudrun Kruip, *Das "Welt" - "Bild" des Axel Springer Verlags: Journalismus zwischen westlichen Werten und deutschen Denk-traditionen* (Munich, 1999). See Tim von Arnim, *"Und dann werde ich das grösste Zeitungshaus Europas bauen": der Unternehmer Axel Springer* (Frankfurt/Main, 2012).
39. Demshuk, *Lost German East*, 21, 106.
40. Feinberg, *Curtain of Lies*, xi.
41. A popular Westdeutscher Rundfunk (WDR) radio show reporting from East Germany but also from Eastern Europe in the early 1960s was named *Wir sprechen zur Zone* (We Speak about the Zone).
42. See Hodenberg, *Konsens und Krise*, 150–61. Mathias Weiss, "Öffentlichkeit als Therapie: Die Medien und Informationspolitik der Regierung Adenauer zwischen Propaganda und kritischer Aufklärung," in *Medialisierung und Demokratie im 20. Jahrhundert*, ed. Frank Bösch and Norbert Frei (Göttingen, 2006), 73–120.
43. Pszon, "Wspomnienia 1947–1956," 12.
44. Ibid., 536.
45. Friszke, "Jerzy Zawieyski," 16–17.
46. Jarocki, *Czterdzieści pięć lat w opozycji*, 76–121.
47. Stomma, *Pościg za nadzieją*, 88–89. For a contextual history of Vilnius during the Second World War and its relations to Poland, Germany, and the Soviet Union, see Šarūnas Liekis, *1939: The Year That Changed Everything in Lithuania's History* (Amsterdam, 2010).
48. Józefa Hennelowa, *Bo jestem z Wilna . . . (z Józefą Hennelową rozmawia Roman Graczyk)* (Cracow: Społeczny Instytut Wydawnictwo ZNAK, 2001), 34–35.
49. Stomma, *Pościg za nadzieją*, 90.
50. Hennelowa, *Bo jestem z Wilna*, 51.
51. Norman Davies, *God's Playground: A History of Poland*, vol. 2, *1795 to the Present*, rev. ed. (New York, 2005), 575.
52. Czeckoslovakia took similar measures. A growing literature on the Polonization of Poland in the 1940s and 1950s has emerged. Thum, *Die fremde Stadt*; Curp, *A Clean Sweep?*; Service, "Reinterpreting the Expulsion," 528–50.
53. Antoni Dudek and Ryszard Gryz, *Komuniści i Kościół w Polsce (1945–1989)* (Cracow, 2003), 24–27. See Porter-Szücs, *Faith and Fatherland*, for a discussion of the position of the postwar Polish Church. See also Friszke, *Opozycja polityczna w PRL*, 39.
54. Władysław Bartoszewski, *Aus der Geschichte lernen? Aufsätze und Reden zur Kriegs- und Nachkriegsgeschichte Polens* (Munich, 1986).
55. For a thorough understanding of *Tygodnik Powszechny*'s role in Poland internally, see Manetti, "Sign of the Times." The Central Office for the Contro of Press, Publications, and Entertainments (GUKPPiW) was established on 5 July 1946. Joanna Szymoniczek, "Polish Public Opinion towards Germany and the Events of the Year 1968 Therein," in *1968 and Polish–West German Relations*, edited by Wanda Jarząbek, Piotr Madajczyk, and Joanna Szymoniczek, translated by Mariusz Kukliński (Warsaw, 2013), 134.
56. Manetti, "Sign of the Times," 72. See also Stanisław Stomma, "Maksymalne i minimalne tendencje społeczne katolików," *Znak* 3 (1946): 265–75.
57. Jarocki, *Czterdzieści pięć lat*, 158.
58. Bolesław Piasecki (1915–79) led the Polish Fascist party Obóz Narodowy-Radykalny during the interwar era and later the even the further right ONR-Falanga. During

the war, he fought for the resistance, but after the Soviet NKVD took him captive he became a communist. In 1947, he founded the pro-communist Catholic organization Stowarzyszenie PAX and its daily newspaper *Słowo Powszechnie*. While the Stowarzyszenie PAX was founded with NKVD support to undermine Catholic nationalism, Kunicki argues in *Between the Brown and the Red* that the organization carried many ONR legacies, such as its anti-German and anti-Semitic stance, into the postwar era.

59. Andrzej Werblan, "The Polish October of 1956—Legends and Reality," in *The Polish October 1956 in World Politics*, ed. Jan Rowiński and Tytus Jaskułowski (Warsaw, 2007), 23. See also Paweł Machcewicz, *Rebellious Satellite: Poland, 1956* (Washington, DC, 2009).
60. "O Polen, deine Qual!" *Der Spiegel* 44, 31 October 1956, 34. For an overview of 1956, see contributions to Rowiński and Jaskułowski, *Polish October 1956*.
61. Jarocki, *Czterdeści pięć lat w opozycji*; Andrzej Friszke, *Koło posłów Znak w Sejmie, 1957–1976* (Warsaw, 2002).
62. Bartoszewski, *Aus der Geschichte lernen?*, 281.
63. Barbara Tyszkiewicz. "Naiwny i heroiczny: Jerzy Zawieyski jako mediator pomiędzy kardynałem Wyszyńskim a Władysławem Gomułką," *Zeszyty Historyczne* 156 (Paris, 2006): 40–2006; Friszke, "Jerzy Zawieyski," 36.
64. An influential thinker on Polish geopolitics, Dmowski founded the modern nationalist movement (Endecja) in Poland and was a lifelong political competitor to Józef Piłsudski. Recent spatial thought on Eastern Europe has posited, as a contrast to Dmowski's vision, that Piłsudski "envisioned a Polish political nation floating above the multinational borderlands he called home." Snyder, *Reconstruction of Nations*, 59. Also discussed in Andrzej Walicki "The Three Traditions in Polish Patriotism," in *Polish Paradoxes*, ed. Stanisław Gomułka and Antony Polonsky (New York, 1990), 34.
65. Stanisław Stomma, "Pozytywizm od strony moralnej," *Tygodnik Powszechny*, 14 April 1957.
66. Stefan Kisielewski, *An dieser Stelle Europas: Ein Pole über Ost und West—und andere Fragen von heute* (Munich, 1964), 263.
67. Marcin Zaremba, *Komunizm, legitymizacja, nacjonalizm: nacjonalistyczna legitymizacja władzy komunistycznej w Polsce* (Warsaw, 2005).
68. Tadeusz Kościuszko led a national uprising in 1794 in Warsaw against Russia and Prussia. After some months of fighting in the summer and fall, it was ultimately defeated. The Polish king was deported, and the Polish kingdom ceased to exist; the uprising's leaders were imprisoned or killed. The uprising in November 1830 began on a small scale but broadened when the Russian tsar demanded unconditional surrender of the Polish nation, leading many additional Poles to take up arms. The conflict lasted for almost a year, and Poles lost the rest of their self-governance. The 1863 uprising lasted sixteen months, and the Russian authorities punished the insurrectionaries by executions and deportations. All traces of the Polish state were erased, and Russia launched a program of Russification of the Poles.
69. Stanisław Stomma, "Pozytywizm od strony moralnej," *Tygodnik Powszechny*, 14 January 1957. Communist schoolbooks lauded Kościuszko for his efforts to liberate the serfs, to include peasants, but emphasized that his uprising failed because of its limited scope. Joanna Wojdon and Jakub Tyszkiewicz, "The Image of Tadeusz Kościuszko in Postwar Polish Education," *Polish Review* 59, no. 3 (2014): 81–94.
70. Winkelried was a Swiss hero who saved an army when he stopped a spear by letting it pierce his own chest. Stanisław Stomma, "Cień Winkelrieda," *Tygodnik Powszechny*, 21 June 1959.
71. Stanisław Stomma, "Pozytywizm od strony moralnej," *Tygodnik Powszechny*, 14 January 1957.

72. Hansjakob Stehle, "Blick nach Ost und West: Hansjakob Stehle stellt den polnischen Publizisten Stefan Kisielewski vor," 13 October 1964, HA-WDR 2502, 48.
73. Stanisław Stomma, "Dlaczego kandyduję do Sejmu," *Tygodnik Powszechny*, 20 January 1957; see also Stehle, "Blick nach Ost und West," 13 October 1964, HA-WDR 2502.
74. Ibid.
75. Wawrzyniak, *Veterans, Victims, and Memories*, 26.
76. Wacław Miziniak, "Polityka Informacyjna," in Wolff-Powęska, *Polacy wobec Niemców*, 142–60. Stefan Garsztecki, *Das Deutschlandbild in der offiziellen, der katholischen un der oppositionellen Publizistik Polens 1970–1989: Feindbild kontra Annäherung* (Marburg, 1997), 15–18. See also the anthology by Katarzyna Pokorna-Ignatowicz, Joanna Bierówka, and Stanisław Jędrzejewski, *Media a Polacy: polskie media wobec ważnych wydarzeń politycznych i problemów społecznych* (Cracow, 2012).
77. Miziniak, "Polityka Informacyjna," 145.
78. Ibid., 147.
79. Szymoniczek, "Polish Public Opinion," 132, 134. Also Jane Leftwich Curry, trans. and ed., *The Black Book of Polish Censorship* (New York, 1984), 125–28.
80. See Anna Wolff-Powęska, "Poszukiwanie dróg dialogu: Świeckie elity katolickie wobec Niemiec," in Wolff-Powęska, *Polacy wobec Niemców*, 374–77.
81. Stanislaw Stomma, "Czy Hitler nie był Prusakiem?" *Tygodnik Powszechny*, 27 September 1964.
82. Stanislaw Stomma, "Dlaczego skapitulowano (katolicyzm w Niemczech)," *Tygodnik Powszechny*, 15 September 1963.
83. See Jerzy Łukaszewski, "Notatki Monachijskie—Reportaż z Niemiec," *Tzgodnik Powszechny*, 24 November 1957, or Antoni Gołubiew, "Mit o Drang nach Osten," *Tygodnik Powszechny*, 26 February 1960.
84. Stanisław Stomma, "Czy istnieje niebezpieczeństwo niemieckie?" *Tygodnik Powszechny*, 19 September 1962.
85. Stanisław Stomma, "Dlaczego kandyduję do Sejmu," *Tygodnik Powszechny*, 20 January 1957.
86. Stanisław Stomma and Jerzy Turowicz, "Pokój i treci świat," *Tygodnik Powszechny*, 23 May 1965.
87. As seen, for example, in Stanisław Stomma, "Gdzie jesteśmy? Dokąd idziemy?" *Tygodnik Powszechny*, 17 January 1960; Stanisław Stomma, "Co naprawdę jest realne?" 4 September 1960; Stanisław Stomma, "Czy spać na bombie atomowej?" 24 September 1961.
88. Klaus Furchner, "Kampf in der Stille: Der Katholizismus in Polen," *Rheinischer Merkur*, 30 July 1954.
89. "Uns heilt kein Balsam," *Der Spiegel* 27 (4 July 1956): 32.
90. "Das ist Wladyslaw Gomulka: Eiserner Wille und fanatischer Mut; Das abenteuerliche Leben des polnischen KP-Führers—Auch er glaubte an Moskau," *Der Tag*, 22 (?) October 1956.
91. Bernd Schaefer, "The GDR, the FRG and the Polish October 1956," in Jaskułowski and Rowiński, *Polish October 1956*, 197–216.
92. "Der stärkste Mann in Polen—Kardinal Wyszynski und der Staat—Die schwierige Lage der reformatorischen Kirche," *Der Tagesspiegel*, 18 July 1958; "Staat und Kirche in Polen," *Neue Zürcher Zeitung*, 5 December 1956.
93. Joanna Olczak-Ronikier, interview with author; Hansjakob Stehle, interview with author. Hansjakob Stehle, "Ludwig Zimmerer +" *Die Zeit*, 2 October 1987.
94. Joanna Olczak-Ronikier, interview with author.
95. Hansjakob Stehle, "Die polnische 'Opposition' im Zwielicht: Chancen und Grenzen eine politischen Katholizismus," *FAZ*, 31 October 1956.

96. Hermann Pörzgen, "Warschau—nicht mehr klein-Paris," *Frankfurter Allgemeine*, 10 December 1956; Werner Marx, "Nach der unblutigen Revolution: Bilanz einer Reise durch Polen," *Rheinischer Merkur*, 16 November 1956.
97. Klaus Skibowski, *Wolken über weitem Land: Eine Familiengeschichte aus Masuren* (Munich, 2003), 310.
98. Klaus Otto Skibowski, "Polen und Europa: Offene Gespräche hinter den Oder-Neisse," *Rheinischer Merkur*, 24 May 1957.
99. Klaus Skibowski, report, private copy in possession of author, 1957, 4.
100. "Aufzeichnung Freiherr von Ungern-Sternberg," 2 August 1957, PAA B 12 596A.
101. Benjamin Kubocz, "Polnisches Reisetagebuch," *Europa-Union*, 20 May 1957. Kubocz was Koppe's pen name in the 1950s. Koppe, *Dreimal getauft*, 168.
102. Ibid.
103. Teresa Łos-Nowak, *Plan Rapackiego a bezpieczeństwo Europejskie* (Wrocław, 1991); David Stefancic, "The Rapacki Plan: A Case Study of European Diplomacy,"*East European Quarterly* 21, no. 4 (Winter 1987): 401. See also Ernst Laboor, *Der Rapacki-Plan und die DDR: die Entspannungsvision des polnischen Aussenministers Adam Rapacki und die deutschlandpolitischen Ambitionen der SED-Führung in den fünfziger und sechziger Jahren* (Berlin, 2003).
104. Stehle wrote about the Rapacki Plan in *Nachbar Polen* (Frankfurt/Main, 1963).
105. Stehle, *Nachbar Polen*, 321. Beitz's Poland trip was also described in the Foreign Office archival sources PAA, B12/589c 6.5.1961 Vermerk betr. Beitz-Besuche in Polen.
106. Stehle, *Nachbar Polen*, 322–33; Krszysztof Ruchniewicz, *Zögernde Annäherung: Studien zur Geschichte der deutsch-polnischen Beziehungen im 20. Jahrhundert* (Dresden, 2005), 121–32.
107. The "Little Stabilization," Gomułka's rollback of reforms, is described, for example, by Andrzej Friszke, *Anatomia Buntu:Kuroń, Modzelewski i komandosi* (Cracow, 2010), 61.

Chapter 2

VICTIMS, HEROES, AND DARK REFLECTIONS
Polish Travelers, West German Journalists,
and the New Relations, 1958–64

Klaus Otto Skibowski told me an anecdote about his first postwar visit to Warsaw in 1958, at the invitation of Cardinal Wyszyński and the Polish episcopate. He and his wife were staying at Hotel Bristol, a large structure in neo-Renaissance style on Krakowskie Przedmieście. Bristol was one of Warsaw's most famous hotels, originally built in 1900. During the hotel's golden age in the early 1920s, Warsaw's political and cultural elites congregated there; at the time of the Nazi occupation (1939–45), high-level German officers took it over. The hotel survived the wartime bombings, which left most of Warsaw in ruins. The Polish state assumed ownership of it after the Second World War, renovating it entirely in the socialist realist style, intended to reflect the desired modernity of the rebuilt communist Poland.[1] A symbol for historical and modern Poland, Bristol served as Warsaw's gateway for foreign visitors. During the communist era, its rooms and meeting spaces were extensively wiretapped. Skibowski had been warned not to use the room telephone for any important phone calls, but he did ignore this warning once, at his wife's suggestion: he called and notified Cardinal Wyszyński's personal secretary that they were receiving terrible service. After that, he assured me, the service improved promptly.[2]

An apt metaphor, the anecdote suggests the dynamics of the interactions between the Polish communist state, the Polish Church, and western visitors in those early years. The anecdote hints at the inconveniences of traveling in communist Poland, and it also exemplifies the respect that hotel staff afforded the Polish cardinal and any guest of his. After Cardinal Wyszyński was released from house arrest in 1956, following the late Stalinist attack on the Polish Catholic Church after 1953, he became a hero in Poland, but he also acquired a considerable reputation abroad

---

Notes for this chapter begin on page 76.

as a success story of the Polish Catholic Church's strength and ability to survive, especially among West European Catholics.[3] In this way, the story illustrates the scope, possibilities, and limitations of Polish–German interactions in 1956. West German and Polish partners' attempts to establish new relations were circumscribed by practical matters and by distrust, only occasionally bridged. Their mutual perceptions were negotiated in limited spaces between appearances and competing versions of reality as well as colored by their own hopes and expectations.

When the Poles began to travel into the Federal Republic to find conversation partners among media personalities and a few sympathetic politicians, they remained isolated from larger West German society, which still showed limited interest in their country and agendas. In parallel developments, the West German journalists and correspondents to Warsaw accessed Poland primarily based on their limited number of contacts, as the Polish state strove to block their access to noncommunist groups, while others were equally uninterested in connecting with visiting Germans. The new generation of West German journalists and correspondents to Warsaw became closely connected to the Znak Circle and the contributors to *Znak*, *Tygodnik Powszechny*, and *Więź* as reliable and accessible sources and translators of the Polish political situation. Through these connections, the Catholic intellectuals could participate in shaping the analysis of Poland in West German media and transmit their vision of communist politics and peace to a broader media sphere across the borders. The Poles and Germans also began in earnest the search for mutually acceptable historical and political memories of the past, particularly of the Second World War.[4]

Soon after the Polish October, Gomułka began the "Little Stabilization," rolling back liberalizing measures, reigning in the freedom of the press, and reducing the number of independent Catholic journals and groups in the Sejm. He and Khrushchev reached a compromise in which Poland remained a loyal supporter of Soviet policy in return for the permission to rule Poland more autonomously.[5] Meanwhile, despite its interest in the Polish developments, the West German Christian Democratic Union (CDU) government held firm to the Hallstein Doctrine. The expellee's political party, Bund der Heimatvertriebenen und Entträchteten (BHE) was losing voters and leaders by the late 1950s. Nevertheless, expellee organizations still participated actively in domestic politics, and West German politicians remained exceedingly careful not to revise the policy on the eastern territories for fear of losing expellee votes.[6] After the Adenauer government's rejection of the Rapacki Plan, while the journalists were still hopeful about the political opening, the actual political and cultural situation in both Poland and West Germany changed rapidly.

The particular outlook of the Warsaw correspondents from the major West German newspapers, found in the dining halls and hallways of Bristol, played a role in updating and changing portrayals of Poland and Polish–German relations in West German public space. The major German newspapers and, increasingly, radio and television stations sent correspondents to Warsaw in the late 1950s. These media representatives generally belonged to an elite media that must be accounted for in order to fully understand the perceptions of Poland transmitted to West German society. After the war, institutions of elite journalism in West Germany attempted to counteract the propagandistic practices and reputation of the wartime German press by creating articles that more closely resembled academic writing. This type of journalism also existed on a cross-European and cross-Atlantic level through such newspapers and journals as *Neue Zürcher Zeitung,* the *New York Times,* the *Washington Post, Le Monde,* and *Figaro.*[7] Adhering to principles of scientific objectivity, respect for credentials, and research, journalists also embraced political moderation, far-reaching identification with the state, and attention to the opinions of their peer networks.

By the late 1950s, a group of journalists, editors, and media outlets, including Marion Countess Dönhoff's *Die Zeit, Der Spiegel,* and Henri Nannen's *Stern,* did become engaged with Polish–German relations. The experts on Poland and Eastern Europe began to produce content for both audiovisual and print media. This eventually introduced new agendas for international relations media coverage compared to the previous Cold War perspectives or omissions. The group of early correspondents to Warsaw included Ludwig Zimmerer for *Die Welt, Süddeutsche Zeitung's* correspondent Jochen Steinmayr, the united television and radio stations, West German Radio's (Norddeutscher Rundfunk, NDR) correspondent Sven Hasselblatt, *deutsche Presse-Agentur* (DPA, the German Press Agency), and Hansjakob Stehle for *FAZ,* who was later replaced by Angela Nacken. Zimmerer became West German radio's Poland correspondent and replaced Hasselblatt. Renate Marsch-Potocka was the correspondent for the DPA. The elite media's audiences, educated and politically engaged groups in West Germany, were limited but still played a crucial role in policy-making.

In Warsaw, the Polish state closely monitored foreign correspondents' and journalists' comings and goings, as well as the content they produced.[8] Journalists had to renew their accreditations every three months. Poland might refuse a journalist for any reason. Even no reason might suffice: there is no evidence that Jürgen Neven-du Mont's 1958 documentary, *Jenseits Oder und Neisse: Polen ist anders* (Beyond Oder and Neisse: Poland is different), had in any way alienated the censors, but Poland barred its producer from returning to Poland between 1959 and 1960 when he began filming his second documentary, *Zwischen Ost und West: Polen 1961* (Between East and West: Poland 1961).[9] A few years later, Ludwig Zimmerer reported in a letter that he was in bad standing with the authorities and suspected that his work visa might be terminated because of critical reports about the communist leadership, which, to make matters worse, had been picked up by American-funded Radio Free Europe.[10] As a consequence of the Polish state's touchiness and the potential for censorship, correspondents strove to strike a balance between reporting critically and retaining accreditations, in some cases their livelihoods, by maintaining a working relationship with the Polish government. In addition, state interference impacted their ability to access all parts of Polish politics, culture, and society.

In the face of the various difficulties and challenges present in Poland, the correspondents of the early years became a community. They helped each other with contacts, with passing on rumors and information about new developments in the communist leadership, and they supported each other practically when possible.[11] At the center of this group stood Ludwig Zimmerer. The journalists' and correspondents' groups also strove to manage the behavior of newly arrived journalists to protect the larger group's position in Poland. In November 1956, a journalist from *Rheinischer Merkur* arrived in Warsaw, insinuating openly and in different social contexts that he had a secret mission of establishing connections to leading communists, which the Foreign Office and the Bundespresseamt had authorized. According to a letter to his employer, the editor in chief of *Die Welt*, Zimmerer, together with two other colleagues, took the journalist aside and gave him a "very firm talk," admonishing him not to alienate the authorities. *Die Welt* forwarded Zimmerer's letter to the Foreign Office, requesting that it rein in the newly arrived journalist.[12] While it is unclear whether the unnamed journalist truly had a mission from the Foreign Office, the incident suggests the collective pressure on correspondents in Warsaw at the time.

Zimmerer had given Stehle the introduction to the PAX group that brought him to Warsaw in 1956.[13] Piasecki was looking for potentially sympathetic left-wing West European media circles. As Mikołaj Kunicki has written, the early postwar period was the "heyday of Left Catholicism," and Zimmerer in particular originally came from this subculture.[14] According to reports from conservative Catholic observers, Stehle belonged to left-wing Catholic circles in the late 1950s as well, which opposed the positions and views of *Rheinischer Merkur*, a right-leaning publication.[15] By 1957, Stehle had become *FAZ*'s permanent correspondent to Warsaw. Stehle lived at times at Hotel Bristol, and he also found a tutor and began learning Polish. Stehle's early articles in *FAZ* emphasized the cooperation of the Polish Catholic Church and Cardinal Wyszyński with the new head of state, Gomułka, in a critical yet highly optimistic fashion.[16]

The early Gomułka era shaped Stehle's understanding of postwar Poland. During these years, he described the relationship between the two institutions as one of somewhat equal players, and he came to believe that this was a larger positive development toward internal reform of East European communism.[17] When the state attempted to limit the influence of the church, negotiations between state and church continued to take place, sometimes through the mediation of the Znak Circle. Stehle noted the church's positivism, its agency, and the relative willingness of the party secretary and cardinal to cooperate with one another.[18] His initial writings also described the limited liberalizing efforts, such as the installation of the small Catholic opposition in the communist Sejm. In January 1957, he emphasized Stomma and Zawieyski as key players on the new political scene.[19] The articles also discussed Stomma's and Kisielewski's open opposition to the reversal of certain church rights in 1959.[20] Stehle's reports often relied heavily on the Znak Circle as informed sources. To him, the Znak individuals symbolized the greater openness and improvements in Poland. On a personal level, he relied on its members as translators of the Polish internal situation.

Stehle's early years in Poland sensitized him to Polish suffering during the Second World War and the lingering memories of German brutality and occupation. Unlike von Bismarck, Neven-du Mont, and Skibowski, he had not served on the eastern front and had no direct experience with the war in the east. Traveling in eastern Poland in the late 1950s brought him face to face with ruined cities and villages as well as with anti-German sentiment among many Poles outside of Warsaw's and Cracow's educated and well-traveled circles.[21] Polish antipathies to Germany featured prominently in Stehle's reportage, and he explicitly contradicted prevalent German victim narratives through these reports. In early efforts to nudge his audiences toward *Vergangenheitsbewältigung* (the process of coming to terms with the past) he used Polish national memories of German atrocities to sensitize the West Germans to their problematic past and to argue that West Germany must take full responsibility for improving relations with postwar Poland.

Stehle had been *FAZ*'s Warsaw correspondent for five years at the time of his breakthrough as *the* expert on Polish–German relations through the publication of his book *Nachbar Polen* (S[amuel] Fischer Verlag, 1963). The book was an amalgamation of his Polish experiences and the topics discussed in the early *FAZ* articles. A journalistic piece, *Nachbar Polen* garnered critical acclaim in Poland and became a bestseller in West Germany.

Nachbar Polen opened as a travelogue, describing the border crossing in Frankfurt/Oder into Słubice and the traveler's first impressions of Poland. Like many of Stehle's articles, as well as the documentary he produced in 1965, it depicts a journey into a country that is simultaneously foreign and familiar, suggesting Poland to be Germany's dark reflection. He described Warsaw as the heart of Poland, where "85 percent of all buildings were destroyed, 800,000 of the 1.3 million inhabitants had perished. In the face of the nearly impossible, many people recommended leaving the ruins in place, raising the city in a new location."[22] Describing how the Poles reconstructed the Old Town stone by stone, this section inspired admiration for postwar Polish accomplishments, but it also appealed for sympathy to a generation of German readers who themselves had experienced rebuilding their cities from rubble. Stehle placed great emphasis on the postwar Polish entrepreneurial spirit and ability to rebound from the enormous damage of the Second World War.

The opening section particularly emphasized the signs of improvement and reform in Polish communist society under Gomułka. Compared to the Stalinist era, Poland after 1956 had experienced moderate improvements in living standards, personal freedoms, access to the Western press, and greater freedom of speech.[23] Chapter 2 focused on the Gomułka government, its strengths and weaknesses from a more analytical perspective, picking up and strengthening the theme of a specific Polish-style communism. Stehle argued that the Polish communist party leadership was more loyal to the idea of the Polish nation than to the Soviet Union.[24] Whereas Gomułka's reforms did not live up to the promises of 1956, they still introduced greater freedoms for the people and showed more Polish independence from the Soviet Union than the other Soviet Bloc countries had acquired. Stehle described Gomułka as a difficult but hard-working and incorruptible man. He argued that the Polish communist party was internally weak and that Gomułka held it together based on a compromise between "Stalinists" and "Partisans," or orthodox communists and reformers.[25] This weakness, according to Stehle, made the regime open to the idea of cooperation with the Federal Republic. Through carefully optimistic descriptions of the new reasonable Polish communist state and a modern and increasingly "western" Polish society, Stehle attempted to combat old German stereotypes of Polish economic incompetence and corruption (*polnische Wirtschaft*). His determination, which he also shared with other Poland experts, would continue to color representations of Poland throughout the Cold War.

As part of the effort to correct un-nuanced anticommunist stereotypes of Poland as an oppressive and oppressed Stalinist state, Stehle also focused on the role, strength, and significance of the Catholic Church and hierarchy to Polish society and politics. The chapter about the Polish Catholic Church centered on the power negotiations between state and church, Stehle's particular interest from the very beginning of his journalistic engagement with Poland. Stehle described the strength, populism, and combative mentality of the Polish Church during the war and after, which he claimed had never been "mute" as "western slogans" suggested—that it "was always fighting and usually winning."[26] The image of the combative and powerful church in Stehle's description countered the image of the church as a helpless and passive victim to the state that had been particularly prominent in the descriptions by the *Rheinischer Merkur*. It suggested the possibility of a balance of power between the church and the state.

Naturally, the Znak Circle also played a key role in Stehle's book. The book mentioned Stanisław Stomma seventeen times and, by contrast, Cardinal Wyszyński only twice. Stehle profiled Jerzy Zawieyski as "the most important man in Znak," Stomma as "the politically leading parliamentarian," and Stefan Kisielewski as the group's "most interesting figure."[27] He considered the Znak group important because it had the weight of the Catholic Church behind it in the parliament. He also explained in detail the political philosophy of Znak, particularly neopositivism. Stehle's reliance on Znak as inside commentators also became evident in that he cited Kisielewski and Stomma in multiple places, on the topics of domestic policy—noticeably in the section discussing the "democratic" efforts of the parliament—and Polish foreign policy vis-à-vis the Federal Republic.[28] His focus meant that he lifted Polish compromisers and "bridge-builders" to the forefront rather than those who were more uncompromisingly against the communist state or West Germany.

In discussing Poland, Stehle had a clear political program, opinions, and agenda with regards to West German foreign policy. In the section on Polish foreign relations, he discussed the effects of the 1958 Rapacki Plan in great detail, emphasizing the damage that the CDU's lack of response had done to West Germany's image in Poland and to Polish–German relations.[29] Stehle also outlined the improving relations between Poland and the United States, its relationship with the German Democratic Republic, and the relationship with the Federal Republic. He wrote,

> The GDR, the actual neighbor, is populated by those Germans with whom the Poles historically had the most frequent contacts: the Prussians and the Saxons. Considering them, the anti-Prussian, anti-Protestant and anti-Stalinist sentiments become mixed in the general consciousness. In the last few years, something like a marriage of convenience—if no great affection—has developed between Warsaw and East Berlin.[30]

He added that the Poles considered the German Democratic Republic much less important than the Federal Republic, and that the GDR was rarely mentioned in the press or in Polish conversation.

Stehle's book became a bestseller in West Germany and was translated into English in 1965 under the title *The Independent Satellite: Society and Politics in Poland after 1945*.[31] Fischer also published an extended second edition of the original German publication in 1968.[32] American academic reviewers of the translation commented that his analysis was particularly valuable because of his sensitivity to Poland as a West German, but a few of them also felt that his description of Polish politics had become dated by the late 1960s.[33] The lingering popularity and international fame of the book meant that Stehle's optimistic interpretation of the Polish developments that Gomułka had initiated in 1956 continued to inform knowledge of Polish communism into the late 1960s, even though the circumstances it described had changed.

In the conclusion to *Nachbar Polen*, Stehle criticized Bonn's failure to capitalize on multiple opportunities to improve Polish–German relations. He outlined the measures he thought West Germany must take to improve its eastern foreign policy. Stehle argued that the Adenauer government had made a grave error in not opening diplomatic relations with Poland between 1956 and 1958, when the Polish state made the recognition of the border and of the German Democratic Republic a precondition for diplomatic relations.[34] He recommended that West Germany begin to prepare audiences and voters for the day when the Federal Republic would be forced to recognize the border since all other options had become unrealistic.[35] The border territories, he argued, were permanently Polish, and any other idea was a dangerous illusion. He concluded, "A key to peace in Europe today lies in correcting the image which the two neighbors construct of one another, in the attempt through continuous official conversations and contacts to remove distrust and win confidence, but also in the decision to take concrete measures."[36] Apart from correcting overly negative stereotypes and misconceptions, Stehle's practical agenda for peace and stability thus focused greatly on state-sponsored initiatives and contacts.

Another leading West German correspondent to Poland was Ludwig Zimmerer. While several correspondents in Warsaw developed good connections to communist and noncommunist Polish partners, Zimmerer's network and insider position were unique. He had arrived in Poland in the mid-1950s because he believed that it might constitute a successful experiment of combining socialism with Catholicism. While he soon lost his idealism with regards to Poland as a country where communism and Catholicism might coexist, he nevertheless fell in love with the country itself, as well as with a particular person, the cabaret actress Joanna Olczak, whom he eventually married.[37] Early on, Zimmerer developed close connections to the Znak Circle, including a personal friendship with Jerzy Turowicz. Through his marriage, Zimmerer gained access to artistic, bohemian, and intellectual circles in Warsaw as well as in Cracow, where Olczak was part of the famous dissident cabaret *Piwnica Pod Baranami*.[38] He also became acquainted with the intellectual and artistic circles surrounding his mother-in-law, the author Hanna Mortkowicz-Olczakowa.[39] In addition, as a collector of Polish peasant woodcuts, he created connections with Polish folk artists in the countryside, mountains, and villages. In short, Zimmerer had access to a much more extensive Polish network than most foreign correspondents.

Zimmerer had some personal tools that helped him as well. First, he had an ear for languages, and had learned Polish as well and as quickly as he had learned French during the late war years. He learned Polish on his own and with the help of his wife's family. Second, Zimmerer had a talent for being liked that also deepened and broadened his professional network and contacts as a journalist. Zimmerer's wages as an employee of a West German radio and television station allowed him to live quite comfortably in Warsaw. He and his wife owned a house at Ulica Dąbrowiecka 28 in the late 1950s, where he began building his collection of Polish folk art as well as entertaining, holding regular open houses every Friday where West German and other visitors could meet and interact with Warsaw's political, literary, and cultural elites.[40] These gatherings became an institution, particularly as there were few other places for West Germans to meet and interact with Poles in Warsaw. Stefan Kisielewski reported about one of his parties:

> I was at a monster-reception at Ludwig Zimmerer's, an odd German journalist who has been here for fifteen years already.... He has an incredible apartment: thousands of saints, wayside figures, naïve paintings—what a collection! The company was bizarre, mixed, Mandalian, Stomma, Rakowski, Małcużyński, Krauts, young people, lots of whisky, a very entertaining Viennese journalist, Mr. Balwany from Switzerland. I spoke with journalists from *Trybuna Ludu* (Luliński).[41]

Zimmerer's ability to make friends helped him to effectively serve as a mediator between Polish and German circles, both of whom trusted him. Through NDR, he became acquainted with Jürgen Neven-du Mont and, by 1962, a warm friendship had developed between the two.[42] Neven-du Mont received updates on the developments in the communist government as well as contacts to Polish intellectuals that enhanced his films through Zimmerer. Zimmerer translated the work of the playwright Sławomir Mrożek into German, and Neven-du Mont helped introduce it and the Polish playwright to German audiences through NDR television.

Zimmerer took on a mentoring role to an entire generation of western correspondents in Warsaw. He mentored Renate Marsch-Potocka, who began working for the DPA in Warsaw in 1965, as well as Angela Nacken, who replaced Hansjakob Stehle as *FAZ*'s correspondent in the late 1950s.[43] Correspondent for the British *Times*, Krzysztof Bobiński, who arrived in Poland in 1976, also described Zimmerer as a protector and teacher.[44] Most West German visitors to Warsaw, whether media representatives, semi-official visitors, business travelers, or politicians, were referred to Zimmerer. Sometimes they simply showed up on his doorstep after someone pointed them to his house. His mediation enabled these West German political and prominent private visitors to meet communists, members of the communist and noncommunist Polish press, and intellectual and artistic elites.

Jürgen Neven-du Mont also visited Poland for the first time after the war in the late 1950s as NDR's reporter and documentary filmmaker. A 1958 letter to his nine-year-old son, Christian, written before his departure to Poland, forecasted "lice in the beds" and "black beetle" infestation in the hotels of Poland's "destroyed cities." Even Warsaw, which was "supposed to be really nice," would be "dreadfully cold." He told Christian to "Take a look at the map at some point" and see that "Poland lies much, much further east than Munich and very close to Russia where it is always terribly cold in the winter."[45] The last time Neven-du Mont had been in Poland was during the final part of the war, at which point the country had been occupied and exploited by the German army for several years. In addition, the winter of 1944–45 was one of Europe's coldest in the twentieth century. Clearly these experiences colored his expectations.

During his 1958 visit, Neven-du Mont revised his image of Poland considerably. He presented his new understanding of Poland in the documentary *Jenseits der Oder und Neisse: Polen ist anders*. This documentary highlighted the extensive reconstruction and rebuilding of Polish cities, the Poles' youth and vigor, and the large number of western plays, newspapers, and music available. The society's openness and relative intellectual freedom impressed Neven-du Mont. He included an interview with the famous Polish literary critic Marcel Ranicki (later Reich-Ranicki, 1920–2013), who was at the time still living in Warsaw. Ranicki spoke about the openness of the cultural climate. Neven-du Mont summarized the interview: "Poland is thus a lot more open than we believed. From a western perspective, it is surely still eastern but from an eastern perspective, it is very western."[46] As already described, western journalists primarily tended to interact closely with Polish elites who already had an existing interest in foreign visitors in the larger urban communities. Consequently, Neven-du Mont's and Skibowski's observations did not necessarily contradict Stehle's reports about surviving Polish anti-German sentiments, which were made in part about encounters in the countryside.

The documentary did remark on the relative poverty of the Poles. After pointing out that bus travel was cheap in Warsaw, Neven-du Mont's narration stated, "This cheap pleasure does not improve the mood of most Poles. They know that they do not live differently than we did before the currency reform, and they know why this is."[47] He also remarked that, as a consequence, alcoholism was widespread. Sociologist Marcin Zaremba has written about the complex, destructive effects of the Second World War on Polish society and psyche, including high levels of alcohol abuse as self-medication, a severe drop in income levels, but also increased levels of violence and a disappearance of morals with regards to circles beyond the immediate ones.[48] Zaremba argues that many of these effects lingered well into the postwar era. Again, his observations do not negate the West German travelers' descriptions of determination, optimism, and progress but adds a dimension to them that the West German observers in the 1950s and 1960s either could not see or did not wish to emphasize to their home audiences for fear of feeding into existing German stereotypes.

Many German travelers and correspondents who came to Poland between 1956 and 1958 expressed surprise at the Poles' intellectual openness, their efforts at rebuilding, and their curiosity vis-à-vis postwar West Germans. These reports countered the prevalent descriptions by expellees in West German media of harsh oppression, destroyed lands and cities, and overall backwardness.[49] Polish society had worked hard to rebuild and recover its central cities after the war. With a few exceptions, the West Germans had access to relatively limited parts of Polish society and tended to spend time mostly in the larger cities: Warsaw, Cracow, and sometimes Wrocław. The journalists' and correspondents' attempts to counter the grim expellee notions of a society in ruins and older stereotypes of a "Polish economy" were influenced by hopes and optimism associated with Gomułka's reforms. Reporting also at least in part reflected the pressure not to irritate communist authorities and endanger their ability to work and function in Poland.

After the Polish October, Poles also traveled more freely and frequently to West Germany for the first time since 1939. This gave the Catholic intellectuals new opportunities to connect to their West European counterparts and participate in pan-European Catholic events and life. In 1957, the Catholic Journalists' Association's conference took place in Vienna. The Union Internationale de la Presse Catholique organized the conference. The arrangers had chosen Vienna specifically in order to facilitate travel from the recently opened Poland.[50] A total of 450 representatives of the Catholic press attended. The Austrian delegation was the largest, with 120 delegates, but the West German group included a respectable 90 delegates. The Polish delegation, the first one from a communist country that had been able to visit the conference, consisted of only eight participants. They represented the newspapers *Przewodnik Katolicki* (the Catholic Guide) from Poznań, *Gość Niedzielny* (the Sunday Guest) from Katowice, *Za i Przeciw* (For and Against) from Warsaw, the Club of Catholic Intellectuals (KIK) from Warsaw and *Tygodnik Powszechny* from Cracow. The Polish October had made this participation possible. The press reported, "Naturally at the center of attention stood the Polish delegation, and the Sejm-representative Stomma from Cracow, a small, graying gentleman whose excellent German has a light Austrian tone, was the most sought-after man during the congress."[51] The conference became a starting point for the Znak Circle's efforts to find conversation partners in the Federal Republic and to influence Polish–German relations.

Western Catholic media understood the release of Cardinal Wyszyński as a triumph of the Catholic Church over the communist state. Consequently, journalists who had absorbed this point of view cheered at the reading of the names of the Polish journalists during the opening ceremony.[52] The Western journalists were especially interested in the representatives from the Znak Circle as they were known to have Cardinal Wyszyński's support and confidence. The West German journalists particularly turned to Stomma because of his already noted fluency in German.

At this time, Stanisław Stomma considered himself not only a representative of the Polish Catholic media but also a state representative. When Gomułka invited him to become part of the Sejm, he had justified his political affiliation with the communists to *Tygodnik Powszechny*'s audiences by arguing that it would give Polish Catholics an opportunity to become involved in international relations, particularly those with the west.[53] The Catholic journalists' conference was an opportunity to begin to implement this agenda. Afterward, he wrote that the most important meeting he had in Vienna was with the West German consul, Carl Hermann Mueller-Graaf. Stomma reported that "an atmosphere of pleasant hospitality" prevailed in his conversation with the consul, which lasted "for over an hour."[54] Ascribing it historical significance, he wrote in his memoirs, "A beginning had been made; an official representative of the government of the Federal Republic had spoken with a Pole, a parliamentary member of the Polish People's Republic, whom he knew to be connected with the Polish episcopate."[55] After this meeting, Stomma felt that West Germany, at least, accepted him as a representative of the Polish state. Stomma reported about the conference to the communist party both before and after the trip. However, he may have misunderstood his position in the eyes of the West German journalists, politicians, and CDU members.

Encouraged by the reception in Vienna, the Znak Circle planned to build serious political partnerships with the members of the ruling Christian Democratic Union whom they considered their natural allies in West Germany. Meanwhile, many of the West German Catholic journalists admired the Znak Circle as symbolic evidence of the church's endurance and strength despite communist oppression. They also considered the Circle's members a reliable source of inside information about the Polish internal situation, but they did not see the interactions as likely to lead to official political contacts. Neither the Christian Democrats nor the Social Democrats were ready to accept a Polish Catholic Sejm representative as a serious political partner. The Poles would have to find other paths to dialogue.

Stomma fully recognized the difficulty of gaining attention for the Polish cause in West German society during his first visit to the Federal Republic in 1958. He traveled at the official invitation of Klaus Otto Skibowski, who at that time was the head of the Catholic News Agency (KNA). Stomma had met Skibowski both in Vienna and during Skibowski's Warsaw visit in 1957. When Stomma and his wife Elwira (Ela) arrived in Bonn in April 1958, they realized to their disappointment that the KNA had arranged no specific program of political meetings for them. Instead, they were taken to a four-day Catholic conference on problems in Africa. Stomma had wished to meet with parliamentary members from the CDU, but it became clear that they had a very limited interest in meeting him.[56] On short notice, the Catholic News Agency and Skibowski tried to arrange meetings with people to whom Stomma hoped to develop political contacts.[57] Through the intervention of the Catholic Central Committee, Stomma was finally able to meet with three parliamentary members, but they were all prominent expellee representatives firmly opposed to the recognition of the Oder-Neisse Line.[58] While the meeting was cordial, Stomma later commented that "the fact remained that I only had the opportunity to meet three deputies who were revisionists."[59]

Stomma's eventual meeting with foreign minister Heinrich von Brentano also turned out to be a disappointment. Stomma particularly recalled von Brentano's comment that "one cannot jump over one's own shadows."[60] Neither the CDU nor the mainstream Central Catholic Committee in West Germany were willing to support Stomma's efforts of finding political contacts or opening a conversation about the territorial question and the establishment of official relations. Ten years later, Stomma commented that his initial impression of the West Germans in 1958 was that they "were so satisfied with their prosperity and with the smaller European solution that they did not at all pay any attention to the difficult contemporary questions."[61] The Christian Democrats and Catholic dignitaries to whom he spoke politely kept their distance.

Recognizing the hesitance of his would-be political contacts, Stomma at this point took the opportunity to establish stronger ties to West German media and with public intellectuals. During the 1957 Catholic conference, Stomma had already noticed the goodwill of West German media, writing that "from the West German journalists, we were met with enormous sympathy, interest and desire with regards to closer cooperation."[62] Catholic center-left publications *Frankfurter Hefte* in West Germany and *Die Furche* in Austria became particularly close partners to *Tygodnik Powszechny* over time.[63] Several of the Catholic journalists who wrote for religious publications in the late 1950s would also move into prominent positions in mainstream media beginning in the early 1960s. They included the editors of the ecumenical journal *Dokumente*, Franz Ansprenger and Paul Botta as well as Heinz Linnerz, who helped and advised Stomma during his time in the Bonn area.[64] Botta eventually became a leader at the political desk at Westdeutscher Rundfunk (WDR) in Köln. The editors of Catholic *Frankfurter Hefte*, Walter Dirks and Eugen Kogon, were hired by WDR and NDR respectively. These transitions also meant that Stomma would go from having contacts in a few Catholic journals to having them in several of West Germany's largest audiovisual media institutes.

Back in Poland, the travelers reported their impressions of West Germany in articles in *Tygodnik Powszechny*. They wrote for an audience that was largely unable to travel and whose experiences with Germans stemmed from the Nazi occupation. In addition, during the 1950s, the communist media had closely observed and reported Adenauer's efforts to reintegrate former members of the Nazi party into West German society.[65] By writing about the "new Germans," the *Tygodnik* contributors challenged the descriptions by the communist media of a West German threat to its borders.[66] In Polish mainstream memories, Germans were on the one hand a military people, cold and brutal. In addition, the communist press focused their reporting on the ways in which postwar West Germans appeared to be entirely without regret or remorse for the atrocities their nation had imposed on Poland at the time of the Third Reich.[67] Given the overwhelmingly negative image of Germans in Polish representations, the Catholic writers' efforts to revamp the image of the West Germans garnered widespread attention. The West German correspondents followed these domestic efforts of the Catholic intellectuals closely as well.[68]

In January 1958, the author Leopold Tyrmand reported his impressions from his visit to the Federal Republic in a *Tygodnik Powszechny* article titled "O quae mutatio rerum ..." (Oh, what a change ...).[69] Tyrmand's emphasis on change over time amounted to a renegotiation of the image of the West Germans. He described an emerging generational conflict in West Germany, arguing that a majority of youth rejected all notions of militarism and exaggerated nationalism. More and more people belonging to the younger generation were critical of Germany's role in the war. In this way, while Germany before the postwar era had been militaristic, anti-Polish, and nationalist, this was changing. The article also argued that an exaggerated materialism had replaced the militarism and nationalism of the Nazi era. Tyrmand noted how well-dressed and elegant the people on the streets were, writing that he could not imagine any of them trading their clothing for uniforms. The postwar West German prosperity had led to anti-imperialism and liberalism. In short, it would be foolish to argue, as many people in Poland did, that "Germany will always be Germany" and that change was impossible.[70] The less-than-flattering descriptions of West German capitalist focus and wealth also pointed to the economic inequality of Polish–West German meetings at this time. Travelogues were not the only efforts by *Tygodnik Powszechny* to offset anti-German sentiments. Other articles reconsidered the myth of the *Drang nach Osten* (drive to the east) and yet others discussed whether it would be possible for the Germans to overcome their nationalist past.[71] The descriptions of West Germany were part of a larger trend, connected to more frequent travels and a more permissive censorship, but *Tygodnik Powszechny* was the most positive with regards to West German progress.[72]

In 1962, Stefan Kisielewski penned the most extensive, controversial, and broadly penetrative travelogues in Polish press, suggesting that Germans could change for the better. Kisielewski's travel articles in *Tygodnik Powszechny*, "Powrót do Niemców" (Return to Germany), "Co mowią Niemcy?" (What Do the Germans Say?), and "Czy Niemcy myślą o Wschodzie" (What Do the Germans Think of the East?) challenged the images of lingering German aggression against Poland.[73] In the articles, Kisielewski adopted the persona of the ironic, observant, and slightly bemused flaneur moving through an unknown space and gauging his own emotional response to it.[74] Kisielewski wrote that one of the first things that struck him when he arrived in Cologne was that all Germans were smiling. Dubbing West Germany "The Country of Smiles," he reported that "the bright, precisely built, not too big airport in Cologne is dominated by smiles, eager friendliness, correctness, diligent helpfulness, speed."[75] Kisielewski reacted with suspicion. He wrote that he could not help wondering what these smiling and polite people had done and where they had been during the war.

Kisielewski particularly noted the economic miracle unfolding in the Federal Republic. According to him, the West Germans lived a luxurious life. He described new cars, spacious homes, and department stores full of beautiful merchandise. He, coming from a poorer society, felt overwhelmed and somewhat jealous of it all. He reported,

> Kaufhaus Merkur—merchandise—here [in a department store], the German love of materialism, their cult of objects, reaches a highpoint. Everything is available here, in unbelievable quantity and quality; food, clothes, underwear, attire, jewelry, sailboats, shoes, beverages, furniture, household items, refrigerators, washing machines, TVs, carpets, crystal, flowers, toys, fruit, books, school articles—the eyes hurt from the color and the riches. I have never been greedy but here the hand reaches out by itself. . . . I would really like to steal something, but I am a bit afraid—they are so honest here.[76]

While he considered the West Germans more harmless in their postwar appearance than they had once been, Kisielewski was not uncritical of them. As an intellectual, he regarded the West German broader public—their consumerism and materialism—unsophisticated like children playing with their toys. As practical and materialist civilians rather than ideologically aggressive Nazi militarists, however, West Germans did not pose a danger to Poland. While somewhat dismissive, his description broke with earlier Polish images.

Kisielewski's articles also covered key disagreements and differences between Polish and German views on topics such as the dominant memories of the Second World War, the expulsions of Germans from Eastern Europe, and the character of Polish communism. From Kisielewski's perspective, the central problem preventing the normalization of relations was the German avoidance of responsibility for the brutalities and atrocities against Poland during the Second World War. The West Germans seemed to him oblivious to their country's invasion and occupation of Poland and completely focused on the present. Their short historical memory disturbed him. With reference to the multiple past German invasions of Poland, he would ask his conversation partners why Germans were so anti-Polish. To his surprise, the people with whom he spoke seemed not to understand this question at all. If anything, he reported, they felt very interested in, and friendly toward, Poland. On the other hand, they cast Germany as victims of Polish and Allied aggressions during and immediately after the war.

> Even the occasional pro-Polish out-migrants say that they "forgive" us everything. "Who should forgive whom?" I ask, somewhat irritated. "Did you have Hitler, or did we?" Unfortunately, this position is perceived as tactless, mean and demagogic. One does not speak about Hitler, just like, in a decent home, one does not mention the wayward daughter.[77]

Kisielewski concluded, "And again, it becomes clear that I am wrong, that my historic-moral right is antiquated and outdated."[78] In this interaction, the Polish memory of the German occupation of Poland clashed with German memories.

Instead, German war memories focused on the Polish expulsions of ethnic Germans and the loss of territory. Kisielewski described these events as a frequent topic of conversation in West Germany. He was not inclined to acknowledge any Polish responsibility for the expulsions of German minorities from Eastern Europe. In 1962, he wrote, "The transfer of the German population (of which a portion had already fled before the approaching Red Army), took place according to the plan by the victorious Allies. Contrary to the anti-Polish propaganda, it was orderly and calm and stood in sharp contrast to that to which Hitler subjected the Poles (not to mention the apocalyptic fate of the unhappy Jewish population)."[79] He placed the main responsibility for the expulsions with the Allies and the Red Army. Furthermore, again drawing on notions of the vitality of homogeneous nation-states, he thought that the expulsions, though unfortunate, had strengthened the postwar Polish state. In his opinion, the disappearance of the Polish minority problem, through the intervention of the Allied powers and the Germans themselves, had ultimately increased the chances for stability and survival of the Polish postwar state and for peace in Europe.[80]

Another central point of disagreement in these early interactions concerned the nature of the communist rule in Poland after 1956. Anticommunism manifesting itself in the reports about the show trials and the repression during the era of high Stalinism had colored West German understandings of communist Eastern Europe. According to Kisielewski, West Germans in general were uninformed about Poland, particularly about Polish communism, believing in "dark fairytales" about the postwar communist society.[81] Once more referring to the Second World War, he pointed out that recent history had proven that these dark fairytales did not at all need to come from the east of Europe but could just as well emerge in the west or in the center of old Christian Europe.

Kisielewski argued that full acceptance of the Oder-Neisse Line would be the only way to avoid the futuristic horror scenario of a new war, one involving nuclear weapons. He pointed out that West Germans were left with no other choice since another border revision would now be impossible without violence. After the Second World War, Poland had been "pushed sideways" to the west. Such a move could only happen in the aftermath of a great conflict. In other words, only a new world war would change the border. "This time," he wrote, "it would be of cosmic and many times more demonic dimensions through the use of nuclear weapons. In the Nuclear Age, a war would be impossible unless the peoples risked a mutual suicide—particularly the centrally located nations such as the

German and Polish ones."[82] Here the elephant in the room was the Soviet Union, as it had insisted on the westward move of Poland's eastern border and would never accept a reversal of that border. Given censorship, Kisielewski was not at liberty to publicly question that border move. In this way, in his agenda for Polish–German contacts, Kisielewski argued for the unconditional recognition of the borderlands as Polish as a precondition not only for improved Polish–German relations but for world peace, a point that Stomma and Turowicz had also made in *Tygodnik Powszechny*. He skillfully used the threat of nuclear war to emphasize the necessity for acceptance of the postwar borders.

Kisielewski claimed that Germans he met were often more interested in Polish perceptions of their own country than they were in Poland itself. Many people in West Germany had asked him what he thought about the German question—should Germany be reunited or not? He had avoided answering this question with a simple "yes" or "no." Instead, he stated that this was a German problem and not a Polish one. "Ulbricht is a German . . . and that is your German business. Besides, [Ulbricht] recognizes our borders and coexists peacefully with us. And Adenauer traveled to Moscow (in 1958) but he did not go to Warsaw since he only cares about those who are powerful."[83] This statement generally harmonized with the official Polish line on East Germany. In addition, the commentary indicated Kisielewski's unwillingness to serve as a sounding board for German conversations about internal German concerns. He did not wish to be a mirror for an ongoing German crisis of identity. However, the West German inclination to use him for this purpose, together with the title and aim of Kisielewski's article "What Do the Germans Think about the East?" show the way in which ongoing renegotiations of national identities in the early 1960s intersected with the establishment of Polish–German reconciliatory dialogue.

Like Stomma, Kisielewski forged his most important connections among West German intelligentsia and media elites. Among these groups, he counted "weekly or monthly journals with a more or less elitist character, with a relatively narrow influence but forming an important and morally relevant tendency."[84] He listed the Protestant intellectuals behind the 1962 Tübingen Memorandum, an Evangelical Memorandum criticizing Bonn's existing eastern policy, the radio stations (particularly Bavarian Radio), and "many authors, journalists, philosophers and theologians." He commented that it was important to use these connections, but he also felt that their interest in Poland was often founded more on German feelings of guilt, on Poland as a symbol for repentance, rather than on Poland in and by itself. Finally, this group of intellectuals was a disappearingly small part of West German society in his estimation.[85]

West German elite media outlets met Kisielewski's reports with great interest and celebrated the author himself. Among Kisielewski's earliest sponsors in West Germany was Hansjakob Stehle.[86] Stehle's and other West German journalists' introductions, articles, and promotion of Kisielewski contributed to his ability to gain an audience in the Federal Republic. Paul Botta, now the leader of the political department of WDR in Cologne, wrote about his expectations before meeting with Kisielewski in 1962 in a radio feature. The feature described the author and his West German travels. "German and Polish friends had told me much about the agile, intelligent and independent-minded Catholic politician and publisher." He continued, "I knew of his large-scale travel reports about Western Europe and the Soviet Union, which had appeared successively in 1960 and 1961 in *Tygodnik Powszechny* and had received a certain attention in Poland at the time."[87]

Botta's introduction in some ways underlined Kisielewski's discomfort with the symbolic usage of Poland in a West German media intent on making its audiences reconsider the past. Botta introduced Kisielewski as a personification of Europe's dark and war-weary, almost oriental Other, a critical observer of and counterpoint to West German postwar prosperity. He wrote, "The first thing I noticed about him was his battered and, for our fashion, far too long brownish trench coat. The second thing was his bright, swift eyes which suddenly, during the course of a conversation, could become very cold, very distanced and scrutinizing." The mention of the author's shabby coat again referenced the economic aspects underlying the relations. While participants in and narrators of Polish–German reconciliation and relations would later downplay that inequality, it nonetheless shaped Cold War interactions in many ways. Botta described how he had proudly showed Kisielewski Bonn's newly built train station. However, Kisielewski's reaction was to ask whether the stands at the station would have Polish newspapers.[88] Botta concluded his description of Kisielewski by stating that he felt honored to meet "this extraordinary, courageous man."[89] It was common for West German media to describe representatives of Polish culture and church in a universalizing fashion as representatives of Polish culture. In truth, these multilingual, sophisticated, highly educated, and internationally connected travelers could scarcely be considered "ordinary Poles" or representatives of the majority. The West German media continually ran the risk of understanding Poland and Polish society based on the smaller numbers of Polish representatives whom they encountered and with whom they were able to have more extensive conversations.

In Poland, the Catholic publishers' optimism vis-à-vis the Federal Republic worried the communist leadership. They eventually mobilized state media into a counterattack and began tightening censorship. In August 1962, communist-loyal PAX publication *Za i przeciw* published an article titled "Zmącony obraz NRF" (Distorted Image of the FRG) that criticized the positive description of West Germany in *Tygodnik Powszechny*.[90] The article argued that *Tygodnik Powszechny* provided a dangerously one-sided, naïve, and overly optimistic image of West Germany. They opposed the descriptions of the "German Economic Miracle," which they claimed was exaggerated, not wishing to admit to the economic disparities between the two countries. They further discredited the "myth" of total destruction of German cities during the Second World War. They presented some anti-Polish West German statements and developments to counter the images of positive change in West German society. As a sign of the pro-German bias in *Tygodnik Powszechny*, *Za i przeciw* pointed out that both Stehle, who was with *FAZ* at the time, and the correspondent of the DPA had reacted favorably to the *Tygodnik Powszechny* articles. It ended by asking why the authors had advanced such a "distorted image" of Germans. They called for the authors to tone down their descriptions of West German progress and for *Tygodnik Powszechny*'s editors to add commentary warning readers that the articles were biased.[91]

About a month after the article in *Za i Przeciw* appeared, Stomma responded to the attacks on *Tygodnik Powszechny* with a programmatic overview of the new situation for Polish–German relations from his and the *Tygodnik*-affiliated journalists' perspective.[92] He argued from a geopolitical perspective that Poland as a state no longer had much to fear from West Germany. While a weak, isolated Poland had stood alone against a united, strong, and aggressive Germany in the past, its alliance with the Soviet Union now protected it, while Germany, on the other hand, was weakened and divided. Further, the Federal Republic's western allies would prevent any renewed aggression.[93] Because of this, Poland could afford to leave its old fears of German revisionism and imperialism behind and instead begin to prepare the way for an improved relationship. Trying to be evenhanded, Stomma did charge the West German government with a problematic foreign policy vis-à-vis Poland. He stated that the "logic of conflict" drove traditional Polish politics. Considering the Cold War and the nuclear threat, this logic was no longer realistic. "Humanity," Stomma wrote, "is calling more and more impatiently for the logic of peace."[94]

Up until this point, Kisielewski had enjoyed an unusual amount of journalistic freedom with regards to the censors, but his 1962 articles upset the authorities. The anger affected the state's relationship with the Znak affiliates, *Tygodnik Powszechny*, *Więź*, and the Catholic intellectuals overall. As a result, the state cut entirely a series of articles in which Kisielewski reported from France in 1963.⁹⁵ The censoring of Kisielewski's articles and the criticism of him in the communist press further raised his profile as a fearless and morally admirable figure in the Federal Republic. Both Stehle and Zimmerer discussed these developments extensively in articles and broadcasts in West Germany.⁹⁶ Stehle also pointed out in his foreword to Kisielewski's book, which was translated into German, that the communist press accused Kisielewski of "disconcerting nonchalance toward the revisionist activities" in West Germany.⁹⁷ Thus the West German journalists used the tension, and the audience's interest in communist oppression, to draw attention to Poland, the Znak Circle, and Kisielewski himself. Of course, stricter censorship made it more difficult for him to reach an audience at home.

Zimmerer lauded Stomma as well as Kisielewski in his radio features. With respect to Stomma's article "Does a German Danger Exist?" he explained that

> Stomma's article is, unlike Zaborowski's, free from all anti-German spite. Nevertheless, it ultimately illustrates how difficult the task of a Polish–German understanding is and would be even if cool-headed people, such as Stomma and Kisielewski, and not Zaborowski and his like-minded friends [*Gesinnungsfreunde*], dictated the tone in Poland today. What Stomma requires from the Germans is not just a friendly gesture but a radical political change.⁹⁸

The West German correspondents, growing impatient with the West German state's policy on Eastern Europe, thus made good use of the Polish debates and domestic anxiety about the German image abroad to promote West German political change.

Interest in Poland continued to grow in West German media in part because of Kisielewski's writings. Two years later, in 1964, Piper & Co. in Munich published a book with an extensive collection of articles by Kisielewski, including the travel reports, translated into German, under the title *An dieser Stelle Europas* (In This Place of Europe). In the book's foreword, Stehle presented Kisielewski as an essayist, journalist, novel author, political publisher, parliamentary speaker, and composer. He also spoke highly of Kisielewski's intelligence, courage, and "roguish shrewdness."⁹⁹ "The court jester of the Polish People's Republic," in Stehle's description, had become the poster child not only for the renewal of the Polish–German relations but also for the "new" Polish state.

An dieser Stelle Europas thus took on a life of its own. Kisielewski's contacts and allies in the West German media championed and marketed it. Paul Botta, Klaus von Bismarck, Marion Countess Dönhoff, and others promoted Kisielewski in West German media. In 1964, Ulrich Gembardt, also at the political desk at WDR, contracted Hansjakob Stehle to write a WDR-feature on Kisielewski in connection with the publication of the book.[100] WDR broadcasted the feature "Blick nach Osten und Westen" on October 13, 1964. Stehle copied much of his foreword into the manuscript, and the program functioned to promote the book to a broader public. It solidified the image that Stehle had already created of Kisielewski. The radio program ended with one of Stehle's favorite quotes from Kisielewski:

> The idea of a Poland within the present borders and in alliance with Russia agrees with me. Perhaps because I cannot imagine another version of the Polish state in contemporary times, or because I am born in this country, have lived my whole life here and want to die here. Because, after all, I am a person of the state and do not like persons without states—regardless of the system of that state and whatever hesitations I may have against that system.[101]

To Stehle, this quote explained why the status quo with the communist leadership must be maintained in the interest of the Polish people. It suggested that the Federal Republic should develop relations with communist leaders and governments in the interest of Poland's security as well as European security and stability overall. In a longer-term perspective, it would mean that West Germans who were invested in Polish–German relations, based on sentiments as the one described above, were willing to go to great lengths to maintain a cooperation with the communist state. However, Stehle's and many West German politicians' heavy focus on connections with a sitting leadership without broader support among its own population may have limited or offset their ability to build strong, neighborly relations or pay sufficient attention to Polish society beyond that leadership.

Kisielewski's writings contributed to the interest in Poland among a new generation of West German intellectuals and journalists. *Dpa* correspondent Renate Marsch-Potocka mentioned it as a contributing factor in her decision to become a correspondent to Warsaw. "I was interested in Poland. I had read Stefan Kisielewski's *An dieser Stelle Europas* and imagined a country which was socialist but where people still thought independently."[102] The Znak Circle's vision of Poland as a reformed socialist state in a compromise with the church and Kisielewski's good standing with the Polish state had eroded by the time *An dieser Stelle* became a West German bestseller in the mid-1960s. The reforms had been rolled back, and Kisielewski had abandoned his position in the Sejm. Nevertheless, his well-formulated argument for a strong and stable Polish state with a communist leadership as introduced in his book continued to reach and convince West German audiences.

Conclusion

Through connections between media and internal Polish reformers, the Polish October shaped the West German media experts' image of postwar Poland, which would remain at the heart of reconciliation narratives after the 1960s and dominate later media representations. The Znak Circle's rise to prominence and its understanding of Poland's place within Europe, neo-positivism, compromise, stability, and reform from within, became part and parcel of West German political thought as well. These ideas depended on notions of the strength and vitality of homogeneous nation-states in peaceful cooperation with one another as opposed to ethnically or religiously diverse spaces such as the prewar empires and borderlands, armed resistance, or antagonism between European neighboring countries. Polish intellectuals would lose their initial optimism with regards to the state's reformability relatively soon after 1956, however. Even as they did so, and a more powerful opposition movement emerged in Poland, these trends in understanding Polish politics would continue to influence media discussions of Poland and Polish–German relations.

The new Polish–German partnerships and emerging dialogues were not without tensions. The Poles and Germans struggled with the limitations imposed on them by their own and the other country's state leaderships, by suspicion, distrust, or disinterest among its inhabitants. West German journalists began to revise the image of Polish communism into more nuanced representations. In conversation, Poles and Germans noted their competing victim narratives and identified disagreements over memories and understandings of the Second World War, the Holocaust and German invasion, the expulsions, and postwar communism. A more optimistic perspective on the new communist leadership, a reaction to dominant anticommunist narratives, began to characterize West German reports from Poland. The West German journalists praised the compromise between the state and the church, the liberalizing measures of society, and the freedom of the media.

While Polish Catholic writers distinguished "new Germans" from the negative German stereotypes stemming from the Second World War, West German journalists' images of the "new Poland" was of a modern, recovering society, avoiding the demonization of communism or reverting to older representations of "polnische Wirtschaft." The communists' visa and accreditation policies vis-à-vis western journalists also shaped German reports, as they made journalists cautious of publishing inflammatory or hostile content. In describing Polish politics and the communist state, West German journalists depended heavily on the information the

Catholic semioppositional writers could give them. Some new stereotypes also developed as a consequence of the postwar meetings and interactions. The West German articles seemed to contain a measure of romanticized orientalism. In West German media, Polish travelers were portrayed as embodying the admirable Polish spirit, battered but irrepressible in accordance with models dating from the mid-nineteenth century.[103] The Poles traveling in the Federal Republic, on the other hand, occasionally portrayed the regular West Germans they met as somewhat infantilized; shallow, consumerist, provincial, and self-centered but, on the positive side, nonthreatening, friendly, and civilian-minded.

West German correspondents and journalists also used Poland and the Poles to educate West Germans on the dark sides of their own recent past, the invasion of Poland during the Second World War. The Polish travelers were asked to mirror back to West German audiences a greater awareness of questions regarding Germany's role in the war. Engagements with each other also caused West Germans and Poles to reflect on their economic disparities and cultural differences. Kisielewski in his travel reports noted that the idea of Poland as a symbol tended to overshadow Poland as an existing country, and he also stated his unwillingness to serve as a mirror in such attempts at *Vergangenheitsbewältigung*. Nevertheless, this mirroring showed aspects of a reconciliatory forgiveness model, the reformulating of the own and the others' identities in less antagonistic and hostile fashions and of the entangled and ongoing negotiations of national identities through the peace process.

Notes

1. The hotel fell into disrepair after 1952, when renovations concluded. It was closed in 1978 and donated to Warsaw University in 1981, but it remained unused until the fall of communism. Ewa Pustoła-Kozłowska and Jacek Pustoła, *Hotel Bristol* (Warsaw, 1985). It reopened again in 1993 as part of a British hotel chain.
2. Klaus Otto Skibowski, interview with author, Bonn, 3 February 2005.
3. Kosicki, "Five—Vatican II and Poland," 142.
4. For German 1950s memories, including war memories, memories of the air raids on German cities toward the end of the war, and expulsions, particularly as an attack on German women, see Charles Maier's classic discussion *The Unmasterable Past: History, Holocaust, and German National Identity* (Cambridge, MA, 1988). For a gendered memory of the expulsions, see Elizabeth Heinemann, "The Hour of the Woman: Memories of Germany's 'Crisis Years' and West German National Identity," *American Historical Review* 101, no. 2 (April 1996): 354–95; Dietmar Süss, "The Air War, the Public and the Cycles of Memory," in *Experience and Memory: The Second World War in Europe*, ed. Jörg Echternkampf and Stefan Martens (New York, 2010), 180–97. In Poland, state-built

public memories of communist resistance and Fascist brutality competed with private memory cultures. See Piotr Madajczyk, "Experience and Memory: The Second World War in Poland," in Echternkampf and Martens, *Experience and Memory*, 70–85. See also discussions about Polish war memories, silences, and exclusions in Wawrzyniak, *Veterans, Victims, and Memory*.

5. Kunicki, *Between the Brown and the Red*, 119–20; Davies, *God's Playground*, 2:439, 441.
6. Ahonen, *After the Expulsion*, 144–45.
7. Lutz Hachmeister and Friedemann Siering, eds. *Die Herren Journalisten: Die Elite der deutschen Presse nach 1945* (Munich, 2002), 14–15.
8. For an overview of the correspondents' life in Warsaw during the Cold War, see Barbara Polak, "Wszystko pod kontrolą: o inwigilacji zachodnich korespondentów z Krzysztofem Bobińskim, Bernardem Margueritte i Krzysztofem Persakiem rozmawia Barbara Polak," *Biuletyn Instytutu Pamięci Narodowej* 11, no. 46 (November 2004): 18–36.
9. Jürgen Neven-du Mont to Juliusz Stroynowski, 9 April 1959, BAK NL1279/34–35.
10. Ludwig Zimmerer to Klaus von Bismarck, 6 December 1964, WDR-HA, Nachlass Klaus von Bismarck, Unterlagen Polen-Reise, Lauf. No. 259.
11. A report based on a two-hour interview with Stehle in 1960 by the Foreign Office described the correspondents' situation. See PAA, "Vermerk betr. Hans-Jacob Stehle, Korrespondent der Frankfurter Allgemeinen Zeitung in Warschau," 14 December 1960, PAA B12/ 589B.
12. Ludwig Zimmerer to Hans Zehrer, 4 December 1956, 18 December 1956, Hans Zehrer to Heinrich von Brentano, Foreign Office, PAA B12 549; Von Eckart, "Aufzeichnung für Herrn von Haase," 12 February 1957, BAK B145/1159.
13. Stehle described this in his 1960 interview with the Foreign Office as well as their friendship in the late 1950s more generally. See PAA, "Vermerk betr. Hans-Jacob Stehle, Korrespondent der Frankfurter Allgemeinen Zeitung in Warschau," 14 December 1960, PAA B12/ 589B.
14. Kunicki, *Between the Brown and the Red*, 88.
15. "Vermerk Betr. Hans-Jakob Stehle. Korrespondent der Frankfurter Allgemeinen Zeitung in Warschau," 14 December 1960. This information came to the Foreign Office from Clemens J. Neumann, *Pressereferent* for the BdV. PAA 12 589B.
16. Hansjakob Stehle, "Die polnische 'Opposition' im Zwielicht: Chancen und Grenzen eines politschen Katholizismus," *FAZ*, 19 January 1956; "Die Wahl der Polen: Einheitsliste mit der Freiheit," *FAZ*, 19 January 1957; "Signale aus Warschau," *FAZ*, 2 January 1958. See Kunicki, *Between the Brown and the Red*, for an overview of PAX's role and position in Polish society in the early Gomułka era.
17. Hansjakob Stehle, "Die polnische 'Opposition' im Zwielicht: Chancen und Grenzen eines politischen Katholizismus," *FAZ*, 1 October 1956.
18. Hansjakob Stehle, "Kardinal und Parteichef unter vier Augen: Im Spannungsfeld polnischer Koexistenz," *FAZ*, 30 January 1960.
19. Hansjakob Stehle, "Der Wahl die Polen. Einheitsliste mit der Freiheit," *FAZ*, 19 January 1957.
20. Hansjakob Stehle, "Der Sejm fordert religiöse Toleranz: Temperamentvolle Debatte im polnischen Parlament," *FAZ*, 13 February 1959.
21. See, for example, Hansjakob Stehle, "Grüne Grenzen, Bunker und Barack," *FAZ*, 30 August 1958, which reports on cries of "This language hurts my ears!"
22. Stehle, *Nachbar Polen*, 15.
23. Ibid., 16, 19.
24. Ibid., 36.
25. Ibid., 31.

26. Ibid., 99. This church at war, or sometimes embattled church, the *Ecclesia militans*, is discussed by Porter-Szücs in *Faith and Fatherland*, 232. In more traditional representations of the *Ecclesia militans*, compromise and coexistence with the communists was simply not an option, and Porter-Szücs's description also omits most mentions of compromise and coexistence with the communist state in the 1950s and 1960s.
27. Stehle, *Nachbar Polen*, 135–36.
28. Ibid., 136, 305.
29. Ibid., 297.
30. Stehle, *Nachbar Polen*, 307.
31. Hansjakob Stehle, *The Independent Satellite: Society and Politics in Poland after 1945*, trans. D. J. S. Thomson (London, 1965).
32. Stehle, *Nachbar Polen*.
33. Stephen Fischer-Galati, "Review of *The Independent Satellite: Society and Politics in Poland after 1945*," *Annals of the American Academy of Political and Social Science* 365, The Peace Corps. (May 1966): 184; Peter Brock, "Review of *The Independent Satellite: Society and Politics in Poland after 1945*," *Political Science Quarterly* 82, no. 2 (June 1967): 328–29; Andrzej Korbonski, "Review of *The Independent Satellite: Society and Politics in Poland after 1945*," *Slavic Review* 25, no. 4 (December 1966), 706–7; Leopold B. Koziebrodzki, "Review of *The Independent Satellite: Society and Politics in Poland after 1945*," *Journal of Politics* 28, no. 3 (August 1966), 689–91; W. W. Kulski, "Review of *The Independent Satellite: Society and Politics in Poland after 1945*," *Russian Review* 25, no. 3. (July 1966), 312–14.
34. Stehle, *Nachbar Polen*, 312.
35. Christian Lotz argued in *Die Deutung des Verlusts* that a majority of West Germans recognized that a return of the territories was simply not realistic, and this contributed to the eventual introduction of Ostpolitik. While Lotz's point is well taken, active lobbying by these media outlets also contributed to the shift. Lotz, *Die Deutung des Verlusts*, 266.
36. Stehle, *Nachbar Polen*, 362.
37. Marta Kijowska, "Die Heiligen spucken uns in die Suppe: Erinnerung an Ludwig Zimmerer, der Sammler polnischer Volkskunst und langjährigen ARD-Korrespondenten in Warschau," *Süddeutsche Zeitung*, 20 September 1997.
38. Barbara Nawratowicz, *Piwnica pod Baranami: Początki i rozwój (1956–1963)* (Cracow, 2010); Joanna Olczak-Ronikier, *W ogródzie pamięci* (Cracow, 2001).
39. Hanna Mortkowicz-Olczakowa (1905–68). Some of her works included *Bunt Wspomnień* (Warsaw, 1961), *Pod znakiem kłoska* (Warsaw, 1962), and *O Stefanie Żeromskim: ze wspomnień i dokumentów* (Warsaw, 1965).
40. Bernd Musch-Borowska, "Im innern der polnischen Volkskunst: Ludwig Zimmerer—erster ARD-Korrespondent in Warschau," radio show, 21 August 2001.
41. Stefan Kisielewski, *Dzienniki* (Warsaw, 2001), 594.
42. Jürgen Neven-du Mont to Ludwig Zimmerer, 27 June 1958, BAK NL1279/32-33; Jürgen Neven-du Mont to Ludwig Zimmerer, 27 November 1962, BAK NL1279/46.
43. Renate Marsch-Potocka, telephone interview with author, 7 July 2005.
44. Polak, "Wszystko pod kontrolą," 18.
45. Jürgen Neven-du Mont to Christian Neven-du Mont, 21 February 1958, BAK NL1279/11.
46. Jürgen Neven-du Mont, "Jenseits Oder und Neisse: Polen ist anders," film manuscript, 1958, BAK NL1279/129-130, 17. Ranicki left Poland for good in 1958. Marcel Reich-Ranicki (1920–2013) was born in a Jewish family and grew up in both Germany and Poland. He was forced to leave Berlin for Poland in 1938 and went to Warsaw, survived the early war years in the Warsaw ghetto, and later fought for the Armia Krajowa. He worked at the University of Warsaw in the early postwar years. After his immigration

to West Germany, he went on to become *Die Zeit*'s literary critic from 1963 to 1973 and eventually the most important literary critic of German literature in the Federal Republic. He was also well acquainted with Hansjakob Stehle during his time in Warsaw in the late 1950s. Hansjakob Stehle, "Człowiek z właściwościami—od Reicha do Ranickiego. Reflekcje przyjaciela" in Pięciak, *Polacy i Niemcy*, 167–80.

47. Neven-du Mont, "Jenseits Oder und Neisse: Polen ist anders," film manuscript, 1958, BAK NL1279/129-130, p. 14. The currency reform took place in 1948 when the Federal Republic went from the Reichsmark to the Deutsche Mark.
48. Zaremba, "War Syndrome," 27–62.
49. Demshuk, *Lost German East*, 21.
50. Reconstructed after the war, the union had organized its first congress in Rome in 1950, followed by Paris in 1954, and now Vienna in 1957.
51. Jerzy Turowicz, "Światowy kongres prasy katolickiej," *Tygodnik Powszechny*, 20 October 1957.
52. Ibid.
53. See for example Stanisław Stomma, "Dlaczego kandyduję do Sejmu?" *Tygodnik Powszechny*, 20 January 1957.
54. Pailer, *Stanisław Stomma*, 67; Stomma, *Pościg za nadzieją*, 173.
55. Stomma, *Pościg za nadzieją*, 173. The West German state pursued multiple contacts with representatives of Poland at this time. In January 1957, a high ranking West German diplomat in Washington, DC, acting on von Brentano's orders, met secretly with his Polish counterparts several times. Chances are that Stomma remained unaware of these meetings, however. The connection with the episcopate was probably of great importance since it granted Stomma an integrity and objectivity that an official representative of Poland would not have. Ahonen, *After the Expulsions*, 127.
56. Klaus Otto Skibowski, interview with author, Bonn, 3 February 2005.
57. Stomma, *Pościg za nadzieją*, 174.
58. Herbert Czaja, Karl Theodor von Guttenberg, and Ernst Majonica. Czaja also mentioned this meeting in his memoirs. Stomma made a positive impression on him, and he regretted that Stomma kept his distance later, such as at the Catholic conventions (*Katholikentage*). However, Czaja commented that "for [Stomma], the recognition of the Oder-Neisse Border was kind of a watershed issue." Herbert Czaja, *Unterwegs zum kleinsten Deutschland? Mangel an Solidarität mit den Vertriebenen: Marginalien zu 50 Jahre Ostpolitk* (Frankfurt/Main, 1996), 203.
59. Stomma, *Pościg za nadzieją*, 175.
60. Pailer, *Stanisław Stomma*, 82–83.
61. Stanisław Stomma, "Poseł Stomma w NRF (wywiad)," trans. Anna Morawska, *Tygodnik Powszechny*, 30 November 1969.
62. Stomma, *Pościg za nadzieją*, 172.
63. Seen for example in correspondences between Jerzy Turowicz and Władysław Bartoszewski in the early 1960s. Letter 17 November 1963 Bartoszewski to Turowicz; postcard 29 May 1965 Bartoszewski to Turowicz; letter 24 April 1965 Bartoszewski to Turowicz, Archiwum Jerzego Turowicza, Cracow.
64. Stomma, *Pościg za nadzieją*, 178.
65. Wawrzyniak, *Veterans, Victims, and Memory*, 168.
66. Wolff-Powęska, "Poszukuwanie dróg dialogu," 365–94.
67. Such an image was created both through Polish film from the postwar era, in school education, in literature, and through individual and collective memories from the occupation era. Mieczysław Tomala, *Deutschland, von Polen gesehen: zu den deutsch-polnischen Beziehungen, 1945–1990* (Marburg, 2000), 117–18.

68. See Wolff-Powęska, "Poszukiwanie dróg dialogu," 365–94.
69. Leopold Tyrmand was born in Warsaw in 1920. Before the Second World War, he studied architecture in Paris. In 1942, the Nazis arrested him and sent him to labor camp. In the first postwar years, he lived in Denmark, Norway, and France; he returned to Poland and stayed there until 1966 when he immigrated to the United States. He contributed articles to *Kultura* and *Tygodnik Powszechny* as well as other journals. After his emigration, he wrote for the *New Yorker*.
70. Leopold Tyrmand, "O Quae Mutatio Rerum . . ." *Tygodnik Powszechny*, 26 January 1958.
71. Antoni Gołubiew, "Mit o Drang nach Osten," *Tygodnik Powszechny*, 28 February 1960.
72. Other descriptions of West Germany were published in 1958, including Mieczysław Rakowski, *NRF z bliska* (1958) and Marian Podkowiński, *Czy zegary NRF chodzą szybciej* (Warsaw, 1959). Podkowiński was the most well-known correspondent to Bonn working for the communist press.
73. Stefan Kisielewski, "Powrót do Niemców," *Tygodnik Powszechny*, 10 June 1962; "Co mowią Niemcy?" *Tygodnik Powszechny*, 17 June 1962; "Czy Niemcy myślą o Wschodzie," *Tygodnik Powszechny*, 24 June 1962.
74. This approach may have something in common with concepts of psychogeography, particularly the approach of Dérive as developed by Guy Debord and the Situationists International. See Vincent Kaufmann, *Guy Debord: Revolution in the Service of Poetry*, trans. Robert Bononno (Minneapolis, MN, 2006).
75. Kisielewski, *An dieser Stelle Europas*, 187. See also original text: Stefan Kisielewski, "Powrót do Niemców," *Tygodnik Powszechny*, 10 June 1962.
76. Kisielewski, *An dieser Stelle Europas*, 192.
77. Ibid., 217, or original Kisielewski, "Co mowią Niemcy?" *Tygodnik Powszechny*, 17 June 1962.
78. Kisielewski, *An dieser Stelle Europas*, 219.
79. Ibid.
80. This is a position that Polish historians of *myśl zachodnia* shared and which coincided with ideas by Roman Dmowski. Prominently, Zygmunt Wojciechowski, the founder of the Instytut Zachodni in Poznań, promoted the idea. Jörg Hackmann, "German East or Polish West? Historiographical Discourse on the German–Polish Overlap between Confrontation and Reconciliation," in *Disputed Territories and Shared Pasts: Overlapping National Histories in Modern Europe*, ed. Tibor Frank and Frank Hadler (New York, 2011), 111, 114.
81. Kisielewski, *An dieser Stelle Europas*, 257. Originally in *Stimme der Gemeinde* (Frankfurt/Main, 1963), later published in *An dieser Stelle*. Never published in Polish.
82. Ibid., 266.
83. Kisielewski, *An dieser Stelle Europas*, 220. Originally published in *Tygodnik Powszechny* as "Twierdza Zachodnia Europa," 1962. Translated for *Dokumente* and published in translation in *An dieser Stelle Europas*.
84. Kisielewski, *An dieser Stelle Europas*, 205, 219. The Tübingen Memorandum is discussed in greater detail in chapter 5 on Polish–German reconciliation initiatives.
85. Ibid., 205, 226.
86. Hansjakob Stehle, "Hofnarr der Volksrepublik: Eine Vorbemerkung," in Kisielewski, *An dieser Stelle Europas*, 9; Kisielewski, *Dzienniki*, 234.
87. Paul Botta, radio manuscript, 11 October 1962, HA-WDR 1674.
88. Although the feature was broadcast in 1964, quite possibly in connection with the marketing of Kisielewski's German book, the comments seem to refer to an earlier visit, at least judging by the content description.
89. Paul Botta, radio manuscript, 11 October 1962, HA-WDR 1674.

90. The regime-loyal Christian-Social Institute (Chrześcijańsko-Społeczny Instytut), an outgrowth of the PAX movement, published *Za i Preciw*, a weekly magazine. Jan Frankowski chaired the Christian-Social Institute. Friszke, *Opozycja polityczna PRL*, 189–90.
91. Jan Zaborowski and Jan Zarański, "Zmącony obraz RFN," *Za i przeciw*, 12 August 1962, 2–3.
92. Ludwig Zimmerer, "Ein Pole sieht Deutschland: Berichte und Ausschnitte über die Artikelserie des polnischen Journalisten Kisielevsky über seine Deutschlandreise und deren Reflexe in der polnischen Öffentlichkeit," 11 October 1962, HA-WDR 1674.
93. Stanisław Stomma, "Czy istnieje niebezpieczeństwo niemieckie?" *Tygodnik Powszechny*, 19 September 1962.
94. Ibid.
95. Zimmerer, "Ein Pole sieht Deutschland."
96. Ibid.
97. Stehle, "Vorwort," 13. Stehle had taken the citation from a Polish communist newspaper, the *Trybuna Robotnicza*.
98. Ludwig Zimmerer, Warsaw, 7 October 1962, HA-WDR 1674.
99. Stehle, *Nachbar Polen*, 10. The book was translated by Wanda Bronska-Pampuch except in the instances where the articles were taken from the pages of Paul Botta's *Dokumente*.
100. Ulrich Gembardt, letter to Hansjakob Stehle, Cologne, 29 July 1964; Hansjakob Stehle, letter to Ulrich Gembardt, Berlin, 16 August 1964; HA-WDR 2502.
101. Hansjakob Stehle, "Blick nach Ost und West: Hansjakob Stehle stellt den polnischen Publizisten Stefan Kisielewski vor," 13 October 1964, HA-WDR 2502, 48.
102. Renate Marsch-Potocka, phone interview with author, 7 June 2005. Renate Marsch-Potocka was born in 1935. In 1961 she had returned to West Germany after living in Paris for a few years. She had taken a job at the German Press Agency in Hamburg. In 1965, the agency wanted to send a correspondent to Warsaw, and Renate Marsch volunteered to go. She was the correspondent for DPA 1965–70 and 1973–96.
103. Kristin Kopp, *Germany's Wild East: Constructing Poland as a Colonial Space* (Ann Arbor, MI, 2012), described the way in which German literary imagination set up Poland as an irrational, emotional other but also lauded Polish revolutionary spirit, a legacy of the "Poland-friendship" sentiments in the 1840s.

Chapter 3

RADIO RELATIONS

Klaus von Bismarck, Poland, and the Audiovisual Media Institutes

Klaus von Bismarck, in addition to his Protestant activism, greatly influenced Polish–German relations in the 1960s as director general of Westdeutscher Rundfunk (WDR), one of the largest federal audiovisual media institutes in West Germany, through institutionalizing relations and allowing them to reach much larger audiences. He spearheaded and protected the more critical approach of the audiovisual institutes' reporters and producers vis-à-vis the Adenauer and Ludwig Erhard governments' eastern policy.[1] He represented the interconnectedness between religious initiatives and audiovisual media, the continuities in German thought from the pre- to postwar era, and the early efforts to utilize *Vergangenheitsbewältigung* as a tool in foreign policy. Radio and television provided an important platform for broadening engagement with Poland and Ostpolitik beyond the narrower spheres of religious and elite print media, giving pro-Polish West German journalists and Polish participants another way to reach a West German audience.

In 1961, when von Bismarck became the director general of WDR, he was a compromise candidate. Hans Hartmann, the institute's director general between 1947 and 1961, had been forced to resign because of a conflict with the Christian Democratic Union (CDU)–affiliated chairman of the radio institute's Administrative Council. The Administrative Council, consisting of representatives from all political parties as well as a number of civil-society organization representatives, appointed the position of director general. Von Bismarck, an independent, was the only candidate the dominant CDU and Social Democratic Party (SPD) Council factions could agree upon.[2]

Notes for this chapter begin on page 101.

WDR was the Cologne-based half of the former Nordwestdeutscher Rundfunk (NWDR), which had been divided in 1955 into WDR and Norddeutscher Rundfunk (NDR), based in Hamburg. Even after the split, NDR and WDR often cooperated closely, sharing correspondents and special projects. Under von Bismarck, WDR took a leading role in promoting Polish–German relations. During his years as director general, he promoted German connections with and expanded reporting on Eastern Europe. In 1961, NDR, WDR, and Sender Freies Berlin established a cooperative instance on the east–west broadcasting, the *Ost-West-Gemeinschaftsredaktion*. WDR also opened two "eastern" television studios, in Warsaw and Moscow, during von Bismarck's tenure.[3] Thus, his contribution to linking reconciliation efforts into public space cannot be underestimated.

Radio had been used for nation-building from its inception in the 1910s, throughout the wars and into the postwar era, making it an interesting vehicle for reconciliation. It was simultaneously closely tied to state missions and able to transcend national borders. From the Weimar era, German elites and politicians tended to regard radio primarily as a means for the state to transmit its value systems, attitudes, and ideologies to a larger society, and to legitimate state leadership.[4] Its state-supporting role was further pronounced as it became the primary propaganda tool for the National Socialists in the 1930s and 1940s. In the postwar era, nation-building continued to be a central aim for West German radio producers and broadcasts as well.[5]

By the late 1950s, however, new generations of media representatives challenged the existing models for political content in audiovisual media. They considered radio a discursive public space where different societal and political forces representing multiple positions should interact—a fifth pillar of democracy.[6] The younger groups in the audiovisual media institutes who would become engaged with eastern questions and eastern policy in a way that contested state policy were, similarly to the groups already described, highly educated and often bi- or multilingual. Ulrich Gembardt, Moscow and Washington, DC, correspondent for WDR, was born in 1919 and had studied at the Frankfurt School of Sociology with Max Horkheimer and Theodor Adorno. He became a reporter for WDR in 1962. Hans Joachim Lange, who was to become closely engaged with the Eastern Policy, had studied languages and art history and begun his media career at the American-led *Neue Zeitung*.[7]

Helmut Drück, the radio director at WDR, who was also involved with the Polish broadcasts, had a law degree from the university in Göttingen as well as a master of law from Harvard. In 1951 he became program director for radio and television at Hessischer Rundfunk, and in 1960 von

Bismarck's predecessor Hans Hartmann recruited him to serve as director for television at WDR. In 1965, he began working for the political desk at WDR and became part of the director general's office with Klaus von Bismarck in 1972. He recruited several other influential journalists who also became involved with international relations questions, resulting in the creation of a faction of leading political reporters involved with the East European questions at WDR.[8] Franz Wördemann left Germany after the war and immigrated to London, where he became a correspondent for the British Broadcasting Corporation (BBC). In 1957, he returned to the Federal Republic as the correspondent to West Germany for the BBC, but soon afterward, WDR recruited him for television. In 1965 he led the TV news magazine *Monitor*.[9]

Paul Botta had originally been involved with the French-German Catholic journal *Dokumente* and was also familiar with the Frankfurt groups and *Frankfurter Hefte*. Already in 1957, he maintained a correspondence with Jerzy Turowicz in Cracow and with Władysław Bartoszewski in Warsaw. Later, as an employee at WDR's political desk, Botta became an expert on Ostpolitik, the Middle East, and France, and was in this way engaged with Polish–German relations as well. Through his intervention, the Polish Catholic intellectuals could reach broader radio and television audiences in the Federal Republic. The distinct goals of the new media elites were to educate Germans into democrats through pluralism in debate, and also to protect the freedom of the media and thus guard against a return of fascism. Still, they too continued to use radio for statist purposes, namely the reeducation and reintegration of citizens into postwar West Germany. To avoid power abuses and state control, West Germany's radio was organized into a federal structure with nine regionally based radio institutes. NDR and WDR were two of the larger of these institutes.

Radio was famously used to penetrate the Iron Curtain during the Cold War era, particularly through the American-funded Berlin radio station Radio in the American Sector (RIAS) and Radio Free Europe, which became focal points of the Cold War conflict and, in Eastern Europe, a favored source of western news and music for many East Europeans.[10] These radio stations, whose staff members were émigrés from the communist countries, initially produced highly anticommunist and propaganda-focused content but later softened their stance to offer entertainment and music as well as shorter news reports. The communist leaderships considered them highly problematic and attempted to block their frequencies, a fate that also befell the West German radio channels when they tried to reach Polish or East German areas with their programming.

In the 1960s, at WDR, West German nation-building frequently focused on forging connections between the two German states, and Polish coverage became something of a side-effect of this project. The Ost-West Redaktion in particular was set up to function as a link across the internal border between the two Germanys.[11] However, it also included broadcasting on Poland and other countries in the eastern bloc. Klaus von Bismarck discussed his views of nation-building in foreign policy as an aspect of the article "Die nationalen Aufgaben von Rundfunk und Fernsehen im Ost-West-Konflikt" (The National Tasks of Radio and Television in the East-West Conflict), stating his belief that radio had a central role to play in spiritually unifying the eastern and western parts of the nation.[12] This presentation focused on the German–German relations, making Poland and other East European countries secondary topics. Poland after 1956 also became important to German–German relations as a positive model for the East Germans. Von Bismarck commented that the "Zone inhabitants" should not be encouraged to wait for communism to fall but should be made aware about the possibilities of development within their existing system. "For this reason, we consciously report from other eastern bloc states, particularly Poland, but more recently also Hungary, because there, communists rule as well but under more humane and sensible conditions than in the Soviet Zone."[13]

Another central topic bridging Polish–German relations and the rebuilding of West Germany concerned democratic dissent, particularly as related to the Oder-Neisse Line. During the era of consensus journalism, the focus of the media had been to integrate the population into the new state and to convince West Germans to support the postwar state wholly in order to prevent a return of extremist politics.[14] Even as radio and television began to challenge consensus journalism, they continued the efforts to assimilate and integrate diverging political opinions and factions, particularly with regards to divisive political questions such as the territorial losses to Poland. As an example, the 1962 radio play *Verzicht auf die Ostgebiete?* (Relinquishing the Eastern Territories?) by Rudolf Fiedler, which was broadcast at 9:00 P.M. on 5 June 1962, addressed these questions without seeking to settle them, modeling polite disagreement in a democratic system.[15] The play was set up as a civilized and democratic debate between "Mr. Pro," who favored giving up the territories, and "Mr. Contra," who opposed it in alternating voices. Nevertheless, journalists, administrative staff, and political commentators constantly worried about domestic disagreements as a potentially destabilizing force, and such concerns came to the forefront in coverage of Polish–German relations.

Radio had the potential to reach larger audiences than print media, but the Poland broadcasts, by their times and format, were often intended for highly educated and politically engaged segments of the West German population. In the 1960s, the role of radio had diminished as a consequence of the growing popularity of television. The listening habits and demographics of radio audiences changed. Between 1958 and 1960, the average radio-listening time per citizen of the Federal Republic per day dropped from two hours and forty-nine minutes to two hours and twelve minutes. Television was taking over and becoming the primary source of information and entertainment during evening hours.[16] As radio became a secondary medium, audiences began to listen to it more passively during the daytime as a backdrop to other activities.[17] In response to these changes, radio stations began to offer more ambitious political programs, in the evenings on the third channel, which at WDR was modeled on the Third Channel of the BBC.[18] These broadcasts, requiring active listening, political knowledge, and a longer attention span, included the more extensive analyses of Poland and Polish–German relations.

In 1963, in addition to his position with WDR, von Bismarck also extended his responsibilities to become the chair of the Arbeitsgemeinschaft der öffentlich-rechtlichen Rundfunkanstalten der Bundesrepublik Deutschland (ARD).[19] This umbrella organization for audiovisual institutes formed in 1950 to respond to and push back against increasing pressure from the state and political leadership. The director generals of all nine radio and television institutes traded off serving as its chair. During von Bismarck's years as chairman for the ARD he undertook two visits to Poland, officially invited by Polskie Radio i Telewizja, to improve West Germany's media contacts with and profile in Eastern Europe.

Overall, West German radio institutes and their employees became more interested in improving popular perceptions of Poland in the early 1960s. Following the Polish October, television broadcasts discussing Poland emerged, as did the publications and travelogues by, among others, Stehle and Kisielewski. Also, politically engaged Protestants published the Tübingen Memorandum, the first of the religious statements pertaining to Polish–German relations, in 1961. The radio broadcasters wished to raise consciousness of and sensitivity toward the "new" Poland. Cities and radio stations arranged so-called "Poland weeks" to create an interest in Polish culture, music, politics, and society. As Radio Bremen's director general Heinz Kerneck stated in his opening speech to the station's 1963 Poland week, "Each report that attempts to show us the situation as is, helps to relieve us of stereotypes."[20] Referring to the expellee attacks against Jürgen Neven-du Mont showed in the 1963 Poland documentary *Polen in Breslau*, he claimed that political factions in West Germany attempted to prevent journalistic work connected to Poland. Norddeutscher Rundfunk also organized a Poland week in April 1963 in its third program and cooperated on a limited basis with Radio Warsaw in doing so.[21] The

NDR and Radio Bremen's Poland weeks included Polish guest artists and featured Polish books and plays. Ludwig Zimmerer contributed with a broadcast titled "Als Deutscher in Polen" (As a German in Poland), and Kerneck himself reported from a trip he had made through Poland and the borderlands.[22]

The coverage of Polish topics and the journalists covering them was also closely connected to the clashes within West German media and between media and state about freedom of speech, dissent, and democratic debate in what Christina von Hodenberg has called the "great time of the media scandals."[23] In the introduction to Radio Bremen's Poland week, Kerneck connected the reporting on Poland directly to the German media's freedom of speech, which had come into sharp focus in the recent Spiegel Affair in the fall of 1962. The affair took place in October 1962 and sharpened the defiance the media brought to the question of state intervention in content of radio and television broadcasts. *Der Spiegel* had long been critical of defense minister Franz Josef Strauss, and on 8 October 1962 it ran an investigative article, based on classified sources, about the weaknesses of the Bundeswehr, the German army. In response, on instructions by Strauss, police raided the offices of *Der Spiegel* and arrested several of its staff members, including the editor in chief, a few weeks later. The confrontation caused an outcry in the media in defense of the constitutionally protected freedom of the press. Over time, *Der Spiegel*'s staff was released, and Minister Strauss was dismissed.[24] The uproar surrounding these events considerably weakened Adenauer's political position and eventually led to Ludwig Erhard replacing him in 1963. To the journalists, the Spiegel Affair and debates over media freedom became analogous to a battle for the future of West German democracy. Criticizing the West German government for their policies on the Oder-Neisse Line and Polish–German relations became an aspect of defending an open and permissive media climate in the Federal Republic.

Referring to the Spiegel Affair and to a recent expellee attack on Jürgen Neven-du Mont and his documentary about the expellee question and Breslau (discussed in the following chapter), Kerneck thus stated that "recently, there have been frequent attempts to subordinate journalistic work to particular political perspectives. These efforts are bound to fail. They contradict the general societal desire for thorough information."[25] This linking of freedom of the media to the coverage of Poland had both positive and negative consequences. On the positive side, Poland received more coverage and attention because of the domestic controversies. However, the audiences' and journalists' attention was also diverted away from the actual developments in Poland toward the political effect of the Polish topics on West German politics. Put another way, Poland became a weapon in the emerging disagreement between various political factions, the sitting government, and media on state–media relations and foreign policy.[26]

Von Bismarck's first official trip to Poland since the war took place in 1964. The trip was the beginning of a more serious engagement with Polish–German relations. On a personal level, he wanted to see his old home in Pomerania once more, and to see for himself the changes in Poland. As director general of WDR and chair of the ARD, he wished to create closer cultural connections between West German and East European radio and television institutes.[27] Creating goodwill for the West German state in Poland was an explicit goal.

In planning the trip, von Bismarck drew on the existing media networks engaged with Polish–German relations. Since Norddeutscher Rundfunk and Radio Bremen had already cooperated with Polish Radio and Television, he asked for advice from these stations' director generals on whom to contact and how to come into contact with them. He also sought the advice of Neven-du Mont.[28] They responded with lists of important dignitaries, such as Janina Kowalikowa, the leader of the foreign desk, who was highly connected in the government through her husband, a public official actively engaged in Germany's foreign relations with Poland.[29]

Von Bismarck also contacted the Foreign Office in April 1963 to inform them of his travel plans and ask for advice, but they were of little or no help. Although West Germany at this point had a trade mission in Warsaw, its representative was isolated from larger Polish society.[30] Von Bismarck's relationship with the West German state was not one of open opposition. As a moderate, he recognized the necessity in the early 1960s to explore Polish–German relations outside of the state's existing framework, questioned state policy, and strove to protect the independence of WDR, but he preferred to work together with state representatives and within existing political structures. The Foreign Office approved of WDR's initiative toward cultural diplomacy, assuring von Bismarck that it was "definitely interested in an intensification of cultural contacts with Poland."[31] The Foreign Office described the Poles as reluctant to develop such contacts with the West Germans. They often let inquiries and proposals go unanswered because they resented the lack of official state relations and the lack of any border recognition. Of course, Polish state contacts were a necessity and a precondition for WDR's work in Poland. Kerneck, Neven-du Mont, and Zimmerer all emphasized the importance of communist and media contacts in their advice.[32]

A better connection than the Foreign Office and within immediate reach of von Bismarck was Ludwig Zimmerer and his Polish contacts. Practically all of von Bismarck's contacts unanimously recommended NDR's correspondent to Warsaw as the most important mediator of Polish–West German relations in Poland. Heinz Kerneck passed on his personal contacts at the Polish radio but emphasized that for all other contacts, authors, actors, journalists, but also high functionaries, von Bismarck should contact Zimmerer, who "probably has the best connections to the elites possible for a foreigner and non-communist journalist in a dictatorship state."[33] Neven-du Mont wrote that "since he lives in Poland, is married to a Pole, has many Polish friends and an excellent knowledge of the situation in Warsaw, it is almost presumptuous of me to still dare to draw your attention to a few things, almost in the hope that Mr. Zimmerer might forget to mention them."[34] Consequently, von Bismarck came to rely heavily on Zimmerer for assistance in preparing the trip.

Zimmerer's response illustrated the breadth and depth of his Polish network. He recommended that von Bismarck meet three groups of people in order to truly understand postwar Poland. The first group was the official contacts, including representatives for radio and television, the media department of the foreign ministry, and possibly also a representative at the foreign ministry. Zimmerer also counseled scheduling a meeting with Dr. Eugen Bernd Mumm von Schwarzenstein, the West German trade mission representative. Secondly, Zimmerer wanted to introduce von Bismarck to the Warsaw intelligentsia, his personal acquaintances. "You could meet a similar circle in Cracow through my mother-in-law, who lives there as an author," he added.[35] Von Bismarck was also instructed to meet the Catholic intellectuals in the Znak Circle, whose names, Zimmerer assumed, were already familiar to von Bismarck. Finally, von Bismarck ought to drive through the countryside and speak with people who lived outside of Cracow and Warsaw, for example a mayor of a small town, a party secretary, and the director of a school. Zimmerer thought it best to select a community in the Oder-Neisse area. "I have frequently found out much that was unknown to Warsaw or Cracow intellectuals in these kinds of conversations," he added. By December 1963, von Bismarck had in his hands a report based on the answers from Zimmerer, Neven-du Mont, NDR's director general Gerhard Schröder, and Radio Bremen's Heinz Kerneck to be used as his main guide in preparing the trip.[36]

The report was written both as advice and as a travel guide for an official German visitor to Poland. The visitor should expect a common distrust of the Germans and be prepared to answer questions about the recent German past. "The years of suffering are unforgotten and almost every family is regretting the loss of one or several victims," the report stated. Furthermore, as to the question of victimhood, it was important for von Bismarck to know that Poles considered Germans the perpetrators of Polish suffering during the Second World War; "Both officially and unofficially, the Poles are of the opinion that the effort toward understanding must come from the German side."[37] This reflected and reinforced the observations Stefan Kisielewski had made during his visit to the Federal Republic in 1962. Finally, the Polish people were united in considering the current territorial status quo beyond question and could not understand the West German stance, which combined the declaration of nonviolence with a refusal to accept the existing borders.

The report also gave several pieces of cautionary advice with regards to the political situation. Von Bismarck ought to keep in mind that the Polish secret service would follow him constantly, tap his telephone, and bug his hotel room. He and his companions should not keep addresses and texts with them when crossing the borders since they would be thoroughly searched, and this could endanger their Polish contacts. NDR's Gerhard Schröder emphasized that the Poles considered the West German radio stations an extension of the federal government and that von Bismarck should insist on WDR's independence from Bonn. Finally, the report treated details of etiquette such as gift-giving, stating that books, records, and, for the ladies, "Kölnisch Wasser" (eau de cologne) were desirable articles and could be given "without embarrassment."[38]

To the extent that his hosts permitted it, von Bismarck followed Zimmerer's advice closely, meeting with both official representatives of the Polish state media, with Catholic representatives, and with Cracow and Warsaw intellectual groups. In addition to attending one of Zimmerer's house parties, he met with the Znak Circle. In Warsaw, he spent an evening with Stanisław and Elwira Stomma, Stefan and Lidia Kisielewski, Dominik Morawski, and Tadeusz Mazowiecki. He remarked on their openness, friendliness, and personal integrity. The conversation touched upon fundamental concerns of "the Polish existence," namely the coexistence of communism and Catholicism.[39] The Znak group described the unwillingness of both the Catholic hierarchy and the communist party to cooperate with each other, making the bridge position of Znak increasingly difficult by 1964.[40] The Warsaw members of Znak still wished to reform the state from the inside, and fundamentally supported the Polish raison d'état, but their position was becoming untenable as Gomułka continued to roll back the 1956 reforms.[41] Von Bismarck wrote in his travel report that of all his meetings in 1964, the one with the Znak Circle was closest to his heart. The Circle's concerns and outlooks corresponded closely with his own during his years at Vlotho and Villigst, and they had in common connections to West German Catholic activists such as their mutual acquaintance Walter Dirks. Von Bismarck would continue to keep in touch with the Circle's members.[42]

For the Bismarcks, the visit to their lost former home after twenty years of exile was a moment of delicate negotiation between personal emotions and diplomatic necessities. Their (in)famous name made the moment more poignant and the necessity of displaying appropriate sensitivity and remorse greater. They turned the visit to Pomerania into an opportunity to model the renewal of Polish–German relations and the rebirth of an alternative national self-representation in their meeting with the current inhabitants of their former property in Jarchlino, formerly Jarchlin. Klaus wrote a carefully edited travel report about the visit, and Ruth-Alice added several pages of information.

An article Ruth-Alice wrote under the title "Hier bin ich geboren . . ." (I Was Born Here. . .) for *Die Zeit* showcased herself and her husband as models of how expellees might relate to the lost territories, still connected to the former home yet willing to give up their rights to it despite their sense of loss and sorrow.[43] The article first described the connection of the Prussian Junkers to their Heimat, and continued by providing a visual of the first glimpse of the former home and the emotions that accompanied that sight. It described the meeting between the former and current inhabitants of Jarchlino as awkward and emotional. Von Bismarck had publicly stated on many occasions that he neither demanded nor expected to ever return to his former estate, yet the interaction remained fraught. During the visit, the von Bismarcks met the present Polish administrator of the estate, who seemed intelligent and "could have been a Pomeranian overseer." Initially, the atmosphere at the meeting was gloomy, but the Polish family handed over some heirlooms belonging to the von Bismarcks.

The dark mood passed as the conversation was directed toward practical matters of farm maintenance, turning to "the question that my husband had anticipated for a long time: 'How in the world are we supposed to find the drainage system?' And now all the internal drive can be channeled into the concentrated effort of retrieving from memory a piece of useful advice for the current situation."[44] The article ended on an optimistic note. The villagers of Jarchlino had kept their distance, but one of the women invited the von Bismarcks to her home late in the visit. Suddenly, the relationship transformed, and the interaction found a new formula: "The expression of anxious insecurity which has met us in almost all faces here is replaced by the warmth and dignity of the host." Overcoming the tensions, the memory of the past, and the property conflict, the meeting's lasting impression consisted of Polish hospitality and German practical aid. Von Bismarck distributed his own travel report as well as Ruth-Alice's article widely within his own media institute, to his religious—Protestant and Catholic—networks, and to his political allies in promoting official relations with Poland and recognition of the Oder-Neisse Line. He also sent the article to Jerzy Turowicz in Cracow.

The efforts to find formulas for interactions in semiofficial and official meetings was even more pronounced during the WDR-sponsored trip to Poland that took place in 1965. The trip had been negotiated and agreed upon in von Bismarck's official meetings with Polish media officials in 1964. Its explicit purpose was to market a positive image of West Germany by showing the documentary *Das Dritte Reich*, one of the first documentaries attempting a self-critical German perspective on the Second World War.[45] As von Bismarck brought it on tour to Poland, he was attempting, on his own initiative rather than as a state-sponsored effort, to use West German *Vergangenheitsbewältigung* to improve Polish–German relations.

The radio and television representatives accompanying von Bismarck to Poland in 1965 included documentary producers Gerd Ruge, Heinz Huber, and Waldemar Besson. Ruge, who was responsible for the journalistic work in the film, had been the first West German correspondent to Moscow.[46] He was at the time the Washington, DC, correspondent for German television. Huber was a reporter at the Süddeutscher Rundfunk (SDR). Waldemar Besson, who functioned as an expert advisor for the documentary, was a progressive professor of political science at the University of Erlangen. Ulrich Schaeffer, who was responsible for international contacts at WDR, also joined the group. The group officially represented West Germany in Poland, participating in visits to memorials, official dinners, and discussions. Through these events and through broadcasting the documentary series, the WDR journalists intended to show that the Germans had gained critical distance from the past and were able to recognize the injustice of the Nazi era. Each member of the group also wrote an individual report on his visit and the impression Poland made. Von Bismarck merged these reports into one document for distribution to a wide variety of contacts.[47]

A reading of the report reveals that once more the West German media representatives met not only official communist but also civil-society representatives, such as members of the Polish intelligentsia, journalists, and artists at a cocktail party Zimmerer hosted. However, Ruge commented that these interactions, while interesting, had not given an opportunity for establishing deeper contacts. "I thoroughly enjoyed the ambiance at the reception by the Zimmerers but am not really able to remember the names of my conversation partners, let alone to judge their importance."[48] Von Bismarck had reconnected with friends such as Turowicz and other Znak Circle members. He wrote in a letter to Jerzy Turowicz a few months later, "Though we were not able to speak in peace and quiet at the joyful fairground of Ludwig Zimmerer's reception, I was still very glad that we met again and that I could give you some information about the things—particularly in the church realm—that have preoccupied me since our last meeting."[49] Waldemar Besson, a first-timer in Poland, also visited Auschwitz and commented particularly on his impression of the concentration camp. Besson stated in his report that the visit to Poland was a "nightmare" in light of the communist persecution of the Polish intelligentsia, of which Zimmerer's acquaintances at the reception spoke, and of the visit to Auschwitz.[50]

During both trips to Poland, Von Bismarck spent the majority of his time in meetings and interactions with state representatives. Particularly in 1965, the Polish communists actively discouraged the participation of mediators such as Zimmerer and tried to prevent the West Germans from meeting with groups outside of the official ones. Waldemar Besson asked the hosts to arrange meetings with some Polish academic colleagues, but his request went unanswered.[51] Also, von Bismarck expressed his disappointment after the 1965 trip that the delegation was unable to meet with people beyond the communist circles. Before the trip, Ludwig Zimmerer had provided von Bismarck with a list of individuals in Warsaw who should be invited to the viewing of *Das Dritte Reich*. WDR sent a request to Polish radio to extend invitations to these individuals, but the Polish Radio and Television officials sidestepped Zimmerer's proposals.[52] When the West Germans did meet with Polish intellectuals at Zimmerer's reception, they became aware of the rollback of liberal measures since 1956. They described the political mood in Warsaw as bleak. Von Bismarck commented that not even the intellectuals' sardonic sense of humor could compensate for this dark mood.[53] In the end, while the 1965 trip was an effort to reach a broader Polish audience with the adjusted German representations of the Second World War, the contacts with the communist circles took precedence over the civil-society contacts. The communist state, which preferred to cultivate anti-German sentiments as a way to build national unity, actively discouraged broader societal contacts. With these restrictions in place, working toward anything approximating a shift in Polish public space was difficult.[54]

At home again, von Bismarck distributed the travel report from the 1965 trip widely to his associates in politics as well as the churches, people known for their support of Polish–German relations. Copies went out to his co-signers of the Tübingen Memorandum accompanied by a letter in which von Bismarck stated that "since the question of an activation of the Eastern Policy was also addressed in our memorandum, I am sending you a report about a trip to Poland which will probably be of interest to you."[55] He sent copies to Berthold Beitz and Marion Countess Dönhoff, who responded and thanked him for the information. A wide variety of politicians, including the ministers Gerhard Schröder and Rainer Barzel, Erich Mende (who was minister for "German-German affairs"), and federal president Heinrich Lübke, whom he wished to influence received the report. They all responded and thanked him for the report, personally or through their offices. He also reported on the trip in person to the members of the WDR radio council (*Rundfunkrat*), which together with the administrative council (*Verwaltungsrat*) served as the highest instances for WDR and to whom he, as the director general, was ultimately responsible.[56]

Stehle had gained access to and was producing broadcasts for WDR and other audiovisual media in the early 1960s. In one of them from 8 June 1964, in honor of the six hundredth anniversary of the Jagiellonian University in Cracow, he described going on a guided tour of the university and interviewing one of its professors. He opened the manuscript by stating that the tour guide, Professor Karol Estreicher, addressed him, the only German tourist present, in German and that no one in the group seemed to mind.[57] Like Ruth-Alice von Bismarck's article in *Die Zeit*, this represented a modeling of new relations, but the setting also directed attention to a change in interactions with German speakers. He emphasized the existence of "good Poles" as well as good Germans.

In his broadcasts, Stehle attempted to influence not only German but also Polish conversation partners toward more positive representations of the other society. This became evident in his conversation with the editors of *Życie Warszawy* (Life in Warsaw, the second largest Polish communist daily at the time) in a 1964 radio interview. The interview was broadcast in the WDR's Third Program and was part of a series titled "Interview with the Press," in which German correspondents and reporters interviewed newspaper reporters in other countries, including the editors in chief of the French *Le Monde* and the Swiss *Neue Züricher Zeitung*. Stehle interviewed five of the leading journalists of *Życie Warszawy* in June 1964.[58] During the interview, Stehle criticized the newspaper's editorial line toward the Federal Republic for its anti-German slant.[59] He questioned the newspaper's conflation of West German "revisionism" with "revanchism." He argued that whereas large numbers of West Germans could be accused of revisionism, the refusal to accept the border move, very few were in actuality revanchists, desiring revenge on the Polish state. He asked the *Życie Warszawy* editors, "What are you doing in your newspaper to oppose the danger of anti-German sentiments . . . or to avoid the emergence of such sentiments?"[60] The overwhelming tendency in the communist press in the mid- to late 1960s when discussing West Germany was "fueling the atmosphere of menace by using texts about imperialism, the Cold War, Poland's chief enemies: the United States and West Germany" and to describe how these countries were striving to "undermine communist society and must be carefully watched."⁶¹ The Polish journalists rejected Stehle's understanding of their work. They responded by stating that as long as the aggressive political line of West Germany ruined any chances for *rapprochement* while the East German political line was beneficial to the relations, they would report this clearly.

On the West German domestic scene, Stehle criticized hardline anti-communist positions and favored more moderate ones. In 1964, he agreed with the minister president of Nordrhein-Westfalen, Franz Meyers, who argued that a total ban on the Communist Party in Germany (Kommunistische Partei Deutschlands, KPD) would only serve to drive the party into the underground. Stehle stated that if the communist party was allowed to exist, it would soon become clear that it had almost no public support and was very weak in the Federal Republic.⁶² He commented that people generally failed to recognize "the difference . . . between an anti-communism which defends democratic freedoms against a totalitarian regime, and a fascist hate of everything foreign, against 'the East,' and 'the Russians,' which is dressed up as anti-communism."⁶³

As in the case with Kisielewski's visits, West German radio broadcasters used Polish opinions to reflect back to West Germans the outside world's image of Germany's role during the Second World War. Hansjakob Stehle's "Im Blick der Nachbarn: Die Polen sehen Deutschland und die Deutschen" (From the Perspective of the Neighbors: The Poles see Germany and the Germans), which was aired on July 3, 1965, was a mosaic description of face-to-face conversations between himself and a larger number of Poles, discussing Polish perceptions of West German politics and society.⁶⁴ It was part of a program series, conceived by Ulrich Gembardt, in which neighboring peoples gave their opinions on the Germans. West German correspondents or experts on various countries, including Czechoslovakia and Denmark, mediated the responses and pieced them together into the scripted manuscripts on which radio shows at this time were usually based. Gembardt stated in his introduction of Stehle, "According to plan, the broadcast that you are about to hear is not kind at all. It is intended to be forthright, and I know that Hansjakob Stehle is nothing if not forthright."⁶⁵ The show thus clearly advertised its intent to force the listeners into self-reflection and reconsideration of their own past and present.

The Polish interviewees did not always go along with the West German agendas. Stehle asked about the division of Germany, the Nazi past, and the Eastern Policy. The Poles frequently confessed being relatively uninterested in these questions.⁶⁶ As an example, Stehle asked a twenty-two-year-old Polish actress whether or not she would like to visit "Germany." She answered that yes, she would like that even if it frightened her. He then asked whether she thought there would be any difference between traveling to the German Democratic Republic (GDR) or the Federal Republic. For her it was much easier to travel to East Germany, as no travel restrictions were in place between the GDR and Poland, but the response did not reference that: "Oh, you know, I think the difference for me would probably be that the Federal Republic had better shop windows."[67] Another person replied that she would probably rather go to the Federal Republic because "the people in the GDR seem much duller and less colorful."[68] Traveling and exchanges between Poland and East Germany were at this point easier and more common, but the comments did not indicate that these closer interactions had contributed to more common ground with regards to the war memories or territorial disagreement on broader or deeper levels of the two societies. On the contrary, the more frequent meetings seemed to have increased antagonism between the Poles and the East Germans at times. A student from Cracow commented especially on her irritation with East German tourists who came to Poland and acted self-confidently and arrogantly.[69] Stehle's Polish conversation partners for the most part professed neither to hate nor to love the Germans. The older generation who had lived through the war stated that the memories of the Nazi occupation of Poland made them fearful and suspicious of German intentions. On the other hand, the younger generation felt less antagonistic.

Zimmerer considered it among his tasks to interpret Poland, Polish society, and Polish attitudes to West German audiences. Between 1963 and 1965, the very public Second Auschwitz trials, in which lower-level camp administrators at Auschwitz were tried, took place in Frankfurt.[70] The trials were broadcasted and followed closely on West German radio, and they also drew attention in Poland as the Polish communists allowed the court, in the interest of fair proceedings, to visit Auschwitz in order to control and confirm the testimonies on the camp grounds. The twentieth anniversary of the liberation of the camp in January 1965 further contributed to the interest. Zimmerer wrote a contribution for *Auf ein Wort* in December 1964, explaining the Polish perspective on the proceedings. He stated that he had hoped to be able to leave the topic of Auschwitz as a symbol of the German past alone for a while and focus on other events, but his Polish friends and acquaintances kept asking for his opinions. Zimmerer stated that most of all the Poles "wanted to know whether the average German really understood what Auschwitz was. They want to know if he is horrified by Auschwitz or if he would prefer to dismiss it as a thing of the past."[71] The Poles struggled with understanding and accepting the visits of the court to Auschwitz as a purely legal concern. They rejected the administrative treatment by a German court of a place, which to them was a central symbol of suffering. In this discussion, Zimmerer followed the Polish practice at that time of treating Auschwitz primarily as a site of Polish significance.⁷² Zimmerer was embedded in Polish society and his focus was on sensitizing West German audiences to the Polish perspective. As a result, his broadcast did not engage with representations of Auschwitz as a Jewish site of suffering, although this understanding was starting to become more common in the 1960s.⁷³

In another feature from 8 January 1965, Zimmerer described the historical relationship between the Polish intelligentsia, the nation, and the state. He commented that the role of Polish intellectuals could not be compared to that of their western counterparts. During the eighteenth and nineteenth centuries when Poland had no state, the intellectuals had been "the politicians, the pedagogues, and the pastors of the nation."⁷⁴ After the war, their position became one of more symbolic importance and growing helplessness. He commented pointedly that because of the great national reverence for intellectuals, even mediocre writers got an exceptional amount of attention in the country. However, while the church and the communist party had many similarities as powerful and state-building institutions in postwar Poland, the writers/intellectuals were entirely without influence on the course of state policy by the mid-1960s.⁷⁵

In the talks during the WDR trips in 1964 and 1965, Polish communist conversation partners had expressed some resistance to devoting particular times to Poland in audiovisual media. They did not want "Polish days" and "Polish weeks" to be the one and only form in which West German listeners received information about Poland, as a form of national curiosa.⁷⁶ Instead, Poland should appear regularly in daily West German cultural and news broadcasts. Von Bismarck made margin comments in his copy of the meeting notes at that time agreeing with this idea. Perhaps as a consequence, WDR never arranged its own Polish week. They did, however, broadcast a variety of Polish political and cultural features. For example, WDR Hörspiele reported in the annual report at the end of 1964 that they had broadcasted a great number of East European plays translated into German, including those of the Polish authors and playwrights Tymoteusz Karpowicz, Zbigniew Herbert, and Ireneusz Iredyński.⁷⁷

In 1965, after von Bismarck's visit to Poland, three Polish journalists and radio officials visited Cologne, and WDR broadcasted two plays by Polish playwrights.⁷⁸ The WDR chamber orchestra Cappella Coloniensis also toured Poland in 1966 as a consequence of the conversations during the trips.⁷⁹ When Polish musicians performed during the Poland weeks on West German radio, or when Cappella Coloniensis toured in Łódź, Warsaw, and Poznań in 1966, radio officials and Polish–German relations promoters strove to create as much publicity as possible around these events as they were intended to represent a new, nonthreatening Germany to the Poles and a sophisticated and culturally advanced Poland to the Germans.

Before the trip of Cappella Coloniensis, the orchestra leader Ferdinand Leitner received instructions from von Bismarck to take every opportunity to create goodwill for West Germany. In Warsaw, Ludwig Zimmerer interviewed Leitner on radio. Leitner described the performance in Łódź as a great triumph and the Polish audience as very enthusiastic. Zimmerer added that since the Polish concert audiences as a rule were somewhat reserved, the performance had really been a great success.[80]

More Polish events and Poland weeks were arranged in West German media throughout the 1960s. In November 1966, the Südwestfunk arranged a Polish cultural week in which, among others, the author Andrzej Szczypiorski participated.[81] In the fall of 1967, the city of Cologne arranged a Polish cultural week, and WDR participated, hosting a "Polish evening" as a part of the festivities. A jazz ensemble from Warsaw named Novi and the singer Ewa Demarczyk performed, as did Stefan Kisielewski's son Tomasz—who was a pianist in the Federal Republic—and the wife of one of the administrative leaders at Radio Warsaw.[82]

A notable aspect of renewal in national images and identities through the travels, exchanges, and broadcasts was avoiding traditional representations, such as folk music and folk costumes, and favoring "modern" and often high intellectual representations of Poland's and the two Germanys' cultures. Also, Zimmerer in his guidance of West German visitors steered clear of broader popular representations of Poland. Before the 1964 trip, he gave von Bismarck a reading list featuring postwar Polish authors, such as the translated plays and short stories by Sławomir Mrożek, *Ashes and Diamonds* by Jerzy Andrzejewski, and *Steinerne Welt* by Tadeusz Borowski.[83] Mrożek, whose work Zimmerer himself translated from Polish into German, satirized the absurdities of the communist state, while Andrzejewski made a more earnest attempt to describe the complexities of postwar Poland in *Ashes and Diamonds*. Borowski was a Polish Holocaust survivor who described the experience of the concentration camp in brutal detail. All three authors supported the Polish communist state in the 1950s but gradually became disillusioned with it. Borowski, who served in Berlin as a diplomat at the Polish military mission after the war, committed suicide in 1951.[84] One should also note, however, the omissions from the list described above of older, but equally famous literature, works describing Poland's glorious struggle for survival during attacks by larger and more powerful neighbors, the Russians and Germans, such as, for example, the novels by Henryk Sienkiewicz. The literary Poland introduced here was high intellectual and devoid of traditional national symbolism or anti-German and anti-Semitic sentiments. It also did not represent the diversity of prewar Polish culture. Noticeably, in Borowski, the experience of the Holocaust was presented from a Polish rather than Jewish perspective.

In the postwar era, as a reaction to Hitler's appropriation of German folk culture, West German elites had shied away from traditional romantic nationalism and folk culture to a greater extent than the Poles. This became apparent in the 1965 conversations between WDR, Süddeutsche Rundfunk, and Polskie Radio i Telewizja about exchanges of documentaries where the West Germans and their Polish conversation partners disagreed on the type of films that could be used to represent national culture in the exchange. The Poles had prepared examples of documentaries suitable for the exchange. Von Bismarck commented that "both sides agree that no folklore should be offered but films about science and education (*Bildung*)."[85] Nevertheless, Poles and Germans disagreed on acceptable representations of the postwar nations. The West Germans rejected the prepared films with the comment that they were "the kind of unbearable and dishonest mix of medieval national history, folklore, flower wreaths and industrial reconstruction so typical for authoritarian states. A partially very good film technique does not make such garbage any easier to digest."[86]

West German radio programming on Poland grappled with ways to neutralize the memories and memory cultures surrounding imperial, minority, and borderlands populations without denying them entirely as well. An interesting example of an effort to integrate a borderlands identity and resituate it in the postwar political and geographic reality as well as in successful Polish–German relations was the 1962 radio broadcast "Gefährliche Vorurteile—bedrohliches Nichtwissen: Zu Czeslaw Miloszs Gedanken über Polen" (Dangerous Stereotypes—Threatening Ignorance: On Czesław Miłosz's Thoughts about Poland).[87] In a late-night hour-long feature, Bastian Müller reported on a new book by Miłosz, which had appeared under the German title *West- und östliches Gelände* (East-West Landscape). Its original Polish title was *Rodzinna Europa* (European Homeland).[88] In his partially autobiographical narrative, Miłosz had claimed that it was extremely difficult to assign clear national belonging to the people living in Eastern Europe and that he came from an area where borders and belonging were fluid and ever-changing categories.

The radio manuscript introducing *West- und östliches Gelände* opened by criticizing older derogatory German stereotypes of Poles as a nonhistorical people of "primitive, somewhat Hunnish diligent work horses, whom one just had to keep on a short leash with a little pork and schnapps and their Cracowiak [a traditional folk dance from Cracow] on Sunday, after the mass of course."[89] It also mentioned the stereotypes of the "beautiful Polish woman" as an erotic orientalist fantasy among western males. Against these prejudices, Müller pitched Miłosz's highly complex and sophisticated image of multicultural and multilingual Polish borderlands and their history and position in Europe.

According to Müller, Miłosz was typically Polish precisely because of the way in which he described himself as part of a European realm, separate from the Soviet Union and "the east." In *Native Realm*, Miłosz had emphasized his own multinational background and his suspicion of nationalism, but he also drew sharp boundaries with the Russian realm. To him, the "native realm" was primarily Lithuania, though he spoke Polish and Russian, and he described himself as having a "mélange of Polish, Lithuanian and German blood."[90] He argued that his home area did not belong to a Slavic east despite its current alliance with the Soviet Union. Based on Christian ideals and the cultural connection with the west since the tenth century, the former Polish commonwealth was European.[91] While Miłosz's book blurred the boundaries between national identities, states, and borders by referring to the federalist past of Poland and Lithuania, Müller used the discussion to argue for the uniquely *Polish* sophistication of thought surrounding history and current political relations. He firmly assigned importance to Miłosz's view and descriptions as representative of the Polish intellectual milieu. Müller repackaged Miłosz's representation as well as the author himself to fit with the postwar project of clear and stable national boundaries.

Conclusion

West German radio became involved in Polish–German relations in the early 1960s. Klaus von Bismarck himself, the radio reporters involved in the relations, and the format of radio greatly influenced the portrayal of Poland and Polish–German relations both by disseminating it further in public space and by influencing the transmitted content. The Polish Catholic intellectuals gained access to West German radio through their previous connections with West German Catholic journalists, initially publishing for Catholic journals, who continued their media careers at the audiovisual institutes. These connections included Walter Dirks, Eugen Kogon, and Paul Botta. The access to radio meant that new versions of Polish–German relations reached larger audiences, though to be fair, given the times of programming and character of the broadcasts, they remained primarily directed at elite audiences.

The trips and networking undertaken in the late 1950s and early 1960s by prominent media personalities, including several of the radio institutes' director generals, especially the two trips by Bismarck and other WDR representatives in 1964 and 1965, furthered West German radio's engagement with Poland. These face-to-face meetings led to cultural exchanges and program exchanges between WDR and Polskie Radio i Telewizja. However, these trips also highlighted West German media representatives' lack of access to broader Polish society and focus, in part based on necessity and sometimes against their personal preferences, on building cooperation with communist partners. This focus was in part counterproductive to broader reconciliatory development in its lack of grassroots anchoring on the Polish side. Only much later did a broader Polish public participate in the cross-border conversations.

The project of educating audiences and of shaping Polish content into appropriate postwar molds carried over into radio broadcasts as well. The West German radio broadcasts prioritized positive representations of Poland, and of the meetings between Poles and (West) Germans. They also emphasized Polish modernity, high culture, and avant-garde. The radio producers attempted to build as well as embody friendly Polish–German relations, to educate audiences about the other country, and to encourage West German self-criticism with regards to the past. In doing so, they reaffirmed, renegotiated, and reconstructed national identities in acceptable directions.

Finally, the entanglements in relations become visible in multiple ways in the radio broadcasts and engagement described. First, radio's nation-building across the internal border with East Germany influenced broadcasts on Poland. Poland after 1956 was held forth as a model that the East Germans might follow toward greater societal openness. Funding and expertise for Polish broadcasts also carried over from the effort to learn about and open a dialogue with "the Zone." Secondly, Polish voices and perspectives of the Second World War were frequently used to raise awareness in West German audiences of Germany's role in the Second World War, as a tool and a method to come to terms with the past. Meanwhile, West German broadcasters also used Polish observers and commenters to gauge the progress of the West German postwar state and to try to determine whether the country's reputation abroad was improving. In Poland, visits to West Germany became a measuring stick against which travelers gauged their own country's economic situation but also their own cultural and political understandings of the past and present.

Notes

1. Klaus Katz, "Die WDR-Intendanten 1956–1985," in *Am Puls der Zeit: Der Sender; Weltweit Nah Dran 1956–1985; 50 Jahre WDR*, Bd. 2, ed. Klaus Katz et al. (Cologne, 2006), 40.
2. Bismarck, *Aufbruch aus Pommern*, 256.
3. Angela Reuber, "Deutschland- und Ostpolitik im Fernsehen: Die Sendungen der Ost-West-Redaktion des Westdeutschen Rundfunks 1966–1969" (master's thesis, Uni-

versität zu Köln, Philosophisches Fakultät, Historisches Seminar, 2003), 11. Jürgen Rühle (1924–86) had been a prisoner of war in the Soviet Union, a convinced communist, and a journalist in the GDR, but he left the country and arrived in the Federal Republic in 1963 and began working for WDR with East German and East European broadcasts. Katz et al., eds., *Am Puls der Zeit*, 2:180.

4. Inge Marszolek and Adelheid von Saldern, "Massenmedien im Kontext von Herrschaft, Alltag und Gesellschaft: Eine Herausforderung an die Geschichtsschreibung," in *Radiozeiten: Herrschaft, Alltag, Gesellschaft (1924–1960)*, ed. Inge Marszolek and Adelheid von Saldern (Potsdam, 1999), 14.
5. See Yuliya Komska, "Introduction: West Germany's Cold War Radio; A Crucible of the Transatlantic Century," *German Politics and Society* 32, no. 1 (110) (Spring 2014): 1–14, and Inge Marszolek, "Unforgotten Landscapes," *German Politics and Society* 32, no. 1 (110) (Spring 2014): 60–73, particularly on the ongoing nation-building project through radio in the 1950s and the continuities from the prewar era.
6. Ibid.
7. Ulrich Gembardt (1913–96). Katz et al., eds., *Am Puls der Zeit*, 2:66. For the special milieu of *Neue Zeitung* and the position of its journalists as cultural brokers between American occupation powers and West German society, see Jessica Gienow-Hecht, *Transmission Impossible: American Journalism as Cultural Diplomacy in Post-War Germany 1945–1955* (Baton Rouge, 1999).
8. *Wer ist Wer 2007/2008* (Lübeck, 2007), 259. Bismarck, *Aufbruch aus Pommern*, 274.
9. Katz et al., eds., *Am Puls der Zeit*, 2:160–61.
10. Nicholas Schlosser, *Battling for the Airwaves: The Radio Propaganda War against East Germany* (Champaign, IL, 2015); A. Ross Johnson, *Radio Free Europe and Radio Liberty: The CIA Years and Beyond* (Redwood City, CA, 2010).
11. Reuber, "Deutschland- und Ostpolitik im Fernsehen."
12. Klaus von Bismarck, *Die nationalen Aufgaben von Rundfunk und Fernsehen: eine Vorlesung des ARD-Vorsitzenden vor Studenten des Instituts für Publizistik an der Universität Münster, gehalten am 9. Mai 1963* (Cologne, 1963), 28.
13. Ibid.
14. Hodenberg, *Konsens und Krise*, 148.
15. Rudolf Fiedler, "Verzicht auf die Ostgebiete? Tatsachen und Irrtümer, Argumente und Illusionen," 5 June 1962, Lauf. No. 162, HA-WDR.
16. Hans Jürgen Koch and Hermann Glaser, *Ganz Ohr: Eine Kulturgeschichte des Radios in Deutschland* (Cologne, 2005), 261.
17. See Marszolek, "Unforgotten Landscapes," 63; Marszolek and Saldern, "Massenmedien im Kontext von Herrschaft," 14. See also Heide Riedel, *Lieber Rundfunk . . . 75 Jahre Hörergeschichte(n)* (Berlin, 1999).
18. Koch and Glaser, *Ganz Ohr*, 263. When NWDR, the predecessor of WDR, was founded in the early 1950s by the British zone, it was modeled in general on the BBC, a large, centralized, relatively independent media institute, as compared to the federal model that the American occupation powers applied in their zone with several smaller stations.
19. Hodenberg, *Konsens und Krise*, 94.
20. Heinz Kerneck to Klaus von Bismarck, 30 September 1963, Nachlass Klaus von Bismarck, Polen-Reise 1964, Lauf. No 259, HA-WDR.
21. Gerhard Schröder to Klaus von Bismarck, 21 October 1963, Nachlass Klaus von Bismarck, Polen-Reise 1964, Lauf. No 259, HA-WDR.
22. PAA, B2/146 17.12.1963 Referat 5 an Büro Staatssekretär. The Foreign Office commented about both broadcasts that they had presented the problem of the border entirely from the Polish perspective.

23. Hodenberg, *Konsens und Krise*, 323.
24. Ibid., 328.
25. Kerneck, letter to Klaus von Bismarck, 30 September 1963.
26. Christina von Hodenberg describes this intensifying disagreement in *Konsens und Krise*.
27. Arbeitsgemeinschaft der öffentlich-rechtlichen Rundfunkanstalten der Bundesrepublik Deutschland (ARD) was founded in 1949–50 by the six media stations in the Federal Republic at the time—NWDR, BR, SDR, HR, SWF, RB—to make cooperation easier and form a united front against efforts by the federal government to assume control over media.
28. Letter from Klaus von Bismarck to Jürgen Neven-du Mont, 27 September 1963.
29. Letter from Heinz Kerneck to Klaus von Bismarck, 30 September 1963, WDR-HA, Nachlass Klaus von Bismarck, Polen-reise 1964.
30. The trade mission was a result of Polish–West German political negotiations through Beitz. Mumm von Schwarzenstein had arrived in early 1964 with instructions from Foreign Minister Schröder to lead the trade mission. Schröder wrote, "Your task will exclude any visible or quick successes. It requires a high measure of patience and tact. You should strive to gradually improve our relationship with Poland. This concerns primarily the economic relations but also, if it proves possible, other limited aspects, such as the cultural relations." Dok. 80, *Akten zur Auswärtigen Politik des Bundesrepublik Deutschlands, 1964*, ed. Hans-Peter Schwarz (Munich, 1989), 376.
31. Letter from Dietrich Sattler to Klaus von Bismarck, 4 May 1965, WDR-HA, Nachlass Klaus von Bismarck, Unterlagen Polen-Reise, Lauf. No. 259.
32. Letter from Klaus von Bismarck to Jürgen Neven-du Mont, 27 September 1963; letter from Heinz Kerneck to Klaus von Bismarck, 30 September 1963, WDR-HA, Nachlass Klaus von Bismarck, Polen-reise 1964; letter from Jürgen Neven-du Mont to Klaus von Bismarck, 25 October 1963, WDR-HA, Nachlass Klaus von Bismarck, Polen-reise 1964.
33. Letter from Heinz Kerneck to Klaus von Bismarck, 30 September 1963, WDR-HA, Nachlass Klaus von Bismarck, Polen-reise 1964.
34. Letter from Jürgen Neven-du Mont to Klaus von Bismarck, 25 October 1963, WDR-HA, Nachlass Klaus von Bismarck, Polen-reise 1964.
35. Letter from Ludwig Zimmerer to Klaus von Bismarck, 17 October 1963, WDR-HA, Nachlass Klaus von Bismarck, Polen-reise 1964.
36. "Erste Informationen zur Polen-Reise," marked: B.5.12, meaning Bismarck read it on 5 December 1963, WDR-HA, Nachlass Klaus von Bismarck, Polen-reise 1964.
37. Ibid. For the prevalence of the narrative of Polish martyrdom in the understanding of Polish memory of the Second World War, see Zofia Wóycicka, *Arrested Mourning: Memory of the Nazi Camps in Poland, 1944–1950* (Wiesbaden, 2013), 64. See also Wawrzyniak, *Veterans, Victims, and Memory*.
38. "Erste Informationen zur Polen-Reise."
39. Klaus von Bismarck, "Reise nach Polen. Entwurf," WDR-HA, Nachlass Klaus von Bismarck, Polen-reise 1964, 5.
40. Bismarck later commented that Jerzy Turowicz in Cracow seemed less critical of the Polish Catholic hierarchy than the Znak members in Warsaw.
41. Letter from Klaus von Bismarck to Jerzy Turowicz, 15 June 1965, Correspondences A–Z, Archiwum Jerzego Turowicza, Cracow. In 1964, Kisielewski also resigned from the Sejm. Friszke, *Opozycja polityczna PRL*, 198.
42. Klaus von Bismarck to Jerzy Turowicz, 15 June 1965, Correspondences A–Z, Archiwum Jerzego Turowicza, Kraków.
43. Ruth-Alice von Bismarck, "'Hier bin ich geboren . . .': Besuch in der pommerschen Heimat—'Merkwürdig, dass man einfach lächeln kann,'" *Die Zeit*, 4 September 1964.

44. Ibid. Bismarck had, in fact, expected that very question and been prepared to answer it since his Leipzig speech in 1954.
45. Compared to 1980s productions, the documentary was still quite limited in its self-critical position in that it projected most responsibility onto Hitler's state and tended to treat the Nazi era as a natural catastrophe over which human agency had little influence. Kansteiner, *In Pursuit of German Memory*, 211.
46. Gerd Ruge was hired by Hans Hartmann in 1947. He worked as a correspondent in various parts of the world, including Korea, the United States, and Moscow. Ulrich Harbecke, "Gerd Ruge," in Katz et al., *Am Puls der Zeit*, 2:179.
47. Bericht über die Polen-Reise der WDR/SDR-Delegation, WDR-HA, Nachlass Klaus von Bismarck, Unterlagen Polen-Reise, Lauf. No. 259.
48. Ruge, report, WDR-HA, Nachlass Klaus von Bismarck, Unterlagen Polen-Reise, Lauf. No. 259.
49. Klaus von Bismarck to Jerzy Turowicz, Cologne, 15 June 1965, AJT correspondence.
50. Besson, report, WDR-HA, Nachlass Klaus von Bismarck, Unterlagen Polen-Reise, Lauf. No. 259.
51. Waldemar Besson (1929–71) was a historian and political scientist as well as a publicist and media personality. He held a chair in political science at the University of Erlangen.
52. Bismarck, "Polen-Reise vom 16.5. bis 25.5.1965. Eindrucke und Ergebnisse," WDR-HA, Nachlass Klaus von Bismarck, Unterlagen Polen-Reise, Lauf. No. 259. In a letter a few months earlier, Zimmerer had also indicated that he was in bad standing with the authorities, perhaps even risking a termination of his work visa, because of his critical radio reports on the communist authorities. To make matters worse, these reports were being translated into Polish and broadcasted back into Poland by Radio Free Europe. Ludwig Zimmerer to Klaus von Bismarck, 6 December 1964, WDR-HA, Nachlass Klaus von Bismarck, Unterlagen Polen-Reise, Lauf. No. 259.
53. Bismarck, report, WDR-HA, Nachlass Klaus von Bismarck, Unterlagen Polen-Reise, Lauf. No. 259.
54. The communist leadership's usage of German hostility to unify Polish groups and society is described by Wawrzyniak, *Veterans, Victims, and Memory*, 167.
55. Klaus von Bismarck to Hellmut Becker, Joachim Beckmann, et al., 9 July 1965, WDR-HA, Nachlass Klaus von Bismarck, Unterlagen Polen-Reise, Lauf. No. 259.
56. Klaus von Bismarck to members of Rundfunkrat, 22 July 1965, WDR-HA, Nachlass Klaus von Bismarck, Unterlagen Polen-Reise, Lauf. No. 259.
57. Hansjakob Stehle, "600 Jahre Krakauer Universität," in "Kulturelles Wort," 8 June 1964, HA-WDR 719. Karol Estreicher (1906–84) came from a well-known family in Cracow. He was an art historian who had been involved with registration of Polish cultural property looted and removed by German occupying forces and with the efforts to have such property returned to Poland. Marek Sroka, "'Nations Will Not Survive without Their Cultural Heritage': Karol Estreicher, Polish Cultural Restitution Plans and the Recovery of Polish Cultural Property from the American Zone of Occupation," *Polish Review* 57, no. 3 (2012): 3–28.
58. Hansjakob Stehle, "Hans Joachim Stehle interviewt Redakteure der polnischen Zeitung 'Zycie Warszawy,'" *Kulturelles Wort*, WDR, Cologne, 17 April 1964, HA-WDR 1682. The interview took place in Polish. Stehle personally translated it into German, and the final forty-five-minute long manuscript was read by four readers in WDR on 17 April 1964. Both translated and edited, the interview was a far cry from today's magazine-style live interviews where interviewers and interviewees pit their rhetorical skills against one another.
59. Ibid.

60. Ibid.
61. Szymoniczek, "Polish Public Opinion," 132.
62. Hansjakob Stehle, *Auf ein Wort*, 4 March 1964, HA-WDR 677.
63. Hansjakob Stehle, "Wir sprechen zur Zone," 31 May 1963, HA-WDR 2748.
64. Hansjakob Stehle, "Im Blick der Nachbarn. Die Polen sehen Deutschland und die Deutschen," 3 July 1965, HA-WDR 3277, 4.
65. Ulrich Gembardt, introduction to Hansjakob Stehle, "Im Blick der Nachbarn. Die Polen sehen Deutschland und die Deutschen," 3 July 1965, HA-WDR 3277.
66. Hansjakob Stehle, "Im Blick der Nachbarn. Die Polen sehen Deutschland und die Deutschen," 3 July 1965, HA-WDR 3277, 21.
67. Ibid., 15.
68. Ibid.
69. The tourist interactions between Poles and West Germans were extremely limited. Mieczysław Tomala stated that between 1966 and 1967, no larger groups of Poles went to the Federal Republic, and only about four thousand West Germans belonging to youth groups entered Poland (Tomala, *Deutschland—von Polen gesehen*, 254). This was also the general conclusion put forth by historian Sheldon B. Anderson about the official Polish–East German friendship and the many state-organized meetings that took place between Polish and East German representatives (Anderson, *Cold War in the Soviet Block*, 62–63).
70. Devin Pendas, *The Frankfurt Auschwitz Trial, 1963–1965: Genocide, History, and the Limits of the Law* (Cambridge, 2006).
71. Ludwig Zimmerer, *Auf ein Wort*, WDR, Cologne, 18 December 1964, HA-WDR 8018.
72. For discussions of Polish cultural and political memory culture surrounding Auschwitz and how it gradually became more internationalized, see Jonathan Huener, *Auschwitz, Poland, and the Politics of Commemoration* (Athens, OH, 2003), 29. See also Wóycicka, *Arrested Mourning*.
73. See the arguments and periodization by Huener, *Auschwitz, Poland*.
74. Ludwig Zimmerer, "Die Schriftsteller und die Partei—die Partei und die Schriftsteller," WDR, Cologne, 8 February 1965, HA-WDR 2504.
75. For a description of the Warsaw intelligentsia in the 1950s and 1960s, see Marci Shore, *Caviar and Ashes: A Warsaw Generation's Life and Death in Marxism* (New Haven, CT, 2006).
76. Janina Kowalikowa to Klaus von Bismarck, 10 April 1964, Nachlass Klaus von Bismarck, Polen-Reise 1964, Lauf. No 259, HA-WDR.
77. "WDR Jahresbuch des Intendanten für die Zeit vom 1. Januar bis 32. Dezember 1964," WDR 1964, 41.
78. Klaus von Bismarck to W. T. Sokorski, 22 December 1965, WDR-HA, Nachlass Klaus von Bismarck, Unterlagen Polen-Reise, Lauf. No. 259.
79. "Erste Informationen zur Polen-Reise."
80. Ludwig Zimmerer, interview with Ferdinand Leitner, NDR, Hamburg, 5 March 1966, Nachlass Klaus von Bismarck, Polen-Reise 1964, Lauf. No 259, HA-WDR. Meanwhile, internal memos showed that WDR had to pay for the trip and that Cappella Coloniensis took a financial loss by touring in Poland.
81. Andrzej Szczypiorski (1928–2000).
82. Kalkulation polnischer Abend Gürzenich/Köln, 27 October 1967, Nachlass Klaus von Bismarck, Polen-Reise 1964, Lauf. No 259, HA-WDR.
83. This is a German translation of Borowski's short stories, *Kamienny Świat*, from his time at Auschwitz. Some of the corresponding stories were translated into English and published under the title *This Way for the Gas, Ladies and Gentlemen*, trans. Barbara Vedder (New York, 1967).

84. Andrzejewski and Borowski were the figures Alpha and Beta in Czesław Miłosz's famous 1953 book *The Captive Mind* about Polish intelligentsia and the communist system in the first years after 1945. Its first edition, *Zniewolony Umysł* was published in 1953 in Paris by Instytut Literackie.
85. Report, Bismarck, WDR-HA, Nachlass Klaus von Bismarck, Unterlagen Polen-Reise, Lauf. No. 259. The absolute rejection of folklore stemmed from its nationalist connotations, which the West German partners considered damaging to Polish–German dialogue.
86. Huber, report, WDR-HA, Nachlass Klaus von Bismarck, Unterlagen Polen-Reise, Lauf. No. 259, 3.
87. Bastian Müller, "Gefährliche Vorurteile—bedrohliches Nichtwissen. Zu Czeslaw Miloszs Gedanken über Polen," WDR, Cologne, 18 May 1962, HA-WDR 1962.
88. *West- und östliches Gelände* (Cologne, 1961) or in original *Rodzinna Europa* (Paris, 1959). The title when the book appeared in an English translation was *Native Realm: A Search for Self-Definition*, trans. Catherine S. Leach (Berkeley, 1968).
89. Müller, "Gefährliche Vorurteile."
90. Miłosz, *Native Realm*, 24.
91. This is a point made by many of the Czech, Polish, or Hungarian intellectuals and artists. For a comparison, see Milan Kundera, "The Tragedy of Central Europe," *New York Review of Books* 31, no. 7 (April 1984): 33–38.

Chapter 4

TELEVISING THE TERRITORIAL CONFLICT
Documentary Portrayals of Polish–German Relations

New life and modernity dominated the image of Poland in Jürgen Neven-du Mont's television documentary *Polen in Breslau*, as he filmed the opening scenes of it in a maternity ward. The camera followed a young woman, Jadwiga Skłodowska, who moved between rows of beds with her newborn charges. The setting was that of a 1960s hospital, starched white sheets and aprons and clean floors, at the time the epitome of hygiene and progress. Meanwhile, the voiceover informed the audience that these babies were Polish, born in Wrocław, not in the formerly German Breslau, and that the city's previous German inhabitants had been expelled. "All of those are the consequences of our past under Hitler."[1] The images spoke of hope and new life, but also of modern healthcare and a functioning welfare state—Poland quite literally reborn out of the ashes.

Polen in Breslau, as well as its sister documentary *Sind wir Revanchisten?* and in particular the altercations in 1963 between their producer, Neven-du Mont, and the expellee organizations, had a great impact on debates and conversations surrounding Polish–German relations in the early 1960s. The television controversies amplified efforts by radio and print media to counter the expellee press's and others' stereotypes of a backward and totalitarian postwar Polish communist society. Television in the early 1960s was particularly well placed to make contributions to the debates and to draw attention to them. Its producers took advantage of a monopoly on broadcast times and the protection of their director generals in the political struggles over media content to further their agendas and topics with regards to the eastern policy of the Adenauer government, the controversial eastern territories, and Polish–German relations.

Television's effectiveness at inserting Polish–German relations into political and media debates was due in part to its emerging status as a lead-

---

Notes for this chapter begin on page 124.

ing media and to the political leadership's anxieties about its potential as a propaganda tool.[2] By 1963, 6.6 million West German households had a television set, and the numbers continued to grow rapidly. Television had begun broadcasting in West Germany in 1954. Up until 1961, West Germany had only one channel, Arbeitsgemeinschaft der öffentlich-rechtlichen Rundfunkanstalten der Bundesrepublik Deutschland (ARD), funded and produced under the aegis of the umbrella organization sharing its name: the German National TV Consortium (Erstes Deutsches Fernsehen after 1984). TV producers for ARD had a fair amount of creative and political freedom even though they remained at the center of an ongoing struggle for control between federal powers, regional authorities, and media institutes.[3] Adenauer was fully aware of television's growing importance to politics and public space as well and attempted to gain more control over its content. The so-called "great television controversy" erupted in 1961, and the victory of the media institutes over federal and regional political interests led to the foundation of Zweites Deutsches Fernsehen (ZDF), the second West German channel, outside of organized state or political control.[4] As a consequence of this, despite frequent controversies, West German television and the documentary makers in the mid-1960s were able to operate in public space relatively freely despite efforts at political control and intervention. Broader media as well as political instances and audiences paid close attention to their productions.

One major catalyst for political controversies and debates involving television was the Norddeutscher Rundfunk (NDR) produced news magazine *Panorama*. Rüdiger Proske founded *Panorama* in 1961 as an avant-garde and controversial voice in German politics. *Panorama* hosted several of the media personalities engaged on a regular basis with Polish–German relations. By 1962, it reached 50 percent of all West German television viewers. Poland and the Federal Republic's eastern policy were regular topics on the show, and Hansjakob Stehle was often found in the studio commenting on Eastern Europe, East Germany, and German–Polish relations. Between 1963 and 1964, Eugen Kogon also worked with and served as a news anchor for *Panorama*.[5] Furthermore, Jürgen Neven-du Mont collaborated with Proske from 1962 when he began working for NDR. In other words, the debates about the media's role in politics and media freedom surrounding *Panorama* and other news magazines were also closely connected to the topics of Poland and Polish–German relations.[6]

Neven-du Mont had left his job at Hessischer Rundfunk in 1962 to join NDR, and he continued working there until 1966.[7] During those years, he produced more than ten documentaries about Poland, the Soviet Union, and the other East European countries. As a producer, he was established and well networked in West German larger media, with supporters defending him publicly against charges of disloyalty, and he had plentiful resources and access to attractive programming hours.[8] That West German television did not depend directly on revenue and audience popularity for its survival was another reason Neven-du Mont could pursue controversial and intellectually challenging topics in his documentaries.

Similarly to radio, television was in one sense an international project possessing the potential to transcend borders.[9] In the debates surrounding the television broadcasts, it is possible to discern something of a public space stretching across the borders, even across the Iron Curtain. However, these documentaries were not, as was at times the case with Radio Free Europe or Radio Liberty, an aspect of Cold War propaganda competitions intended to convince audiences of the own ideological system's superiority.[10] Instead, the West German television documentaries presented complimentary and sometimes overly bright pictures of communist Poland in their efforts to challenge existing German perceptions. In the polarizing climate of the times, audiences and critics sometimes interpreted such positive representations of Poland and Eastern Europe as signs of the producers' communist sympathies. However, the pro-Polish television producers maintained an alternative and more complex agenda of educating postwar Germans on Poland, cultivating a more critical stance in German society toward the Nazi past, and finally, when possible, raising postwar West Germany's profile abroad.

While the producers, with the help of their director generals, were able to secure creative and intellectual freedom in their own media institutes, they still had to depend on Polish authorities to work with television productions in Poland. Even more than radio broadcasting and print media, television productions required the cooperation of the Polish state. The production teams needed multiple visas and accreditations to enter and film in Poland. They also needed the state to permit Polish technicians to work for the West German productions, as standard practice was to use Polish expertise for parts of the productions. The Polish communist state was sensitive about the way in which its cities and territories were represented in western media. Historian Gregor Thum has shown with regards to Wrocław that the postwar Polish leaders, in particular in the 1950s and 1960s, allocated resources to rebuild the cities in the western territories in part to offset German stereotypes of Polish and communist mismanagement of those areas.[11] The Polish authorities developed a certain amount of trust in both Neven-du Mont and Stehle over the course of the 1960s. Nevertheless, political developments, such as the failure of the Rapacki Plan, created problems for the documentary makers. Neven-du Mont waited a few weeks in February 1958 for his entrance visa to make his first documentary, and at least a year to enter to make his second one.[12]

With the threat of delays and inconveniences, the documentary-makers, even more than newspaper and radio employees, had to take into account the sensibilities of the Polish side.

Neven-du Mont's and his associates' ongoing disagreements with the expellee press and organizations' representations of Poland influenced the content of the documentaries as well. The expellee press and films had previously described the formerly German territories as filled with fallow fields, destroyed cities, empty houses, and unusable roads. These images were based on the destruction in the late 1940s and also on the expellees' negative comparisons of postwar Poland with the prewar areas they had known.[13] Neven-du Mont's 1958 documentary by contrast particularly noted that the filmmakers did not see any "uncultivated farmland" and that Wrocław, which the expellee press had frequently used as an example of Polish inability to manage the former German territory, was becoming more and more developed.[14]

In his two initial documentaries about Poland, Neven-du Mont addressed the question of Poland's disappearing minorities. In 1958, in *Jenseits der Oder und die Neisse*, he commented on the Jewish past in Warsaw and described the activities of Warsaw's almost defunct Yiddish theater. The documentary described how the Ghetto had been razed to the ground and houses built on the rubble. However, the narrator presented a clear break with the past, stating that "time has moved on. Other people live here now, not without sorrows but finally without fear, without mortal danger, and without hunger."[15] As was the case in similar article series and radio productions, *Jenseits der Oder und die Neisse* balanced out descriptions of the tragedy of the Jewish and other minority communities' diminishing importance with celebrations of the return of peace and order to Central Europe. In general, 1960s documentaries on West German television commonly celebrated Jewish heritage or mourned its disappearance without directly linking it to German responsibility or German actions during the war.[16] In 1961, *Zwischen Ost und West* discussed the disappearance of Jews, Belarusians, Poles, and Ukrainians from eastern Poland, particularly in a village named Kruszyniany close to the Belarusian border. The documentary paralleled the experiences of the Poles from the eastern territories to the experiences of the German expellees in Silesia with an emphasis on the necessity of peace. Neven-du Mont interviewed a farmer, Władysław Dochniak, who said, "When I hear that there are people who once more want to expel me, I become afraid. I don't want a war. I've lived here for sixteen years. This has become my new home. I would like to tend to my fields in peace."[17] These late 1950s and 1960s productions thus connected the past existence of minorities with suffering, chaos, and war, and the present reality of homogeneous communities with stability and peace.

Zwischen Ost und West: Polen 1961, broadcast in the midst of the crisis created by the construction of the Berlin Wall, also made clear that the Polish cities had been further reconstructed and that Poles were enjoying economic advances and new freedoms. Comparing Warsaw's and Poland's situation to 1958, and to his last visit, Neven-du Mont reported that people were now dressed considerably better and that the Stalinist architecture had been plastered over.[18] The camera team followed a day in the life of a young, educated Warsaw woman. The film described her hopes for the future, her efforts to dress fashionably despite shortages and a lack of access to western fashion, and the cultural and intellectual activities in which she was involved. The documentary humanized life in communist Poland and offset the catastrophist representations of high politics precisely at this tense moment in east–west relations.

Neven-du Mont's 1963 two-part series on Poland for NDR, *Polen in Breslau* and *Sind wir Revanchisten?* took the argument about the Polish western territories one step further. While Neven-du Mont's earlier documentaries had contradicted the 1950s media images of mismanaged borderlands and of harshly authoritarian rule in Poland, *Polen in Breslau*, which aired in May 1963, made television history by removing the West German expellees entirely from the narrative of the city.[19] Neven-du Mont focused exclusively on the young and ambitious Polish citizens of Wrocław, their professional advancement, entrepreneurship, and plans for the future. It pointed out that fifty thousand Poles in Wroclaw were going back to school:

> This means that every fifth Polish adult from Breslau spends fifteen hours a week in the classroom. These people want to complete their primary schooling or finish their diploma. They want to fill in the gaps in their education that emerged because they came from the countryside or had to carry out forced labor during the war.[20]

Neven-du Mont interviewed a Polish headmaster of a school in Wrocław and filmed the university and school areas to underscore the city inhabitants' dedication to education. Even as it erased West German expellees, the documentary pointed to the historical and cultural anchoring of this society in the past by emphasizing the significance of the Catholic Church to Poland's recovery. It commented on the fact that Polish families could be both members of the communist party and good Catholics at the same time.

The documentary was reviewed in multiple newspapers. West German press largely criticized the omission of the expellees. The opening scene of the documentary featuring the newborn Polish babies was particularly controversial to the critics.[21] Expellee newspaper *Schlesische Rundschau* wrote, "A whole lot of children were no doubt born there during this time but where is that not the case? However, that has nothing to do with the fact that Poland taking over the German eastern territories violated international law (*war völkerrechtswidrig*)."²² The more mainstream Christian Democratic *Pressedienst* mentioned, and rejected, the emotional appeal of the newborn Polish babies as well.²³

Most media responses to *Polen in Breslau* initially reinserted the memories of the expulsions and their victims in their discussion of the film. *Frankfurter Allgemeine Zeitung* commented that the film by necessity must evoke painful emotions in expellees who had once lived in Breslau.²⁴ The press reported expellee protests of the film as well as its sequel.²⁵ The newspapers frequently turned to leading spokesmen for the *Landsmannschaften* and Bund der Vertriebenen (BdV) for public statements about the broadcasts. Even the newspaper commentaries that challenged the expellee perspective primarily engaged in the debates on the expellees' terms. The Polish communist press also paid close attention to the expellees and their relationship to Wrocław in their response, particularly because they sought to emphasize the continuous West German threat to Poland.²⁶

Other commentaries criticized the fact that Neven-du Mont's documentaries were intentionally provocative and divisive. The moderate weekly *Die Zeit*'s television reviewer noted that Neven-du Mont's sole intent was to educate "those thickheaded groups among the German Silesia-expellees, who insist on the inability of the Polish population to administer and further develop the German provinces."²⁷ The reviewer criticized the result as flat and uninteresting. *Polen in Breslau* and *Sind wir Revanchisten?* were pointed contributions to the internal West German debates in the spirit of challenging the government and the political opposition, similarly to *Panorama*. At the same time, the debates concerned truth: the true character of the contested territories and the true sentiments of the former populations of Wrocław.²⁸ Neven-du Mont carefully fact-checked the information he presented and tried to hold the high ground of truthful representation by introducing multiple perspectives into his productions. He accused the expellee media of misrepresenting Poland and the expellee leadership of misrepresenting sentiments among expellees in West Germany. Over time, the debate became increasingly polarized: the more the expellee media lamented poverty, corruption, and mismanagement, the more the documentaries celebrated success, modernization, and progress. The more the expellees insisted on their place in the history of Polish lands, the more the documentaries downplayed the expellee perspectives.²⁹

Polen in Breslau and *Sind wir Revanchisten?* reached much larger audiences than traditional media and evening radio had done. The polls concerning the public reactions to *Polen in Breslau* showed that 48 percent of

West German households owning a television viewed the documentary.[30] It also created waves of reactions and debate in print media and political circles in West Germany. Cold War polarization and fears of communism shaped print-media responses to the documentaries.[31] Neven-du Mont's supporters responded to accusations that the documentaries were slanted by describing them as necessary correctives to extreme and blind anticommunist sentiments in West Germany. Center-right press considered them overly optimistic, while far-right and expellee press dismissed them as communist propaganda. *Die Welt's* television reviewer felt that no reports on instances of modern art or western dance events should overshadow the fact that the Poles had limited democratic freedom under the communist leadership.[32] The far-right commentators considered the positive receptions of *Polen in Breslau* by the Polish press clear evidence of a conspiracy between West German television and East European communist parties. *Deutsche Nationalzeitung* wrote that they had already published true reports from the area and that "our correspondents were not guests of the Soviet-Polish propaganda institutions; they did not describe Potemkin villages."[33] The *Deutsche Ostdienst* (DOD) and *Der Schlesier* went so far in their accusations that Neven-du Mont successfully took them to court for libel. In the fall of 1965, the editor in chief for *Der Schlesier* had to pay a fine, and the editor in chief for DOD had to issue an official apology to the filmmakers.[34]

In 1963, the conflict between Neven-du Mont and the expellee activists reached its boiling point. A few weeks after *Polen in Breslau* had aired in June 1963, the Silesian Meeting, the annual meeting of the Schlesische Landsmannschaft, took place in Cologne. Jürgen Neven-du Mont and a camera team from Norddeutscher Rundfunk filmed at the meeting. They set up a platform right across from the stage to film the speeches, which they were planning to include in the second documentary, *Sind wir Revanchisten?* During Minister Erich Schellhaus's speech, which sharply criticized West German television for its recent biased and pro-Polish portrayals of the expellee question, a group of young Silesians began to advance on the platform and tried to attack Neven-du Mont. They shouted, "Down with that swine! Send the man to Poland! Jewish pig! Communist! Polish dog! Kill him!"[35] Neven-du Mont was forced to leave the area under police escort.

This attack, in connection with the conflict surrounding the establishment of Zweites Deutsches Fernsehen and the Spiegel affair, enhanced the journalists' and larger media's sense of defending not just Poland's postwar border but West German media freedom and democracy itself. The incident proved extremely damaging for the public image of the *Landsmannschaften*. The West German media cast Neven-du Mont as a fearless supporter of Poland and of media freedom and cast politically active expellees as an anachronistic danger to democracy.

Sind wir Revanchisten? was broadcast on 2 July 1963. It included interviews with West German political leaders and polls of the expellees' and the broader West German population's opinions, showing that the majority of expellees from Breslau were well integrated into West Germany. The film's introduction stated, "Some beliefs that were expressed—and some words that were spoken here, caused people in Germany and abroad both in the East and the West to think that the expellees—all of us—are revanchists, meaning people vengefully waiting for the day of reckoning."[36] The statistics and information in the documentary challenged the perception of Germans as violent and revanchist, and once more strove to improve the German reputation abroad.

In terms of content, *Sind wir Revanchisten?* attempted to present a balanced, pedagogical, and objective answer to the question of whether the Germans actually wished to take back the eastern territories. Relying heavily on interviews and polls, it explained German attitudes and beliefs about Poland in relation to broad layers of the West German population. Neven-du Mont polled twenty-one thousand former inhabitants of Breslau as well as a broader sample of West Germans on their feelings about the eastern borderlands. He interviewed West German politicians from both sides of the political spectrum. The documentary was produced in a talk-show style, using studio interviews with political representatives, interspersed with black-and-white screens displaying statistics garnered from the polls.

Despite being politically confrontational, Neven-du Mont's message in *Sind wir Revanchisten?* remained focused on integration and internal coherence within West Germany. Referring in the documentary's final minutes to the attack on himself at the Silesian meeting, he stated that most attendees were already leaving the stage to head for dinner before the attack began. "What they missed was no doubt despicable," he said of the attack, "but was not evidence that all Silesians are revanchist, or that all Germans are without manners."[37] Neven-du Mont did not believe that the aggressors or expellee leaders actually represented any form of broader opinion. The polls in *Sind wir Revanchisten?* had proven that a large majority of expellees were integrating successfully into West German society, with 76 percent saying they felt completely at home not only in their *Heimat* but also in West Germany, and 92 percent of expellees under thirty agreeing.[38] He also stated that only 25 percent of the expellees maintained membership in the *Landsmannschaften*, and only 17 percent of the overall population and 39 percent of the expellees expressed their support of the expellee organizations' political positions and activities.[39]

At the same time, however, the visual aspects of the documentary footage created a menacing image of smaller groups of still-active expellee protesters. The footage showed expellee leaders speaking in the same oratorical style as Hitler and expellee youth organizations marching in uniforms, wearing folk costumes, and carrying flags. These were important signifiers of fascism to audiences who still clearly remembered the Nazi journal films and visuals from twenty years before. The statements and actions of some of the expellee leadership in the footage projected an image of militarism, violence, and nationalism. In a voiceover, Neven-du Mont condemned them: as long as a few Germans "are allowed to act and speak without sense, we must endure that people give us false names that we don't deserve." He concluded: "Ladies and gentlemen, we live in a democracy. Our state will only be what we make of it."[40] In other words, it was the responsibility of everyone to make sure that the integration of the expellees into West German society progressed successfully. The journalistic qualities of the broadcast impressed the West German media establishment, and *Sind wir Revanchisten?* won German television's most prestigious award, the Adolf Grimme Prize, in 1963. Also, the larger audience response was positive. Of the polled viewers, 27 percent reported that they found the documentary "excellent," 52 percent found it "good," 8 percent reported that it was "satisfactory," 10 percent "fair," and 3 percent "very bad."[41]

Both major parties, the Social Democratic Party (SPD) and the Christian Democratic Union (CDU), issued early statements after the attack on Neven-du Mont in Cologne, saying that the expellees' reaction was understandable in light of the "dubious" content in *Polen in Breslau*.[42] *Sind wir Revanchisten?* itself included the CDU's representative Fritz Erler commenting on the need for understanding and tolerance for expellees in light of their losses and experiences during the war. Unsurprisingly, expellee leaders took exception to *Sind wir Revanchisten?* as well. Drawing on the television statutes' calls for objective political reports, the expellee leaders accused the media institutes of political bias. Christian Democratic parliamentarian and Silesian expellee Clemens Riedel explained that "it is not part of the competency of radio and television as public institutions to be the stage for this kind of manipulation of opinions."[43] The expellee leadership also actively pressured the state to intervene against the media institutes using the perceived numbers and strength of their membership as leverage. Indeed, even before the broadcasts of *Polen in Breslau* and *Sind wir Revanchisten?* the state gathered information about the content of the documentaries and attempted to control it.

Neven-du Mont's message ran contrary to the state's preferences on another level as well: many state representatives preferred to cultivate the image of the German expellees as restive with regards to the border areas. State officials felt that they stood to lose a bargaining chip in power political negotiations for a future reunification of Germany because of Neven-du Mont's image of a satisfied and settled West German expellee population. The use of polls in *Sind wir Revanchisten?* to probe Germans' true opinions with regards to the former territories in the east particularly disturbed these officials. The Federal Press Office commented in internal memos on the importance of preventing "this completely unnecessary" line of inquiry. It said, further, that preventing "unrest in the eastern bloc," meaning the possibility that Poland would place demands on West Germany, was only possible if the West German state continued "insist[ing] on the reintegration of these territories into Germany."[44] At the same time, the Press Office acknowledged that interest in reintegration was weakening even among expellees, and cited the NDR documentaries' content as evidence.[45] The Press Office commentary also showed that the government had informal agreements with some but not all of the polling institutes to avoid broader polling on the attitudes in expellee and larger population layers with regards to the eastern territories. The media elites and the state differed widely in their views about which image of these relocated Germans would best serve national interests.

Before the Poland documentaries were broadcast, the West German state made censorship-like efforts to control its content, the forms in which it would reach public space, and its reception. State representatives wrote directly to the director generals of the media institutes to ask them to moderate the content of the documentaries. The letter from State Secretary Karl-Günther von Hase to NDR director general Gerhard Schröder, for example, pled, "I would ask you to understand these considerations as an expression of my concern that the legal position of the Federal Republic could become eroded." He concluded with a caution: "I surely do not need to elaborate on what that might mean," but he clearly pleaded with Schröder to act out of concern for Germany rather than obligation to the government.[46] Von Hase also wrote to von Bismarck, and another Federal Press Office employee put in a phone call to Neven-du Mont himself.

Officials also tried to turn public opinion against the documentaries. When *Polen in Breslau* was broadcast, an internal remark of the West German Press Office stated that it had contacted friendly television reviewers with its reservations about the documentary, alerting them to the fact that Neven-du Mont's work was more positive about Breslau than West German television had ever been "about [any] city or ... country in the West or in the neutral areas."[47] The West German state's worries about the documentaries' influence was great, but its actual influence over them was limited.

Sind wir Revanchisten? and *Polen in Breslau* contributed to the shift in mainstream media's treatment of Poland and Polish–German relations. Mainstream media's neutral or more positive treatment of the documentary was also a consequence of its reaction to the Spiegel Affair and the attack on Neven-du Mont at the Silesian Meeting. Even reports by such conservative news outlets as *Rheinischer Merkur* and *Die Welt* condemned the attack on Neven-du Mont and the expellee organizations' and their state supporters' efforts to curtail information about the situation in Poland or the sentiments of the expellees.[48] *Die Welt* wrote,

> It is not a question of protecting the television writer Neven-du Mont against the criticism which many Silesians—and not only they—want to direct at his film "Polen in Breslau." It is however a question of protesting against the methods of this criticism. In this country, Freedom of Speech rules![49]

In this way, the reviewers shifted the attention from the content and quality of the documentary to the ongoing debate about freedom of speech, democracy, and media freedom.

The waves of controversy surrounding the Poland documentaries also reached Polish media and reporters. In 1963, Polish television broadcast a discussion about *Polen in Breslau* called "Casus Neven-du-Mont" with brief excerpts from the original film. Polish television announcers explained they were not broadcasting the film in its entirety because of a lack of time—a claim transparently manufactured by extending a report from Moscow about the quarterfinals in boxing by half an hour.[50] The broadcast was discussed by some of the leading communist press, including *Trybuna Ludu*. They highlighted the negative responses and the expellee group's political power, referencing the *Deutsche National-Zeitung*'s claim that nothing about Neven-du Mont's portrayal of Poland was Potemkian. *Trybuna Ludu* announced, "Neven-du Mont—sees what he wants, talks with whom he wants and films what he wants. Poland is not afraid of the truth."[51] The newspaper acknowledged the debates surrounding the film as a positive tendency toward change in West German journalism, but expressed doubts about a broader societal shift in West Germany. *Trybuna Ludu* pointed to other, more disturbing trends: West German authorities had arrested a German Democratic Republic (GDR) correspondent and initiated an action against another "progressive" TV reporter, Gert von Paczensky.[52]

Coverage of Eastern Europe grew swiftly between 1961 and 1965, as did the media institutes' investment in television at large. During these years, Westdeutscher Rundfunk (WDR), together with NDR and Sender Freies Berlin, opened two television studios in Warsaw and Moscow. Jürgen Rühle led the Ost-West Redaktion from 1963 in beginning to profiling the political east–west questions more strongly on television.[53] Shortly after his second trip to Poland, von Bismarck also set about recruiting Stehle to WDR. Hansjakob Stehle's career had been taking off in the early 1960s. He worked for *Die Zeit* and *Stern* in 1964/1965, and as a radio broadcast and documentary producer for multiple media institutes before von Bismarck hired him as WDR's Southeastern Europe correspondent with residence in Vienna.[54] While Stehle had continued to work for print media, his engagement with radio and television had been growing since the early 1960s. In 1964, he produced a documentary titled *Deutschlands Osten—Polens Westen?* for West German television. The opening scene of this documentary showed people strolling in Old Town and the harbor of Gdańsk on a typical Sunday interspersed with historic footage of the German invasion near Westerplatte in 1939. The voiceover cited Hitler's writings about Gdańsk and Poland.[55] Stehle's images of the rebuilt city centers and young, healthy, and happy Poles enjoying themselves at the waterfront communicated the same upbeat and positive image of a progressive Poland as Neven-du Mont's documentaries.

Deutschlands Osten—Polens Westen? responded directly to the controversies surrounding *Polen in Breslau*. Together with a film team from Hessischer Rundfunk, Stehle traveled in the end of July 1964 through the Oder-Neisse areas, filmed, and spoke with the Polish inhabitants there.[56] The team covered over thirty-four hundred miles in the formerly German territories. The documentary focused heavily on the lives, hopes, and dreams of young Poles growing up in the borderlands. Stehle continued to highlight the progress and modernity of Poland and its population, describing its rebuilding efforts, entrepreneurship, and plans for the future in the former German territories. He did show images of ruins and rubble but contrasted them with evidence of rebuilding.[57] He explained that the castle belonging to the German noble family Nostitz had been left as a ruin because the cost of its reconstruction would be more than "small, comfortable houses for the 54 estate workers and their 122 children."[58] In the film, Stehle portrayed the German minority in Poland as a disappearing problem, calling the Germans who had remained or returned to the borderlands "the last victims, one hopes, of the fates of peoples, which only time can heal."[59] Stehle stated that few people in the former German territories now knew the German place names and history of the areas. He pointed out that Poland had the highest birthrates in all of Europe, and that almost half of the population in the former German territories was born after 1945.[60] After the film was broadcast, Stehle reported that in the polls made by the media institutes, three-fourths of the viewers had a positive response to the documentary and that the percentage of total West German viewers watching—five million television sets or half of all TVs existing in the Federal Republic—was one "that TV producers nowadays can only dream about."⁶¹

In the mid-1960s, as the Adenauer era came to its close, the West German state, which had funded and supported earlier expellee-produced journal films about Poland, began to question the expellees' representations of Eastern Europe. After *Sind wir Revanchisten?* was broadcast, an internal commentary in the Press Office stated that the documentary ultimately was a fair and balanced analysis of the situation. The memo added that the office should look into withdrawing federal subsidies from the expellee press because of the biases in its reporting. Similarly, it proposed that the office withdraw films that presented a biased and outdated view of the situation in the Oder-Neisse areas.⁶² In the debates following Stehle's documentary, the minister of internal affairs declined to make a statement against it a few weeks later, saying he had not seen it himself.⁶³ Even the center-right political representatives had begun to disassociate themselves from the politically contentious and increasingly problematic expellee questions. The expellees' attempt to control public space through lobbying political leaders—using the expellee vote as leverage—was beginning to fail.

The cooler reception to the political lobbying did not deter the expellee press. In its criticism of *Deutschlands Osten—Polens Westen?*, the expellee news agency Deutsche Ostdienst wrote that "the 'Poland-expert' Stehle, who is responsible for the direction of the film, was and is persona gratissima in Red Warsaw thanks to his continued labor of love and the fact that he in barely cloaked form pleads for the renunciation of the Polish territories."⁶⁴ While such accusations were predictable, mainstream media had grown skeptical of them. In a letter dated 19 October 1964, Werner Höss, the director general of Hessischer Rundfunk, stated that television's role, in his view, was to further knowledge about the current situation in the eastern territories and that Stehle's documentary fulfilled this task. He accused the expellee leaders of "terror of opinion" (*Meinungsterror*).⁶⁵ *Frankfurter Rundschau* wrote that the actions of the expellees showed a lack of insight about the way democracy and democratic media functioned. When Wenzel Jaksch, a prominent SPD representative and Sudeten German expellee leader, attacked West German television for not allowing dissenting opinions in 1965, he was in turn criticized by other SPD representatives and by the media.⁶⁶ He eventually left the SPD.

Stehle himself published records of the more hostile expellee reactions. After the broadcast of *Deutschlands Osten* and the protests by various expellee representatives, Stehle published the full script, media discussions, and expellee responses in a thin book titled *Deutschlands Osten—Polens Westen? Eine Dokumentation* (Germany's East—Poland's West: A Documentation) with Fischer in 1965.[67] The book included article excerpts from major newspapers as well as the expellee press and political statements in response to the documentary. The publication transmitted an impression of the violent nature of politically organized expellee organizations in West Germany. Overall, it contributed to the image of expellees as dangerous, antidemocratic, and militant. While truthful to its sources, the book did not make visible the silent majority of expellees who did not comment or threaten violence as a result of *Deutschlands Osten*. As was the case at the Silesian meeting in 1963, the book highlighted the loudest, most disturbing responses, simply because those most upset were the ones who took the time to write to the newspapers or to Stehle himself. In mainstream media, as a consequence, the expellees, especially those connected to the *Landsmannschaften*, became more and more firmly associated with antidemocratic violence and revisionism.

Stehle's documentary, like Neven-du Mont's, had an impact in Poland as well. Polish television's introduction to its December 1964 broadcast of *Deutschlands Osten — Polens Westen?* referenced the sentiments that Stehle's book collected when it pointed out that the "revisionist press" was critical of the film.[68] With the support of his employer Stern-TV, Stehle granted Polish television the right to broadcast the film in Poland, but only on the condition that the introduction to the film not include any polemical statements against Bonn and that the general positive response to the film in West German media be mentioned.[69] Stehle also required that Polish television broadcast the film in its entirety to avoid a situation in which Polish television, as in Neven-du Mont's case, introduced carefully chosen excerpts supporting their preferred representation of West German attitudes toward Poland. Polish television complied but added the caveat about the "revisionist press." The Polish state remained ambivalent about the new trends in the documentaries on West German television. They approved of the positive image of Poland that the documentaries disseminated in the Federal Republic, and of the efforts to secure the western border, but they were not ready to give up impressions of West German anti-Polish sentiments and revanchism. The December broadcast date reflected a period of consideration; the agreement had been made in October.

The introduction to what Polish television titled *Germany's East* described German expellees' efforts to create an opinion against the film and its producers. It described the film as an "attempt" to show Polish reality in the western territories, partially dismissing Stehle's representation. According to the presenter, Stehle had shown "our daily problems and our difficulties ... in a fairly one-sided and distorted way as a critic of the communists ruling Poland."[70] Polish television concluded that the film was only a break with the common negative images of the former German territories dispersed in the Federal Republic.

It is difficult to determine how the Polish audiences received or interpreted the West German documentaries, or even how many Poles watched the broadcasts. Television was first broadcast in Poland in 1952.[71] The price of televisions was lowered by 9 percent in 1959 to encourage the public to buy them, but the number of TVs registered in Poland, 238,440, remained lower than in West Germany.[72] On the other hand, evidence suggests that Poles gathered with friends or extended family to watch television, broadening the medium's reach and raising the numbers of viewers. Another question is whether audiences trusted the government-mediated discussion about the West German documentaries. Here research indicates that Polish audiences generally relied more heavily on radio broadcasts, particularly Radio Free Europe, western newspapers, or underground publications, to receive trustworthy news.[73] Television was more a source of entertainment than of information, and as elsewhere audiences favored entertainment such as theater and music.

While the response to *Deutschlands Osten—Polens Westen?* came at a time of tightening censorship in Polish media, some of the commentary reflected the fact that the media freedom following the Polish October still lingered. While *Trybuna Ludu* commented positively on the broadcast "Casus Neven-du Mont," it complained about the fact that it had not included the full film.[74] *Życie Warszawy* ran an interview with Neven-du Mont by its West German foreign correspondent a few months after the broadcast, giving evidence to the ability of the West German audiences to create a conversation in Poland.[75] *Sztandar Młodych* and *Słowo Powszechne* were cautiously positive as well.

West German television productions also played a role during the second WDR trip to Poland in 1964. The purpose of this trip was to bring three episodes of the fourteen-part WDR documentary *Das Dritte Reich*, a West German production about Germany's role in the Second World War, to be shown to select audiences in Poland. Von Bismarck saw the broadcasts as a means to amplify the "objective" West German perspective on the two nations' mutual past to Polish audiences. He wrote in internal correspondences that the series was "an important cultural political contribution to reconsidering the German history as well as *rapprochement*."[76] The touring of *Das Dritte Reich* became a form of *Vergangenheitsbewältigung* as Polish–German cultural diplomacy, and Bismarck's hope was to eventually make such productions accessible to Polish television audiences, also with the purpose of improving West Germany's standing in Poland.

Das Dritte Reich had appeared on West German television in late 1960 and early 1961. It was made in a new spirit of German self-criticism, but it still downplayed the broad popular support among the middle classes for Hitler.[77] It focused on the violence and repression of the Nazi regime, which tended to excuse German compliance, and emphasized resistance attempts.[78] This emphasis on German resistance was consistent with larger television trends in regards to the coverage of the Second World War and the Holocaust during the 1960s.[79] The series had drawn large audiences in West Germany. According to a letter von Bismarck sent, Polish and West German radio officials felt the film was a good way to "familiarize [Poles] with a [West German] scrutiny (*Auseinandersetzung*) of the past through television."[80] The statement indicated how central it was for von Bismarck and others to improve the image of West Germany in Poland by marketing it as a civilized and modern country and to emphasize its efforts toward coming to terms with the past.

The episodes broadcast in Poland, "Der SS-Staat," "Die Gleichschaltung," and "Totaler Krieg und Wiederstand," discussed the Nazi takeover of press and society beginning in 1933, the terror apparatus in the Third Reich, and the Nazi state's war in Europe, but also German resistance, in particular the 20 July movement in the German army in which a few officers tried unsuccessfully to assassinate Hitler. Von Bismarck and other media institutes' associates traveled to Poland for a screening of the three episodes back to back in Warsaw and Wrocław.

While the screenings were limited to party elites and loyal communist circles, the German visitors did manage to reach a slightly larger group of Poles than the state intended. According to von Bismarck's memoirs, someone knocked on the door to his hotel room in Wrocław after the screening he provided for the party faithful. The visitor asked if he would be willing to show the episodes once more to a group of nonsanctioned viewers. The group assembled in a private home, where a "long, very straightforward and interesting discussion" followed the screening.[81] Clearly curiosity about the film was high, but the Poles were critical of the slant of the film and the ways in which it seemed to reduce German culpability.

The effort was a success in that Polish television did ask WDR to make the remaining eleven episodes of *Das Dritte Reich* available for broadcast in Warsaw, and WDR and Südwestfunk (SWF) promised to make it happen. However, political and financial issues forced the West German audiovisual institutes to abandon this plan. The many different owners of the rights to the footage in the series required high license fees, which the Polish cooperation partners were unable to pay. Some of the owners also placed conditions on the use of the film, which the WDR leadership knew the Polish side would not accept.[82]

Conclusion

The period from 1961 to 1967 saw the building of the Berlin Wall, the presidency and murder of John F. Kennedy, and the growing American investment in the Vietnam War. It was a time of intensifying political turbulence in the Federal Republic. Television and radio were at the center of political controversies. Criticism of Adenauer led to his replacement by Ludwig Erhard in 1963. However, Erhard's coalition with the Free Democratic Party (FDP) fell apart over budget issues in 1966 as his FDP finance minister Walter Scheel resigned. Meanwhile, Willy Brandt, the extremely telegenic leader of the SPD, had become a force to be reckoned with in national and international politics.[83] In 1966, the CDU's Kurt Georg Kiesinger formed the Grand Coalition together with the SPD. Willy Brandt became vice chancellor and minister of foreign affairs. The Grand Coalition was based on extensive compromises between the two leading parties and precluded a functioning opposition party. Many West Germans mistrusted it, and, as in several other countries, a radical student opposition began to emerge. The coalition was not prepared to openly recognize the Oder-Neisse border or open diplomatic relations with Poland. As the battle lines became drawn between the expellee lobby, the conservatives, and the student radicals, these developments hardened political positions and made compromise positions in domestic as well as foreign policy increasingly difficult to accomplish. In the continuing stalemate in Polish–German relations and given the positive signals that Willy Brandt sent regarding a policy change, the media activists moved forward their positions and increased their efforts to lobby for change.

Director generals and producers in West Germany were relatively successful in protecting their institutes' independence vis-à-vis the state. Television allowed for renegotiated representations of Poland and discussions of Polish–German relations to reach wider audiences and, because of its high public profile, drew more attention from West German political circles. The television producers' privileged positions and access to mass audiences made their contributions to Polish–German relations central to a broader societal break with the earlier representations of Poland. The political attention given to television documentaries and productions allowed for a reorientation and reframing of Polish representations and Polish–German relations. Pertti Ahonen has argued that the building of the Berlin Wall in 1961 and changing foreign political situation altered the attitudes toward expellees and their representation of Poland and the eastern territories.[84] In addition, audiovisual and print media outlets actively worked to convince audiences that change and progress had taken place in Eastern Europe since 1945, that older representations of Poland had become slanted and outdated, and that the expellees posed a danger to West German progress and stability unless they were willing to fully integrate and assimilate.

The West German television controversies reached Polish public space in a limited form, however. While the West German producers and media personalities made concerted efforts to introduce their debates and new images to Poland, and while some members of the Polish communist press corps and television institutes were interested in those efforts, overall state censors and leadership distrusted the signs of change and, for domestic political purposes, thought it best to preserve the image of West German hostility and revisionism in Polish media. Nevertheless, in more limited circles, among city and political elites in Warsaw and Wrocław, the efforts had an effect and resulted in dialogues about the representations of the mutual past.

Notes

1. Jürgen Neven-du Mont, "Polen in Breslau: Porträt einer Stadt; Sending am 7.Mai 1963-20.15 Uhr," BAK NL1279/131, 1.
2. For agenda-setting of leading media, see Jürgen Wilke, "Leitmedien und Zielgruppenorgane," in *Mediengeschichte der Bundesrepublik Deutschland*, ed. Jürgen Wilke (Cologne, Weimar, Vienna, 1999), 302–29. By "agenda-setting," media researchers mean the identification and introduction of a topic to a larger public, while "framing" is the creation of reference frames for an existing topic.
3. William Uricchio, "Television as History: Representations of German Television Broadcasting, 1935–1944," in *Framing the Past: The Historiography of German Cinema and Television*, ed. Bruce A. Murray and Christopher J. Wickham (Carbondale, 1992), 171.
4. Brack, *German Radio and Television*, 36–37. Also see discussion in Hodenberg, *Konsens und Krise*, 150–51, on the debates between state and journalists on the role and independence of the media vis-à-vis the state.
5. Hodenberg, *Konsens und Krise*, 302–5.
6. Before 1970, correspondents and journalists abroad often reported and worked both for television and radio. Katz et al., eds., *Am Puls der Zeit*, 2:86.
7. *Panorama* was launched in 1958 by Rüdiger Proske as a controversial news show, a visual counterpart to *Der Spiegel*. Hodenberg, *Konsens und Krise*, 302ff.
8. Reuber, *Deutschland- und Ostpolitik im Fernsehen*, 11.
9. For television and the West German national past, see Kansteiner, *In Pursuit of German Memory*; Michael E. Geisler, "The Disposal of Memory: Fascism and the Holocaust on West German Television," in Murray and Wickham, *Framing the Past*, 220–60. See also Christoph Scheurle, *Die deutschen Kanzler im Fernsehen: Theatrale Darstellungsstrategien von Politikern im Schlüsselmedium der Nachkriegsgeschichte* (Bielefeld, 2009); Woo Seung-Lee, *Das Fernsehen im geteilten Deutschland (1952–1989): Ideologische Konkurrenz und programmliche Kooperation* (Potsdam, 2003). For transnational media research, see for

example Jean K. Chalaby, ed., *Transnational Television World Wide: Towards a New Media Order* (New York, 2005).
10. Important research on such efforts have been done on Radio Free Europe and Radio Liberty. See for example A. Ross Johnson, *Radio Free Europe and Radio Liberty: The CIA Years and Beyond* (Washington, DC, 2010), or for the larger cultural Cold War, Giles Scott-Smith and Hans Krabbendamm, eds., *The Cultural Cold War in Western Europe, 1945–1960* (London, 2009); Frances Stonor Saunders, *The Cultural Cold War: CIA and the World of Arts and Letters* (New York, 2001); see also Feinberg, *Culture of Lies*.
11. Thum, *Die Fremde Stadt*, 209ff.
12. Letter Jürgen Neven-du Mont to Christian Neven-du Mont, 21 February 1958, BAK NL1279/11.
13. For more extensive discussions of German stereotypes of Poland that may have influenced the expellee productions, see Hubert Orłowski, *Polnische Wirtschaft: Zum deutschen Polendiskurs im Neuzeit* (Wiesbaden, 1996), and Hasso von Zitzewitz, *Das deutsche Polenbild in der Geschichte: Entstehung—Einflüsse—Auswirkungen* (Cologne, Weimar, Vienna, 1991) or Jarochna Dąbrowska, *Stereotype und ihr sprachlicher Ausdruck im Polenbild der deutschen Presse* (Tübingen, 1999). An example of the type of reporting the documentaries were trying to oppose is "25 Tage in der alten Heimat," *Pommersche Zeitung* 8, 15 March 1958, 4.
14. Neven-du Mont, "Jenseits der Oder und die Neisse," 14.
15. Ibid., 6.
16. Kansteiner, *In Pursuit of German Memory*, 112.
17. Neven-du Mont, manuscript "Zwischen Ost und West: Polen 1961; Sendung am 21.8.1961 um 20.30 Uhr," BAK NL1279/131-132, 13.
18. Ibid., 2. Gregor Thum writes that though the rebuilding of Polish cities in the early 1950s was highly characterized by socialist realism, this ideal weakened after 1956 and even further in the 1960s and 1970s. Thum, *Die Fremde Stadt*, 236–40.
19. "Polen in Breslau," 7 May 1963, NDR/ARD, BAK, N/1279, 131, Neven-du Mont BAK NL1279/131.
20. Ibid.
21. Ibid., 1.
22. "Deutsche ohne Verantwortung," *Schlesische Rundschau*, 17 May 1963.
23. "Vertriebene kritisieren Breslau-Sendung: Verzerrung der gegenwärtigen Verhältnisse/ Wieder Protest gegen Befragung," *FAZ*, 10 May 1963.
24. "Breslau," *FAZ*, 9 May 1963.
25. "Kritik an Breslau-Fernsehsendung," *Süddeutsche Zeitung*, 10 May 1963. Hans Krüger was president of the BdV at the time. He resigned in 1963 due to controversies over his Nazi past.
26. "Rozmyślania przy telewizorze: Nauka nie idzie w las," *Trybuna Ludu*, 23 December 1964.
27. "Blasses Breslau," *Die Zeit*, 17 May 1963.
28. In *A Curtain of Lies*, Melissa Feinberg discusses the alternative Cold War treatment of the concept of truth. She points to two trends relevant here: first, the obsession with proving the truth—that is to say, "our" version of any given event—or the lies on the opposite side, and second, the way in which this approach to truth and exaggerating was shared by all sides of the debate. Feinberg, *Curtain of Lies*, xix.
29. As Thum showed in *Die Fremde Stadt*, Polonization of Breslau took a relatively long time to complete after the war. Meanwhile, historians such as James Bjork (*Neither German nor Pole*) and Peter Polak-Springer (*Recovered Territory: A German-Polish Conflict over Land and Culture 1919–1989* [New York, 2015]) have described the multinational ele-

ments present in the cultural fabrics of borderlands populations in Silesia. Thum, *Die Fremde Stadt*, 338–431.
30. "Infratest," 7 May 1963, BAK, Neven-du Mont, BAK NL1279/93.
31. See Patrick Major, *The Death of KPD: Communism and Anti-Communism in West Germany, 1945–1956* (Oxford, 1998) for a political overview of the development of American and West German anticommunism after the Second World War.
32. "Breslau—ein fälliges Nachwort," *Die Welt*, 15 May 1963.
33. "Bundesdeutsche Instinktlosigkeiten: 'Die Uhren der polnischen Wirklichkeit gehen anders,'" *Deutsche National-Zeitung und Soldaten-Zeitung*, 24 May 1963.
34. "Rechtsverfahren," *Rheinische Post*, 25 October 1965.
35. "Vertriebene: Zorn im Fackelschein," *Der Spiegel* 17:25, 19 June 1963, 17.
36. Jürgen Neven-du Mont, "Manuskript: Sind wir Revanchisten? Die Deutschen und die Oder-Neisse Linie," Hamburg, 26 June 1963, BAK NL1279/132, 1.
37. Neven-du Mont, "Sind wir Revanchisten?" 24.
38. Ibid., 13.
39. Ibid., 20.
40. Ibid.
41. "Infratest," 7 May 1963, BAK, Neven-du Mont, BAK NL1279/93.
42. Ahonen, *After the Expulsions*, 171.
43. Clemens Rieder, "Heute Breslau, Morgen Berlin?" *Bayern-Kurier*, 18 May 1963. The protests against the poll were also mentioned in two articles in *Frankfurter Allgemeine*: "Breslau," 9 May 1963, and "Vertriebene kritisieren Breslau-Sendung: Verzerrung der gegenwärtigen Verhältnisse/Wieder Protest gegen Befragung," 10 May 1963.
44. "Vermerk Ruth Müller," 17 April 1963, BAK B145/2858.
45. Ibid.
46. Karl Günther von Hase to Gerhard Schröder, 23 May 1963, BAK B145/2858.
47. Vermerk, Dr. Ludwig Maria Freibüter, 13 May 1963, BAK B145/2858.
48. "Der Wirbel um 'Polen in Breslau': Gespräch unseres Bonner Redakteurs P W Wenger mit dem Fernsehreporter des NDR Neven-du Mont," *Rheinischer Merkur*, 21 June 1963.
49. "Leidenschaften," *Die Welt*, 10 June 1963.
50. Leszek Goliński, "Rozmyślania przy telewizorze: Czego najbardziej nie lubią tygrysy," *Trybuna Ludu*, 5 June 1963.
51. "To co stare—i to co nowe," *Trybuna Ludu*, 17 May 1963.
52. Hodenberg, *Konsens und Krise*, 357. Gert von Paczensky (1925–).
53. Reuber, *Deutschland- und Ostpolitik im Fernsehen*, 11.
54. Hodenberg, *Konsens und Krise*, 302–23. Letter exchange, HA-WDR 3968. Interestingly, Stehle was hired on the precondition that WDR would allow him to take over the position as the network's foreign correspondent to Rome in 1969, as the current correspondent was due to retire then.
55. Stehle, *Deutschlands Osten—Polens Westen?*, 40.
56. Ibid., 28.
57. Ibid., 60.
58. Ibid., 47. The castle he referred to was probably Schloss Laasan in Łazany in Lower Silesia.
59. Ibid., 44.
60. Ibid., 51.
61. Ibid., 65. Hansjakob Stehle, interview by author.
62. "Aufzeichnung betr. Fernsehaufführung von Neven-du Mont, Ruth Müller," 3 July 1963, BAK B145/2858.

63. Stehle, *Deutschlands Osten—Polens Westen?*, 98, Fragestunde der 141. Sitzung, 23 October 1964, Protokoll S. 7047 ff. Bundesminister des Innern, Höcherl; Ahonen, *After the Expulsions*, 172.
64. Stehle, *Deutschlands Osten—Polens Westen?*, 82, DOD, October 1964 (41).
65. Ibid., 97.
66. Ibid., 104. Ahonen, *After the Expulsions*, 58.
67. Stehle, *Deutschlands Osten—Polens Westen?*
68. Since 1959, Polish television had bought seventy-four French and twenty English films produced between 1930 and 1950 to broadcast. Pokorna-Ignatowicz does not, however, mention any purchases of German films in her report. Katarzyna Pokorna-Ignatowicz, *Telewizja w systemie politycznym i medialnym PRL: Między polityką a widzem* (Cracow, 2003), 60.
69. Stehle, *Deutschlands Osten—Polens Westen?*, 123.
70. Ibid., 126.
71. Pokorna-Ignatowicz, *Telewizja w systemie politycznym i medialnym*, 44.
72. Ibid., 57.
73. Ibid., 54.
74. Leszek Goliński, "Rozmyślania przy telewizorze: Czego najbardziej nie lubią tygrysy," *Trybuna Ludu*, 5 June 1963.
75. Ryszard Wojna, "Prawda o Wrocławiu w zachodnioniemieckiej TV," *Życie Warszawy*, 9 May 1963; "Zycie rozmawia z Neven-du Montem autorem audycji telewizji NRF o Wrocławiu," *Życie Warszawy*, 9 September 1963.
76. Bismarck, *Aufbruch aus Pommern*, 281.
77. Hodenberg, *Konsens und Krise*, 272; Peter Zimmerman, "Vergangenheitsbewältigung: Das 'Dritte Reich' in Dokumentarfilmen und Fernsehdokumentationen der BRD," in *Der geteilte Himmel: Arbeits, Alltag und Geschichte im ost- und westdeutschen Film*, ed. Peter Zimmerman and Gebhard Moldenhauer (Konstanz, 2000), 57–75.
78. Once more, this model followed standard 1950s media treatments in allocating all responsibility for the Holocaust and the Third Reich to Hitler's regime and treating the Nazi era as a natural catastrophe over which human agency had little influence. Kansteiner, *In Pursuit of German Memory*, 211.
79. Ibid., 114.
80. Klaus von Bismarck to Hubert Meller, 20 July 1964, WDR-HA, Nachlass Klaus von Bismarck, Unterlagen Polen-Reise, Lauf. No. 259. Gerd Ruge also proposed creating a shorter version of the series for U.S. audiences as a means to market West Germany as a self-critical society that had attained a healthy distance from its past to its western allies. Hodenberg, *Konsens und Krise*, 272.
81. Bismarck, *Aufbruch aus Pommern*, 282.
82. The responsible person estimated the licensing cost at 250,000 DM in the event of a decision to broadcast the films on Polish television. Internal WDR communication, Otto Heuft to Klaus von Bismarck, 15 August 1965, WDR-HA, Nachlass Klaus von Bismarck, Unterlagen Polen-Reise, Lauf. No. 259.
83. The media particularly highlighted Brandt's youth and dynamism as compared to the elderly Adenauer. In addition, they paralleled Brandt to the equally young and vibrant John F. Kennedy. Daniela Münkel, "Als 'deutscher Kennedy' zum Sieg? Willy Brandt, die USA und die Medien," *Zeithistorische forschungen*, 1 (2004): 172–94.
84. Ahonen, *After the Expulsions*, 165.

Chapter 5

OF FORGIVING AND FORGETTING
The Religious Memoranda and the Media, 1961–68

On 18 November 1965, the Polish Catholic bishops sent their letter of reconciliation to the German Catholic bishops. In the letter, they asked for a dialogue about the troubled Polish–German relations and invited the Germans to the Polish Novena, the one thousandth anniversary of the conversion of the Polish nation to Christianity in 966, the following year. The most-quoted line of this letter was "We forgive and ask for forgiveness."[1] It was a powerful statement admitting suffering and wrongdoing, and while it was not widely supported in Polish society at the time it first appeared, it would echo across Polish and German media for the remainder of the twentieth century.

In an interview about the letter some thirty years later, the *Tygodnik* journalist Józefa Hennelowa recalled that it had upset her and other young Catholics in Poland. She stated,

> What caused this reaction was not the "we forgive" part, but the words "we ask for forgiveness." . . . We knew that as Christians we were called upon to forgive even when it is difficult. But we could not understand why the bishops said, "we ask for forgiveness." Back then, this was a completely black hole in which we could not find one another. And I have to say that Karol Wojtyła [the archbishop of Poland, later Pope John Paul II] never really convinced us in this discussion.[2]

Over time, the bishops' act of writing the letter acquired multiple and shifting layers of significance in both the Polish and German context. In Poland, people began to see the bishops' initiative as a signal of the church's resistance to and eventually triumph over the communist state. West German media activists utilized the initiative as an aspect of their ongoing campaign to raise Poland's profile and to improve Polish–German re-

---

Notes for this chapter begin on page 149.

lations. The conservative West German press interpreted the state–church conflict surrounding the letter as an ominous sign of the growing communist threat.

The 1965 Polish Catholic Bishops' Letter of Reconciliation to the German Catholic Bishops was one of a number of religious statements on reconciliation that helped bring in new awareness of Polish–German relations to public discourse. Other statements in this era included the 1962 Tübingen Memorandum, the 1965 Protestant Expellee Memorandum, the 1966 German Catholic Bishops' response to the Polish Catholic letter, and the 1968 Bensberger Memorandum. Discussions of reconciliation activism also often include mentions of the travels and initiatives toward penance by the East German Aktion Sühnezeichen.[3] Both larger histories of Central Europe in the postwar era and special commemorative writings and anthologies have celebrated the memoranda as civil society initiatives toward improving Polish–German relations.[4] The statements were deeply integrated within the media networks discussed in earlier chapters. Elite journalists, correspondents, and public intellectuals active in Polish–German relations co-wrote some of the memoranda and provided advice or feedback on others. Sympathetic media outlets also played crucial roles in interpreting and packaging the memoranda to have the greatest possible effect on the public. In doing so, they interpreted the documents within the context of existing domestic debates concerning territory, the Eastern Policy, the freedom of the media or the state–church struggle in Poland. This chapter will discuss how the church memoranda's significance to reconciliation and Polish–German relations was mediated by their political context and through the media's transmission of them to the public.

From the late 1940s to the mid-1950s, as Robert Żurek has pointed out, Polish as well as German churches prioritized national dialogue at the cost of cross-border conversations.[5] Their focus was logical considering the challenges of stabilizing the Central European nations after the war. In the 1960s, West European societies seemed to become increasingly secularized. Both Catholic and Protestant spiritual communities struggled to adjust to this and to salvage their roles in rapidly changing societies. Their relationship to the media was ambivalent. The new generation of media personalities and editors challenged the churches' traditional authority on a variety of topics, but the churches were also successful in carving out space in public media to reach the larger population.[6] The concern about secularization and a perceived need to provide moral leadership were some of the motivations for the religious engagement in politics, and key reasons behind the memoranda. The Polish Catholic Church, as discussed earlier, held a strong position in Polish society and had its own print media but no access to the dominant communist print and audiovisual media.

Germany's two major churches underwent drastic changes in the 1950s. In the German Protestant Church, a new pluralism entered the church structure as debates on democratization intensified in the early 1960s.[7] On the other hand, the mainstream Catholic establishment on the whole resisted trends such as public transparency and two-way communication with a larger public space in spite of the Second Vatican Council's encouragement, until at least the 1970s.[8] The German Catholic Church did, however, gradually introduce some changes as it strove to adjust to postwar societal change.[9] Vatican II provided an impetus for greater democratization, ecumenical work, and dialogue, the consequences of which became crucial to actors involved in Polish–German relations.[10]

The first church memorandum published on Polish–German relations was the Tübingen Memorandum, "The Memorandum of the Eight," in November 1961. Klaus von Bismarck, who had recently become director general at Westdeutscher Rundfunk (WDR), was one of its initiators, thus contributing to the overlap between religious reconciliatory initiatives and audiovisual media in yet another way. The other signers included a number of Protestant intellectuals and academics, such as Hellmut Becker, a sociologist, legal expert, and president of the Deutscher Volkshochschulverband; Joachim Beckmann, president of the Protestant Church in the Rhineland; Werner Heisenberg, Nobel Prize winner and professor of astrophysics; Dr. Günter Howe of the Evangelisches Studiengemeinschaft in Heidelberg; Dr. Georg Picht, active in pedagogy and religious philosophy; from Hinterzarten, professor of law Ludwig Raiser, who was in the leadership of the church, particularly as member of its advisory board; and Professor Carl Friedrich von Weizsäcker, also active within the field of astrophysics and in philosophy.[11] The document was not initially a public statement. It intended to open conversation among all actively Protestant parliamentary members in Bonn.

The memorandum criticized several aspects of the Federal Republic's politics, including some of its social policies and the discussions about rearmament after the North Atlantic Treaty Organization (NATO) began to consider stationing nuclear weapons in West Germany in 1957.[12] Its primary focus was foreign policy and the possibility of German reunification, criticizing Bonn's passive eastern policy as an obstacle to reunification. The document pointed out that Germany had the world's attention and support in the wish for freedom for the East Germans, particularly after the erection of the Berlin Wall. However, the memorandum argued, the state had no international support for its demand for a reinstitution of the borders from 1937.[13] Thus, West Germany must seriously consider relinquishing the eastern territories to create goodwill that would eventually lead to a reunification, which both the eastern and western powers would support.[14] If the West German political establishment pursued the short-term goal of courting an electorate unwilling to accept the loss of the eastern territories, they would not be acting in the long-term interest of the German state.

Given the prominence of the signees, the Protestant parliamentary members took the Tübingen Memorandum seriously, and met with its authors. The memorandum might have remained only one internal document among many others circulating in Bonn had not parts of it been leaked to *deutsche Presse-Agentur* (DPA) four months later. In early March 1962, the Tübingen Memorandum entered the media scene and became the subject of intense public debate. The already existing interest in Poland and the border among journalists, the high profile of the document's authors, the forthrightness of its claims, but also the attacks and calls about "betrayals of the nation" from right-wing groups and expellees brought considerable attention to the memorandum.[15] At that point, the authors elected to make the full text public to avoid rumors and misinterpretations. The text appeared in the *Evangelisches Amtsblatt*, the Protestant Church's newsletter.

Die Zeit and *Süddeutsche Zeitung* both republished the seven-page memorandum in its entirety within days. They and *Frankfurter Rundschau* were the most supportive of the memorandum, but all three major mainstream publications dismissed the possibility that Bonn would recognize the Oder-Neisse Line. In *Die Zeit*, Marion Countess Dönhoff wrote that whereas she considered the authors of the Tübingen Memorandum voices of reason and their political commentary well worth thinking about, she still questioned whether postwar Germans even had the right to give up lands where their forefathers had lived for seven hundred years.[16] *Frankfurter Rundschau* stated that the authors had every right to pose the questions in the Tübingen Memorandum. It called the document's suggestions realistic and justified but avoided commenting on the territorial question altogether. *Rundschau* remarked that the lack of serious political discussion in West Germany was worrisome, and it applauded lay Protestants' attempt to promote political dialogue.[17] In this article, the theme of threatened media freedom and the efforts by the state to suppress any questioning of the Adenauer government's stance on the territorial issue informed the commentary as well.

The conservative, expellee, and right-wing Catholic papers protested.[18] Landsmannschaft Schlesien and *deutsche Soldatenzeitung* called the memorandum a betrayal of the nation, indicating that older understandings of German boundaries and of what it meant to be German still prevailed.[19] *Frankfurter Allgemeine* wrote that although some of the criticisms in the memorandum were to the point, the document's commentary about political taboos on the territorial question was a strange accusation given that the authors themselves had not originally made the document public. They claimed there were currently no realistic solutions available to the border question, so it was reasonable to continue to postpone discussions.[20] The media commentary also reflected the Germans' shocked reaction to the recently erected Berlin Wall, both in the liberal media's insistence that change was necessary and conservative media's wish to avoid destabilizing the political situation further. Overall, the Tübingen Memorandum had intended to continue the praxis of limiting sensitive discussions to political elites and experts in order to protect the internal consensus politics. The leaks and media intervention caused the memorandum to play a different and more public role in West Germany.

The religious memoranda also became part of political agendas and disagreements. In late March, as multiple newspapers reported, Willy Brandt, at the time Berlin's mayor and the Social Democratic Party's rising star, lent support to the Tübingen Memorandum while using it to further his new political program of a "policy of small steps."[21] At the same time, he commented, he himself opposed some of the statements in the memorandum, noting that the memorandum had unfairly included the Social Democrats in criticisms that should be directed primarily to the Free Democratic Party (FDP) and the Christian Democratic Union (CDU). At this moment, he was less concerned with the Oder-Neisse Line and Poland than with the division of Germany and the existence of the Berlin Wall. Given the existence of the wall, it was important to focus on Soviet politics and the possible security threat toward Berlin. Nevertheless, he complimented the writers on the memorandum, saying that a "troublesome democrat is a thousand times more preferable than a half-hearted follower."[22] In such statements, the Social Democrats and Brandt, while still restrained, were preparing to initiate new agendas with regards to Eastern Europe and Poland.

The expellee organizations harshly condemned the Tübingen Memorandum. They wrote to Klaus von Bismarck and WDR directly, as well as to several other media institute representatives. Von Bismarck received from widely differing groups numerous letters and communications that ranged from threats to long discussions about the expellee situation.[23] Hans Bausch, director general for the Süddeutscher Rundfunk, forwarded the statement expellee organizations had sent to him with a note saying he would not be responding to them.[24] A leading representative of the radio institutes' umbrella organization Arbeitsgemeinschaft der öffentlich-rechtlichen Rundfunkanstalten der Bundesrepublik Deutschland sent a similar note. The expellee politicians had clear difficulties in gaining access to audiovisual media.

Von Bismarck himself did not entirely welcome the public controversy at this time since he wished to focus on his new position at WDR and worried that the negative publicity connected to it would also carry over to WDR as a whole. In April 1962 he turned down a request to write an editorial in the *Kölner Stadtanzeiger*, stating that "after the publication of the memorandum, I have my hands full with answering questions about it, and defending its arguments where necessary. I would like to lay low with other statements in the public space for the time being."[25]

The Tübingen Memorandum also made an impression on Polish observers and media representatives. The correspondent for *Trybuna Ludu* in Bonn, Marian Podkowiński, reported by telephone on the memorandum, and his reports were immediately published in Warsaw.[26] Poles were surprised that von Bismarck, a Prussian, whose family name was firmly connected to the "Drang nach Osten" lore in Polish national mythology, and that German Protestants, traditionally considered hostile to Poland and Polish Catholicism, had authored and signed it. Von Bismarck had already drawn some attention with his 1954 speech before the Annual Protestant Congress. The Tübingen Memorandum further contributed to his reputation in Poland and facilitated his efforts during his official visits in 1964 and 1965.

Further, the Tübingen Memorandum initiated an internal discussion on the eastern questions within the German Protestant Church. The Ostkirchenausschuss, which consisted of Protestant clergy and dignitaries from the former German eastern parishes, had dominated the Church's eastern policy since the late 1940s. On March 5, 1962, the Ostkirchenausschuss issued an official comment on the Tübingen Memorandum, criticizing its disregard of the *Recht auf Heimat* and its naiveté concerning Soviet power politics in Poland. The memorandum's suggestion that an official recognition of the Oder-Neisse border would improve relations with Poland was an illusion "in light of the Polish public opinion within and, unfortunately, also outside of the communist-controlled country."[27] However, in internal conversations, other leaders of the Protestant Church began floating the idea of issuing an official statement representing the entire church on the eastern territories in 1963. The Ostkirchenausschuss asked for restraint and a united front.[28] The discussions developed into a drawn-out dispute about whether the church should hold back from the political questions of relinquishing the territory, continuing to support expellees' rights to them.[29]

The Protestant Church leaders in favor of engagement with the question became increasingly aware that other countries in Western Europe as well as the United States were pressuring West Germany to accept the postwar borders. *The Times* reported that some of the Protestant Church leaders who endorsed the Tübingen Memorandum had first visited the United States and become aware of American and other western expectations in this regard.[30] In 1963, the Kammer für öffentliche Verantwortung (the Section for Public Responsibility), under the leadership of Ludwig Raiser, began to prepare a general memorandum on the situation of the expellees, which came to be known as "The Situation of the Expellees and the Relations of the German People to Its Eastern Neighbors" or, more commonly, the Protestant Expellee Memorandum, which was published in 1965.

The Tübingen Memorandum had mainly concerned the West German political sphere. However, East German clergy were also included in the Protestant Memorandum in 1965 as the document represented the entire church. The Kammer für öffentliche Verantwortung especially invited representatives of the East German Protestant Church to participate in preparing the memorandum. These representatives were initially hesitant, fearing that the expellee controversies would spill over into the German Democratic Republic as well, leading to general unrest. On the other hand, both sides agreed that the Protestant Church should not be divided into eastern and western parts, and ultimately the eastern representatives signed as well.[31] The Kammer für öffentliche Verantwortung solicited opinions of expellee representatives as well but were unable to reach any agreement as to content with them.[32]

The memorandum appeared in several editions published by the Protestant Church's publishing house Verlag des Amtsblattes der Evangelischen Kirche in Deutschland in 1965. The Protestant Expellee Memorandum was much more carefully phrased than the Tübingen Memorandum, yet it drew more attention and created greater controversy. The document redefined the Protestant Church's stance on the eastern territories and the expulsions. Its introduction assured readers that the Church was not attempting to make policy, a task it left to elected political representatives.[33] The church was also not responsible for formulating detailed political goals and solutions. "However, it belongs to the political service of Christianity to represent the structural and human preconditions for politics that serve humanity and peace," it said. As Christians, German Protestants were responsible for their political leaders' mistakes, including the existing eastern policy, which it felt the state should reformulate.[34]

Although expellee groups had refused to sign on to the statement, the memorandum still strove to address their concerns. Stating that it was not the Protestant Church's task to determine the right time to develop a new active policy toward Poland and Eastern Europe, the text nonetheless rejected the argument that all such considerations would have to "postpone indefinitely" a more permanent settlement of the border questions in light of "the fundamental questions which come into play here."[35] The memorandum acknowledged that the expellees had a right to compensation for their loss of land and property. Yet such compensation would invoke questions about compensation for losses German actions had caused Polish and other eastern neighbors. Finally, the memorandum suggested that addressing such questions might lead to the conclusion that the German state and nation should not be allowed to keep its territory from 1937, given German crimes in the east.

The Protestant Memorandum has been widely cited as a watershed moment in West German public debates. It shocked the public that a central civil institution would break the taboo surrounding the conversation about the eastern territories and propose a change of state policy. Media from all parts of the political spectrum reacted by discussing the necessary conciliatory aspects of Polish–German relations in 1965, with widely differing conclusions.[36] In *Die Zeit*, Countess Dönhoff commended the attempt at reconciliation with the eastern neighbors but added, "This is only possible if the church can accomplish a reconciliation among its own however. And that is precisely what has been neglected." The memorandum did cause several divisions and conflicts within the church. The Ostkirchenausschuss protested sharply, and Bishop Reinhard Weiter, who was responsible within the church for remigration and expellee questions, officially asked to be relieved of his position. Further, a number of prominent Protestants formed the Emergency Community for Protestant Germans (Notgemeinschaft Evangelischer Deutschen) in Stuttgart in the spring of 1966 since they felt that the mainstream church's leadership did not represent them anymore.[37] Other observers were also troubled by the threat the memorandum posed to internal West German unity and stability. *Rheinischer Merkur* argued under the title "Necessary Appeal for Reconciliation" that the critics had misunderstood the memorandum. It never intended to change policy, only to begin a dialogue in the spirit of reconciliation.[38] *Die Welt*'s article writer concurred with Countess Dönhoff that the fact that expellee organizations had not signed it doomed the ambition of achieving a spirit of reconciliation.[39] Critical as well as sympathetic commentators understood the Protestant Church's position on the border question as a matter of seeking consensus and unity *within* West German society rather than an invitation to a pluralistic understanding of a potential change in Polish–German relations. Meanwhile, no echo of the correspondence reached the larger East German society at the time, neither positive nor negative reactions.[40]

In West Germany, Polish–German relations received even more attention as the debates about the Expellee Memorandum coincided with the 18 November 1965 publication of the Polish Catholic Bishops' Letter of Reconciliation to the German Catholic Bishops. The letter invited the German bishops to the Polish Church's millennial celebration in 1966 and addressed historic and present Polish–German relations in new ways. Bolesław Kominek, archbishop of Wrocław, was its principal author. Bishop Kominek, born in 1903, had grown up in Silesia and spoke both Polish and German. After the war, he became a close associate of the Catholic intellectuals in the Znak group and a regular contributor to *Tygodnik Powszechny*.[41] Bishop Kominek firmly believed that Poland needed and had the right to the Oder-Neisse territories. According to some sources, he had actively encouraged German priests to leave Silesia after the war. He had also played a crucial role in integrating newly arrived Polish Catholics from the east into the diocese of Wrocław.[42] Like most postwar European elites, he had become convinced that a culturally and ethnically homogeneous Polish nation was key to the country's peace and stability. At the same time, he rejected anti-German, victimhood-centered, and ultranationalist understandings of Polish–German relations and believed on political and personal grounds that positive relations with Germans were needed. A bilingual person from the borderlands, he cultivated friendships with Germans and professed admiration for German culture.[43] Bishop Kominek's nontraditional Polish patriotism made it easier for him to reach out and find connections among sympathetic Germans, among them Walter Dirks and Hansjakob Stehle.

It was Bishop Kominek's different approach to Polish–German relations compared with Cardinal Wyszyński that initially caught Hansjakob Stehle's attention and interest. While agreeing that Poland should retain the ceded territories, the two men differed as to the rationale. Cardinal Wyszyński claimed, at least publicly, that Poland should retain the lands because they were ancient Polish holdings. Bishop Kominek meanwhile argued that the terrible consequences of the Second World War, not ancient rights, justified Poland's possession of these territories.[44] He also emphasized the existence of many positive contacts between Poles and Germans, including among the "representatives of the German episcopate."[45]

The initial contact between Stehle and Kominek followed an article Stehle published in *Die Zeit*, criticizing Cardinal Wyszyński while being slightly more complimentary toward Bishop Kominek. Bishop Kominek wrote a letter to the editor of *Die Zeit*, criticizing the article for having been based on false information and contributing to making the domestic situation for the Polish bishops more difficult.[46] Stehle responded in a personal letter, including copies of the materials on which he based his article. He also published the full text of Kominek's letter in *Die Zeit* as a correction. In the letter, Stehle stated that he had no intention of making the situation in communist Poland worse for the bishops. He had heard that Kominek possessed a copy of *Nachbar Polen* and he should thus be familiar with Stehle's perspective. Kominek would surely understand, based on *Nachbar Polen* and articles, why Stehle was critical of Cardinal Wyszyński.[47] Kominek replied and this exchange began their correspondence. In these days, Kominek frequently worried that Stehle would present the Polish Church in an unfavorable light. Cardinal Wyszyński's rhetorical stance with regards to the Germans and the borderlands would remain an issue of contention between them in the years to come.

Despite their disagreements, Bishop Kominek and Hansjakob Stehle continued their conversation about the major issues of Polish–German relations. In a letter dated May 1965, Bishop Kominek wrote, "I confirm your letter from May 10th. I will certainly be at home in Breslau on June 15th. In the meantime, I have been able to ponder the problems that we spoke about in Rome in April. I am grateful for your openness in many things."[48] In this letter, the bishop also discussed his hesitance to become a "political bishop" if he got caught up in the ongoing debates.

Stehle again made an unfavorable distinction between Cardinal Wyszyński and Bishop Kominek in September 1965, when the cardinal again held a sermon in Wrocław in which he claimed that these border territories were ancient Polish property. Stehle compared the sermon negatively to Bishop Kominek's statements of "facts, practical common sense, and patriotism without national narrow-mindedness" on the same occasion.[49] The bishop wrote to Stehle and thanked him, with some reservations, for the media reports. Then he wrote worriedly that he had heard that Stehle was preparing a radio feature on Poland and religion: "This gave me a fright: what are you making of it?! It is not a question of my own person, but more about not contrasting me with the Cardinal as a sensible friend of the Germans—and the Cardinal as a completely bad guy (*schwarzen Mann*)."[50] On the positive side, the journalist and the bishop shared a great concern with Polish–German questions. In addition, Stehle's contacts in West German media and television would help Bishop Kominek reach larger audiences in West Germany. Stehle gained a reliable insider connection in the Catholic Church of Poland and found another figurehead in addition to Gomułka and the cardinal, neither of whom had entirely lived up to his expectations, for improved relations and a new progressive Poland.

On 9 November, ten days before the Polish bishops released their letter, Bishop Kominek wrote to Stehle and thanked him for his work in *Deutschlands Osten—Polens Westen?* and *Gott im Osten* (God in the East). The latter focused on the Polish Catholic Church and its relations with the state and the people. While Bishop Kominek still disagreed with Stehle's criticism of Cardinal Wyszyński, his reproach had a half-serious and tolerant quality. He emphasized his appreciation for the positive light in which Stehle portrayed Polish religious life.⁵¹ By this time, Kominek had a draft of the letter ready. The role of media and media actors here went well beyond merely reporting on the letter after it became published. These sources indicate that Kominek's conversations with Stehle and other German journalists and activists such as Walter Dirks earlier that same fall in Rome played an important role in its content and timing, as did the publication of the Protestant Expellee Memorandum. At the letter's early stages, only a few members of the Polish hierarchy, notably the bishop of Cracow, Karol Wojtyła, the future Pope John Paul II, supported it.⁵² Cardinal Wyszyński was hesitant to approve the initiative. He suspected that the letter could become a point of contention with the state; he also did not consider relations with the Germans a matter of primary importance to the Polish Catholic Church. Bishop Kominek's later reminiscences largely figured German bishops as advisors and conversation partners during the development of the text. Yet the failure of the West German Catholic Church to respond in spirit to the letter suggests that this cooperation was not extensive.

Bishop Kominek was aware that Polish–West German relations was a sensitive topic to Poles as well as Germans. However, he failed to appreciate fully how controversial his letter would become to the Polish state. The bishop had kept Ignacy Krasicki, the representative for the Polish People's Republic in Rome, updated on the progress of the statement and also provided him with a copy of the full text before publication. Bishop Kominek may have expected Krasicki to forward the text to Warsaw, noting its origin and author and requesting approval. According to Stehle, however, Krasicki sent the letter to Gomułka and claimed that he had intercepted it, confirming Gomułka's suspicions that the episcopate was going behind his back in foreign policy questions.⁵³ Bishop Kominek published the letter on 18 November 1965 without having heard anything further from Warsaw in terms of an official approval.

The letter, signed by all Polish Catholic bishops, consisted largely of a narration of Polish–German relations from a very traditional Polish Catholic perspective, from the baptism of Mieszko I in 966, when Poland became a Christian country, to the present. The letter described the origins of the Polish–German enmity as beginning with the Teutonic Knights' settlement on Polish territory in the thirteenth century. The letter also mentioned those Germans who contributed to the increasing fear and hatred of Germany in Poland: "Albrecht of Prussia, Frederick the so-called Great, [Otto von] Bismarck, and finally Hitler."⁵⁴ In terms of national self-understanding, the letter used a rigid definition of Polish national identity as equated with Catholicism. It stated that "the symbiosis between Christianity, Church and State existed in Poland from the beginning and was never really disrupted. Over time, it created the almost universal Polish notion: to be Polish is to be Catholic."[55] The letter also confirmed Polish national historical narratives of victimology. While it precluded more inclusive understandings of Polish national belonging, the letter emphasized the positive aspects of the historical relationship with Germans, such as medieval cultural exchanges, including that of the German craftsman Veit Stoss (Wit Stwosz), who came to Cracow from Nuremberg and made the famous altar plates in the Church of Mary, and Queen Hedwig, a German princess who came to Poland in the thirteenth century through marriage and became one of its national saints. The final few pages finally focused on the present day. The letter stated, "Despite this almost hopelessly historically burdened situation, precisely from this situation, honorable brothers, we call out to you: 'Let us try to forget! No polemics, no more Cold War, but the beginning of a dialogue.'"[56]

To pro-Polish West German journalists and intellectuals, the bishops' initiative illustrated, firstly, that powerful representatives of the spiritual Polish nation desired reconciliation and, secondly, that a major Polish civil society institution was willing to challenge the state on Polish–German matters. It also forcefully reminded the western public that Poland was more than a communist puppet state in Soviet hands. Conservative media, such as *Die Welt*, still insisted on the helplessness of both German and Polish actors in the Cold War context and Soviet power politics.[57] Others, however, interpreted the bishops' letter as a hopeful sign since it was a voice of "historical Poland" as opposed to "communist Poland."[58] The letter had reintroduced noncommunist Poland into the West German public awareness. To the media activists, the Polish bishops and especially Bishop Kominek suddenly emerged as new powerful symbols and potential allies for improved relations.

In their initial reactions, the West German media concerned itself with the nature of the German bishops' response. The writers wondered whether the German Catholic leadership would make a gesture toward recognizing the Oder-Neisse Line, similar to the Protestant Memorandum. Some West German political factions hoped for such a response; others feared it. The Poles hoped, based on earlier statements by Cardinal Julius Döpfner and in the context of the Protestant document, for such a gesture as well. Walter Dirks wrote in his report in *Frankfurter Hefte* from Rome, "Finally, the message of the Polish episcopate was silently being prepared. Since the message is one its fruits, will the Council in its last moments help to ease certain domestic German tensions?"[59]

Bishop Hengsbach of Essen dashed these hopes on 2 December when he explained to the *Frankfurter Rundschau* that "it is not for the bishops to be involved in categories of state law (*staatsrechtliche Kathegorien*) and the

Oder-Neisse Border is a political matter."⁶⁰ Conservatives generally and the Catholic expellee leaders in particular breathed a sigh of relief. Hengsbach was one of the preparers of the German bishops' response to the Polish letter, which appeared three days after his remarks in the *Frankfurter Rundschau*. The German Catholic bishops' response was much briefer than the Polish one. "Terrible things were done by Germans and in the name of the German people to the Polish people," they stated.⁶¹ They assured the Poles that the expellees had no aggressive intentions with regards to the Oder-Neisse territories and hoped that the territorial question would find "a solution which is just and satisfactory to all sides."⁶² Removed from its political context, this message was friendly and showed goodwill. However, in the context of the Tübingen Memorandum, the Protestant Expellee Memorandum, and the Polish bishops' letter, it seemed too cautious and made no significant political gestures or concessions. Ultimately, it disappointed the Polish bishops as well as those who had hoped for a clearer commitment toward accepting the border from the episcopate.

The Polish communist party had remained silent during the first ten days after the bishops' letter became public. Following the release of the German bishops' response, the communist media launched a full-scale attack on the Polish Church, coordinating for the first time ever television, radio, and press to condemn the Polish bishops.⁶³ Zooming in on the particular phrase "We forgive and ask for forgiveness," they accused the bishops of betraying the nation and usurping the role of the state in foreign policy matters. The communist press called the phrase "[We] ask for forgiveness" the most controversial aspect of the message. "In whose name," asked *Życie Warszawy* in its headline, "are you asking for forgiveness?"⁶⁴ Playing to the widespread Polish self-perceptions of heroism and victimhood during the war, the newspaper suggested that it was outrageous to ask Germans for forgiveness. The Polish bishops' letter had called the Oder-Neisse area the "Potsdam western territories." According to the Polish communist media, who objected to the word choice, these lands were ancient Polish holdings, and by questioning this fact the Polish bishops in yet another way had failed their nation.⁶⁵ Through this attack, the significance and interpretive context of the letter exchange shifted in Poland as well as in West Germany.

Evidence indicates that the letter was indeed unpopular in large sections of the Polish population. Over 50 percent of the parish priests in Poland opposed it.⁶⁶ The notion of Polish innocence, heroism, and victimhood during the war was firmly anchored in national consciousness at the time. The Znak group might have been natural allies to the bishops, but they disapproved of the letter and resented being excluded from its preparation. Jerzy Zawieyski wrote in his diary on 22 December that the letter was "hard" and "brutal" in its tone and that the Cardinal had gone to great lengths to make clear that the church would in no way cooperate with the communists.[67] Conflicts that had continued throughout the Vatican II Council between Wyszyński and the Znak group as well as other lay Catholics about who had the right to represent Poland abroad, the independence of the lay movement, and the relationship of Poland's Catholics with the communist regime became part of the controversy.[68] In the discussions in the Sejm surrounding the letter, only Jerzy Turowicz came to its defense. This silence on behalf of the Znak Circle led to a more pronounced conflict with Cardinal Wyszyński when he returned from Rome.[69]

The "new Left," which would gain attention in 1967 and 1968 as the opposition movement, also reacted negatively to the letter. One of its most prominent members, Adam Michnik, later acknowledged that he did not read the letter properly until ten years later. Criticizing his own unquestioning antipathy to the bishops' statement in an essay, he wrote,

> Now that I have read it carefully, the truth is that I can find in it nothing, absolutely nothing, that could justify the surprisingly hostile reaction it elicited in otherwise quite civil people. Nor can I find anything that might explain the unexpected susceptibility of these critics to the demagogic arguments of officialdom.[70]

Michnik's statement showed the extent to which he and the larger population based their opinions not on the letter's actual content but on the way it was reported in the media or on their own preconceived notions of the church–state conflict.

As a consequence of the domestic uproar, the church retreated from the notion of asking for forgiveness, the most criticized part of the letter. When Cardinal Wyszyński returned from Rome, he and several bishops, including Bishop Kominek, Bishop Choromański of Warsaw, and Bishop Wojtyła, set out to explain the letter and reassure their dioceses. The Polish Catholic Church had fewer media channels through which to respond to the attack, but, unlike other East European churches, it could still effectively reach large numbers of the Polish public because it had retained control over the churches as meeting places and because of the high church attendance. Wyszyński's strategy became to turn the society's attention away from the letter and toward the common accepted enemy, the communist state. He asked his audiences to trust the bishops above the state media, something they were inclined to do at any rate. About the media attacks, he stated ironically that the communists must always be correct "since they are the wisest of the Polish people . . . wiser even than the bishops and everyone else."[71] He also assured his audiences that at least two-thirds of the letter had focused on the German cruelties against

Poland during the war and that the phrase "[We] ask for forgiveness" was thus taken out of context in the state's campaign.

The church–state battle continued into the early months of 1966 and turned the Polish people's sympathy back to the church. The secret police's attacks on ceremonies and symbols of the church during the celebration of its one thousandth anniversary brought the population together in opposition to the communists and in defense of the bishops. In May 1966, in front of thousands of Poles who had gathered on Jasna Góra, one of Poland's holiest places, Cardinal Wyszyński had the enormous crowds chanting again and again, "We forgive! We forgive!"[72] "We ask for forgiveness" made no appearance in the chants. The message had been realigned to fit better with the church's resistance to the state and with dominant national memory.

Many West German observers now chose to disregard the call to a dialogue and interpret the bishops' letter and its consequences as just another phase in the church–state battle, an internal Polish matter. Several West German newspapers predicted that communist persecution of the church would intensify in Poland.[73] Only about half of the *Frankfurter Allgemeine*'s coverage of the bishops' correspondence concerned the content of the letters. The other half focused on the escalating state–church conflict in Poland. This elevated the Polish bishops' status in West German media as independent and heroic resisters but also distracted observers away from the question of the border recognition and diocesan settlement that the Polish bishops had wanted to bring to West German awareness.

The West German activists who supported reconciliation kept the debate alive and used it to support their political agenda with regards to the eastern policy. They also brought attention back to the original intent of the letter. Stehle interviewed Bishop Kominek in person on *Panorama* on 10 January 1966.[74] Stehle had advised Bishop Kominek to appear on television in order to clear up the misunderstandings surrounding his letter. Stehle had also attempted to get Cardinal Döpfner to appear together with the Polish bishop, but the German cardinal turned down the request.[75] In his solo appearance, Bishop Kominek told the West German public that the greatest misunderstanding surrounding the letter was the assumption that it was a political document. He had only intended to begin a religious dialogue. In response to accusations that he had betrayed Poland, he emphasized that the bishops had never questioned that the Oder-Neisse territories belonged to Poland. He called the Oder-Neisse border "a precondition of existence for the Polish people."[76] What he meant was that the vitality of the Polish nation depended on the territory it had gained in the west since it had also lost a considerable amount of territory in the east, to the Soviet Union.

In the interview, Stehle compared the Polish bishops' letter to the Protestant Memorandum, a connection that Bishop Kominek had wished to emphasize in the letter but which his German Catholic contacts had asked him to omit. Bishop Kominek said that the Protestant Expellee Memorandum had been positively received in Polish circles. The interview concluded with a statement of optimism about the future and a request for the German people's understanding that the Polish people still feared their power and potential aggression. West Germans received the interview very well, sending Bishop Kominek letters of support. Bishop Kominek credited Stehle with the success. "This time, you have really outdone yourself," he wrote enthusiastically from Schärding in Switzerland, where he was spending some retreat time in January 1966, "and I am very grateful for all of it."[77] He thanked Stehle for advising him to do the interview. He ended by assuring Stehle that "in Breslau, the door is always open to you and the heart even more." The exchanges indicated that Bishop Kominek had depended on Stehle's expertise in managing the public relations crisis in 1966. With Stehle's help, he had employed a strategy much like that which international relations experts Kathryn Sikkink and Margaret Keck have called a "boomerang effect."[78] He entered into a cross-border alliance and gained access to more resources or to public opinion abroad, thereby gaining the ability to counter the accusations from the communist media at home. The exchange showed the significance of entanglements and cross-border networks not only in creating but also in defending and marketing the reconciliation initiatives.

Like Stehle, Jürgen Neven-du Mont defended the Polish Church against the state's accusations on West German television in the spring of 1966. He described Cardinal Wyszyński as fully loyal to the Polish *raison d'état*, but also pointed out that the population was more loyal to the church than to the state. He added that the church had "kept the ideals of the Polish nation, whose existence had so often been threatened, alive."[79] Neven-du Mont acknowledged a conflict between Gomułka's demand for the "unconditional surrender" of the Germans with reference to the territorial question and what he saw as the Polish cardinal's search "for a way toward compromise." Crediting Cardinal Wyszyński with the now-famous phrase about forgiveness, Neven-du Mont ended his commentary by stating that Christians in the Federal Republic would do well to think and act in a less political and more Christian spirit.[80]

Walter Dirks, who initially had reported enthusiastically about the Polish letter and the German response, gradually became convinced that West German Catholics had lived up neither to Polish expectations nor to the Protestant initiatives. Together with a group of associates, many connected to the Catholic peace organization Pax Christi, and other associates from media circles, Dirks began planning yet another document on Polish–German relations in 1966.[81] He drafted a letter to like-minded Catholic circles in West Germany inviting them to the founding of the Bensberger Circle. It read in part:

> We owe not only an answer but also a supplement; the community of faith with the Polish Catholics gives us specific sources of recognition, relations, and responsibilities. We also owe the Polish bishops an answer to their appellation, which on a foundational level goes beyond the German bishops and addresses us all.[82]

Dirks referenced the need to follow up on the efforts made at the Second Vatican Council and to contribute a Catholic voice to the 1965 Protestant document. At least fifty people met on 7–8 May 1966 in the Thomas-Morus Akademie in Bensberg, near Cologne. They elected a Poland Commission, which composed a text on the Polish–German relationship during the following two years. The committee over time came to include Gottfried Erb, Karlheinz Koppe, and Manfred Seidler among its leading members and spokespersons.[83]

During their first meetings, rather than having a leader or chairman, the group nominated speakers (*Sprachrohre*) to represent them in the public space. A letter exchange between Gottfried Erb and Walter Dirks agreed that the gathering should be a group of Catholic laity independent of church structures and Pax Christi, which was led by Cardinal Döpfner, in order to make it "politically freer and more flexible."[84] These considerations reflected the increasingly politicized West German media scene as well as an awareness of publicity issues. The membership recognized that, since they lacked the backing of the Catholic establishment, they would need to cultivate public attention in order to create the broader Catholic debate they hoped to initiate.

Dirks originally worked with Eugen Kogon to draft the group's public statement, the Bensberger Memorandum, although ultimately Erb would play a greater role than Kogon. Under the leadership of these men, the Bensberger Circle combined left-wing politics with Catholicism in the spirit of the Second Vatican Council. On a spiritual level, they considered the foundation for improved relations with Poland an internal process of confessing Germany's own guilt, overcoming hostility, and giving and receiving forgiveness. The memorandum stated, "The Christian message of salvation refers in its central promises—reconciliation, justice, peace—also to the world changing forces of contemporary society. In the service of this message, Christians are charged to assume public responsibility in a critical and liberating manner."[85] Contextualizing the suggested action by Catholic theology and dialogue, the memorandum pointed out that the two most recent popes, John XXIII and Paul VI, and the Second Vatican Council had attempted to communicate this need for reconciliation, and it called on West German Catholics to enact the council's message of peace.[86] The memorandum chastised German Catholics for their failure in this regard, saying that "the terrible injustice committed against the Poles" required that German Catholics act "beyond all diplomacy and political calculations" to seek peace. The memorandum referenced Jesus's clashes with the "official powers of his time" to proclaim his message of peace.[87] It called on Christians to follow their conscience against the decisions of the ruling authorities as well as church authorities.

Two concepts were at the foundation of the memorandum's political vision of Polish–German relations. First, it built on the notion of stable nation-states in postwar Europe. The authors of the memorandum were of course aware that a large segment of the West German population belonged to the very ethnic minority that had been forced to leave the formerly multiethnic border areas. The Bensberger Memorandum, like the other German memoranda, was forced to address the problem of peace with this group in mind. It had to balance the trust in homogeneous nation-states as a precondition for peace with sensitivity to the loss of the borderlands and the division of Germany. The memorandum stated, "We Germans experienced the loss of East Germany as an amputation."[88] On the other hand, Poland's loss of the eastern territories to the Soviet Union meant that the nation now depended on the new western territories for its very survival. The memorandum thanked the authors of the Polish Catholic Bishops' Letter for "placing the emphasis of their argumentation for the Polish territorial claims on the contemporary facts: the territorial loss in the east of Poland, the hardship in its middle part where the war passed through twice, and life and work for the new settlers."[89] In the interest of peace and the survival of an independent Poland, it called on Germany to accept the current postwar nation-states and their borders, even as it acknowledged the pain of the territorial loss and uprooting of the German ethnic minorities.

Second, the creators of the Bensberger Memorandum believed that Polish–German reconciliation required official political relations and cooperation with Poland's existing (communist) state. On its second page, the memorandum assured the reader that German Catholics would "support with all their powers, [the perspective] that the German people respect the Polish people's national right to existence."[90] The phrase came out of the intertwined Polish–German past, encompassing the Prussian participation in the partitions of Poland, the Nazi Occupation, and the Molotov–Ribbentrop Pact. As the memorandum hinted, the Polish nation had been stateless and occupied by foreign powers (including Prussia) for over one hundred years. From both a geopolitical and historical perspective, according to the memorandum, Bonn ought to recognize the existing Polish state and ensure the security of the nation before any form of reconciliation could take place. In this line of reasoning, the Bensberger Circle arrived at the necessity of coexistence with Poland's communist state in the interest of peace and Poland's survival, a stance that it also shared with the West German liberal media and with the Znak Circle. Their position would, however, create some tensions with the Polish episcopate.

Long before the draft was complete, the media interest in the memorandum was already great. Rumors about its content kept surfacing in the press throughout 1966 and 1967. Between 1966 and 1968, the Bensberger Circle collected over fifteen hundred press clippings concerning issues related to its work.[91] The media attention at times had unintended effects on the circle's work. Between the summers of 1966 and 1967, the work on the memorandum almost stalled. Eugen Kogon had developed an outline for a draft but had not found time to write the full text. Walter Dirks was in poor health and also otherwise engaged.[92] A third member of the commission, Hans Werhahn, felt that the memorandum would not be interesting to a greater public if its publication was delayed for too long. He kept urging the commission to use the momentum of the earlier church documents and finally wrote a first draft of the memorandum in their stead. A majority of the circle rejected Wehrhahn's draft, but it did serve the purpose of spurring the commission into renewed action. In June 1967, Dirks and Erb retreated to the Black Forest for a week and developed an alternative draft, which became the foundation of the memorandum in its final form.[93]

As with the Tübingen Memorandum, leaks about the content to the press determined the Bensberger Memorandum's final date of publication. In the fall of 1967, a conservative Catholic weekly, *Echo der Zeit*, reported dramatically in an article that the Bensberger Circle would be releasing a memorandum expressing a "radical leftist orientation of German Catholics" and that it would demand the recognition of the German Democratic Republic.[94] Alarmed, Cardinal Döpfner wrote to the Bensberger leadership and wanted more information about the group's work since people were now "writing to [him] from all sides."[95] In this way the media attention forced the West German episcopate to become involved with the document, however hesitantly.

At the episcopate's urging, on 4 February 1968, representatives of the Bensberger Circle met with representatives from the Catholic expellee organizations to investigate whether the groups could find common ground concerning the content of the memorandum. Nine expellee representatives who had read the draft participated in the meeting. They had many criticisms, but the most frequent was the memorandum's ignorance of the role of the Soviet Union controlling Poland and placing demands on Poland's relationship with the west. The expellee representatives argued that Poland and the Federal Republic could not have a decisive impact on Cold War political relations, given their small size, and that smaller independent groups like the Bensberger Circle would have even less impact. Consequently, the publication of the memorandum would be a futile effort. The two groups were unable to come to any agreements.[96]

These meetings may have led to the leaking of the memorandum's text to the media. Later that month, DPA gained access to full drafts of the text through an unknown source and published them.[97] The Bensberger Circle decided to go ahead and publish the text in its entirety. The Bensberger Memorandum was released to the public in March 1968. Those responsible for the leaks may have hoped to sabotage the circle's work and efforts to find agreement with other groups in the larger church. In fact, the circle found the leaks problematic at the time. The media attention alienated moderate and conservative Catholics and disturbed the ongoing negotiations with the Catholic organizations of German expellees from the Polish borderlands. At the same time, the media's involvement through the leak once more impacted the document's timing as well as content. Gottfried Erb later proposed that the quality of the memorandum improved after the Poland Commission came under external pressure from the press.[98] The media brought the memorandum into the public eye, prevented its marginalization, and forced the authors to sharpen their arguments.

The fallout from the Polish bishops' letter to the German Catholic bishops as well as the political climate of 1968, including the Prague Spring and the internal purge in Poland, influenced Polish readings of the Bensberger Memorandum. The Znak Circle welcomed the memorandum as a specifically Catholic document contributing to Polish–German reconciliation.[99] It had improved relations with the episcopate since the break over the episcopate's letter in 1965.[100] Cardinal Wyszyński also expressed appreciation for the Bensberger Memorandum, while noting pointedly that it was the German bishops who should have responded more emphatically to the 1965 letter with a recognition of the Polish rights to the borderlands. His September 1968 letter to the Bensberger Circle thanked the authors cordially in the name of the Polish hierarchy for their "courageous phrasing," adding, "As shepherds of the Polish people, we evaluated the letter less from a political than from a social-religious point of view." The letter commended the Bensberger Circle's "Christian courage, honest good will, and international outlook on the world."[101]

Conclusion

Did the bishops' letter actually accomplish any kind of true reconciliation? Some authors have argued that the emerging state–church conflict in the aftermath of the 1965 letter's publication became the Polish Catholics' primary focus and that this stunted the reconciliatory developments entirely.[102] While this is true in the short-term perspective, it does not tell the full story of the developments the document set in motion in Polish–German cultural relations. The Polish Catholic bishops' letter must be studied in the context of the other religious memoranda in the 1960s and the full spectrum of media discussion and commentary over an extended time period. The publication of the letters and memoranda turned into media events, acquired shifting long-term symbolic weight, and contributed to religious institutional changes over time. The memoranda pushed the boundaries for the religious groups' and churches' involvement in politics and their ability to influence public space. They also became powerful political tools in West German public space at the time and later.

Beyond doubt, newspaper, radio, and television writers' agendas of changing Polish–West German relations and the ongoing political disputes greatly influenced the reports and public understanding of the religious documents. These controversies also pressured the authors of the Bensberger Memorandum and the Polish Catholic bishops to simplify and explain their messages. By doing so, they also removed some of the complexity of the original texts. Thus, once more, the participants in the dialogue adjusted the complex Central European past to the Cold War polarizing political scene. In the Polish case, in leading the chants on Jaśna Góra, Cardinal Wyszyński removed the problematic message that Poles should in any way feel remorse for atrocities or injustices during and after the Second World War. In German media short term, the Polish Catholic letter primarily became a symbol of the church–state battle as the communist leadership launched its attack on the message and its authors. The West German activists also focused on the letter's reconciliatory sections, authored by Kominek, while ignoring the sections reflecting a more traditional Polish patriotism. Often, their discussion turned to questions of the West German borders and the internal unity, that is, to the disagreements with the expellee organizations.

As the memoranda entered public space and as their authors attempted to stand their ground in public controversies, the interpretations of them also became more closely tied into national interests and existing national myths. They came into existence as internal conversations and elite discourses among Polish–German relations groups in the churches and media. In the larger media sphere, they were attacked, and their authors were forced to firm up and sharpen their messages. Thus, public reactions transformed their significance. At the same time, media and political debates adapted religious elements and imagery. The media, conservative, moderate, and liberal, were inspired to take ethical questions into account in high political discussions about the border territories, Cold War concerns, or national interests. Particularly, the moral and ethical authority of the Polish bishops, whose status was enhanced by the state persecution they endured, left its imprint not only on the "pro-Polish" press but also on sympathetic conservative Christian media, such as *Christ und Welt* or *Rheinischer Merkur*, and on publications such as *Die Welt*. The Christian concept of reconciliation (*Aussöhnung*) was at the forefront of media debates on Polish–German relations and gave shared Christian values a greater emphasis. The West German media actors acquired a powerful symbolic ally, a representative simultaneously of a historic, noncommunist Poland. Meanwhile, the Polish Church and Polish lay Catholics appeared on the West German and international media stage through the conduit of media allies such as Stehle and other journalists, interpreters, and correspondents.

Notes

1. "Die Botschaft der polnischen Bischöfe an die deutschen Bischöfe, Rom, 18. November 1965," in Jacobsen and Tomala, *Bonn-Warschau*, 139.
2. Józefa Hennelowa, "'Die Zeit ist reif für einen neuen Brief der Bischöfe': Gespräch mit Józefa Hennelowa," in *"Wir vergeben und bitten um Vergebung": Der Briefwechsel der polnischen und deutschen Bischöfe von 1965 und seine Wirkung*, ed. Basil Kerski, Thomas Życia, and Robert Żurek (Osnabrück, 2006), 202. Hennelowa is referring to meetings in the Catholic milieu with Karol Wojtyła, later Pope John Paul II, and his young mentees that he had gathered around himself in Cracow as archbishop. Also Jerzy Zawieyski disapproved of the idea that Poles ought to ask the Germans for forgiveness. Friszke, "Jerzy Zawieyski," 41.
3. A volume discussing these initiatives is Boll et al., *Versöhnung und Politik*.
4. They are mentioned by Timothy Garton Ash, *In Europe's Name: Germany and the Divided Continent* (New York, 1994), 298ff., Dieter Bingen, *Polen-Politik der Bonner Republik von Adenauer bis Kohl 1949–1991* (Baden-Baden, 1998), 87–89, and also in specific essays and books such as Piotr Madajczyk, *Na drodze do pojednania: Wokół orędzia biskupów polskich do biskupów niemieckich z 1965 roku* (Warsaw, 1994), and Edith Heller, *Macht, Kirche, Politik: Der Briefwechsel zwischen den polnischen und deutschen Bischöfen im Jahre 1965* (Cologne, 1992).
5. Żurek, *Zwischen Nationalismus und Versöhnung*, 364.
6. For an extensive discussion of the churches and the media in the postwar era, see Nicolai Hannig, *Die Religion der Öffentlichkeit: Kirche, Religion und Medien in der Bundesrepublik 1945–1980* (Göttingen, 2010).

7. Martin Greschat, "Protestantismus und Evangelische Kirche," in *Dynamische Zeiten: Die 60er Jahren in den beiden deutschen Gesellschaften*, ed. Axel Schildt, Detlef Siegfried, and Karl Christian Lammers (Hamburg, 2000), 552.
8. Benjamin Ziemann, "Öffentlichkeit in der Kirche: Medien und Partizipation in der Katholische Kirche der Bundesrepublik, 1963–1972," in Bösch and Frei, *Medialisierung und Demokratie*, 179–206; Żurek, *Zwischen Nationalismus und Versöhnung*; see also Greschat, "Vom Tübinger Memorandum," 29–51.
9. Karl Gabriel, "Zwischen Aufbruch und Absturz in die Moderne: Die katholische Kirche in den 60er Jahren," in Schildt, Siegfried, and Lammers, *Dynamische Zeiten*, 528–43.
10. Ibid.
11. "Das Memorandum der acht evangelischen Persönlichkeiten zur Bonner Politik: Wortlaut der Stellungnahme veröffentlicht/Ursprünglich Grundlage für interne Gespräche mit Abgeordneten," *Süddeutsche Zeitung*, 26 February 1962. See also Greschat, "Protestantismus und Evangelische Kirche," 555.
12. Anderson, *Cold War in the Eastern Bloc*, 204.
13. "Das Memorandum der Acht: Wissenschaftler warnen vor Selbstgefälligkeit und Illusionen," *Die Zeit*, 2 March 1962.
14. Ibid. *Die Zeit* and *Süddeutsche Zeitung* published the memorandum in its entirety.
15. The expellees were cited in, for example, "Diskussion über das Memorandum eines evangelischen Kreisse: Nicht harten Entscheidungen asuweichen/Anerkennung der Oder-Neisse-Linie gefordert/Wiederspruch der Vertriebenen," *Frankfurter Allgemeine Zeitung*, 26 February 1962, "Oder-Neisse-Grenze anerkennen: Denkschrift von acht führenden deutschen Protestanten," *Die Welt*, 24 February 1962.
16. "Das Memorandum der Acht," *Die Zeit*, 2 March 1962.
17. "Verkümmernde Freiheit,"*Frankfurter Rundschau*, 28 February 1962.
18. "Stellungnahme des Ostkirchenassuschusses der Evangelischen Kirche in Deutschland zum 'Memorandum der Acht' vom 6.November 1961," *Ostkircheninformationsdienst*, Sondernummer, 5 March 1962; "Memorandum der Acht," *Die Welt*, 22 March 1962.
19. "Gegen den Dolchstoss der Acht!" *Landsmannschaft Schlesien Rundbrief der Bundesgeschäftstelle*, 16 March 1962; "Sie verraten den deutschen Osten," *deutsche Soldatenzeitung*, 9 March 1962.
20. "Stachel ins Fleisch," *Frankfurter Allgemeine Zeitung*, 26 February 1962.
21. "Brandt fordert aktive Ostpolitik: Scharfe Kritik an Bonner Koalition.Tübinger Acht nicht allein," *Frankfurter Rundschau*, 26 March 1962; "Brandt zum Memorandum der Acht. In einigen Punkten der gleichen Meinung—aber auch ernste Bedenken," *Süddeutsche Zeitung*, 26 March 1962; "Brandt zum Memorandum der Acht," *Stuttgarter Zeitung*, 26 March 1962.
22. "Brandt zum Memorandum der Acht," *Süddeutsche Zeitung*, 26 March 1962.
23. Anonymous letter from May 1962, Franz Rendel (Pommersche Landsmannschaft) letter to Klaus von Bismarck, 5 April 1962, Lauf. No. 163, Nachlass Klaus von Bismarck, HA-WDR.
24. Hans Bausch, letter to Klaus von Bismarck, 24 May 1962, Lauf. No. 163, Nachlass Klaus von Bismarck, HA-WDR.
25. Klaus von Bismarck, letter to Christoph von Imhoff (Kölner Stadt-Anzeiger), 2 April 1962, Lauf. No. 163, Nachlass Klaus von Bismarck, HA-WDR.
26. "Echa wystąpienia działaczy ewangelickich w sprawie Odry i Nysy," *Trybuna Ludu*, 25 February 1962.
27. "Sondernummer: Stellungnahme des Ostkirchenaussschuss der Evangelischen Kirche in Deutschland aus 'Memorandum der Acht' vom 6.November 1961," Ostkirchen-Informationsdienst, Hannover, 5 March 1962.
28. W. Schweitzer, letter to Klaus von Bismarck, 10 November 1965, and Martin Niemeyer,

letter to W. Schweitzer, 20 January 1963, Lauf. No. 163, Nachlass Klaus von Bismarck, HA-WDR.
29. Bishop Kunst and Bishop Kurt Scharf were the most prominent voices for a more general statement. Greschat, "Protestantismus und Evangelische Kirche," 559.
30. "Church Challenges Politicians of Bonn," *The Times*, 1 December 1965.
31. Greschat, "Protestantismus und Evangelische Kirche," 564.
32. Ibid., 563.
33. "Die Lage der Vertriebenen und das Verhältnis des deutschen Volkes zu seinen östlichen Nachbarn: Eine evangelische Denkschrift," 5th ed. (Hannover, 1965), 5.
34. Ibid., 41.
35. "Auszüge aus der Denkschrift der Evangelischen Kirche in Deutschland: 'Die Lage der Vertriebenen und das Verhältnis des deutschen Volkes zu seinen östlichen Nachbarn,' Hannover, 1.Oktober 1965," in Jacobsen and Tomala, *Bonn-Warschau*, 134.
36. This point was also noted by Arnold Sywottek, "Nationale Politik als Symbolpolitik: Die westdeutsche Deutschland- und Aussenpolitik in gesellschaftsgeschichtlicher Perspektive," in Schildt, Siegfried, and Lammers, *Dynamische Zeiten*, 354.
37. Marion Dönhoff, "Kontroversen in die Kirche," *Die Zeit*, 29 October 1965; Greschat, "Protestantismus und Evangelische Kirche," 568.
38. Paul Wilhelm Wenger, "Notwendiger Appell zur Versöhnung: Die umstrittene Denkschrift der Evangelischen Kirche in Deutschland," *Rheinischer Merkur*, 22 October 1965.
39. Bernd Conrad, "Die Grenzen im Osten: Eine kirchliche Denkschrift," *Die Welt*, 19 October 1965.
40. Konrad Weiss, "'Polen hatte eine Vorbildfunktion.' Gespräch mit Konrad Weiss," *Wir vergeben und bitten um Vergebung: Der Briefwechsel der polnischen und deutschen Bischöfe von 1965*, ed. Basil Kerski, Thomas Kycia, and Robert Żurek (Osnabrück, 2006), 188–89.
41. Porter-Szücs, *Faith and Fatherland*, 42.
42. This according to Thomas Urban, *Die Vertreibung der Deutschen und Polen im 20. Jahrhundert* (Munich, 2004), 134.
43. For a full biography, see Tomasz Serwatka, *Kardynał Bolesław Kominek (1903–1974) Duszpasterz i polityk. Zarys biograficzny* (Wrocław, 2013). See also *Wokół Orędzia: kardynał Bolesław Kominek, prekursor pojednania polsko-niemieckiego*, ed. Wojciech Kucharski et al. (Wrocław, 2009).
44. Bolesław Kominek, "Ziemie Zachodnie: Mandat sprzed 20 lat," *Tygodnik Powszechny*, 30 May 1965.
45. Ibid.
46. Hansjakob Stehle, "Polens Kardinal isoliert sich: Der Papst mahnt Wyszynski zum Ausgleich mit Gomulka," *Die Zeit*, 17 January 1964.
47. Hansjakob Stehle, letter to Bolesław Kominek, Berlin, 28 February 1964, copy in private possession of author.
48. Bolesław Kominek, letter to Hansjakob Stehle, 15 May 1965, copy in private possession of author.
49. Hansjakob Stehle, "Zwanzig Jahre polnisches Breslau: Die Kirche feierte Vergangenheit und Gegenwart in den Oder-Neisse Gebieten," *Die Zeit*, 10 September 1965.
50. Bolesław Kominek, letter to Hansjakob Stehle, Rome, September 1965, copy in private possession of author.
51. Ibid.
52. Brian Porter-Szücs in *Faith and Fatherland* discusses the modernizing influences with regards to Polish patriotism that were carried and expressed by *Tygodnik Powszechny* and, at that time though not later, Bishop Wojtyła. Porter-Szücs, whose main concern is the Polish Catholic Church's interaction with modernity, shows that *Tygodnik*'s positions

and outlooks were limited to a small, highly intellectual leadership. However, he argues that the one tendency that the Polish episcopate took from Vatican Council II was the greater openness toward the world, including the Germans. Porter-Szücs, *Faith and Fatherland*, 40, 265. There were, incidentally, also those among the hierarchy who spoke Italian and had spent time abroad. Kosicki, "Five—Vatican II and Poland," 149.

53. Hansjakob Stehle, *Eastern Politics of the Vatican, 1917–1979*, trans. Sandra Smith (Columbus, OH, 1981), 344.
54. "Die Botschaft der polnischen Bischöfe an die deutschen Bischöfe, Rom, 18. November 1965," in Jacobsen and Tomala, *Bonn-Warschau*, 139.
55. Ibid., 136.
56. Ibid., 141.
57. *German–Polish Dialogue*, 118, translated excerpt from *Die Welt*, 4 December 1965.
58. *German–Polish Dialogue*, 124, translated excerpt from *Bayern-Kurier*, 29 January 1965.
59. Walter Dirks, "Im Rom, Spätherbst 1965," *Frankfurter Hefte*, January 1966, 34.
60. "Hengsbach wünscht Gespräch in versöhnlichem Geist," *Frankfurter Rundschau*, 2 December 1965.
61. "Die Antwort der deutschen Bischöfe an die polnischen Bischöfe, Rom 5. Dezember 1965," in Jacobsen and Tomala, *Bonn-Warschau*, 143.
62. Ibid., 144.
63. Pokorna-Ignatowicz, *Telewizja w systemie politycznym*, 77.
64. Ibid.
65. "Wobec 'orędzia' do biskupów niemieckich: W czyim imieniu?" *Życie Warszawy*, 10 December 1965.
66. Kosicki, "*Caritas* across the Iron Curtain," 225.
67. Jerzy Zawieyski, *Dzienniki: Tom II, Wybór z lat 1960–1969* (Warsaw, 2011), 627.
68. Kosicki, "Five—Vatican II and Poland," 166.
69. Andrzej Micewski, *Cardinal Wyszyński: A Biography*, trans. William R. Brand and Katarzyna Mroczkowska-Brand (San Diego, 1984), 258.
70. Adam Michnik, *The Church and the Left*, trans. David Ost (Chicago, 1993), 87.
71. Stefan Wyszyński, "Fragmenty kazania wygłoszonego w Warszawie w kościele Najczystszego Serca Marii 19 grudnia 1965 r. dotyczące 'Orędzia' biskupów polskich do biskupów niemieckich," in *Orędzie biskupów polskich do biskupów niemieckich: Materiały i dokumenty* (Warsaw, 1966), 129.
72. Heller, *Macht, Kirche, Politik*, 171.
73. Angela Nacken, "Die umstrittene Botschaft: Der Briefwechsel mit den deutschen Bischöfen steht zwischen Staat und Kirche in Polen," *Frankfurter Allgemeine Zeitung*, 14 December 1965.
74. Hansjakob Stehle, "Die Allianz der Kalten Krieger: Wie die Bischöfe in Polen und Deutschland missverstanden wurden," *Die Zeit*, 17 December 1965; Hansjakob Stehle, "Versöhnung mit der Grenze: Eine bedeutsame Rede im polnischen Parlament," *Die Zeit*, 24 December 1965. Most likely the article to which Kominek was referring was Hansjakob Stehle, "Kein Pass für den Kardinal: Der Bischofsbriefwechsel und seine politische Folgen," *Die Zeit*, 14 January 1966.
75. Hansjakob Stehle, "Seit 1960: Der mühsame katholische Dialog über die Grenze," in *Ungewöhnliche Normalisierung: Beziehungen der Bundesrepublik Deutschland zu Polen*, ed. Werner Plum (Bonn, 1984), 162.
76. Full text of television interview in "Wir bitten um Verständnis," *Petrus-Blatt*, 23 January 1966, and "Ich bin Optimist . . .," *Christ in der Welt*, date unknown.
77. Bolesław Kominek, letter to Hansjakob Stehle, Schärding, 20 January 1966, copy in private possession of author.

78. Keck and Sikkink, *Activists beyond Borders*, 4.
79. Jürgen Neven-du Mont, "Der Kommentar: Gomułka und der Kardinal," 9 March 1966, BArch N1279, 103.
80. Ibid.
81. See also Boll, "Der Bensberger Kreis," in Boll et al., *Versöhnung und Politik*, 77–116, and Gottfried Erb, "Verständigung mit Polen: Die Arbeit des Bensberger Kreises—eine persönliche Bilanz," in Boll et al., *Versöhnung und Politik*, 357–65.
82. Bensberger Circle, letter to Heinz Missala, 13 April 1966, Bensberger Kreis, BK Protokoll, Erklärungen, Bensberger Kreis 54, FES.
83. Gottfried Erb (b. 1931) became a leading member of the Bensberger Circle. Erb wrote his dissertation with Eugen Kogon as his advisor at the Technische Hochschule in Darmstadt and also became a co-editor of *Frankfurter Hefte*. Also his father, Alfons Erb, was engaged with Polish–German relations. Alfons Erb was the vice president of peace organization Pax Christi, and founded the Maximilian-Kolbe-Werks, a charity to assist concentration camp survivors. Kerski, Kycia, and Żurek, eds., *"Wir vergeben und bitten um Vergebung,"* 173. Manfred Seidler (1922–2007) was another expellee, from Königsberg (later Kaliningrad). His family originally came from Salzburg, he had a PhD in German literature and pedagogy, and he later became a teacher and headmaster at a gymnasium in Bonn. In addition to his engagement with Polish–German relations, he also later worked with German–Jewish relations.
84. Walter Dirks, letter to Gottfried Erb, 4 January 1966, Nachlass Walter Dirks, Box 128, FES.
85. Bensberger Memorandum, 7.
86. Kosicki, *"Caritas* across the Iron Curtain," 217–18.
87. Ibid., 7.
88. Bensberger Memorandum, 8.
89. Ibid., 20.
90. Ibid., 4.
91. Gottfried Erb, "Das Memorandum des Bensberger Kreises zur Polenpolitik," 182. Folders with press clippings also in Friedrich Ebert Stiftung.
92. Manfried Seidler, letter to the members of the "smaller circle" of the Poland Commission, 31 May 1967, Bensberger Kreis, Polen, Mi 60, FES.
93. Norbert Greinacher, letter to Manfred Seidler, 1 September 1967, Bensberger Kreis, Polen, Mi 60, FES.
94. "Ostdruck bei den Katholiken: Kardinal Döpfner's Bistumsblatt für Anerkennung der Oder-Neisse-Grenze," *Die Zeit*, 24 November 1967.
95. Julius Döpfner, letter to Alfons Erb, 6 December 1967, Bensberger Kreis Polen, Polen, Mi 60, FES.
96. Manfried Seidler, "Das Polenmemorandum des Bensberger Kreises: Wirkung in Deutschland und Polen," in Pflüger and Lipscher, *Feinde werden Freunde*, 105.
97. Gottfried Erb, "Das 'Bensberger Memorandum'/Geschichte und erste Stellungnahmen," *Frankfurter Hefte*, April 1968, 219.
98. Erb, "Das Memorandum des Bensberger Kreises zur Polenpolitik," 182.
99. Tadeusz Mazowiecki, "Polska-Niemcy i memorandum 'Bensberger Kreis,'" *Więź*, 1968, 5, 4–5. Jerzy Turowicz, "Memorandum 'Bensberger Kreis,'" *Tygodnik Powszechny*, 17 March 1968. See also Kosicki, *"Caritas* across the Iron Curtain," 226.
100. Jarocki, *Czterdzieści pięć*, 221; Pailer, *Stanisław Stomma*, 103.
101. Stefan Wyszyński, letter to the Bensberger Circle, 12 September 1968, Bensberger Kreis, Polen 60, FES.
102. Kosicki, *"Caritas* across the Iron Curtain," 234.

Chapter 6

BRANDT-ING RECONCILIATION
Politics, Media, and New Relations, 1968–72

In a 1968 radio interview in *Kontraste: Ein Ost–West Magazin*, produced by Sender Freies Berlin, Willy Brandt, the foreign minister of the Great Coalition, compared Polish–German relations to French-German relations. In light of the Second World War, he stated, Polish–German reconciliation required particular circumstances to occur. He said that he was very interested in improved relations with Poland but stated that "we are moving in an unknown territory."[1] Brandt introduced his official program of Ostpolitik at the Social Democratic Party (SPD) Convention in Nuremberg in March 1968, where he argued that the recognition of the Oder-Neisse Line and diplomatic relations to the East European states were a political necessity.[2] In the United States and western Europe, student protests erupted that spring. The same year also saw significant political unrest in Poland and Czechoslovakia. Reform communist Alexander Dubček was elected first secretary of Czechoslovakia in January. He instituted partial reforms and a rollback of censorship, the so-called Prague Spring. Poland had protests as well, largely by university students.

Since 1967, Gomułka had struggled with controlling the country while also being involved in an internal power struggle. In 1968, in response to the student protests, he engaged in an intensified nationalist and anti-Zionist—meaning anti-Semitic—campaign intended to allow him to regain control over the Polish Communist Party. The campaign attacked the student protests as some of its leaders had Jewish backgrounds, but it also extended the attacks to reform-minded and liberal members of the Polish communist party, the university system, and other societal groups.[3] In August 1968, the Red Army, with military support from the German Democratic Republic (GDR), Bulgaria, Hungary, and Gomułka's Poland, invaded Czechoslovakia, violently ending the Czech reforms. Poland's

---

Notes for this chapter begin on page 174.

participation in the ending of the Prague Spring and the 1968 anti-Zionist campaign were extremely disconcerting to the groups in West German society in support of Brandt's Ostpolitik.

Traditionally, participants and scholars considered the time from the late 1960s into the early 1970s a high point of reconciliation. However, the political struggles during this time period further limited societal participation in the dialogue. It also curtailed the dialogue about Polish–German relations and calcified the phrases and formulas that media and participants used in narrating them. The political developments in 1968, and the perceived need to protect Ostpolitik, and developing state-level agreements strongly shaped media representations of Polish–German reconciliation. Ostpolitik further simplified the narrative of Polish–German relations into a two-dimensional political relationship of steady linear improvement between Poles and Germans as media actors strove to protect the claim that reconciliation had succeeded by marginalizing instabilities and problems in Eastern Europe. On some level, Ostpolitik also rendered Polish–German relations increasingly asymmetrical as the West German political program took precedence over Polish and East European developments in the late 1960s. The question is, then, to what extent did Ostpolitik actually contribute to and to what extent did it undermine the long-term reconciliation process?

Several events congregated in the spring of 1968. After the Arab–Israeli Six-Day War, the Polish communist party, following the Soviet lead, initiated a propaganda campaign against Israel and "the Zionists" in the summer of 1967. Polish–Israeli relations had steadily worsened from that point onward, and anti-Semitic sentiments had become more common in the circles around Gomułka, particularly among the so-called partisans.[4] In addition, Gomułka's popularity had decreased, and he faced societal as well as political internal challenges. In early 1968, the student protests in Warsaw demanded expanded intellectual freedoms and a loosening of official censorship, particularly after the authorities had banned the play *The Forefathers' Eve* in January. When the student protests led by a younger generation of dissidents, prominently Adam Michnik, began, Gomułka used the anti-Zionist campaign to regain control of an internal power struggle in his own party.[5] The communist leadership and press argued that Zionists constituted a fifth column in the Polish communist party as well as at the university, which had caused the domestic unrest.[6] They stepped up the anti-Zionist propaganda and dismissed a number of party members, some of whom had been at the forefront of the 1956 Polish October developments. The dismissed party members included minister Adam Rapacki and university professors such as Leszek Kołakowski and Zygmunt Bauman. Almost half of the Jews still remaining in Poland—

thirteen thousand of twenty-five to thirty thousand—emigrated following these events.[7] The party purge seriously reduced the possibility for moderate opposition, compromise, or change from within in the Polish party system. At the same time, it galvanized a broader opposition movement in Poland, the Secular Left.[8] The Polish Catholic Church did not especially sympathize with the atheist and left-wing student opposition in the direct line of fire. Nevertheless, it issued a statement protesting the violence against the students.[9]

Among activists and in West German liberal circles, the Prague invasion and Polish purge were disconcerting, not only because they represented a step toward a more authoritarian system in Eastern Europe but, more importantly, because of their potentially harmful impact on Ostpolitik. Piotr Madajczyk argues in a recent essay that a focus on reactions and effects in East Berlin and Ulbricht, the lack of knowledge about Poland among journalists, and their interest in the economic potential of East European markets were the reasons that West German media downplayed the seriousness of the purge and the intervention in Prague.[10] This interpretation overlooks the groups within elite and audiovisual media with an interest in Poland and their political reasons for downplaying the crisis. As we will see, engaged journalists intentionally protected the SPD's political agenda in the wake of the 1968 events by downplaying those aspects that might threaten public support for Ostpolitik.

Initially, despite the anti-Semitism and signs of a hardening party control, in the context of the Prague Spring and western student protests, the student demonstrations were occasionally interpreted as a sign of hope.[11] As the purge intensified, and the Prague Spring ended violently, the German newspapers modified their positive interpretations. *Die Zeit* wrote on 22 March, "Poland's students are precipitating the regime's deepest crisis to date."[12] After the Soviet invasion of Czechoslovakia in August, Kiesinger and Brandt criticized the invasion sharply, calling it a clear violation of Czechoslovakia's sovereignty. Three days after the invasion, however, they also stated that they would continue the efforts toward détente, the nuclear-control talks with Moscow, and the German–German talks with Ulbricht because "there are no other alternatives."[13] Brandt's entire political profile, platform, and electoral campaign hinged on foreign policy reform in Eastern Europe. Jürgen Tern wrote an editorial that appeared in *Frankfurter Allgemeine* arguing for a practical, not an emotional, approach to the developments in Prague. He wrote that although the "painfully prepared roads of our Ostpolitik now seem barricaded," normalization still remained a necessity.[14]

Hansjakob Stehle also strove to save Ostpolitik. He had been closely allied with the Social Democrats and their political agenda since his years in Berlin in the early 1960s. In fact, Stehle's connections with the Polish as well as the West German political leadership had made him an intermediary in the political overtures preceding Ostpolitik. In early 1968, he hosted a secret meeting in his apartment in Vienna where Egon Bahr, the primary engineer of the Social Democratic Ostpolitik program, met with the counselor at the Polish Embassy to Austria, Jerzy Raczkowski.[15] During this meeting, they discussed the possible premises of the new policy should SPD gain power in the coming elections.[16] According to Bahr, the report that Raczkowski wrote about their meeting in Stehle's apartment in early 1968 had become lost in the paper mills of Polish bureaucracy. In February 1969, when Stehle met Zenon Kliszko, Gomułka's closest associate, at the party congress of the Italian communists in Bologna, Kliszko complained about the silence and passivity in Bonn. At that point, Stehle told him about the meeting in Vienna, and the document was consequently tracked down and studied more closely in Warsaw.[17]

Given his personal investment in Ostpolitik, Stehle went to some length to salvage Gomułka's reputation as a statesman and distance him from the purges later that year. "Has Gomułka really saved the power balance of his 'little stabilization,' which for ten years relied on tactical compromises with the right and left wing of his party?" Stehle asked in an article that appeared in *Die Zeit* in June. According to his line of argument, Gomułka knew that the anti-Zionist sentiments could quickly become anti-Soviet sentiments. Stehle noted that Gomułka's "statesman-like instincts" had distanced him "from those partisans, to whom his actual sympathies belong."[18] Stehle portrayed a man involved in a complex domestic political power struggle, but still a statesman who might master the internal unrest and remain a reliable international partner for West Germany.[19] Stehle's article described the internal conflicts and tensions within the party and their expression in the communist press. He placed the main responsibility for the purges and anti-Zionist campaign with Mieczysław Moczar's faction within the communist leadership. Moczar was a leader of the veterans' organization ZBoWiD (the Society for Fighters for Freedom and Democracy) and a minister in Gomułka's government since 1964.[20] Stehle wrote optimistically that by the time he was yet again allowed to travel into the country, the situation had stabilized considerably, and it seemed like Gomułka would retain his control over the state. The West German foreign policy establishment on the whole shared Stehle's assessment of Gomułka's remaining distant from or standing in silent opposition to the anti-Semitic campaign.[21] As Marcin Zaremba and others have pointed out, Gomułka was in reality the initiator of the campaign.[22]

The article ascribed the political foundations of the "absurd" anti-Zionist rhetoric and anti-Semitic attacks to specific cliques and to internal communist party conflicts dating back to the end of the Second World War. Stehle's explanation positioned the anti-Semitic rhetorical stance in political maneuvering within the communist party. He implied that broader Polish opinion had no connection to the anti-Semitic campaign while also emphasizing that several leading Polish communists had distanced themselves from the extreme measures and opinions that had developed in March 1968. He concluded that three months later, the tenor of opinion on foreign policy in Warsaw had moderated, that the overcoming of the March crisis and the stabilization of Czechoslovakia had made Polish communists relaxed and secure enough to venture toward a more open Ostpolitik.[23] In reality, the ultra-nationalist, anti-German, and anti-Semitic wing of the communist party had moved its positions forward since 1964, and Moczar's appointment as minister of internal affairs was indicative of that shift. The Polish Internal Ministry and the Polish army had, as an example, produced special lists of their members who had a Jewish background.[24] While the Polish relationship with West Germany would improve until the 1970s, the Israeli–Polish relationship would remain troubled into the late 1970s.[25]

Zimmerer took a darker view than Stehle on the protests. He wrote in *Die Zeit* that while the protests seemed similar to western student protests, Poland had no "Rudi Dutschkes."[26] The Polish student leaders had already been arrested and jailed. He also pointed out that despite western media reports, the students had no broader support in Polish society. The intellectuals and authors supporting them were a helpless minority, and Cardinal Wyszyński held back from the protests because, according to Zimmerer, he was ultimately uninterested in contributing to an overturning of the state or to large-scale protests.[27]

In August, Zimmerer still saw the situation in more negative terms than Stehle had. His second report on the aftermath of the party purge cited Gomułka's statements in a recent meeting of the central committee. The party leader had called for dialogue and conversation that would include the nation as well as the party. However, Zimmerer warned that Polish communist rule had not relaxed. In their "open conversations," the party members who were still active had agreed that they had been far too tolerant toward their enemies. They "declared unanimously that the fight against their main enemy, revisionism—meaning the leftwing liberals, the reformers of Marxism, the promoters of market economy, the western-influenced Sociologists—had been undertaken too leniently." "The professors who were chased as seducers of young innocent minds; the publishers who were categorized as reactionaries, fools or criminals, and the parliamentary members of the Polish Znak-group who were declared enemies of the people" were also excluded.[28] Gomułka's conciliatory position was little more than a rhetorical stance to pacify public opinion and western critics, according to Zimmerer.

Contributors to the religious memoranda also expressed concerns about the political development. Fourteen days after the invasion of Czechoslovakia, Klaus von Bismarck appeared at the West German Catholic Day in Essen as the invited keynote speaker. He began by saying the invasion had made it impossible for him to give the speech he had initially intended. He spoke of fear and the sense of threat, but he also stated that Ostpolitik was a matter of world peace, and for Christians it had to take priority above "reunification, even in the interest of protection and the essence of the German people."[29] Von Bismarck was deeply invested in the relationship with the East European countries, yet he considered West German security and goals as paramount. At the same time, he reaffirmed the importance of connections to Poland and Eastern Europe.

> Since the brutalities of the Third Reich there is still fear of the Germans in the East and the West. Therefore, we, the citizens of the Federal Republic, despite the last fourteen days, cannot grow tired in ensuring Poles, Czechoslovaks, and of course also the Russians, that we want to overcome the burdensome National Socialist and recent past. Each of us here who maintains a personal relationship to a member of any of these peoples does a great service.... In the service of peace, something more than rationality has to come into play, which we could call freedom, sovereignty, or simply love of thy neighbor [*Liebe zum Nächsten*].[30]

To justify a continuation of relations with Eastern Europe despite the crushing of the Prague Spring, von Bismarck invoked the need to overcome Germany's Nazi past and argued for the Christian duty to love one's neighbor. He also highlighted the nonpolitical and spiritual aspects of international relations as a way to circumvent troubled politics.

Meanwhile, moderate and conservative media outlets and journalists opposing Ostpolitik and recognition of the eastern border took advantage of the Polish state's anti-Semitic campaign and attacks on the students and intellectuals to question Brandt's and Bahr's emerging vision of Ostpolitik. They paid close attention to the "witch hunt" of the opposition, Jewish party members, and academics.[31] East European states proved decisively that they would back up their authoritarian system with armed intervention if necessary. The invasion of Czechoslovakia undermined the assurances of West Germany's major communist partners that they were interested in negotiation and European peace.[32]

The Znak Circle criticized the initial attacks and therefore, like many other liberal groups, came under attack. After the group issued an interpellation of protest in the Sejm, Jerzy Zawieyski lost his position on the State Council. State-controlled press and radio accused the Znak Circle of disloyalty to the Polish state, of "Zionist" sympathies, and of sympathy for foreign powers. A particular direction of official thought promoted by communist media and in particular by the bestselling 1967 book *Israel a NRF* (Israel and the Federal Republic) by Tadeusz Walichnowski also underlaid the criticism directed at the Znak Circle. Walichnowski argued that Israel and the Federal Republic had entered into a partnership to promote American imperialism at the expense of Poland and its international reputation.[33] Consequently, the state could now equal the Znak Circle's efforts to create improved relations with West Germany with a pro-Israeli stance—that is, with "Zionism" and disloyalty to Poland. The communist party also accused the Circle of utilizing and cultivating connections to foreign media, particularly to Radio Free Europe. One of the points of accusation read during parliamentary sessions specifically stated that "the interpellation [of protest against the attacks] was directed to the public and the diversionary loudspeakers of Radio Free Europe."[34]

The attacks by the communist party and media effectively silenced the Znak Circle and the editorial boards of the Catholic press. Further protests would have been, as Stomma wrote in his memoirs using one of his favorite expressions, a Winkelriedian gesture, but one that would not have reached a larger Polish public, as the media was so harshly censored at the time.[35] In the spring of 1969, elections for a new Sejm approached, and it was unclear whether the party would allow the Znak group to retain its seats. Ultimately, Gomułka allowed four Catholic parliamentarians to remain, but he made sure that they belonged to different Catholic camps to further weaken their voice in the public and political realm. Stomma was one of them. At this point, the domestic role and influence of the Znak Circle was all but over.[36] Following his removal from the Sejm, which became clear in April 1969, Jerzy Zawieyski fell ill and died suddenly on 18 June after a fall from the third floor in the hospital in which he was treated. The official sources suggested that he committed suicide, and this is also what Sefan Kisielewski assumed in his diary.[37]

At this moment, a curious split occurred for the Polish individuals involved with the Znak Circle and in Polish–German relations. Their domestic situation and influence were deteriorating, while their status and public roles in West Germany were steadily improving. For a year or more after the 1968 events, the Polish state prevented them from traveling abroad. When they were once more allowed to cross the border, they continued to describe reconciliation as successful. From a West German public relations perspective, relations were progressing. In September 1969, Brandt was elected chancellor of the Federal Republic at the helm of an SPD–FDP coalition. His platform included a program of change in the eastern policy, Ostpolitik, and the notion of *Wandel durch Annäherung* (change through rapprochement), a development that increased attention on Polish–German relations in West German politics. This election was headline news in the Polish press.[38] Soon thereafter, the Federal Republic's government-initiated negotiations with the Polish, East German, and Soviet representatives.

In Brandt's political program, German–German relations took precedence, followed by Soviet–West German relations and Polish–West German relations. In his government declaration on October 1969, Willy Brandt recognized the de facto existence of two German states, and he met with the East German prime minister Willi Stoph twice that fall.[39] On the Polish side, relations with West Germany had to be coordinated with Ulbricht and the GDR. Ulbricht insisted that the West German recognition of the GDR as a state must be a part of a Polish–West German agreement and suspected Gomułka of going behind his back to establish connections with West Germany. Meanwhile, Gomułka equally distrusted the German–German negotiations taking place in his absence.[40] Even more, the Polish communists distrusted the negotiations between West Germany and the Soviet Union, given the historically negative experiences of Poland with German–Russian or Soviet agreements at the cost of Polish interests, including the Molotov–Ribbentrop Pact in 1939. The treaty with Moscow was a precondition for both the East German and Polish negotiations, particularly in light of the intervention in Czechoslovakia in 1968, but the Polish leadership worried about being passed over and included in a "package deal" between the Federal Republic and the Soviet Union.[41]

In October 1969, when Stanisław Stomma visited the Federal Republic, he treaded carefully in the aftermath of the Polish upheavals. He celebrated the progress in relations and shared the West German partners' optimism with regards to the future of Polish–German relations. However, this was not a time for him to draw attention to the Znak Circle or to seem as though he were acting as a representative for Polish foreign policy. During his trip, he gave an interview to the small West German Catholic journal *Publik*. In it, he emphasized that he was not speaking for the state.[42] He stated that he hoped for an agreement between Poland and the Federal Republic, as many had suggested in public discussions, but he made this statement as a private Catholic visitor rather than an official representative. He also emphasized that this was the only public interview he would make during his visit. It was not the time for him to take the role of a statesman.

Nevertheless, Stomma was at this point something of a celebrity in West Germany. He thoroughly enjoyed the contrast of this attention compared to his trips in the late 1950s. Stefan Kisielewski, who could no longer get a visa to travel abroad, noted in his diary that he had met Stomma as he returned and that Stomma had been "very excited" about the recognition the Znak Circle had received.⁴³ Stomma shared the West German media actors' belief in the importance of Ostpolitik, and of the recognition of the Oder-Neisse Line, and took seriously the need to support the bilateral agreement publicly in West Germany. In fact, by reinventing Polish–German relations as a nonpolitical and spiritual relationship, he began to separate them from political developments, just as Bismarck had done.

The Bensberger Circle also focused on the continuation of Ostpolitik and the establishment of official relations. They had almost completely overlooked internal Polish developments after the events in 1968. In May 1968, the Bensberger Circle had invited Jerzy Turowicz and Władysław Bartoszewski to the Protestant-Catholic publisher's gathering in Loccum, but they were unable to travel because of the political turmoil in Poland.⁴⁴ In May 1969, a year later, Bensberger Circle member Winfried Lipscher traveled to Poland with Aktion Sühnezeichen. He reported after his return that the Bensberger Memorandum was known and well regarded in Polish society.⁴⁵ At this time, the Bensberger Circle began discussing the publication of yet another Poland memorandum. The group wished to reinforce the importance of détente in light of the new stabilization in the eastern bloc and Gomułka's offer to the Federal Republic of an official treaty, and in spite of the Soviet intervention in Czechoslovakia.⁴⁶ The preparatory writings and the content of the document made no mention of the Polish internal purge. They steadfastly suggested that the protests by West German expellee organizations were the main obstacle to an improvement in relations.⁴⁷

In April 1970, a delegation from Bensberger Circle traveled to Poland at the invitation of the Znak Circle. The delegates arrived in Warsaw in a snowstorm, where their welcoming committee consisted of members not from Znak or the Catholic intelligentsia clubs but from Piasecki's government-loyal PAX. The next day, Piasecki's newspaper *Słowo Powszechne* published an article about the friendly meeting between PAX and the West German visitors. Karlheinz Koppe, who arranged the trip, remembered the meeting with government-sponsored Catholic groups as a prearranged condition for the group to receive their entrance visas at all.⁴⁸ As a consequence of this meeting and article about it, Cardinal Wyszyński canceled his audience with the Bensberger Circle.

PAX's intervention signaled competition between the Polish state and Catholic Church over foreign relations. The intervention seemed acceptable to the Bensberger Circle, but not to the Polish primate. Their statements and correspondences suggest that the left-wing Bensberger Circle considered the Polish state an essential participant in reconciliation and in a peaceful coexistence between Poles and Germans, whereas the Polish Church wanted to keep a more pronounced distance from the communists, particularly after 1965. Karlheinz Koppe explained in his memoirs that the cardinal had chosen not to meet with them because they were not Christian Democrats and because "we also spoke with other Catholic groups."[49] After the cardinal had removed himself from the interaction, Stomma tried to mediate between the church and the visitors. In the end, the Catholic Church leadership agreed to a compromise. Bishop Kominek received the group in Wrocław in the name of the Polish episcopate. Wyszyński was interested in reconciliation, and both Winfried Lipscher and Stanisław Stomma testified later to his personal sympathy for the Bensberger Circle.

Emphasizing the visit's positive impact, Stomma published an article about it in *Tygodnik Powszechny* in 1970. In it, he inserted the circle's work within a larger Christian narrative of improving Polish–German relations and changing the course of history. He described the religious and church developments leading up to the Bensberger Circle representatives' visit in Poland thus: "But history is made not only by official government policies. Social currents ... also make history."[50] After the war, the lack of a broader support for improvement in Polish–German relations had discouraged Polish initiatives, but the church memoranda were part of a new beginning according to his article. Stomma mentioned Lothar Kreyssig's Aktion Sühnezeichen as the first initiative, but he commented that the initiative was too limited to have a real effect on Polish opinion. In his view, the Protestant Expellee Memorandum was the real breakthrough and the Bensberger Memorandum another high point, both because the German bishops' answer had been so disappointing and because a large group of Catholics rather than Protestants had signed the memorandum.

Stomma assured his readers that the Bensberger Circle had no intention of interfering in politics: "Their goal is to clear away the enmity in the relations between the Polish and German nations."[51] In this statement, following Polish traditions, he differentiated clearly between the state and the nation, whereas the Bensberger Circle understood them as much more closely linked, an interpretation that contributed to its concept of détente and reconciliation in close proximity. By emphasizing the spiritual aspects of the initiative, Stomma also separated the Bensberger Circle from the troublesome association with PAX and from communist politics. This was another way of moving away from emphasizing state contacts to emphasizing spiritual and societal contacts. From the perspective of reconciliation studies, it is an interesting adjustment because it was a reaction to limitations imposed by the state. It also allowed the narrative of reconciliation to survive the fall of that same state in 1989.[52]

Relations between Cardinal Wyszyński and the German episcopate remained tense. In the Federal Republic, the Bensberger Circle was isolated from the more mainstream Catholic Central Committee as well as from the episcopate. The question about the dioceses in the Oder-Neisse territories also remained unsettled. The Vatican, strongly supported by the German Catholic Church, argued that such a regulation could only follow the political settlement of the border question in a peace treaty. In November 1969, Bishop Kominek met privately with the prominent SPD representatives Herbert Wehner and Georg Leber in Rome to discuss how the diocesan question could be connected to the Bonn–Warsaw negotiations about a border treaty.[53] In October 1970, after the Bonn–Moscow Treaty, Cardinal Wyszyński also met with Cardinal Döpfner in Rome and attempted to convince him to support a regulation of the diocesan question.

Stehle followed and reported closely on the interactions between Cardinal Wyszyński and the larger church. Critical of the German episcopate's stance, he believed that Cardinal Döpfner did not fully comprehend the urgency of Polish Church's agenda.[54] In November and December 1970, the two cardinals exchanged letters that, while not written for the public, came into Stehle's hands.[55] They both felt that the reconciliation dialogue had progressed since the early 1960s but also that the two churches' priorities and understandings still differed widely from one another. Cardinal Wyszyński expressed his disappointment with the German bishops' message from 1966. He objected to the German episcopate's continuing rejection of a diocesan adjustment as well as its hesitance to publicly recognize Polish right to the border territories. In his answer, Cardinal Döpfner reiterated his desire for dialogue and his acceptance of Polish retention of the border territories. Yet he said that he would not publicly recognize the territories as Polish because of the German Catholic Church's duty to represent German expellees and encourage their integration into West German society. Ultimately, he wrote, a "peaceful atmosphere in our people is more important than a concrete treaty."[56] Cardinal Döpfner also assured Cardinal Wyszyński that the German Catholic Church would be willing to support the diocesan settlement after a political treaty had been made. Stehle found the letter problematic, particularly because, in a handwritten note on the typed letter, Cardinal Döpfner suggested that Cardinal Wyszyński had written to appease the Polish communist leaders by applying political pressure on the West German episcopate.[57] Overall, the exchange and Stehle's careful coverage of it indicated the political questions at stake in these church contacts, but also the political importance of the churches to the developments in official relations.

Brandt signed the agreement between Poland and the Federal Republic, which recognized the border and established the preconditions for official relations, on 7 December 1970.[58] The real price he paid for the treaty was of course the official West German acceptance of the border, although the full recognition remained postponed until a peace treaty could be concluded with a reunited Germany. The agreement involved sacrifices on both sides of the negotiating table. No compensations for the Polish victims of German war crimes would be paid, and the agreement did not include any clauses concerning German family reunions either. The West German side made their concessions for the sake of stability, peace, and the establishment of official relations, as well as, as Brandt emphasized in a television talk from Warsaw, for moral reasons.[59] However, the agreement still had to be ratified by the Bundestag. An intense campaign of lobbying to support the ratification thus took place between 1970 and 1972. This campaign played a significant role in shaping media reports with regards to Polish–German relations, similarly to the way the feelings of optimism and completion coupled with political objectives of European unity would shape them in the early 1990s.

As 1970 came to an end, the public appearance of the relations—in the visits, summits, and ceremonies that the agreements entailed—became more important than ever. When Willy Brandt traveled to Warsaw to sign the agreement with Gomułka, he also invited a number of private guests to visually mark the significance of the pre-1970 nongovernmental exchanges. His guests included Klaus von Bismarck, *Stern* editor Henri Nannen, Krupp director Berthold Beitz, and authors Siegfried Lenz and Günther Grass.[60] Bismarck, Beitz, Lenz, and Grass all originated from the former German areas in Poland. Brandt had invited Marion Countess Dönhoff to attend as well but she ultimately felt unable to do so.[61] Bismarck took her place instead at short notice.[62]

In his official speeches and appearances in Warsaw, Brandt paid homage to the idea of a spiritually founded reconciliation. During the stay, Brandt visited the Ghetto Monument, erected in memory of the Jewish uprising in 1943. According to protocol, he was to place a wreath by the monument in a ceremony. While he was there, on an impulse, he fell to his knees in a gesture of asking forgiveness in front of the monument. *Süddeutsche Zeitung* published what may have been the most vivid description of the impulsive gesture:

> A guide, who wants to explain to [Brandt] the suffering which Polish Jews had experienced here is unable to finish his lecture. He falls silent as he sees how the chancellor, overcome with troubled emotions, falls to his knees. Brandt takes seconds, which seem endless to his witnesses, until he stands up again.[63]

Brandt himself described the moment in his memoirs: "I hadn't planned anything but had left Wilanow Palace, where I was staying, with the feeling that I had to do something to commemorate the special nature of the ceremony by the Ghetto Monument. . . . I did what people do when words fail them."⁶⁴ While atheist, Willy Brandt still used a religious gesture of atonement to express his feelings before the Warsaw Ghetto Monument. The gesture in connection with the border recognition became a key moment in apology studies and conflict resolution.⁶⁵ However, in order to function as such, media had to interpret it and also highlight its importance.

The kneefall before the Ghetto Monument became a visual symbol of the reconciliatory aspects of Ostpolitik. The significance of the gesture emerged particularly through the descriptions in West German and international media but was only mentioned briefly in the Polish communist press.⁶⁶ For the Polish communist leadership at the time, the gesture had several troubling dimensions, including its marking of Jewish rather than Polish suffering. Meanwhile, Poland was experiencing a deep crisis as the regime decided, during Christmas week, to increase food prices by 20 percent. The price increases led to unrest and violence in Szczecin, Gdańsk, and Gdynia, places with large, organized groups of industrial workers. Gomułka was eventually forced to resign and Edward Gierek replaced him.⁶⁷ Thus, the significance of Brandt's gesture was not a primary focus for Polish media and state, distracted as they were by the domestic crisis. The following media reports had to highlight, reinterpret, and give it significance as a trope of improvement in German-Polish relations.⁶⁸

Stehle, who was in Warsaw at the time of the signing, published an article for *Die Zeit* interpreting the kneefall. He challenged the cynics among his Polish and German contacts who suggested the gesture was pre-planned. Stehle described Brandt as falling to his knees because he was "overcome by the memory of the monstrosities."⁶⁹ Meanwhile, like the Polish communist press, the West German conservative press at least initially downplayed or omitted mentioning the kneefall.⁷⁰ Also, the Polish Catholic press covered the agreement with the Federal Republic and, indirectly, Brandt's gesture. On 13 December, Stomma interviewed Klaus von Bismarck in *Tygodnik Powszechny* about the treaty and about his decision to accompany Brandt on his official visit to Warsaw. Asked whether it was difficult for him to participate, von Bismarck said that he had not hesitated to accompany Brandt, but it was nonetheless painful for him. He believed that signing and confirming the treaty was a way to take responsibility for the war that Germany had started without reason. At the moment of signing, however, he thought of those, many of them his close acquaintances, who could not accept the loss of their homes.⁷¹

Von Bismarck described the agreement in moral terms:

> I believe that neither simple rational reasons nor sensible though painful perspectives on German history dictated this necessary solution. The decision by the Chancellor was above all a decision of a moral nature, taken in consideration of the Poles living in those areas today as well as of the Germans, whom

one must help to find the right outlook on reality. In this way, it was a humanitarian decision. For me as well humanitarian reasons are incomparably more important than legal arguments.[72]

Stomma proposed that the Brandt government also had a political motive. Von Bismarck responded that this motive was long-term peaceful coexistence with Eastern Europe. He described reconciliation as an inner process, adding that it could only take place if it was accompanied by pain.

Stomma celebrated the signing of the bilateral agreement by sending two congratulatory telegrams, to Manfred Seidler in the Bensberger Circle and to Lothar Kreyssig in East German Aktion Sühnezeichen. He explained in his memoirs that to him they were the "Germans who had been especially engaged in the agreement."[73] He also attended festivities and dinners in connection with the signing of the treaty, sitting next to von Bismarck at those occasions. These actions all supported Stomma's particular version of the reconciliation narrative as a cultural and ecumenical event.

While West German press and audiovisual media representatives considered 1970 a positive moment in Polish–German relations, they were also well aware that the Bundestag had not yet ratified the agreement. Thus, their efforts to anchor Ostpolitik more broadly through writings and broadcasts intensified. In March 1970, Westdeutscher Rundfunk (WDR) broadcast a longer feature that Stehle had authored. The transcript, titled "Polen hinter Oder und Neisse," treated the now-familiar theme of life in the borderlands. Compared to its 1964 counterparts, the borderlands portrait was similar, although the description of Polish economic development and entrepreneurship had been toned down. The 1970 feature continued to celebrate the industrial and agricultural progress in Poland but also noted that production was very low compared to Western Europe. Stehle described these numbers as "reflect[ions of] both the progress and the backwardness of the country." The comments considered the economic crisis in Poland and also expressed the hope that the new Ostpolitik would contribute to stabilizing the Polish economic situation further through business cooperation and a new psychological sense of security.[74]

Post-1970 productions also continued to try to come to terms with the question of the minorities in the borderlands. This was true for Stehle's "Polen hinter Oder und Neisse," which once more described the painful experiences of multilingual and multinational borderlands populations but connected their disappearance to a needed modernization project.[75]

Other media representations embraced a similar narrative. The television documentary *Weichsel—Kirschen und Lorbeer: Polens Jubiläum zwischen Ost und West* was broadcast on 21 January 1971 on (ARD).[76] The producer, Olrik Breckhoff, carefully covered the multiethnic past of the area surrounding Chełm near the Ukrainian border, describing the concentration camps that had existed there and also covering the removal of Ukrainians from Poland and Poles from Ukrainian territory. The documentary described those removals as a "painful but perhaps healthy" development.[77] A discussion of the remaining Jewish minority once more focused on the Yiddish State Theater in Warsaw, including its difficulty finding Yiddish-speaking actors for its performances.[78] The theater's director Ida Kamińska had left Poland in 1968, and only five of the original Yiddish-speaking actors remained after that year. The documentary also discussed the apartment buildings that had been built in the place of the destroyed Ghetto in Warsaw. Like other documentaries discussed, *Weichsel — Kirschen und Lorbeer* emphasized the vitality of Catholic faith and culture in Poland, as well as the ongoing baby boom, and pointed to signs of westernization and modernization in Polish society. In this way, it attempted to balance out the mission of positive relations and overcoming old negative stereotypes of Poland without completely ignoring the reality of the disappearing minorities.

Ostpolitik also impacted media's reporting. By 1971, Ludwig Zimmerer wrote more favorably of Gomułka, who had been removed a month earlier. He stated that the 1968 March events had presented a serious challenge to Gomułka because he had to overcome the student protests, handle the witch hunt perpetrated by the national Bolsheviks on several different groups, and repel attacks on himself. On balance, Zimmerer said, Gomułka had been "a significant Polish statesman." Condemning the price increases, he also called the ejected leader "a terrible dilettante with respect to the economic policies."[79] Whereas Zimmerer's immediate experience of the Polish student protests and the state's response made him more pessimistic than Stehle in 1968, the opening of relations in the winter of 1970/1971 caused him to reconsider Gomułka in a more positive light. The successes of Brandt's policy led Zimmerer as well as many other West German politicians and journalists to support the particular attitude that Timothy Garton Ash later called "stability before liberty."[80]

Stehle also published a new book in 1971. It had the title *Nachbarn im Osten: Herausforderung zu einer neuen Politik* and was dedicated to Willy Brandt. Stehle stated in its introduction that despite occasionally being critical of the East European communist leaderships, he nevertheless wanted his book to contribute to the new political opening between West Germany and the East European countries.[81] Unlike Zimmerer, Stehle had become more critical of Gomułka over time. At this time, Stehle mentioned the speech given by the former communist leader on 19 June 1968 that opened the door to the purge.[82] Since Gomułka had already been replaced by Gierek, Stehle no longer had any reason to protect the former's reputation as a partner in the Polish–German cooperation. Stehle also mentioned the broader anti-Semitic sentiments in the late 1960s as a moment of "psychosis that was difficult to control" in the Polish state offices, bureaucracy, and the army.[83] However, he emphasized that the society seemed to come to its senses again later on and that the anti-Zionist rhetorical stance in Gomułka's closest circles had more to do with attempts to distance Poland from Soviet influences, thereby also emphasizing Gomułka's readiness to engage in closer relations with Bonn.

Both audiovisual media and the press expanded their cooperation with Polish radio and television and celebrated the advances made through Ostpolitik while also discussing the continuing tensions and steps needed to improve relations further. In January 1971, a feature titled "Durch polnische Augen" (Through Polish Eyes) appeared as a co-production on Sender Freies Berlin, WDR, NDR (Norddeutscher Rundfunk), SDR (Süddeutscher Rundfunk), and Polish Radio.[84] The program was part of the cross-border cooperation that Polish Radio and WDR had initiated after 1964 and attempted to measure the progress in relations. Similar to Stehle's 1965 manuscript *In the Eyes of the Neighbors*, it consisted of interviews and statements by Poles about Germans. The radio program featured voices from a younger generation of Poles who considered war a thing of the past. A small number of the interviewees had even begun to interact with and speak more positively about the younger postwar German generation. One of the interviewees mentioned Brandt's chancellorship as a sign of positive development. The larger point of the feature was to detect whether Ostpolitik had improved the Poles' opinions of the Germans. Statements made by Polish interviewees still mentioned experiences during the war as their main reference points for evaluating Germans. The older generation in particular expressed their lingering fear and distrust, indicating the need for broader exchange programs and opportunities for changing these negative perceptions, or for more time to pass.

Angela Nacken, Ludwig Zimmerer, and Ulrich Gembardt participated in an expert panel commenting on the questions of progress and change after Ostpolitik, following the feature. They spoke about the developments following the treaty and the new Ostpolitik in some detail.[85] The commentators agreed that the Second World War continued to play a central role in Polish perceptions but also that there was a difference between the older and younger generation of Poles. They made the point that intense traditional Polish patriotism was an obstacle to the relations but suggested that it was becoming outdated and would likely disappear over time.

A positive development in official Polish–German relations following the 1970 agreement according to Zimmerer was the more extensive and fairly accurate coverage of West German topics in the Polish communist media. Nacken agreed but added that interest in West Germany and Polish–German relations was greater in Poland than vice versa. Zimmerer also described an increasing normalization after 1969 and his hope that the trend would continue. Given the Second World War, the Germans would always have to contend with some Polish distrust. But the expert panel asserted that the new treaties had brought positive changes. They said that praise of Brandt was widespread in all levels of Polish society. The continued improvement, according to these Poland experts, would depend on economic cooperation, cultural exchange, and further relaxation of the state-level interactions. They also felt that the interviews in the original show could not have been recorded a year earlier because people would not have dared to answer the questions honestly before the Polish state had sanctioned improved relations. Thus, they were overwhelmingly optimistic with regards to the post-1970 developments in light of the new political leadership and policy in West Germany.

In a separate commentary that followed the panel, Ryszard Wojna, the longtime German expert and correspondent with Życie Warszawy, introduced a Polish perspective.[86] He emphasized the role of West Germany's decision to recognize the border in eventual improvement, should the Republic ratify the treaty. He contrasted its situation with the GDR's treaty with Poland in 1950, which, he said, had speeded the normalization that was only just starting with West Germany.[87] He called Angela Nacken and Ludwig Zimmerer overly optimistic, given that the treaty had not yet been ratified. Wojna also commented that his West German colleagues were confusing psychological and political developments. Whereas the political situation could find an immediate solution, the psychological change might take generations. In his commentary, he clearly separated East and West German relations with Poland, whereas the Polish interviewees tended to consider all Germans as one group with a few exceptions. In this way, the significance and the larger interpretation of the agreement differed considerably between the West German journalists and the Polish one.

In several of his radio programs from 1971 and 1972, Zimmerer expanded on the changes in relations after the treaty was signed. He particularly emphasized that Polish perceptions of Germans had previously been distorted by limited interaction with postwar Germans. The older generation associated "the Germans" with those soldiers they had met during the occupation between 1939 and 1945, while the younger generation knew the German people only from the stories the older generation told them. However, starting in 1969, the communist newspapers were finally publishing accurate and nuanced descriptions of the Federal Republic and of West German society, politics, and conversations about Poland, which also contributed to new insights in broader groups of the Polish people.⁸⁸ The propaganda image of the revisionist and aggressive Germans had done much to damage the Polish perspective on the Germans according to Zimmerer. It was now subsiding, however.

In West Germany, the social-liberal coalition struggled to stay in power. Several members of the SPD and FDP switched party affiliation to the Christian Democratic Union (CDU) after 1970. Emboldened, the CDU attempted to introduce a motion of no confidence to replace Brandt in April 1972. However, Brandt remained in power by a thin margin of two votes. The Warsaw agreement was finally ratified after negotiations with the CDU faction in May 1972. Since his party lacked a majority in the parliament, Brandt asked for a vote of confidence for parliament, and the ensuing nationwide election led to the dissolution of the parliament and new elections, which were held in November 1972. Brandt won the reelection, and the SPD–FDP gained a majority in the parliament, securing Ostpolitik in a more definite way.⁸⁹ From Warsaw, Zimmerer commented that historians of Polish–German relations would surely consider 19 November 1972 a key date.⁹⁰

Less than two months after the reelection, Zimmerer described a "surprising[ly]" rapid disappearance of traditional distrust of Germans in broader Polish society, which he credited both to the treaty and the SPD victory. Through the recognition of the border, he said in a broadcast on 20 November 1972 that Poles had begun to emphasize the positive potential of Polish–German relations. The new interactions held the promise of a Polish–German symbiosis where both cultures and peoples contributed something of their unique culture to the cooperation, particularly its economic aspects.⁹¹

Politically, Ostpolitik and the recognition of the Oder-Neisse Line was a great success for the FDP–SPD's Polish–German relations. The official relations also paved the way for further cultural exchanges and meetings across the border. However, activists in Poland and the Federal Republic were critical to the new partnership, and the recollections of the young opposition in Poland suggest they felt marginalized by the emphasis on state relations. In an interview in 1989, Adam Michnik acknowledged the positive effects of Ostpolitik, yet he called the reconciliation "a rapprochement of states rather than one of nations."

> From that moment on, the only "partner" of the Germans in Poland was the Communist government. Poles began to feel that as a nation, as an issue, not only did they cease to exist at diplomatic conferences, they also ceased to exist in the minds of Westerners.⁹²

The comments showed the extent to which the state was able to frame and circumscribe relations. Polish–German official events frequently excluded the Polish Catholic groups in order to avoid alienating the official state-level conversation partners. Gomułka had removed the Znak Circle from Polish domestic politics in 1968. Minority voices and remaining questions were too sensitive to be part of official communications and statements. The communist state objected to any greater involvement of the church in official relations. Finally, the relations did not always include East German representation. This simplification of topics and adjustment of a narrative acceptable to dominant voices on each side were all part of the unfolding of reconciliation and the creation of a consensus.

Throughout 1969 and 1970, writer Anna Morawska had published a series of observations on the Federal Republic and Polish–German relations and reconciliation in the *Frankfurter Hefte*. Morawska was born in 1922 and had a degree from the Jagiellonian University in Cracow. In the early postwar years, she was a member of the PAX movement, but she left it in 1955 and began writing for *Więź*, *Znak*, and *Tygodnik Powszechny*. She also translated texts from German to Polish and published two books, one on Dietrich Bonhoeffer and the other on religion in the Third Reich. Her comments are clear-sighted and helpful in contextualizing Polish–German reconciliation and relations morally and religiously at this particular moment of time. She was forthrightly critical of the lingering German attitudes toward the border issue and the Nazi past. In 1969, she sympathized with the German student opposition, describing it as a group seeking the truth about the Nazi past.

According to Morawska's observations, the Federal Republic was built on three myths after the war. The first was about the rebuilding effort, in which the population forgot about the past and focused on recovery. The second was the "anticommunist" myth, which allowed them to focus on the present rather than the past and to see themselves as fighting on the side of the good. The final myth was the myth of the "free world" in which they became incorporated in a West European community, supported by both the leading world powers and the pope.[93] Ultimately, she felt that after 1970 Poles and Germans must come to terms with each other's conflicting "frames of reference." These comments on the short-term political goal of reaching consensus and minimizing conflict foreshadowed the work that was to come, regarding conflicting German and Polish memory cultures and the incorporation of the silenced voices and memories of other groups with a stake in Central European history, such as the expellees and the surviving Polish Jewish population. Finally, with regards to Polish–German relations in 1970, she believed that the dialogue had suffered on both sides from each side trying to please rather than being honest with and trying to understand the other.[94]

Conclusion

The 1968 developments decisively changed the position and role of the Znak Circle in Poland. Their position in Polish society and their neopositivist experiment had played out for the time being. The Znak Circle's members invested more heavily in their international relations work instead, sometimes primarily as figureheads, while at the same time beginning to rewrite the relations by separating them more clearly from domestic political developments and emphasizing their moral and spiritual aspects. Internationally, considering the high profile of Polish–German relations in the West German political debates, they retained their prominence.

As the West German media activists became increasingly invested in the foreign policy program that Brandt and the SPD–FDP coalition launched, their commentary about Poland and Polish–German relations was stylized to fit with the story of progress. This politicization became especially clear during and after the anti-Zionist campaign and the internal purge of the Polish party in 1968. For the most part, West German journalists engaged with Polish–German relations did not harshly condemn the Polish internal campaigns. They would not risk Brandt's electoral platform in 1969 by harshly criticizing the purge and its instigators. Instead, they developed multiple strategies to downplay Gomułka's involvement in the purge. They also downplayed the possibility of the existence of a broader anti-Semitism in Polish society, and the turn to violence in the suppression of protests.

Ostpolitik was a necessary step to stabilize the borders and the east–west relations in 1970. However, Ostpolitik did have problematic legacies on Polish–German relations and raised interesting questions about reconciliation at large. The media representatives in support of Ostpolitik crafted a streamlined narrative of Polish–German relations intended to protect and support the SPD's policy. While the activists, including Brandt (who had spent years in Scandinavia and been a Norwegian citizen), had entered into Polish–German relations as multilingual actors with loosened or alternative national identities embedded in international networks, the public performance of these relations and their political realities shaped their identities as integrated in postwar nation-states with stable and eternal borders. In the meantime, Michnik's and Morawska's commentary showed the dangers of this political campaign. While Ostpolitik and official relations created the desired stability, it closed multiple sensitive topics and silenced parts of the dialogue between the two societies. The narrative of reconciliation lost much of its complexity and openness to pluralistic perspectives due to its importance in electoral politics. The developments raise significant questions for scholars of conflict resolution: Should reconciliation efforts prioritize short-term or long-term stability and improvement? To what extent must the state be included in the process? What options and strategies do participants in reconciliation have in order to work around problematic or hostile state actions? Finally, this chapter invites us to consider the relationship of reconciliation to democracy and democratization since, in this particular case, participants on the German side tended to consider cooperation with an openly antidemocratic state key to successful reconciliatory developments.[95]

Notes

1. *Kontraste: Ein Ost–West Magazin*, Sender Freies Berlin, ARD, 18 January 1968, Deutsche Kinemathek, Berlin.
2. Bingen, *Polen-Politik der Bonner Republik*, 105. For thorough discussions of Brandt's relationship with Poland, see the contributions to the recent volume *Nie mehr eine Politik über Polen hinweg: Willy Brandt und Polen*, ed. Friedhelm Boll and Krzysztof Ruchniewicz (Bonn, 2010).
3. Marcin Zaremba makes the point about the strong Dmowskian overtones in the campaign in *Komunizm, legitymizacja, nacjonalizm*. He also places the responsibility of the campaign with Gomułka himself. See also Dariusz Stola, "Fighting against the Shadows: The Anti-Zionist Campaign of 1968," in *Antisemitism and Its Opponents in Modern Poland*, ed. Robert Blobaum (Ithaca, NY, 2005), 286–87. "Gomulka nimmt Stellung," *Frankfurter Allgemeine Zeitung*, 20 March 1968.
4. Jacob Abadi, "The Road to Israeli–Polish Rapprochement," *Middle Eastern Studies* 41, no. 6 (November 2005): 873
5. See Friszke, *Anatomia Buntu*.
6. Stola, "Fighting against the Shadows," 286–87. "Gomulka nimmt Stellung," *Frankfurter Allgemeine Zeitung*, 20 March 1968.
7. Feliks Tych, "The 'March '68' Antisemitic Campaign: Onset, Development, and Consequences," in *Jewish Presence in Absence: The Aftermath of the Holocaust in Poland 1944–2010*, ed. Feliks Tych and Monika Adamczyk-Garbowska, trans. Grzegorz Dąbowski and Jessica Taylor-Kucia (Jerusalem, 2014), 463.
8. Maryjane Osa, *Solidarity and Contention: Networks of Polish Opposition* (Minneapolis, MN, 2003), argues that the initial failures of 1968 forced leaders such as Adam Michnik to rethink the foundation of an opposition in Poland, which ultimately led to the solidifying of a countrywide opposition network in Poland and Solidarność in the late 1970s and early 1980s.
9. Dudek and Grys, *Komuniści i Kościół w Polsce*, 266. "Bischöfe Polens stellen sich hinter Studenten, Brutale Gewalt verurteilt," *Die Welt*, 25 March 1968.
10. Piotr Madajczyk, "The Impact of the Events of the Year 1968 on the Forming of the Image of Poland and the Poles in Public Opinion in the Federal Republic of Germany," in Jarząbek, Madajczyk, and Szymoniczek, *1968 and Polish–West German Relations*, 21, 63–64.
11. Larger recent works about 1968 as a global protest development include Gerard J. De-

Groot, *The Sixties Unplugged: A Kaleidoscopic History of a Disorderly Decade* (Cambridge, MA, 2008). Other recent works studying 1968 as transnational protest include Ingo Cornils and Sarah Waters, eds., *Memories of 1968: International Perspectives* (New York, 2010), and Jeremi Suri, *Power and Protest: Global Revolution and the Rise of Détente* (Cambridge, MA, 2003).

12. "Polens Studenten stürzten das Regime in seine schwerste Krise seit Oktober 1956," *Die Zeit*, 22 March 1968.
13. "Bonn verurteilt den Einmarsch," *Frankfurter Allgemeine Zeitung*, 22 August 1968, "Bonn hält an Entspannung fest,"*Die Welt*, 24 August 1968.
14. Jürgen Tern, "Folgen für die deutsche Politik," *Frankfurter Allgemeine Zeitung*, 23 August 1968.
15. Wanda Jarząbek describes several other conversations as taking place through "unofficial channels" that year, for example between the SPD's Helmut Schmidt and Polish Bonn correspondent Ryszard Wojna. Jarząbek, "Impact of the Events," 35.
16. Hansjakob Stehle, "Eine vertrackte Vorgeschichte: Zum Warschauer Vertrag; Wie ein Schlüsseldokument verschwand und wieder auftauchte," *Die Zeit*, 7 December 1990; Egon Bahr, *Zu meiner Zeit* (Munich, 1996), 232. Of course, Bahr was himself a radio journalist who had worked for Radio in the American Sector (RIAS) between 1950 and 1960; Bahr, *Zu meiner Zeit*, 62, 104. He reported from Bonn in the 1950s. His biography does not mention if he was familiar with Stehle from those years or if he first made his acquaintance in Berlin in the early 1960s.
17. Bahr, *Zu meiner Zeit*, 234.
18. Hansjakob Stehle, "Gomulkas Gang auf schmalen Grat: Machtkampf mit Jungtürken und Opportunisten." *Die Zeit*, 21 June 1968.
19. His opinion was also shared by the correspondent for *Frankfurter Allgemeine Zeitung* (probably at this time Angela Nacken); "Studenten mit Gomulkas Antwort nicht zufrieden," *Frankfurter Allgemeine Zeitung*, 21 March 1968.
20. Wawrzyniak, *Veterans, Victims, and Memory*, 184–85; Abadi, "Road to the Israeli–Polish Rapprochement," 873.
21. Madajczyk, "Impact of the Events," 81.
22. Zaremba, *Komunizm, legitimacja, nacjonalizm*.
23. Hansjakob Stehle, "Gomulkas Gang auf schmalem Grat: Machtkampf mit Jungtürken und Opportunisten," *Die Zeit*, 21 June 1968.
24. Karol Sauerland, "Polen und Juden innerhalb der polnischen Erinnerungskultur," in *Perspektiven einer Europäischen Erinnerungsgemeinschaft: Nationale Narrative und Transnationale dynamiken seit 1989*, ed. Wolfgang Stephan Kissel and Ulrike Liebert (Münster, 2010), 62.
25. Abadi, "Road to the Israeli–Polish Rapprochement," 874.
26. Rudi Dutschke (1940–79) was a leader for the Sozialistischer Deutscher Studentenbund (SDS), the student opposition in West Germany, in the 1960s.
27. Ludwig Zimmerer, "Gomulka zeigt die starke Faust: Es kam zum Aufruhr weil die Reformer fehlten," *Die Zeit*, 22 March 1968.
28. Ludwig Zimmerer, "In der Schwebe. Weiche Töne—Harter Kurs," *Die Zeit*, 19 July 1968.
29. Klaus von Bismarck, "Unruhe in der Welt—Verantwortung aller Christen," *Essen*, 6 September 1968; in a letter to Jerzy Turowicz, 26 November 1968; Archiwum Jerzy Turowicza.
30. Ibid., 7.
31. "Warschauer bringen Esspakete: Studenten werben um Sympathie und Unterstützung von Seiten der Arbeiter," *Süddeutsche Zeitung*, 23/24 March 1968, "Polens Klerus auf Seiten der Studenten," *Süddeutsche Zeitung*, 25 March 1968, "Warschau erwartet eine

Säuberungswelle: Hexenjagd auf Hintermänner der Demonstrationen," *Frankfurter Allgemeine*, 19 March 1968, "Studenten in Warschau setzen Sitzstreik fort: Polizei hält sich zurück," *Die Welt*, 23 March 1968, "Bischöfe Polens stellen sich hinter Studenten: Brutale Gewalt verurteilt," *Die Welt*, 25 March 1968.

32. "Die falsche Strategie des Westens," *Rheinischer Merkur*, 30 August 1968, "Was nützt ein Moskauer Gewaltverzicht? Die Bundesregierung muss ihre Aussenpolitik scharf überprüfen," *Die Welt*, 23 August 1968.
33. Sauerland, "Polen und Juden," 63.
34. Stomma, *Pościg zą nadzieją*, 141.
35. Ibid., 144.
36. Kosicki, "*Caritas* across the Iron Curtain," 233.
37. Kisielewski, *Dzienniki*, 243; Friszke, "Jerzy Zawieyski," 50.
38. "Czy zmieni się dotychczasowy układ sił? Dziś wybory w NRF," *Życie Warszawy*, 28/29 September 1969, "Wyniki wyborów w NRF. CDU/CSU ciągle najsilniejszą partią: Umiarkowy sukces SPD. Brandt ubiega się o urząd kanclerza," *Życie Warszawy*, 30 September 1969.
39. Garton Ash, *In Europe's Name*, 127.
40. Tomala, *Deutschland—von Polen gesehen*, 284.
41. The implications of a Soviet–German agreement above the heads of the Poles is treated, for example, in Bartoszewski, *Und reiss uns den Hass aus der Seele*, 106.
42. The article was translated by Anna Morawska, a journalist and *Znak* associate, and published in *Tygodnik Powszechny*. "Poseł Stomma w NRF," *Tygodnik Powszechny (wywiad)*, 20 November 1969.
43. Kisielewski, *Dzienniki*, 296.
44. J. Pawliczek, letter from the Bensberger Kreis to Jerzy Turowicz, Freiburg, 2 April 1968, correspondences, AJT.
45. Winfried Lipscher, "Report Polen-Reise," 20 May 1969, FE Erb, Bensberger Kreis, FES.
46. Gottfried Erb, "Anregungen für ein zweites Polenmemorandum des Bensberger Kreises," 27 May 1969, FE Erb, Bensberger Kreis, FES.
47. Gunthar Lehner, draft of the second Poland memorandum, 12 June 1969, FE Erb, FES, 3.
48. Karlheinz Koppe, interview with author, 23 February 2005. See also description by Seidler, "Das Polen-Memorandum des Bensberger Kreises," 109–10.
49. Koppe, *Dreimal getauft*, 171.
50. Stanisław Stomma, "'Bensberger Kreis' w Polsce," *Tygodnik Powszechny*, 26 April 1970.
51. Ibid.
52. In works such as Siri Gloppen, Elin Skaar, and Astrid Suhrke's volume, *Roads to Reconciliation* (Lanham, 2005), the definition of reconciliation emphasizes societal developments, the anthropological notion of "rituals of healing," while the actions and roads to reconciliation require a functioning state. Meanwhile, several of the states discussed in the volume, such as Bosnia Herzegovina, were or are fragile creations (pages 4–10).
53. Stehle, "Seit 1960," 165.
54. Ibid.
55. Stefan Wyszyński, "Schreiben des Kardinals Wyszyński an Kardinal Döpfner, Rom, 5.November 1970 und Antowrtbreif des Kardinals Döpfner an Kardinal Wyszyński, München, 14. Dezember 1970," in Jacobsen and Tomala, *Bonn-Warschau*, 209–13.
56. Julius Döpfner, letter to Stefan Wyszyński, 14 December 1970, in Stehle, "Seit 1960," 169–71.
57. Ibid., 172.
58. Tomala, *Deutschland—von Polen gesehen*, 304.
59. Garton Ash, *In Europe's Name*, 438; Bingen, *Polen-Politik der Bonner Republik*, 140–46.

60. "Heute Unterzeichnung des deutsch-polnischen Vertrags," *FAZ*, 7 December 1970.
61. Willy Brandt, *Erinnerungen* (Frankfurt/Main, 1989), 237.
62. Stanisław Stomma, "Zob. Von Bismarck Klaus: O układzie Polska-NRF—(Wywiad dla T.P.)," *Tygodnik Powszechny* 51–52 (1143–44), 13 December 1970.
63. "Der Kanzler unterschreibt mit schweren Hand," *Süddeutsche Zeitung*, 8 December 1970.
64. Brandt, *Erinnerungen*, 214.
65. See, for example, Elazar Barkan and Alexander Karn, *Taking Wrongs Seriously: Apologies and Reconciliation* (Stanford, CA, 2006).
66. Tomas Wolffsohn and Michael Brechenmacher, *Denkmalssturz? Brandts Kniefall* (Munich, 2005), 26.
67. Davies, *God's Playground*, 2:444.
68. See discussion of Polish–German reconciliation as a hybrid case in Long and Breckle, *War and Reconciliation*, 99. The authors do not doubt that the gesture can be used in their model of publically signaling forgiveness. However, both Christoph Schneider, *Der Warschauer Kniefall* (Konstanz, 2006), and Wolffsohn and Brechenmacher indicated the complications involved in interpreting the kneefall in this way. Schneider points to the fact that the gesture found more response nationally in the West German and German public realm than anywhere else, and Wolffsohn and Brechenmacher developed the complexity that stemmed from the Jewish element involved in the gesture through the ghetto monument.
69. Hansjakob Stehle, "Schlusspunkt unter die Vergangenheit: In Warschau wurde ein neues Kapitel aufgeschlagen," *Die Zeit*, 11 December 1970.
70. "Noch ein Ersatz-Frieden: Auch der Polenpakt braucht Zweidrittelmehrheit," *Rhenischer Merkur*, 11 December 1970.
71. Stomma, "Zob. von Bismarck Klaus."
72. Ibid.
73. Stomma, *Pościg za nadzieją*, 201.
74. Hansjakob Stehle, "Polen hinter Oder und Nesse," 7 March 1970, HA-WDR 2565.
75. Ibid. Eagle Glassheim argues in an article that the phenomena of ethnic cleansing, communist social engineering, and late industrial modernity were closely related to each other in the project of high modernity in the Central European borderlands. Stehle might have agreed with this except that he would have argued for the positive improvements of the territory through high modernism rather than the environmental devastation, which is Glassheim's point. "Ethnic Cleansing, Communism, and Environmental Devastation in Czechoslovakia's Borderlands, 1945–1989," *Journal of Modern History* 78, no. 1 (March 2006): 65–92.
76. "Weichsel—Kirschen und Loorbeer: Polens Jubiläum zwischen Ost und West," WDR/ARD January 21, 1971, Deutsche Kinemathek, Berlin.
77. Ibid.
78. The full name of the theater is Teatr Żydowski im. Estery Rachel i Idy Kamińskich w Warszawie. For more information, see Joanna Nalewajko-Kulikov and Magdalena Ruta, "Yiddish Culture in Poland after the Holocaust," in *Jewish Presence in Absence: The Aftermath of the Holocaust in Poland 1944–2010*, ed. Feliks Tych and Monika Adamczyk-Garbowska (Jerusalem, 2014), 353–394. Krystyna Gucewicz, *Symon Szurmiej* (Warsaw, 2007). Symon Szurmiej was the director of the theater 1970 to 2014.
79. Ludwig Zimmerer, "Das Abenteuer der Öffnung nach Westen," WDR, 3 Program, 19 January 1971, HA-WDR 4715.
80. Garton Ash, *In Europe's Name*, 279.
81. Hansjakob Stehle, *Nachbarn im Osten: Herausforderung zu einer neuen Politik* (Frankfurt, 1971), 12.

82. Stehle, *Nachbarn im Osten*, 48.
83. Ibid., 277.
84. Witold Zadrowski (Polish manuscript), Peter Leonhard Braun (German manuscript), "Mit polnischen Augen," NDR, H1572.
85. Ludwig Zimmerer, Angela Nacken, Ulrich Gembardt, and Hans Zielinski, "Diskussion über die Sendung: Mit polnischen Augen," coproduction SFB, NDR, WDR, SDR, Radio Polskie, 3 January 1971, NDR H001572.
86. Ryszard Wojna, "Kommentar von Ryszard Wojna, Chefredakeur einer polnischen Tageszeitung," 3 January 1971, NDR, H1572. Ryszard Wojna (1920–2003), studied in Cracow and France and became a journalist for *Życie Warszawy* and a correspondent to the Federal Republic.
87. Historians dispute this rosy picture of friendly Polish–East German relations. See Tomala, *Deutschland—von Polen gesehen*, 140–98, as well as Anderson, *Cold War in the Soviet Bloc*, 61.
88. Zimmerer et al., "Diskussion über die Sendung."
89. For discussions of the 1972 elections, see Bernd Faulenbach, *Willy Brandt* (Munich, 2013); Rainer Barzel, *Ein gewagtes Leben: Erinnerungen* (Stuttgart, Leipzig, 2001); Czaja, *Unterwegs zum kleinsten Deutschland*, 345–54.
90. Ludwig Zimmerer et al., "Bundestagswahl 1972; Königin Elizabeth; Silberhochzeit; Paris, London; Rom; Warschau; Ostberlin; Den Haag; Washington; Stockholm; BRD," 20 November 1972, NDR F804320.
91. Ludwig Zimmerer, "Alte und neue Heimat: Die Aussiedlung der Deutschen und ihre Probleme aus polnischer Sicht," 30 December 1972, NDR F803134.
92. Adam Michnik, "On Détente: An Interview with Adam Michnik," In *The New Detente: Rethinking East–West Relations*, ed. Mary Kaldor, Gerard Holden, Richard A. Falk (New York, 1989), 119.
93. Anna Morawska, "Die BRD: Bestandsaufnahme von Eindrucken," *Frankfurter Hefte* 9 (September 1969): 631–36
94. Anna Morawska, "Den polnisch-deutschen Beziehungen," *Frankfurter Hefte* 4 (1970): 153.
95. Colleen Murphy, in *A Moral Theory of Political Reconciliation* and drawing on reconciliation as part of transitional justice after civil conflict and violations of human rights, considers whether reconciliation must by necessity precede successful democratization; Murphy, *Moral Theory*, 9. However, here the idea was for reconciliation, as a religious development, to precede and perhaps in the best case scenario contribute to successful democratization.

Chapter 7

REMEMBERING AND REWRITING RECONCILIATION
The 1990s

In the early 1990s, the movement toward Polish–German reconciliation gained new currency in the politics of both countries following the fall of communism and the signing of the final peace treaty.[1] In fact, the word "reconciliation" (*Aussöhnung, pojednanie*) was used so frequently in the media, politics, and official circles that journalist Klaus Bachmann coined the concept of "reconciliation kitsch" to denote the apparent lack of substance behind the utterance of the word in public space.[2] Although politicians, media, and public speakers regularly repeated the word, there was no clear consensus on who the participants were or what the chronology was for Polish–German reconciliation. However, at this point the politics surrounding reconciliation had become a joint intellectual project that aimed to reinforce an emerging postcommunist European status quo by generating the appearance, if not the reality, of unity and common ground. The historicization of this carefully negotiated project was illustrated through a number of volumes, eyewitness descriptions, and personal statements about reconciliation from the 1990s to the 2000s.[3] Most salient to studies of memory and forgetting is the fact that for a "European" political consensus to emerge between Poles and Germans, certain aspects of Polish–German history had to be emphasized, and others downplayed. Yet other aspects made a reappearance in the early 1990s. In addition, in the early 1990s, the Europeanization or regionalization of memories competed with the dynamics of the nationalization of memories during the earlier postwar era.[4]

Notes for this chapter begin on page 196.

Background

After the 1970s, Poland and the Federal Republic maintained official diplomatic relations with one another despite the fact that the border question was not fully regulated. The existence of official channels of relations meant that the importance of nonstate actors diminished somewhat as did the need for media's intervention. At the same time, the nonstate actors multiplied and expanded their efforts to build cultural contacts across borders, now aided by state support. In West Germany, the Maximilian-Kolbe-Werk, a humanitarian support group for concentration camp survivors, was founded in the early 1970s as well as the Anna Morawska seminar, named for Anna Morawska who died quite early and unexpectedly in 1972.[5] In 1972, the German-Polish Textbook Commission was also established, in which historians from both countries participated and reviewed school materials covering the mutual past to make recommendations about appropriate changes.[6]

Hansjakob Stehle had become Westdeutscher Rundfunk's (WDR) correspondent to Rome in 1970. He continued to follow the developments of the Catholic Church in Eastern Europe closely and published a well-received book, *Die Ostpolitik des Vatikans, 1917–1975*, also translated into English a few years later after Cardinal Karol Wojtyła had become Pope John Paul II.[7] Between 1964 and 1971, Winfried Lipscher studied theology with Cardinal Joseph Ratzinger, the future Pope Benedict XVI and a signer of the Bensberger Memorandum, but never worked in a religious office. Instead, he became an interpreter for the German consulate in Warsaw from 1971 to 2003.[8] He also translated Polish literary works and biographies into German. Karlheinz Koppe left West Germany again, spending 1970–71 in Singapore, building up the Asian Media and Information Centre there.[9] Later, he returned to the Federal Republic to be the leader of the Deutsche Gesellschaft fur Friedens- und Konfliktforschung, later Arbeitsstelle Friedensforschung Bonn, until 2007. Klaus von Bismarck remained the general director of WDR until 1976. He became president of the Goethe-Institut in Munich in 1977 and remained there until 1989. Under his leadership, the institute opened branches in Cracow and Warsaw. Angela Nacken died in the 1980s, and Renate Marsch-Potocka remained in Poland, working as a correspondent. In 1974, Willy Brandt had to resign as chancellor in the wake of a scandal, as one of his close associates, Günter Guillaume was exposed as an East German agent. The Social Democratic Party's (SPD) Helmut Schmidt replaced Brandt and ruled until 1982, when Helmut Kohl became chancellor and West Germany was once more governed by the Christian Democratic Union (CDU). Schmidt continued to adhere by the political agreements from 1970 with regards to Eastern Europe.

Jürgen Neven-du Mont died early as well, in 1979 in Munich. Ill and knowing he had limited time left, he wrote his own eulogy. Trying to take stock of his accomplishments, he mentioned his own contributions to French–German and Polish–German reconciliation as his life's most important work. "I went as the first TV producer to Poland, made six films, and I believe I was able to contribute a little bit to off-set the old stereotypes."[10] He wrote that he believed that Polish–German reconciliation was left incomplete in part due to the Polish government's dependence on the Soviet Union and in part because it was very difficult to get past the crimes the Germans committed during the Holocaust. He spoke of his time as a soldier on the eastern front when Germany invaded Poland and added, "I have never gotten over what we did there."

In Poland, Edward Gierek ruled until 1980. As stated before, the Znak Circle had mostly played out its role in domestic politics, but Stanisław Stomma continued to represent the Catholic groups in the Sejm into the 1970s. Polish opposition to the communist rulers continued to grow throughout the 1970s, partially due to the economic failures that caused the party to raise food prices in 1970, 1976, and 1980.[11] These raises caused riots that were brutally suppressed by the state. In 1976, members of the Polish intelligentsia founded the Workers' Defense Committee (KOR), which tried to support those arrested with legal, financial, and medical help.[12] Stomma became noted in 1976 for an act of civil courage as the only Sejm member refusing to vote for a change to the constitution, language in which the leading position of the PZPR, the communist party, was confirmed as well as the close cooperation and friendship with the Soviet Union. He was consequently excluded from the Sejm.[13]

In 1978, Cracow's archbishop Cardinal Karol Wojtyła became the first non-Italian pope since 1523, John Paul II. Pope John Paul's legacy was ambivalent. His rule was staunchly culturally conservative, and he centralized power within the church to his own office. However, he was also one of the most well-traveled world leaders in the twentieth century, visiting 129 countries during his pontificate, and a supporter of ecumenical dialogue. He followed the model set by peace efforts in the 1960s and 1970s in that he issued more official apologies on behalf of the Catholic Church for past injustices than any other pope preceding him.[14] The pontiff's first official visit to Poland, where thousands came to see him, was a testimony to the size and power of the church compared to the communist regime.[15]

The Solidarity movement emerged in the summer of 1980. It was the result of another attempt at a compromise between the Polish state and workers on strike protesting steep price increases in multiple cities, including Warsaw and Gdańsk. The agreement was struck at the end of August 1980 and signed by Lech Wałęsa. By the next spring, Solidarity had seven to eight million members. Former Znak member Tadeusz Mazowiecki was an advisor to Solidarity and the editor of its first weekly newspaper.[16] Also Władysław Bartoszewski became active in the union. On 13 December 1981, General Wojciech Jaruzelski, the Polish prime minister, appeared on television and radio to inform the population that he had discontinued Solidarity and declared martial law. Large parts of the Solidarity leadership and many members, including Mazowiecki and Bartoszewski, were imprisoned.

The martial law and 1981 developments exposed the downsides of the SPD and the German establishment's dedication to the status quo and Polish communist leadership more clearly than the events in 1968 had done. *Zeit* editor Marion Dönhoff in August 1980 refused to support Solidarity given the risk of alienating the Soviet Union. In general, West German official visitors to Poland in these years were not prepared to meet with the leaders of Solidarity and risk their official cooperation partners.[17] Gottfried Erb described on the other hand how a group from the larger Bensberger Circle, the Dortmund group responsible for meetings with Polish partners, actively participated the 1980s package action from West Germany in support of the Solidarity members who were no longer able to work or support their families.[18]

At the outset of the Kohl era in the Federal Republic, Polish politicians and observers were anxious about Helmut Kohl's stance on Ostpolitik and its implications for the Polish–German relationship. However, Kohl continued the political program of the 1970s.[19] In 1981, Ludwig Zimmerer, who was still working for West German radio as its Warsaw correspondent, had a stroke. After this, he was unable to work but survived another six years, nursed by his second wife, Joanna Olczak, until he passed away in 1987. Zimmerer's folk art collection has been the subject of speculations and division. He had wanted it to become a museum, but nothing came of it, and it remained in the house on Dąbrowiecka 28, reminders of a man who once fell in love with Poland.[20] Eugen Kogon held a chair at the Technical University in Darmstadt. He retired in 1968 but continued as editor for *Frankfurter Hefte*. He retired to Königstein in Taunus and died in 1987. Walter Dirks continued as editor in chief for *Frankfurter Hefte* and was also engaged in the leadership of the Catholic peace organization Pax Christi. He died in 1991 in Wittnau bei Freiburg im Breisgau.

Despite the communists' and Jaruzelski's efforts, Solidarity continued to exist throughout the 1980s and was at the forefront of the democratic movement as communism ended in 1989. Several members of the one-time Znak Circle now became members of Poland's first democratic government and parliament. Tadeusz Mazowiecki became Poland's first democratically elected prime minister and was a member of the parliament, representing the moderate Christian Democratic wing of politics until 2001. He died in Warsaw in October 2013.[21] Stanisław Stomma participated in the Round Table negotiations in 1989 and became a member of the first democratic senate.[22] Władysław Bartoszewski became Poland's consul to Vienna from 1990 to 1995 and its foreign minister in 1995. In the early 1990s, as Poland began negotiations for entrance into the European Union and NATO, the Cold War nonstate actors moved to the center of the new political scene. Poland would join NATO in 1999 and the EU by 2003. The great focus on Polish–German reconciliation in the early to mid-1990s was contextualized on the one hand by the optimism that followed the fall of communism and on the other by the effort to become incorporated in these military and economic alliances.[23]

In understanding the 1990s discussions of reconciliation, studies of collective memory become central. They were also central to politics at the time because of their ability to define national boundaries or boundaries between political groups.[24] The two Germanys and Poland had been redefined geographically, demographically, and politically as new states, and ideological systems replaced the earlier ones in 1945 and 1950, and once more after 1989.[25] As a consequence, the memory of the past became hard political and intellectual currency for those concerned with European integration as well as national recovery. This interest in the past was followed by an upsurge of scholarship on national and European memory.[26] In the national upheaval and memory transitions after 1989, the contributors to these volumes on early reconciliation efforts attempted to protect the story of gradual progress in Polish–German relations during the Cold War era as a context to the plans for the EU expansion, their "reinvented nations" as well as to explain their own roles within them through publishing their memories and memoirs.

European Integration and Christian Foundations

The participants in the reconciliation efforts and the subsequent contributors to commemorative volumes preserved the model of reconciliation while reinserting some of their personal histories into their 1990s narratives. In the 1990s, particularly within the context of reconciliation and dialogue, they wished to be good Europeans, constructing a narrative in which Polish–German relations were an early key development in European integration and where the postwar requirement of absolute national loyalties had become loosened. To be sure, their personal experiences as expellees, bilingual activists, or borderlands populations fit awkwardly with the homogeneous nation-state models of the World Wars and the Cold War but better with European integration.

At the heart of the 1990s agendas of reconciliation and of these volumes was still the editors' and contributors' ambition to resolve past antagonistic nationalist constructions by finding common denominators such as the idea of a common European civilization and a Christian heritage.[27] This search for a European memory also intended to support the search for a "community of interests" between Poland, Germany, and, to some extent, France, with the aim of supporting democratic Poland's entrance into NATO and the European Union.[28] Since most of the Polish activists were public intellectuals and journalists in the semi-independent Catholic press, their search for common denominators focused on the shared religious heritage.

However, in their identities as religious activists, universalizing factors such as the necessity for dialogue and forgiveness was sometimes contradicted by the longstanding notion of the Polish Catholic Church as the true soul of the nation. The reconciliation-minded Polish Catholics, the German Protestant Church, and the East German Sühnezeichen became important reconciliatory symbols in Polish–East German relations, and their members became spokesmen for reconciliation in the 1990s. More importantly, the documents that the reconciliation volumes held forth as decisive moments of change in the 1960s, such as the memoranda and the bishops' correspondence, were Christian documents.

Contributors and politicians narrating Polish–German relations emphasized that the religious beginnings of the cross-border dialogue as a unifying factor had begun at a time when the nation-states were still at odds with each other. Rita Süssmuth, president of the German Bundestag, wrote in her introduction to *Feinde werden Freunde: Von den Schwierigkeiten der deutsch-polnischen Nachbarschaft* (Enemies become Friends: About the Difficulties of the German–Polish Coexistence): "Our road to understanding and partnership began in Poland. It was the Polish bishops who first helped to build new bridges between Germans and Poles, and whose hands, stretched out in reconciliation, the German side gratefully grasped."[29] Friedbert Pflüger, CDU politician and editor of *Feinde werden Freunde*, also emphasized that whereas the political relations between the Federal Republic and Poland were frosty for twenty years after the war, "German and Polish theologians began already in the early 1960s to call for reconciliation with great response."[30] The notion of the religious beginnings of the dialogue challenged those commentators who argued that the Cold War and communist oppression made Polish–German relations impossible in the 1960s.[31] Separated from state politics, these religious origins seemed to represent the Polish and German nations' desires for overcoming the divisive past and uniting in a common European realm.

Religious activists in the three societies considered religion and personal meetings as ways to overcome political tensions and divisions in the Cold War relations. Günter and Brigitte Särchen, East German religious activists in Aktion Sühnezeichen wrote,

> whoever believes that reconciliation is a theological problem, belonging to the inner sphere of the church and that as a political act it is unusable or exclusively belonging to church and state dominions, should turn to the address "Mietek Pszon, Cracow." Thinking and acting between political categories of citizen or practicing Catholic, Mieczysław Pszon is a living example that reconciliation, defined as relations between people, is a source of joy, a contagious and healing effect carried from group to group.[32]

In terms of East German relations, this religious aspect was particularly important in light of the "forced friendship" and state restrictions on Polish–East German relations. After 1990, these East German activists could also show that they as representatives for the East German population were not completely bound by the totalitarian regime and that political change happened on a grassroots level. The same was true to an even higher extent for the Polish attitude toward religious activism in the relations. The Polish Catholic Church held enormous prestige in postcommunist Poland, and many Catholics considered it the true representative of the Polish nation-state and bulwark against communism.[33] By focusing on religious relations, the activists indirectly claimed that the Polish spiritual nation, as represented by the church and not the communist state, had wanted a change in Polish–German relations.

Polish as well as German contributions focusing on the Polish–German Catholic bishops' correspondence tended to give the impression that the reception of the documents was overwhelmingly positive. Catholic groups that had initially been hesitant were in favor of the project in hindsight. For example, Bartoszewski, Stomma, and Mazowiecki as well as Bensberger Circle member Winfried Lipscher had described the Central Committee of Catholics in the Federal Republic as passive and unwilling to engage in dialogue during the 1960s. However, in the 1996 volume, a representative of the Central Committee of Catholics who became a liaison between the Polish and German Catholic Churches recounted the committee's longstanding commitment to the "road of reconciliation."[34]

Also, Stomma downplayed his initial opposition to the 1965 Letter of Reconciliation. He had originally been unhappy with the Polish Catholic bishops' correspondence because he felt that the bishops should have consulted the Znak groups and because he thought it was politically ill advised. He had refused to make a statement in its support in the Sejm in 1965 and 1966.[35] During the 1980s, Stomma gradually revised his position in favor of the bishops' initiative. In 1989, he wrote that though the episcopate's letter created a crisis in Poland and was not politically thought through, it was still a brave and important initiative.[36] In an interview with Basil Kerski, Tomasz Kycia, and Robert Żurek in 2006, Stomma praised the Polish bishops' initiative as "an act of great courage." He continued:

> The words "we ask for forgiveness" had a moral meaning of almost heroic consequences and went far beyond the general consciousness of the Polish people. It even awoke their opposition. The consequences of this appellation show the heroism of this step forward. As you know, the "German letter" of the Episcopate in Poland called forth a deep political and societal crisis.[37]

In the interview, he mentioned his disappointment at the German bishops' cautious answer but claimed to be sympathetic to their reasoning and convinced of their good will. By omitting his own hesitance about the Polish letter, he attached himself to the exchange at a time when it was celebrated and drew on the status of the Catholic Church in Poland to create an impression that Polish–German reconciliation was a broader unified movement among the Polish Catholics and that its success was immediate in the 1960s.

In the later volumes on Polish–German relations, the religious and media actors frequently stressed their support for good relations with the Polish Catholic Church and downplayed their efforts to find common ground with the communist state. The members of the Bensberger Circle emphasized their good relations with Cardinal Wyszyński. They mentioned the meeting with the PAX group in Warsaw during the trip in 1969 and the resulting canceled audience with the cardinal, but they ascribed it to being taken by surprise, not to their understanding at the time of the communist state as a necessary partner in successful relations.[38]

In the early 1990s, in the midst of the EU negotiations, the contributions emphasized to a much higher extent the idea of a unifying European realm as a key aspect of reconciliation. They spoke of the way in which the Polish–German initiatives and dialogue had overcome national divisions. Władysław Bartoszewski in 1996 outlined his understanding of European civilization and culture as a cultural, not a geographic, concept, which involved the freedom of the individual, human rights, Judeo-Christian traditions, and a high cultural legacy.[39] European civilization here represented openness, rule of law, and liberal values, which brought Poles and Germans together. In the Polish activists' descriptions, the economic asymmetry of the early relations did not feature very prominently. Poland as a nation was equal to France and Germany in that it was a prominent carrier and protector of European culture.

In postcommunist Europe, these contributions imagined Poland, France, and Germany as playing key roles in European integration, located as they were on a "European main axis."[40] In a postcommunist world, the contributors felt that this threesome would merge in an even closer political cooperation through the "Weimar Triangle," a loose association of the three countries' heads of state, foreign ministers, and ministers of national defense meeting occasionally between 1993 and 2007.[41] The thought that Polish–German reconciliation was a key aspect of European East–West integration also mixed easily with the Polish notion from the 1830s of the Polish nation's mission to act "for your freedom and ours."[42] Tadeusz Mazowiecki commented in 1993,

> Here the European dimension of Polish–German relations becomes highlighted. Both countries lie in the middle of the continent. On the road to European unity, the quality of these relations gains increasing importance. . . . The striving for reconciliation and understanding between the Polish and the German people, in itself a valuable aim, must be accompanied by a feeling of responsibility and duty toward the other peoples of Europe.[43]

Poland as a key to European integration harmonized well with older Polish national concepts and also heightened Poland's sense of its significance to a future Europe.

Meanwhile, the German contributors emphasized the European aspect of Polish–German relations as well. Richard von Weizsäcker, CDU politician and Protestant Church member involved in the Protestant initiatives, also president of the Federal Republic from 1984 to 1994, stated in a speech in Poland that "European history and culture connect us with one another."[44] At the same time, the German media and politicians remained somewhat less prone to see the relationship as absolutely equal or Poland as a major partner in Europe. Germany was still economically stronger than Poland, and it was already a member of the European Union. Consequently, the Germans saw the Weimar Triangle as a patronage as much as a partnership to "pave the Polish road to the European Union, to a common European fatherland, *Heimat* Europe."[45] To Polish intellectuals such as Bartoszewski, this mindset was disappointing. He commented about Polish–German relations during the Cold War that "on the German side, we were in reality not perceived as partners to be taken seriously in contrast to the French or the small west European peoples. Unfortunately, this is still the case today."[46] Even within the unifying European framework, the ambitions for a European common space came into conflict with national consciousness that focused on the role of democratic Poland in the "new" Europe.

The 1990s allowed these groups to reintroduce more complex ethnic maps and belongings compared to the Cold War era. During the Cold War, they had been politically engaged in the reconstruction of the postwar nations within the borders determined at the Potsdam Conference in 1945. They remained deeply concerned with the strength, reputation, and territorial integrity of their own postwar nations. For the sake of peace and stability, they had also been committed to the status quo, which expulsions, population transfers, border moves, and absolute ethnic nationalist frameworks had enforced in Central Europe. A majority of the German participants had been active in the Federal Republic's political and foreign political discourses. In the 1960s, those West Germans interested in Polish–German dialogue leaned toward left-wing politics and the Social Democrats. These conversation partners included members of the Bensberger Circle, journalists working for radio, television, and elite media such as *Die Zeit* and *Frankfurter Allgemeine Zeitung*.[47] A few Social Democratic politicians also contributed to the volumes, including Carlo Schmid and Willy Brandt. Later, in the 1990s, CDU politicians also participated in the efforts. The editor of the volume *Feinde werden Freunde*, Winfried Pflüger, was a Christian Democratic politician, and other contributors, including Richard von Weizsäcker and expellee politician Rainer Barzel, were Christian Democrats. One of the volumes also included Mieczysław Rakowski, the former communist editor in chief of a leading autonomous political weekly and later prime minister and first secretary of the Polish communist party, as a representative of the moderate communists who had been involved with the early relations.[48]

Despite ambitions to overcome national antagonisms, the reconciliation memories in the 1990s and 2000s volumes continued to reflect the legacy of the nation-state building during the first half of the century. Polish–German relations during the Cold War were frequently geared toward arriving at an acceptance of the existing geographic and demographic status quo, a project that fit awkwardly with the recent violent demographic and geographic changes and with the displacement of large populations of not just Poles and Germans but also of Poles, Ukrainians, Belarusians, and Jews.

In their writings from the 1950s, neither Koppe nor Skibowski identified as expellees or made any mention of their prewar connections to Poland. However, in the memoirs he published half a century later, Koppe described seeing the ruins of Wrocław and being unable to find his old house. He wrote, "I cried; not because I had lost my *Heimat* but simply because I was overcome by the memory. I had to think about the many people who had become victims of a senseless war and senseless violence and were still suffering from it today."[49] He added that the trip sensitized him to the necessity of recognizing the Oder-Neisse Line "as a precondition for a free existence of Poland." Thus, Koppe reinserted his own past into the narrative, using it as a motivating factor in his pacifism and activism for Polish–German relations and European integration. The difference between the narrative he presented in 2004 and the one he published in 1957 suggest the ways in which it later became possible to integrate private and public narratives and memories.

Another example of the difficulties to incorporate the presence of multiple groups and perspectives into the narrative of Polish–German dialogue and reconciliation was the memories of the activities of Aktion Sühnezeichen.[50] The Polish and East German writers described Sühnezeichen's activities as directed primarily toward the Polish nation, although the spaces for its activities, the concentration camps, were also Jewish memorial spaces.[51] Sühnezeichen member Konrad Weiss described the group's mission in traveling to Poland and working in the concentration camps: "Unlike normal German tourists, we wanted to perceive of this journey as a sign of atonement, as asking for forgiveness."[52] Their travel days included five daily hours of silence and prayer, and of course the work on the memorial sites. The group's extended times of silence and prayer gave the participants freedom to dedicate their efforts toward any victims who died at Auschwitz or Majdanek. In constructing their memories to fit with Polish–German relations agendas, the German participants and the Polish recipients of the group struggled to balance out their attention to history of the Jewish and the Polish victims in this space.[53] The work of Sühnezeichen was remembered as a concern between the Polish and German religious activists. Interestingly, the inclusion of Aktion Sühnezeichen itself became important in memories of reconciliation in that the organization represented the East German spontaneous and grassroots participation in reconciliation and thereby the inclusion of the former German Democratic Republic (GDR) into postcommunist cultural European integration.

One reason for the omission of ethnic groups other than Poles and Germans was the close connection between these volumes and political perspectives of state building. In a realm of state politics, the borderlands could not be multicultural or have fluid borders but had to belong to one or the other state or people. In discussing the Polish–German borderlands, Prime Minister Mazowiecki stated about the territories' national belonging that "at some point, they became Polish."[54] This statement was perfectly true from a foreign relations perspective. In politics, national gray zones, mixed borderlands, or autochthones would have complicated or even endangered the carefully established consensus on the mutual past of Poland and Germany. Authors and literary critics could reject national belonging or embrace the fluid character of the borderlands; political representatives, on the other hand, needed stability, firm borders, and firm national belongings.[55]

On the Polish side, the Polish–German narrative during the Cold War was circumscribed by communist censorship, whose legacy of interference continued to shape the memories into the 1990s. Because of state interference, Polish participants had been unable to discuss Soviet responsibility for the lost eastern borderlands before 1989.[56] In certain cases, the memories were also influenced by undigested conflicts over Vilnius and Galicia, and with the Jewish minorities in Poland.[57] On the German side, sensitivity to the needs of their Polish conversation partners to avoid controversial or censored topics helped shape the memories. In addition, similarly to the Polish case, hard political realities and possibilities to stabilize, or normalize, the postwar relations determined the agendas of the German memory politics. Political leaders used a certain acceptable formula of Polish–German relations in their official statements and presentations during the Cold War, which survived into the late 1990s and early 2000s. Thus Willy Brandt, remembering the relations, made no mention of the Polish eastern borderlands and omitted potential inclusions of Lithuanians, Ukrainians, and Belarussians in his decisions connected to the 1970 agreement.[58]

The absence after 1945 of larger numbers of ethnic minorities within the Polish borders did surface in other forms of memories of postwar Polish–German relations. Reinhold Lehmann wrote about Mieczysław Pszon: "Mietek showed us his country. He knew different dishes, not just Polish but also Jewish or Lithuanian, for example those small pierogies floating in soup."[59] Before 1945, Jews and Lithuanians had been present in the cityscapes of Poland and the borderlands, but they were absent by the late 1960s and 1970s, and only occasional traces of their cultures and impact on society remained.

The contributors to these volumes had individual memories involving a time when Poland was a multicultural space, however, and by the 1980s and 1990s they developed ways to acknowledge that reality without endangering the status quo of official relations. Władysław Bartoszewski and Jerzy Turowicz became deeply engaged in Polish–Jewish relations from early on. Perhaps reflecting Jerzy Turowicz's individual engagement with the Polish–Jewish relations in the 1980s, the *Denkschrift* to Polish–German activist and long-term *Tygodnik Powszechny* writer Mieczysław Pszon in 1996 by the Znak Publishing House remarked on the centrality of Central Europe's Jewish past to Polish–German mutual history. The volume also approached the difficult aspects of the Polish historical relationship with the Jews. Jerzy Turowicz stated in the volume's foreword that "in this biography, it is worth emphasizing yet another facet [of Pszon's life]: his relationship with the Jews. In his youth, as an activist in Młodzież Wszechpolska (*All-Polish Youth*) and Stronnictwo Narodowe (*the National Party*), he was undoubtedly in some sense an anti-Semite."[60] Turowicz continued to say that Pszon was later "fully cured" from the disease of anti-Semitism by the knowledge that it had led to the Holocaust and to the terrible fate of the Jews.[61]

Also, a number of the 1996 *Księga pamiątkowa* essays were dedicated to questions concerning Polish–German–Jewish relations, such as Stehle's text on the German literary critic Marcel Reich-Ranicki and Klaus Bachmann's discussion about memories of Auschwitz.[62] Nevertheless, these contributions did not merge Polish–German relations history with Polish–Jewish relations history or ease up the strict national categorizations in the memories. They recognized formally the minorities' role in history as parallel (yet separate) histories to that of Polish–German relations. The Jewish topics in the volume dedicated to Pszon or the 1993 *Feinde werden Freunde* were chronologically and spatially separated from rapprochement, reconciliation, and normalization.[63] By addressing the Jewish presence, the 1990s contributors addressed the Polish–German–Jewish needs for reconciliation while still excluding the eastern borderlands (Ukraine, Lithuania, Belarus).

In Stomma's memoirs, Polish–German relations were separated out from the history of Znak's position in 1968, as the Polish communist party completed an internal purge and an anti-Semitic media campaign that caused most of the remaining Jews in Poland to emigrate. Stomma described how the communist party attacked the Znak Circle during the course of the purge, accusing them of pro-Zionism, and how the purge also created internal conflicts in the circle.[64] In a separate description of reconciliation, he spoke of the 1968 Bensberger Memorandum and his West German visit in 1969 with no mention of the difficulties the Znak members experienced in Poland during this time.[65] The positive West German political developments and the German Catholic memorandum in 1968 could not be incorporated with the domestic crisis in Polish politics at the time. More importantly, however, the 1968 purge made no appearance in the descriptions by the Bensberger Circle's members of their interactions with Poland in the late 1960s, although the events impacted their planned activities and attempts at a dialogue with the Poles.[66]

The 1970 agreement between the Federal Republic and the People's Republic of Poland confirmed the inviolability of the Polish existing borders. From a political perspective, the agreement made Ukrainians and Lithuanians potential participants in Polish–German relations as well, particularly given the background of some Polish activists, such as Stanisław Stomma and Józefa Hennelowa.[67] However, the official narration of Polish–German relations also in this case separated out these memories. Again, in the 1996 volume dedicated to Pszon, Hennelowa wrote an article titled "Moja utracona ojczyzna" (My Lost Fatherland) about her native city of Vilnius, which was paralleled with expellee and Protestant creator of the Tübingen Memorandum Klaus von Bismarck's "Moja ziemia rodzinna, która teraz jest w Polsce" (My Family Lands That Are Now in Poland).[68] Meanwhile, discussions about the 1970 bilateral agreement omitted discussions of the border issues outside of the Oder-Neisse Line so as not to appear to challenge the existing borders. Only the occasional critical individual considered the 1970 agreement against the background of its recognition of the eastern as well as western Polish border.[69]

As in his description of the 1968 party purge and anti-Semitic campaign in Poland, Stomma separated his stance on his own background and relationship with Lithuania from his memories of Polish–German relations. As early as 1966, Stomma had stated that it was a political necessity for the Poles to leave their former homes in Lithuania.[70] In his memoirs, he described how he decided to leave Vilnius in 1944 when it became clear that it would soon become part of the Soviet sphere of influence, but he did not dwell on the experience or draw parallels to the German expellee experience or Polish–German relations. When asked about his relationship with the city in 2004, Stomma answered, "My heart pulls me there, but I understand that it is politically impossible. One has to live with the existing situation and without violence, it is not possible to change the situation. Today, Wilna has become the capital of Lithuania and we also want to have good relations with Lithuania."[71] While Polish–German official interactions and the formalized communicative memories of reconciliation required acceptance of the existing Polish–Lithuanian border in the spirit of overcoming past territorial conflicts, Stomma on an individual level still mourned his lost home. His personal experiences and individual memories could for the entire Cold War rarely be incorporated into his communicative and reconciliatory memory of Polish–German relations.

In an interesting contribution to *Feinde werden Freunde*, Stomma chose to write about a German Catholic priest in Vilnius during the First World War.[72] Father Muckermann was an army chaplain accompanying the German army on its eastern campaigns during the First World War. Muckermann became increasingly interested in Polish religious life, studied the language, interacted with the local people, and finally "went native." He left the German army and remained in Vilnius, greatly popular and cultivating connections to Poles, Germans, and Lithuanians alike. In Stomma's perspective, Muckermann encompassed the spirit and curiosity about "the Other" central to reconciliation. Through his example, Stomma could indirectly connect his intellectual and personal background to the Polish–German reconciliation narrative.

However, the story also illustrated the sharpening ethnic divides during the interwar era and the two World Wars as Muckermann, the great bridge builder between Vilnius's different ethnic groups, was imprisoned and later prevented from returning to the city. Disillusioned, Muckermann returned to Germany permanently, and his contacts with Poland during his later years were practically nonexistent.[73] In other words, while the moments of breakdown and chaos in war sometimes created transgressive experiences, individuals functioning across the borders were increasingly forced to choose exclusive national affiliations as order was restored in the interwar and early postwar eras. These pressures sharpened national divisions, and the wars created increased homogeneity in Central Europe. The memory volumes and contributing activists further reinforced the clear-cut national identities of lands and peoples even though the contributors privately showed regrets and longing for looser constellations and spaces.

The previous existence of two German states presented a challenge in the 1990s descriptions as well. Officially, the German Democratic Republic had merged with the Federal Republic into one reunited Germany. However, as several scholars have pointed out, the two Germanys did not have a united memory culture.[74] In the 1990s, it became clear how much East and West Germany had grown apart between 1945 and 1990. Did the East Germans then reconcile with the Poles in the 1950s and 1960s, in the 1970s, and through the Border and Friendship Treaties in the 1990s together with the West Germans?

The individual memories of relations with a broader layer of East German Catholics showed a troubled Cold War relationship, centered on the so-called "forced friendship."[75] In addition, the East Germans exerted pressure on the Polish leadership to minimize West German and Polish official interactions, as mentioned by SPD politician Carlo Schmid, who traveled to Poland in 1958.[76] Also, the West German partners in dialogue were cautious during the Cold War of direct interactions involving East Germans since such interactions could be constructed in the West German media sphere as an implicit recognition of the German Democratic Republic together with the Oder-Neisse Line.[77] Finally, the sense of competition between the two German states should not be underestimated in its shaping of Cold War Polish–German interactions or their later memories.

As part of the forced friendship, the Polish state requested that the Catholic intellectuals in the Catholic Intelligentsia Clubs and surrounding *Tygodnik Powszechny* maintain relations with regime-sanctioned Catholic groups in the GDR. Stomma commented, "We met with them [the regime-loyal Catholics from the GDR] in consideration of our government, to get passports for the Federal Republic, and they met with us to show the West Germans that these independent Catholics from Poland, who were socially acceptable in Bonn, did not shy away from contacts with them. The people from 'Aktion Sühnezeichen' were completely different."[78]

In the reconciliation volumes after 1989, Aktion Sühnezeichen was described as the true representative of East German reconciliation. The group's activities, unlike the forced friendship, were described as broader expressions of the East German population's wish to begin a dialogue with Poland. Mazowiecki wrote extensively on his relations with Aktion Sühnezeichen and particularly with Lothar Kreysig, the person behind the group. Similarly, Stomma remembered that when the 1970 agreement had been signed in Warsaw, he sent two congratulatory telegrams, one to Manfred Seidler in the Bensberger Circle and the other to Lothar Kreysig.[79] This symmetric celebration drew in East as well as West Germans into the first political success of Polish–German relations.

The memories after 1989 tended to universalize the West German reactions and experiences to include both East and West Germans. In his 1993 description of the Polish–German schoolbook commission, Władysław Markiewicz stated that the recommendations concerned "the character of the descriptions of Polish–German relations from the earliest times to the end of the Second World War as well as the relations between the Polish People's Republic and the Federal Republic of Germany in the consideration of the time period between 1945 and 1949, as the Federal Republic of Germany was an occupation zone of the three western powers."[80] The schoolbook commission's work was largely concerned with Polish–West German relations, and East Germans were not always part of reconstructing a mutually acceptable past. Though the contributions spoke about the divisions between East and West Germans during the Cold War, they also did not closely consider the specific challenges of Polish–East German relations after 1989 but quickly referred to Polish–German relations as a unified whole.[81] In the ambitions of an improving Polish–German relationship set within a European space, the East Germans' distinct relationships to Poland and the Poles faded from public statements very quickly.

Conclusion

The complex strategies that the contributors used in negotiating their own personal experiences, their ambitions to protect the status quo of postwar borders and demography and to find a consensus between Poles and

Germans in dialogue, included developing memories that emphasized a common "European" and Christian foundation to the relations. Implied also were the more secular ideals, such as values of civil society, and an independent press but not at the cost of stable borders and stable interstate relations. In the 1990s and 2000s, the activists narrated their early religiously framed efforts to initiate dialogue as an important contribution to European integration. They considered the common Christian heritage an important element in circumventing the divisive and difficult political climate during the Cold War and in finding ways to deal with change and loss. Despite their ambitions of establishing common ground after 1990, they were also committed to Cold War ambitions to rebuild and unify their respective nation-states after 1945, and to protect the postwar borders. These two projects coexisted uneasily in the memories.

Even more noticeable, their commitment to new national models conflicted with their personal and individual experiences as borderlands populations, expellees, and cross-border activists. The history of the borderlands was one of multiple ethnic relationships, conflicts and territorial issues. In their attempts to recognize the historical presence of multicultural populations and their own individual experiences, the contributors included separate and parallel narratives recognizing the presence and roles of ethnic minorities in the Polish–German mutual history. They made only very few attempts to create postwar narratives integrating multiple ethnic groups. Exceptions existed, indicating that additional space for alternative experiences and interpretations had opened by the 1990s.[82]

The relationship in these volumes between memory politics, individual memories, and cultural national memories raises an important point about the relationship between reconciliation and memory. Officially, the contributors arrived at a consensus on the Polish–German past as a religiously founded dialogue between ethnic Poles and ethnic Germans that led to European integration. However, the private memories of the contributors were profoundly shaped by the experiences of discontinuity, upheaval and displacement in East Central Europe. In the words of Richard von Weizsäcker, reconciliation is about taking the past seriously, but the Polish–German reconciliation memories were equally concerned with selecting certain memories and omitting others to fit with the overarching goals of consensus and protection of the status quo. In international relations theory of reconciliation, exercises of truth-telling should precede exercises of consensus-building. In the memories after 1989, Polish–German reconciliation shows that the problematic relationship between consensus-building and truth-telling in an actual historical situation of multiple societal and state upheavals is not so easily disentangled.

Notes

Parts of this chapter have been previously published in Annika Elisabet Frieberg, "Reconciliation Remembered: Early Activists and the Polish-German Relations," in *Re-Mapping Polish-German Memory: Physical, Political and Literary Spaces since World War II*, ed. Justyna Beinek and Piotr Kosicki (Bloomington, IN: Indiana University Press, 2011), 127–58. Republished with permission of Indiana University Press.

1. Dieter Bingen, "Einübung in erwachsene Partnerschaft: Die politischen Beziehungen zwischen Deutschland und Polen," in *Erwachsene Nachbarschaft: Die deutsch-polnische Beziehungen 1991 bis 2011*, ed. Dieter Bingen, Peter Oliver Loew, Krysztof Ruchniewicz, and Marek Zybura (Wiesbaden, 2011), 33.
2. Klaus Bachmann, "Versöhnungskitsch," *tageszeitung*, 5 August 1994. Clarifying his definition of the word and its later uses, Klaus Bachmann, "Versöhnungskitsch nach 10 Jahren—was davon übrig blieb," in Hahn, Hein-Kirchner, and Kochanowska-Nieborak, *Erinnerungskultur und Versöhnungskitsch*, 17–20.
3. Including Stomma, *Pościg za nadzieją*; Pailer, *Stanisław Stomma*; Władysław Bartoszewski, *Und reiss uns der Hass aus der Seele: Die schwierige Aussöhnung von Polen und Deutschen* (Warsaw, 2005); Marion Countess Dönhoff, *Polen und Deutsche: Die schwierige Aussöhnung* (Frankfurt/Main, 1991); contributions in Pięciak, *Polacy i Niemcy*; contributions in *Feinde werden Freunde*; contributions in *"Wir vergeben und bitten um Vergebung"*; Koppe, *Dreimal getauft*; Skibowski, *Wolken über weitem Land*.
4. Traba, "'Region,' 'Regionalismus,' 'Identität,' 'Identifikation,'" 33–42; see also Robert Traba, *Przeszłość w teraźniejszości: Polskie spory o historię na początku XXI wieku* (Poznań, 2009), 170–71.
5. "Chrześcijanka: Wspomnienie Anny Morawskiej," *Znak* 685 (2012): 61–63.
6. Katarzyna Stokłosa, *Polen und die deutsche Ostpolitik 1945–1990* (Göttingen, 2011), 375; see also He, *Search for Reconciliation*, 79–81.
7. Hansjakob Stehle, *Die Ostpolitik des Vatikans, 1917–1975* (Munich, Zurich, 1975). In English, *Eastern Politics of the Vatican, 1917–1979* (Athens, OH, 1979).
8. Lipscher, "Rückkehr in die Heimat," in Pflüger and Lipscher, *Feinde werden Freunde*, 429.
9. Koppe speaks about his continued engagement with pacifism and politics in his autobiography; Koppe, *Dreimal getauft*.
10. BAK NL 1279/200. Grabrede.
11. Stoklosa, *Polen und die deutsche Ostpolitik*, 443, 457.
12. Ibid., 445.
13. Jarocki, *czterdzieści pięć lat w opozycji*, 235.
14. Michael R. Marrus, "Papal Apologies of John Paul II," in *The Age of Apology: Facing Up to the Past*, ed. Mark Gibney et al. (Philadelphia, 2008), 259–70.
15. George Weigel, *The Final Revolution: The Resistance Church and the Collapse of Communism* (New York, 2012), 131.
16. Stokłosa, *Polen und die deutsche Ostpolitik*, 460–61.
17. Ibid., 467–68. See also Erb, "Verständigung mit Polen," 363.
18. Erb, "Verständigung mit Polen," 360.
19. Stokłosa, *Polen und die Deutsche Ostpolitik*, 490–91.
20. Hansjakob Stehle, "Ludwig Zimmerer +," *Die Zeit*, 2 October 1987.
21. "Tadeusz Mazowiecki nie żyje. Miał 86 lat. 'Uczył nas pokory w polityce,'" *Gazeta Wyborcza*, 28 October 2013.
22. *"Wir vergeben und bitten um Vergebung,"* 81.
23. For context to the "golden" 1990s, see Bingen, "Einübung in erwachsene Partnerschaft," 32–37.

24. See Kansteiner, *In Pursuit of German Memories*. Richard Ned Lebow, "The Memory of Politics in Post-war Europe," in *The Politics of Memory in Post-War Europe*, ed. Claudio Fogu, Wulf Kansteiner, and Richard Ned Lebow (Durham, NC, 2006), 1–39; Jan-Werner Müller, "Introduction: The Power of Memory, the Memory of Power and the Power over Memory," in *Memory and Power in Post-War Europe: Studies in the Presence of the Past*, ed. Jan-Werner Müller (Cambridge, MA, 2002), 1–38.
25. For the continuous redefinition of Germany and German history, see Konrad Jarausch and Michael Meyer, *Shattered Past: Reconstructing German Histories* (Princeton, NJ, 2003). For the postwar reconstruction of German national boundaries, see Jan-Werner Müller, *Another Country: German Intellectuals, Unification and National Identity* (New Haven, CT, 2000). For discussions about Polish postcommunist memories, see, for example, Traba, *Przeszłość w teraźniejszości*; Paweł Śpiewak, *Pamięć po komunizmie* (Gdańsk, 2005); or Dobrochna Kałwa, "PRL w polskiej świadomości/pamięci historycznej," in *Pamięc polska pamięc niemiecki: Od XIX do XXI wieku*, ed. Krzysztof Mikulski and Zdzisław Noga (Toruń, 2006).
26. Konrad Jarausch and Thomas Lindenberger, *Conflicted Memories: Europeanizing Contemporary Histories* (New York, 2007), and earlier works such as Jeffrey Herf, *Divided Memory: The Nazi Past in the Two Germanys* (Cambridge, MA, 1997), Norbert Frei, *Vergangenheitspolitk: Die Anfänge der Bundesrepublik und die NS-Vergangenheit* (Munich, 1996). In Poland, examples of immediate postcommunist memory studies included Anna Sawisz and Barbara Szacka, eds., *Czas przeszły i pamięć społeczna: przemiany świadomości historycznej inteligencji polskiej 1965–1988* (Warsaw, 1990), or Martha Kurkowska, "Archiwa pamięci—oral history," *Historyka*, 1998: 28.
27. The concern with European foundations to the relations also had a political aspect. Poland applied for European Union membership in 1990 and was admitted in 2003. As a result, the EU negotiations were ongoing at the time when many of these publications appeared.
28. Bingen, "Die politischen Beziehungen," 35.
29. Rita Süssmuth, "Gute Nachbarschaft gründet sich auf Versöhnung und Partnerschaft," in Pflüger and Lipscher, *Feinde werden Freunde*, 2. Also Willy Brandt assured his readership of the importance of the Protestant Memorandum in opening a dialogue with Poland in the 1960s. Willy Brandt, *My Life in Politics*, trans. Anthea Bell (New York, 1992), 102.
30. Friedbert Pflüger, "Grenze und Partnerschaft: Die deutsch-polnische Verträge von 1990/1991," in Pflüger and Lipscher, *Feinde werden Freunde*, 12.
31. For example, Klaus Otto Skibowski, interview with author, Bad-Godesberg, 3 February 2005. Skibowski argued that true dialogue did not emerge until communism ended. Also Bartoszewski felt that the religious dialogue's importance was overrated. He dated true and meaningful interactions to the late 1970s when a broader Polish opposition developed. "Die Wahrheit ist, dass alle Eliten uasser einzelnen Menschen, nicht reif genug waren, um die Wichtigkeit der Beziehungen zwischen unseren beiden Völkern zu begreifen," in *"Wir vergeben und bitten um Vergebung,"* 115.
32. Günter Särchen and Brigitte Särchen, "Adres: Mietek Pszon, Kraków," in Pięciak, *Polacy i Niemcy*, 39.
33. The truth was a lot more complicated. Postwar church–state relations in Poland were based on a troublesome and hesitant cooperation, which on the one hand allowed the Polish Church certain privileges, unheard of in other communist countries, such as religious education and certain financial independence; on the other hand, it was required to support the state's foreign policy and raison d'etat. While the cardinal's rhetorical stance drew on romantic nationalism, his political course was generally positivist in

nature, focused on the church's survival in Polish society. See Stehle, *Die Ostpolitik des Vatikans*; Dudek and Gryz, *Komuniści i Kościół w Polsce*; Żurek, *Zwischen Nationalismus und Versöhnung*.

34. See Vincens M. Lissek, "'Łączy nas filozofia, a nawet sztuka kulinarna...'" in Pięciak, *Polacy i Niemcy*, 97–113; Winfried Lipscher, interview with author, Berlin, 18 May 2005. Stomma mentioned briefly in his memoirs a meeting with the Central Committee in 1969. Stomma, *Pościg za nadzieją*, 198.
35. In fact, a crisis emerged between Cardinal Wyszyński and the Znak Circle in early 1966 as a consequence of the Znak group remaining silent on the memorandum in the Sejm. Only Jerzy Turowicz came to its defense at the time. Micewski, *Cardinal Wyszyński*, 258. For a comment on Stomma's negative stance on the letter, see Bartoszewski, *Und reiss uns den Hass aus der Seele*, 90.
36. Stomma, *Pościg za nadzieją*, 188.
37. Stanisław Stomma, "Christliche Ethik gilt auch in den internationalen Beziehungen," in *"Wir vergeben und bitten um Vergebung,"* 81–95.
38. Manfried Seidler, "Das Polen-Memorandum des Bensberger Kreises—Wirkung in Deutschland und Polen," 110; Erb, "Verständigung mit Polen," 359.
39. Władysław Bartoszewski, "Pół wieku później," in Pięciak, *Polacy i Niemcy*, 194.
40. Ibid., 450.
41. Bartoszewski, "Pół wieku później," 198. The Weimar Triangle refers to a loose association between France, Germany, and Poland that came into existence in 1992. Initially aimed at supporting Poland in its transition period out of communism, it included meetings between heads of state, foreign ministers, and defense ministers of the three countries. The most recent meeting took place in 2007.
42. The concept was not just used historically during the 1830s but also in the Polish national independence movement and the 1840s Springtime of Nations. It has been used for a variety of recent developments; for example, the Polish participation in the Battle of Britain and the 1980s Solidarity movement. See Giles Hart, ed., *For Our Freedom and Yours: A History of the Polish Solidarity Campaign of Great Britain, 1980–1994* (London, 1995); L. G. Marsh, *Polish Wings over Britain, for Your Freedom and Ours* (London, 1943).
43. Tadeusz Mazowiecki, "Von der Gegenwart zur neuen Nachbarschaft," in Pflüger and Lipscher, *Feinde werden Freunde*, 444–45.
44. Richard von Weizsäcker, "Rede beim Staatsbesuch des Präsidenten der Republik Polen am 30.3.1992," in Pflüger and Lipscher, *Feinde werden Freunde*, 291.
45. Konrad Weiss, "Ojczyzna—Polska, ojczyzna—Niemcy, ojczyzna—Europa," in Pięciak, *Polacy i Niemcy*, 82.
46. Bartoszewski, "Die Wahrheit ist, dass alle Eliten," 121.
47. These included the editor in chief of *Die Zeit*, Marion Countess Dönhoff; *Die Zeit*, *Stern*, and WDR journalist and correspondent Hansjakob Stehle, but also WDR director Klaus von Bismarck; and other WDR and NDR employees, such as Ludwig Zimmerer and Paul Botta.
48. Rakowski also became the last communist minister president of Poland for a few months as a result of the roundtable negotiations in 1989.
49. Koppe, *Dreimal getauft*, 168. Skibowski, *Wolken über weitem Land*.
50. Särchen and Särchen, "Mietek Pszon," 23–33; Friedrich Magirius, another member, cited Kreyssig as stating that the sign of reconciliation should be directed to "Poland, Russia and Israel." However, his chapter is dedicated to the meetings with the Poles. Friedrich Magirius, "'Znaki Pokuty'—próba bilansu," in Pięciak, *Polacy i Niemcy*, 44. Weiss, "Polen hatte eine Vorbildfuktion," Ludwig Mehlhorn mentioned the suffering

of Jewish victims in the concentration camps once in his chapter; Ludwig Mehlhorn, "Szara eminencja," in Pięciak, *Polacy i Niemcy*, 52.
51. Several works have appeared on Auschwitz as a site of competing Polish, German, and Jewish memories. See for example Huener, *Auschwitz, Poland*; Wóycicka, *Arrested Mourning*. From these volumes, see also Klaus Bachmann, "Spory o Auschwitz: Obóz zagłady w oczach Niemców, Polaków i Żydów," in Pięciak, *Polacy i Niemcy*, 228–42.
52. Weiss, "'Polen hatte eine Vorbildfuktion,'" 186.
53. Stomma did not mention it in *Pościg za nadzieją*, nor did Mazowiecki and Pszon in connection with "Sühnezeichen"; see Mieczysław Pszon, "1956–1989," in Pięciak, *Polacy i Niemcy*, 536–49. Pszon did discuss the Jews in Poland and his relationship with them in the interwar era and the 1940s. See also Bartoszewski, "Pół wieku później," 190.
54. Mazowiecki, "Die polnische Gesellschaft," 99.
55. For examples of such literary transcendence of national categories and thought, see Czesław Miłosz's treatment of his own background and the Polish–Lithuanian lands, *Rodzinna Europa* (Paris, 1980). Stehle wrote about Marcel Reich-Ranicki that he claimed that not Germany or Poland, but German literature, was his nation. Hansjakob Stehle, "Człowiek z właściwościami—od Reicha do Ranickiego" in Pięciak, *Polacy i Niemcy*, 179.
56. Bartoszewski, "Pół wieku później," 190.
57. See for example Huener, *Auschwitz, Poland*, for censorship surrounding the Jewish presence during the Second World War, and Iwona Irwin-Zarecka, *Neutralizing Memory: The Jew in Contemporary Poland* (Brunswick, NJ, 1989). For Polish-Ukrainian relations, see Snyder, *Reconstruction of Nations*. As for the Ukrainians, in the volume *"Wir vergeben und bitten um Vergebung,"* the editors Kerski and Żurek mention in the introduction that the 2003 Ukrainian and Polish Catholic bishops' mutual appeal to reconciliation was modeled on the Polish 1965 letter. Robert Żurek and Basil Kerski, "Einführung," in *"Wir vergeben und bitten um Vergebung,"* 7–54.
58. Willy Brandt, "Der Kniefall vor Warschau," in Pflüger and Lipscher, *Feinde werden Freunde*, 51–59.
59. Reinhold Lehmann, "Mietek Pszon: On pokazał nam, dlaczego powinniśmy pokochać Polaków i ich kraj," in Pięciak, *Polacy i Niemcy*, 29.
60. Jerzy Turowicz, "Przedmowa," in Pięciak, *Polacy i Niemcy*, 12 (emphasis mine).
61. Ibid.
62. Stehle, "Człowiek z właściwościami," 167–82; Klaus Bachmann, "Spory o Auschwitz: Obóz zagłady w oczach Niemców, Polaków i Żydów," in Pięciak, *Polacy i Niemcy*, 228–42.
63. In *Feinde werden Freunde*, only one chapter concerned a Jewish topic: Hanna Krall, "Drei Monate später beschloss Axel von dem Busche, Adolf Hitler zu töten," 113–22. The essay concerned events in 1940s.
64. Stomma, *Pościg za nadzieją*, 137–43.
65. Ibid., 193.
66. Seidler, "Das Polenmemorandum des Bensberger Kreises," 109; Koppe, *Dreimal getauft und Mensch geblieben*.
67. Hennelowa, *Bo jestem z Wilna*.
68. Józefa Hennelowa, "Moja utracona ojczyzna," in Pięciak, *Polacy i Niemcy*, 296–310; Klaus von Bismarck, "Moja ziemia rodzinna, która teraz jest w Polsce," in Pięciak, *Polacy i Niemcy*, 283–95.
69. Klaus Otto Skibowski, interview with author, Bad-Godesberg, 3 February 2005. Skibowski's main intent with the statement was not to include the ethnic conflicts on the

eastern borders but to undermine the political decisions of Egon Bahr and Willy Brandt as well as their rapport with the Polish people.
70. Pertti Ahonen, Gustavo Corni, Jerzy Kochanowski, et al., *People on the Move: Forced Population Movements in Europe in the Second World War and Its Aftermath* (New York, 2008), 163. In general, Ahonen, *People on the Move*, argues that the expulsions seemed like minor tragedies compared to the Nazi mass extermination and labor programs in Poland, and, partially, the communist and Stalinist censorship of Polish life in the "Kresy" distorted and suppressed expellee memories or narratives from Polish public space.
71. Stanisław Stomma, interview with author, 7 October 2004.
72. Stanisław Stomma, "Pater Muckermann—ein Vorläufer der Versöhnung in Wilna," in Pflüger and Lipscher, *Feinde werden Freunde*, 130–44.
73. Ibid., 139.
74. Herf, *Divided Memory*; Jarausch and Geyer, eds. *Shattered Past*.
75. Ludwig Mehlhorn, "Die Polenpolitik der DDR," in Pflüger and Lipscher, *Feinde werden Freunde*, 223–29.
76. Carlo Schmid, "Politische Reisen: Polen 1958," in Pflüger and Lipscher, *Feinde werden Freunde*, 29–39.
77. See, for example, CDU politician Clemens Rieder, "Heute Breslau, Morgen Berlin?" *Bayern-Kurier*, 18 May 1963, in connection with Jürgen Neven-du Mont's documentary *Polen in Breslau* for an attempt to connect the border question with the recognition of the GDR.
78. Stomma, "Christliche Ethik," 89.
79. Ibid., 94.
80. Władysław Markiewicz, "Erziehung zur Verständigung: Die deutsch-polnischen Schulbuchempfehlungen," in Pflüger and Lipscher, *Feinde werden Freunde*, 185.
81. See Süssmuth, "Gute Nachbarschaft," 1–8, or some of the contributions to *"Wir vergeben und bitten um Vergebung,"* for example Joseph Homeyer, 80; Tadeusz Mazowiecki, 108–9; and other final statements on Polish–German relations today that draw no distinctions between differences among former East and West Germans and that focus primarily on political challenges.
82. Turowicz's mention of Pszon's early anti-Semitism in "Przedmowa," 12, was such an example, as was Stomma's description of Father Muckermann in Pflüger and Lipscher, *Feinde werden Freunde*.

Conclusion

> After every war
> Someone has to tidy up.
> Things won't pick
> Themselves up after all.
> . . .
> Those who knew
> What this was all about
> Must make way for those
> Who know little.
> And less than that.
> And at last nothing less than nothing.
>
> —Wisława Szymborska[1]

In the 2010s, scholars followed journalist Klaus Bachmann's pointed remarks about "reconciliation kitsch" in commenting that the current state of Europe and "these times of crisis" leave no place for "European platitudes."[2] Scholars continued to describe Polish–French and Polish–German relations as successful overall, but they also identified some of the continuing tensions in relations. They pointed to five main areas of tension. First, starting in the 1950s and 1960s, participants perceived of the expellees, and in particular the expellee organizations, as the greatest obstacles to Polish–German reconciliation. Scholars in the 2010s continued to attribute returning tensions in Polish–German relations to activities among German expellees, focusing their attention on Preussische Treuhand (an organization that asked for compensation from the Polish government for lost German territory), the expellee politician Erika Steinbach, and the debates surrounding the construction of a Center Against Expulsions.[3] A second source of tension went back to the inception of Ostpolitik: differences in Polish and German opinions on the (West) German attempts at improved relations with the Soviet Union, including financial ties between Germany and Russia in the postcommunist era.[4] Third, as the Polish opposition to

---

Notes for this chapter begin on page 208.

communism grew stronger in the early 1980s, the focus of West German politicians, including that of Willy Brandt, on developing relations primarily with the communist leadership caused tensions with opposition leaders, which also problematized postcommunist relations.[5] A fourth source of tension is the way in which certain Polish politicians have utilized both perceived threats from outside enemies and anti-German and victimhood-centered Polish national memory to gain popular support.[6] Of course, the activities of groups on the German side, including Steinbach and Preussische Treuhand, provided useful fodder for Poland's anti-EU movement and politicians. Fifth, differing economic and historical visions and experiences led to disagreements between Poland and Germany regarding the ongoing refugee crisis in Europe. However, when tracing efforts toward reconciliation back to the 1950s, it becomes clear that some of the frailties were also inherent to the peace process itself.

Let us first consider the effects that these initiatives had on political and cultural developments in postwar Polish–German relations. Civil-society initiatives and the individual agency of particular individuals—their transnational or cross-border backgrounds, preferences, and outlooks—played a role in shaping political developments important to the improvement of Polish–West German relations in the 1950s and 1960s. The close study of nonstate participants in international dialogue on a civil society and media level brings alternative concerns and perspectives of relations to the fore compared to earlier studies. The Catholic intellectuals and media elites described here worked patiently to find common ground, mutually acceptable formulas, and frameworks for past and present Polish–West German relations separately from détente and from Willy Brandt's efforts to launch the Policy of Small Steps and Ostpolitik before the initiation of official state relations. Their efforts had several important consequences for postwar Polish–German relations, including contributing to the development of "deep reconciliation" in Yinan He's words.[7]

The media efforts and civil society contributed, more actively than Pertti Ahonen suggested in *After the Expulsions*, to a shift away from the expellee representations of the lost *Heimat* and mistreatment of Germans in Poland that had dominated earlier media representations of Poland.[8] They shifted the framework for discussing Polish–German relations and the former German territories in the east in West German public space to more optimistic approaches to communist Poland and its current inhabitants. They broke taboos around discussing the relinquishment of the eastern territories, and they also offset the narratives of corruption and incompetence or of overwhelming Soviet oppression in Poland. The Polish Catholic publishers in a more limited way attempted to do the same in Polish public space, replacing understandings of the West German militancy, and revisionism, and lack of repentance with models of civilian-minded and nonaggressive Germans of a younger generation. As sole voices in a largely hostile or indifferent environment, their efforts, while limited, received disproportionate attention by politicians and elites in their own and the other society, and this points to the power of individual agency in accomplishing political change. Their access to radio and television amplified their voices and enabled them to reach larger audiences and garner more attention.

The Polish and West German writers introduced the possibility of alternative models to foreign policy instead of Cold War ones that were based on bargaining, displays of strength, distrust, and competition. The elite media outlets and particularly the experts on Eastern Europe and Polish–German relations also played crucial roles in developing, introducing, and interpreting the 1960s religious memoranda and the Polish bishops' letter in 1965 to a larger public. Without their mediation, these memoranda would not have reached a larger public sphere or would have reached them in a different form. Finally, the elite media writers played important roles in interpreting and formulating the problematic West German media approaches to the 1968 Polish Purge and the Czech invasion.[9] Their responses were based on the perceived necessity to protect Ostpolitik and the emerging cordial relations with the existing communist leaderships, particularly in Poland. Overall, the Poland experts and their media outlets formulated the narrative of reconciliation and distributed it widely, gaining increasing support for it in mainstream society. The narrative of reconciliation was partially developed in interaction with Polish conversation partners, such as the Znak Circle, and moderate communists in the late 1950s and early 1960s. Initial meetings and conversations, as well as key "interpreters" such as Zimmerer, mediated the models and approaches that would be acceptable or unacceptable in the other country. The models these media elites and their Polish conversation partners developed centered on the possibility of changing communism from within, the necessity of stability in Europe, and finally the preference for homogeneous nation-states. The models, especially the intellectual foundations of neopositivism, did not necessarily originate in the German context, though they harmonized with certain German understandings of communism. They were based on historical Polish understandings about how to operate within a hostile or oppressive state.

Entangled nation-building remained a crucial aspect of the reconciliatory process. The elite writers and public intellectuals engaged not only with protecting the borders of postwar nations but also with assimilating their own audiences, German and Polish citizens, into clearer ethnonational categories during the 1950s and 1960s. Creating these homogeneous categories involved pressuring expellees and displaced populations to cease all protests of the loss of territory and instead to assimilate fully into the postwar states. In addition, West German journalists and correspondents reporting on Poland strove in their articles, radio coverage, and documentaries to neutralize and offset painful memories of disappearing borderlands populations. In doing so, they connected homogeneous postwar nation-states to order, prosperity, modernity, and peace, while multicultural areas and populations, or the memories of them, were associated with confusion, times of war, conflict, and pain, characteristics that were rapidly becoming distant history. Journalists referred to the "unmixing" of Central Europe as a painful "but perhaps healthy" development, and this was also the prevalent image of the borderlands introduced in the 1960s media.[10] The religious memoranda further supported the reinforcement of ethnonational categorizations and stable states as essential to European peace. The Polish Bishops' Letter introduced the model of the "Polak-Katolik," as an eternal reflection of the Polish nation, although members of the episcopate, particularly Cardinal Wyszyński and Bishop Kominek, continued to disagree on the necessity to essentialize the Polishness of the western borderlands. While the 1960s memoranda promoted friendly relations between the national populations, they largely precluded the notion of fluid boundaries or populations in their discussions of relations.

In West Germany, the discourse surrounding Polish–German relations and the future recognition of the Oder-Neisse Line also overlapped with other central debates about postwar West Germany, such as the freedom of media, democratization of West German society, and the emerging efforts toward *Vergangenheitsbewältigung*. The Polish–German relations debate intersected with fears among the media elites of a reversal into authoritarianism in West Germany. They accused the expellee leaders not only of opposing improved relations with Poland or a debate about relinquishing the borderlands but also of being enemies of democratic debates in postwar West Germany. *Vergangenheitsbewältigung*, the process of coming to terms with the past, also played a role in relations, partially as an approach to cultural diplomacy, such as in von Bismarck's 1964 and 1965 travels to Poland while touring with the television documentary *Das dritte Reich*, and in the West German journalists' tendency to utilize Polish voices to engage their audiences into reflections on Germany's dark past, its responsibility for atrocities in Poland during the Second World War.

Another nation-building debate intersecting with Polish–German relations was the postwar concerns with German–German relations in the media institutes. Poland after 1956 and again in the 1980s occasionally served as a model for a potential opening in East Germany. In addition, the very establishment of studios, television and radio stations, and expertise on Eastern Europe, including Polish reporting, became connected to funding and expertise channeled toward strengthening German–German relations. Polish observers and visitors to West Germany occasionally felt irritated about the prioritizing of the German questions in conversations and events ostensibly connected to Poland. However, the tendency showed the close and multilayered connection between reconciliation and entangled postwar nation-building.

In Poland, relations with West Germany became a catalyst for state and society to consider the role and authority of the church in postwar society. In the late 1950s, as West Germans visited Poland, but even more so in 1965 in connection with the Bishops' Letter of Reconciliation, the church's involvement in foreign contacts and relations threatened the state leadership and caused it, particularly Gomułka, to worry about the church's international reputation and attempts to take over the state's role in foreign relations. The church's initiatives caused competition for control over public space, over the Polish population's sympathies, and over relations with West Germany, also on a civil-society level. The state had a monopoly on television, radio, police, and military, but the church had the great respect and sympathy that the population traditionally afforded it, as well as an international reputation. The reconciliation narrative became a compromise between the two institutions' preferred representations of Poland's recent past and current role in the world. Also, while the Polish bishops' letter was an effort to break with a distrustful and hostile image of the Germans, many of the priests, bishops, and occasionally Cardinal Wyszyński himself continued to cultivate more traditional anti-German stances, grounded in historical myths and memories. Finally, the Znak Circle's and Catholic intellectuals' involvement in relations with West Germany by necessity involved considerations of Polish–Soviet relations as well. Stanisław Stomma argued in 1957 that Soviet sponsorship allowed Poland to cultivate a more relaxed relationship with West Germany.[11] Meanwhile, on an unstated level, the Catholic publishers' Polish–West German relations efforts in part aimed at decreasing Polish dependence on Soviet protection. Bishop Kominek's and other participants' argument that the western border was a necessity for Poland's postwar survival depended on the implicit assumption that the moved eastern border and Poland's territorial loss in the east to the Soviet Union was an unassailable and irreversible fact.

These cultural Polish–German relations in the 1950s and 1960s, during their very inception, revealed some long-term legacies that would continue to haunt relations into the postcommunist era. First, the close study of the early stages of Polish–German relations shows the extent to which these relations were dominated by elites. Elites outside of organized politics were regularly the creators and audiences of reconciliation, and the new understandings of the other country became founded on the interaction with elites across the border. West German correspondents and travelers frequently understood Poland through the lens of visits to Warsaw, Cracow, and occasionally Wrocław. Their comprehension of political developments sometimes strongly reflected their reliance on mediators, the Catholic intelligentsia, and moderate communists such as the Polish correspondents to Bonn. The question is, once the reconciliation narrative had emerged, was there a space for challenges and alternative voices from other societal groups, or for less positive interpretations of the relations in it?

Second, the great focus on developing and maintaining state relations was in hindsight limiting to reconciliation as a broader exercise of healing between the two societies. Even as these groups challenged existing state policy or strove to establish contacts through alternative political channels, they considered state relations—that is, official relations with and through the communist state—an absolute priority. Of course, cultural and media relations depended on state funding, visas, travel permits, and state-granted access to public space. However, considering the limited popularity and fragility of the Polish state, the great investment in it, and the neglect of civil society groups in Poland, such as the New Left and sometimes the Znak Circle (both of which would move into mainstream politics in the 1990s), was erroneous. By this excessive statist focus, West German elite participants and political figures may have damaged broader participation and connections to potential long-term cooperation partners in Poland. Thus, on a level of comparative reconciliation, conflict-resolution efforts need to take seriously the fragility of nondemocratic, unpopular, or economically struggling states and acknowledge even more the potential of powerful nonstate groups and individuals when directing efforts toward building relations.

The focus on state contacts also involves a question of the value and significance of democracy in processes of conflict resolution. If reconciliation with an authoritarian or nondemocratic state is difficult, or perhaps even impossible, are there alternative paths to establish and improve relations? In Polish or East German state-coordinated engagement of larger groups in state-sponsored and state-initiated friendship events and meetings, sometimes the participation lacked conviction, sincerity, or staying power because it was neither grassroots initiated nor voluntary.

Finally, relations suffered because of the participants' great focus on avoiding all forms of dissent. The streamlining and nationalizing of reconciliation narratives was a consequence of the focus on short-term political goals and of the institutional pressures toward assimilation and agreement. However, the attempt to find consensus closed down pluralistic open-ended dialogues too soon, to the detriment of larger societal groups' involvement and ability to shape relations. Even when models became more inclusive in the 1990s, they separated the simpler linear narrative of dualistic progress and steady improvement in the relations from more complex memories engaging with diverse experiences and political developments. Ultimately, the memories nationalized actual events and overemphasized stability and positive aspects, a natural but problematic tendency that left many groups dissatisfied and ready to dismiss the notion of reconciliation entirely or to reinsert their perspectives at a later time, usually in the late 1990s.

When Stanisław Stomma passed away on 21 July 2005, *Tygodnik Powszechny* wrote in his obituary:

> The twentieth century ended last Thursday, 21 of June 2005. On that day, Stanisław Stomma died: one of the founders of *Tygodnik Powszechny* and *Znak*, a pioneer of Polish–German relations, an anti-communist who still between 1956 and 1976 was the leader of the only legal opposition in the Polish People's Republic. His biography reflected, as if in a mirror, the Polish dilemmas of this century.[12]

Stomma had truly been part of all the major developments in Poland during the twentieth century. He had experienced the first German eastern occupation during World War I, been displaced as a consequence of the Second World War's border moves and attempted to work for change in Cold War communist Poland. He witnessed the positive political developments in Polish–German relations in the early 1990s, the final settlement of the border, the Two Plus Four Agreement in 1990, and the Polish–German Friendship and Good Neighborhood Treaty in 1991, a time of great optimism in the relations, and later the EU enlargement as Poland joined in the union in 2004. He died just as French and Dutch voters rejected the EU constitution in the summer of 2005. Perhaps it is no coincidence that the first clear cracks in the grand experiment of the postwar European peace project became visible precisely at the time when he and his generation passed away. Perhaps they were not only the initiators but also the glue that held it together. Regardless of what is left of reconciliation, we would do well not to forget the role these groups and their outlooks played in postwar political developments or the lessons the reconciliatory processes taught us about twentieth-century Europe and about ourselves.

Notes

1. Excerpt from "The End and the Beginning," from *View with a Grain of Sand: Selected Poems* by Wislawa Szymborska, translated from the Polish by Stanislaw Baranczak and Clare Cavanagh. Copyright © 1995 by Houghton Mifflin Harcourt Publishing Company. Copyright © 1976 Czytelnik, Warszawa. Reprinted by permission of Houghton Mifflin Harcourt Publishing Company. All rights reserved.
2. Corinne DeFrance et al., "Vorwort," in *Deutschland-Frankreich-Polen seit 1945: Transfer und Kooperation*, ed. Corinne DeFrance et al. (Brussels, 2014), 9.
3. Karl Cordell, "The Federation of Expellees and the Impact on Memory on Polish–German Relations," *German Politics and Society* 31, no. 4 (109) (Winter 2013), 102–20. On Erika Steinbach, see Kristin Kopp and Joanna Niżynska, "Between Entitlement and Reconciliation: Germany and Poland's Postmemory after 1989," in *Germany, Poland, and Postmemorial Relations: In Search of a Livable Past*, ed. Kristin Kopp and Joanna Niżynska (New York, 2012), 1–24.
4. Cornelius Ochmann, "Neue Ostpolitik der EU. Das Beziehungsgeflecht Deutschland – Polen – Russland – Ukraine," in *Erwachsene Nachbarschaft. Die deutsch-polnische Beziehungen 1991 bis 2011*, ed. Bingen, Loew, Ruchniewicz, and Zybura (Wiesbaden, 2011), 62–76.
5. See Bernd Rother, "Zwischen Solidarität und Friedenssicherung: Willy Brandt und Polen in den 1980er Jahren," in Boll and Ruchniewicz, *Nie mehr eine Politik über Polen hinweg*, 220–64.
6. Lisa Bicknell, "Polnisch-deutsche Versöhnungsinitiativen seit den 1960er Jahren," in DeFrance et al., *Deutschland-Frankreich-Polen seit 1945*, 209.
7. He, *Search for Reconciliation*, 4.
8. Ahonen, *After the Expulsions*, 265.
9. As mentioned by Madajczyk, "Impact of the Events." Madajczyk quotes heavily from Warsaw correspondent Angela Nacken in *FAZ*. One should note that Nacken as well was invested in Polish–German relations as presented here and closely acquainted with Zimmerer and Stehle, the latter her predecessor at *FAZ*.
10. "Weichsel—Kirschen und Loorbeer: Polens Jubiläum zwischen Ost und West," WDR/ARD 21 January 1971, Deutsche Kinemathek, Berlin.
11. Stomma, "Czy istnieje niebezpieczeństwo niemieckie?"
12. "Stanisław Stomma (1908–2005)," *Tygodnik Powszechny*, 31 July 2005.

BIBLIOGRAPHY

Interviews

Karlheinz Koppe, Bonn, 23 February 2005; 28 February 2005.
Winfried Lipscher, Berlin, 18 May 2005.
Renate Marsch-Potocka, telephone, 7 July 2005.
Joanna Olczak-Ronikier, Cracow, 29 October 2004.
Klaus Otto Skibowski, Bad-Godesberg, 3 February 2005.
Hansjakob Stehle, Vienna, 17 June 2005.
Stanisław Stomma, Warsaw, 7 October 2004.

Archival Sources

Archiwum Jerzego Turowicza (AJT)

Correspondence A-Z.
Estate, Jerzy Turowicz.

Friedrich Eberth-Stiftung (FES)

Binder, "FES B2 Bensberger Kreis Polenmemorand. Manuskripte."
Binder, "Bensberger Kreis. Polen Abstimmungen. Mi 68."
Binder, "FE Bensberger Kreis. Polen. Mi 60."
Binder, "FE BK Protokoll, Erklärungen, Bensberger Kreis 54, 1966–1973, Bensberger Kreis, Gottfried Erb, Dokumentation zum Polen-Memorandum des BK (Anerkennung der Oder-Neisse-Linie) 1967–1972."
Binder, "Bensberger Kreis, Gottfried Erb, Bensberger Kreis, Karlheinz Koppe 1970, Polenreise."
Nachlass Walter Dirks, WD 23–WD 139.

Historisches Archiv Westdeutscher Rundfunk (HA-WDR)

Bestand Klaus von Bismarck.
Lauf. No. 462, Polen-Reise 1964.
Lauf. No. 259, Unterlagen Polenreise, 1964–1967.

Lauf. No. 163, Memorandum Allgem. Korresp. A–Z.
Lauf. No. 162, Memorandum (Anerkennung Oder-Neisse-Grenze) Presse, Rundfunk, Ostkirchenaussch. III.

WDR-HA 677.
WDR-HA 719.
WDR-HA 1344.
WDR-HA 1352.
WDR-HA 1674.
WDR-HA 1682.
WDR-HA 1964.
WDR-HA 2502.
WDR-HA 2504.
WDR-HA 2543.
WDR-HA 2553.
WDR-HA 2565.
WDR-HA 2628.
WDR-HA 2748.
WDR-HA 2764.
WDR-HA 2750.
WDR-HA 2888.
WDR-HA 3979.
WDR-HA 3968.
WDR-HA 5257.
WDR-HA 5258.
WDR-HA 5259.
WDR-HA 5320.
WDR-HA 6146.
WDR-HA 6149.
WDR-HA 6374.
WDR-HA 7535.
WDR-HA 8018.
WDR-HA 10337.
WDR-HA 12005.

WDR Jahrbücher.
WDR Jahresberichte.

Stadtarchiv Hamburg

Bestand Nr. 621-1, Akte Nr. 972, Ludwig Zimmerer 1961–1965.

Norddeutscher Rundfunk (NDR)

Wortarchiv H001572, Diskussion über die Sendung: Mit polnischen Augen.
Wortarchiv F804320, Die Bundestagswahl 1972.

Wortrachiv F802756, Kommentar von Ludwig Zimmerer.
Wortarchiv F803134, Die Aussiedlung der Deutschen und ihre Probleme aus polnischer Sicht.
Wortarchiv F802715, Die fortschreitende Normalisierung der Beziehungen zwischen Deutschen.

Evangelisches Zentralarchiv (EZA)

Bestand 2: 1378, 1379, 1380, 1392, 1393.
Bestand 6: 1109, 1110, 7065, 7067.

Bundesarchiv Koblenz (BAK)

B136/3465.
B145/1159, 6670, 14611.
B145/2858 Sind wir revanchisten.
B145/2891.
NL1279/1, 1b.
NL1279/6, 7, 8, 11, 12–18.
NL1279/18 M-Z 1963–1965.
NL1279/32–35.
NL1279/40–41.
NL1279/46.
N/1279/93 Kritiken "Polen in Breslau" (1963), Ausländische Presse.
N/1279/131.
NL 1279/85–88.
NL 1279/90–92.
NL 1279/137.
Z23/8.
Z23/31.
Z23/35.

Politisches Archiv des Auswärtigen Amt

B2	64
B2	81
B2	86
B2	110
B2	113
B2	143
B2	146
B2	176
B11	571
B12	548
B12	549
B12	549a

B12   589b
B12   589c
B12   596a
B12   597
B12   601
B12   605c
B12   615a
B12   615c
B12   641a
B12   641b
B12   649

Document Copies in Private Possession

Klaus Otto Skibowski, report, 1957.
Hansjakob Stehle, correspondence with Bishop Bolesław Kominek, 1964–74.

Newspapers, News Agencies, and Magazines

Bayern-Kurier, May 1963.
Deutsche National-Zeitung und Soldaten-Zeitung, May 1963.
Deutsche Presse-Agentur (DPA).
Deutsches Ostdienst (DOD).
Frankfurter Allgemeine Zeitung, October 1956–December 1970.
Frankfurter Hefte, 1946, 1965–69.
Frankfurter Rundschau, October 1956–December 1970.
Katholische Nachrichtenagentur (KNA).
Norddeutscher Rundfunk Information, 1987.
Observer, May 1963.
Ostkirchen-Informationsdienst, March 1962.
Petrus-Blatt, January 1966.
Polska Agencja Prasowa (pap).
Pommersche Zeitung, March 1962.
Rheinische Post, October 1965.
Rheinischer Merkur, October 1956–December 1970.
Schlesische Rundschau, May 1963.
Stuttgarter Zeitung, March 1962.
Süddeutsche Zeitung, October 1956–December 1970.
Der Tag, 1956.
Taz, 1994.
The Times, December 1965.
Trybuna Ludu, 1946–December 1970.
Tygodnik Powszechny, October 1956–December 1970, July 2005.
Die Welt, October 1956–December 1970.

Więź, 1968.
Wprost, 2005.
Za i przeciw, 1962.
Die Zeit, October 1956–December 1970, December 1990, May 2004.
Życie Warszawy, October 1956–December 1970.

Other Sources

Abadi, Jacob. "The Road to Israeli-Polish Rapprochement." *Middle Eastern Studies* 41, no. 6 (November 2005): 863–88.
Adamczyk-Garbowska, Monika, and Felichs Tych, eds. *Jewish Presence in Absence: The Aftermath of the Holocaust in Poland, 1944–2010*. Jerusalem: Yad Vashem, 2014.
Adler, Bruni. *Geteilte Erinnerung: Polen, Deutsche und der Krieg*. Tübingen: Klöpfer und Meyer, 2006.
Ahonen, Pertti. *After the Expulsion: West Germany and Eastern Europe 1945–1990*. Oxford: Oxford University Press, 2003.
Ahonen, Pertti, Gustavo Corni, Jerzy Kochanowski, et al., eds. *People on the Move: Forced Population Movements in Europe in the Second World War and Its Aftermath*. New York: Berghahn Books, 2008.
Alvis, Robert E. "Holy Homeland: The Discourse of Place and Displacement among Silesian Catholics in Postwar West Germany." *Church History* 79, no. 4 (December 2010): 827–59.
Anderson, Benedict. *Imagined Communities: Reflections on the Origins and Spread of Nationalism*. Revised edition. New York: Verso, 2006.
Anderson, Sheldon B. *A Cold War in the Soviet Bloc: Polish–East German Relations 1945–1962*. Boulder, CO: Westview Press, 2001.
Bachmann, Klaus. "Spory o Auschwitz: Obóz zagłady w oczach Niemców, Polaków i Żydów." In *Polacy i Niemcy pół wieku później: Księga pamiątkowa dla Mieczysława Pszona*, edited by Wojciech Pięciak, 228–42. Cracow: Wydawnictwo Znak, 1996.
———. "Versöhnungskitsch nach 10 Jahren—was davon übrig blieb." In *Erinnerungskultur und Versöhnungskitsch*, edited by Hans Henning Hahn, Heidi Hein-Kirchner, and Anna Kochanowska-Nieborak, 17–20. Marburg: Herderinstitut, 2008.
Bahr, Egon. *Zu meiner Zeit*. Munich: Karl Blessing Verlag, 1996.
Barkan, Elazar, and Alexander Karn. "Group Apology as an Ethical Imperative." In *Taking Wrong Things Seriously: Apologies and Reconciliation*, edited by Elazar Barkan and Alexander Karn, 3–32. Stanford, CA: Stanford University Press, 2006.
Bar-Tal, Daniel. "From Intractable Conflict through Conflict Resolution to Reconciliation: Psychological Analysis." *Political Psychology* 21, no. 2 (June 2000): 351–65.
Bartoszewski, Władysław. *Aus der Geschichte lernen? Aufsätze und Reden zur Kriegs- und Nachkriegsgeschichte Polens*. Munich: dtv, 1986.

———. "Pół wieku później." In *Polacy i Niemcy pół wieku później: Księga pamiątkowa dla Mieczysława Pszona*, edited by Wojciech Pięciak, 183–204. Cracow: Wydawnictwo Znak, 1996.

———. *Und reiss uns den Hass aus der Seele: Die schwierige Aussöhnung von Polen und Deutschen*. Warsaw: Deutsch-Polnischer Verlag, 2005.

———. "Die Wahrheit ist, dass alle Eliten ausser einzelnen Menschen, nicht reif genug waren, um die Wichtigkeit der Beziehungen zwischen unseren beiden Völkern zu begreifen." In *Wir vergeben und bitten um Vergebung: Der Briefwechsel der polnischen und deutschen Bischöfe von 1965*, edited by Basil Kerski, Thomas Kycia, and Robert Żurek. Osnabrück: Fibre, 2006.

Barzel, Rainer. *Ein gewagtes Leben: Erinnerungen*. Stuttgart, Leipzig: Hohenheim Verlag, 2001.

Baum, Gregory. "The Role of the Churches in Polish–German Reconciliation." In *Reconciliation of Peoples*, edited by Gregory Baum and Harold Wells. New York: Orbis Books, 1997.

Beattie, Keith. *Documentary Screens: Nonfiction Film and Television*. New York: Palgrave McMillan, 2004.

Behrens, Petra, ed. *Regionalismus und Regionalisierung in Diktaturen und Demokratien des 20. Jahrhunderts*. Leipzig: Leipziger Universitätsverlag, 2003.

Berger, Thomas. "The Power of Memory and Memories of Power: the Cultural Parameters of German Foreign Policy-Making since 1945." In *Memory and Power in Post-War Europe: Studies in the Presence of the Past*, edited by Jan-Werner Müller. Cambridge: Cambridge University Press, 2002.

Berghahn, Volker. *America and the Intellectual Cold War in Europe: Shepard Stone between Philanthrophy, Academy, and Diplomacy*. Princeton, NJ: Princeton University Press, 2001.

Bet-El, Ilana R. "Unimagined Communities: The Power of Memory and the Conflict in Yugoslavia." In *Memory and Power in Post-war Europe*, edited by Jan-Werner Müller. New York: Cambridge University Press, 2002.

Bierówka, Joanna, Katarzyna Pokorna-Ignatowicz, and Stanisław Jędrzejewski. *Media a Polacy: polskie media wobec waznych wydarzeń politycznych i problemów społecznych*. Cracow: Krakowska Akademia im. Andrzeja Modrzewskiego, 2012.

Biess, Frank. *Homecomings: Returning POWs and the Legacies of the Defeat in Postwar Germany*. Princeton, NJ: Princeton University Press, 2006.

Bigsby, Christopher. *Remembering and Imagining the Holocaust: The Chain of Memory*. Cambridge: Cambridge University Press, 2006.

Bingen, Dieter. *Die Bonner Deutschland Politik 1969–1976 in der polnischen Publizistik*. Frankfurt a. M: Herausgegen von Bundesministerium für Innendeutsche Beziehungen/ Alfred Metzner Verlag, 1982.

———. *Die Polenpolitik der Bonner Republik von Adenaer bis Kohl 1949–1991*. Baden-Baden: Nomos Verlagsgesellschaft, 1998.

———. "Einübung in erwachsene Partnerschaft: Die politischen Beziehungen Deutschland und Polen." In *Erwachsene Nachbarschaft: Die deutsch-polnische Beziehungen 1991 bis 2011*, edited by Dieter Bingen, Peter Oliver Loew, Krzysztof

Ruchniewicz, and Marek Zybura, 29–50. Wiesbaden: Harrassowitz Verlag, 2011.
Bingen, Dieter, Peter Oliver Loew, Krzysztof Ruchniewicz, and Marek Zybura, eds. *Erwachsene Nachbarschaft: Die deutsch-polnische Beziehungen 1991 bis 2011*. Wiesbaden: Harrassowitz Verlag, 2011.
Bismarck, Klaus von. *Aufbruch aus Pommern: Erinnerungen und Perspektiven*. Munich: Piper GmbH&Co, 1996.
———. *Die nationalen Aufgaben von Rundfunk und Fernsehen: Eine Vorlesung des ARD-Vorsitzenden vor Studenten des Instituts für Publizistik an der Universität Münster, gehalten am 9. Mai 1963*. Cologne: Westdeutscher Rundfunk, 1963.
———. *Die Verantwortung eines Intendanten für Rundfunk und Fernsehen*. Cologne: Westdeutscher Rundfunk, 1967
———. *Über den Umgang mit Menschen in Fernsehen*. Cologne: Westdeutscher Rundfunk, 1972.
———. "Ein evangelischer Christ erfährt Polen." In *Ungewöhnliche Normalisierung: Beziehungen der Bundesrepublik Deutschland zu Polen*, edited by Werner Plum. Bonn: Verlag Neue Gesellschaft, 1984.
Bismarck, Klaus von, Oswald von Nell-Breuning, and Karl Kühne. "Konsequenzen für eine soziale Ordnung (Gespräch)." In *Christen oder Bolschewisten*. Stuttgart: Alfred Kröner Verlag, 1957.
Bjork, James. *Neither German nor Pole? Catholicism and National Indifference in a Central European Borderland*. Ann Arbor: University of Michigan Press, 2008.
Blanke, Richard. *Orphans of Versailles: The Germans in Western Poland, 1918–1939*. Lexington: Kentucky University Press, 1993.
———. *Polish-Speaking Germans? Language and National Identity among the Masurians since 1870*. Cologne: Böhlau, 2001.
Bloomfield, David. "Reconciliation: An Introduction." In *Reconciliation after Violent Conflict: A Handbook*, edited by David Bloomfield, Teresa Barnes, and Luc Huyse. Halmstad: Bull Tryckeri AB, 2005.
Boll, Friedhelm. "Der Bensberger Kreis und sein Polenmemorandum (1968): Vom Zweiten Vatikanischen Konzil zur Unterstutzung sozial-liberaler Entspannungspolitik." In *Versöhnung und Politik: Polnisch-deutsche Versöhnungsinitiativen der 1960er Jahren und die Entspannungspolitik*, edited by Friedhelm Boll et al., 77–117. Bonn: Dietz, 2009.
Boll, Friedhelm, Wiesław Wysocki, and Klaus Ziemer, eds. *Versöhnung und Politik: polnisch-deutsche Versöhnungsinitiativen der 1960er Jahren und die Entspannungspolitik*. Bonn: Dietz, 2009.
Boll, Monika. "Kulturradio: Ein Medium intellektueller Selbstverständigung in der frühen Bundesrepublik." In *Demokratie und Medialisierung im 20. Jahrhundert*, edited by Frank Bösch and Norbert Frei. Göttingen: Wallstein Verlag, 2006.
Borodziej, Włodzimierz, Jerzy Kochanowski, and Bernd Schäfer, eds. *Grenzen der Freundschaft: Der Sicherheitsorgane der DDR und der Volksrepublik Polen zwischen 1956 and 1989*. Dresden: Hanna Arendt Institut für Totalitarismusforschung e.V. an der Technischen Hochschule Dresden, 2000.

Bourdieu, Pierre, and Jean-Claude Passeron. *Reproduction in Education, Society and Culture*. Translated by Richard Nice. London: Sage, 1990.
Brandt, Christoph-Mathias. *Souveränität für Deutschland: Grundlagen, Enstehungsgeschichte und Bedeutung des Zwei-Plus-Vier-Vertrages vom 12. September 1990*. Cologne: 1993.
Brandt, Willy. *My Life in Politics*. Translated by Anthea Bell. New York: Viking Adult, 1992.
———. "Der Kniefall vor Warschau." In *Feinde werden Freunde: Von den Schwierigkeiten der deutsch-polnischen Nachbarschaft*, edited by Friedbert Pflüger and Winfried Lipscher, 51–59. Bonn: Bouvier, 1993.
Brawand, Leo. *Der Spiegel—Ein Besatzungskind: Wie die Pressefreiheit nach Deutschland kam*. Hamburg: Europäische Verlagsanstalt, 2007.
Breed, Ananda. "Performing Reconciliation in Rwanda." *Peace Studies* 18, no. 4 (October–December 2006): 507–13.
Bröckling, Ulrich. *Walter Dirks: Bibliographie*. Bonn: Archiv der sozialen Demokratie, 1991.
———. *Katholische Intellektuelle in der Weimarer Republik: Zeitkritik und Gesellschaftstheorie bei Walter Dirks, Romano Guardini, Carl Schmitt, Ernst Michael und Heinrich Mertens*. Munich: Verlag Wilhelm Flink, 1993.
Brubaker, Rogers. *Citizenship and Nationhood in France and Germany*. Cambridge, MA: Harvard University Press, 1992.
———. *Nationalism Reframed: Nationhood and the National Question in the New Europe*. New York: Cambridge University Press, 1996.
———. "Migrations of Ethnic Unmixing in the 'New Europe.'" *International Migration Review* 32, no. 4 (1998): 1047–65.
Brykczynski, Paul. "Reconsidering 'Piłsudskiite Nationalism.'" *Nationalities Papers* 42, no. 5 (2014): 771–90.
———. *Primed for Violence: Murder, Antisemitism, and Democratic Politics in Interwar Poland*. Madison: University of Wisconsin Press, 2016.
Buchhofer, Ekkehard, and Bronisław Kortuś, eds. *Polska i Niemcy: Geografia sąsiedztwo w nowej Europy*. Cracow: Universitas, 1995.
Bucur, Maria, and Nancy Wingfield, eds. *Gender and War in Twentieth Century Eastern Europe*. Bloomington: Indiana University Press, 2006.
Butler, Judith. *Gender Trouble: Feminism and the Subversion of Identity*. New York: Routledge, 1990.
Chalaby, Jean K., ed. *Transnational Television World Wide: Towards a New Media Order*. New York: I.B. Tauris, 2005.
Chapman, Audrey R., and Hugo van der Merwe. *Truth and Reconciliation in South Africa: Did the TRC Deliver?* Philadelphia: University of Philadelphia Press, 2008.
Charbonneau, Bruno, and Genevieve Parent, eds. *Peacebuilding, Memory and Reconciliation: Bridging Top-Down and Bottom-Up Approaches*. New York: Routledge, 2012.
Chu, Winson. *The German Minority in Interwar Poland*. Cambridge: Cambridge University Press, 2012.

Coleman, Peter. *The Liberal Conspiracy: The Congress for Cultural Freedom and the Struggle for the Mind of Postwar Europe*. New York: Free Press, 1989.
Cordell, Karl. "The Federation of Expellees and the Impact on Memory on Polish–German Relations." *German Politics and Society* 31, no. 4 (109) (Winter 2013): 102–20.
Cornils, Ingo, and Sarah Waters, eds. *Memories of 1968: International Perspectives*. New York: Berghahn Books, 2010.
Curp, David. *A Clean Sweep? The Politics of Ethnic Cleansing in Western Poland 1945–1960*. Rochester, NY: University of Rochester Press, 2006.
Czaja, Herbert. *Unterwegs zum kleinsten Deutschland? Mangel an Solidarität mit den Vertreiebenen; Marginalien zu 50 Jahre Ostpolitik*. Frankfurt/Main: Verlag Josef Knecht, 1996.
Dąbrowska, Jarochna. *Stereotype und ihr sprachlicher Ausdruck im Polenbild der deutschen Presse*. Tübingen: Gunter Narr Verlag, 1999.
Dabrowski, Patrice. *Commemorations and the Shaping of Modern Poland*. Bloomington: Indiana University Press, 2004.
David-Fox, Michael. "Introduction" In *Fascination and Enmity: Germany and Russia as Entangled Histories, 1914–1945*, edited by Michael David-Fox, Peter Holquist, and Alexander M. Martin. Pittsburgh, PA: University of Pittsburgh Press, 2012.
Davies, Norman. *God's Playground: A History of Poland*. 2 vols. New York: Columbia University Press, 2005.
Dean, Martin. "Where Did All the Collaborators Go?" *Slavic Review* 64, no. 4 (Winter 2005): 791–98.
DeFrance, Corinne, et al. "Vorwort." In *Deutschland-Frankreich-Polen seit 1945: Transfer und Kooperation*, edited by Corinne DeFrance et al. Brussels: Peter Lang, 2014.
DeGroot, Gerard J. *The Sixties Unplugged: A Kaleidoscopic History of a Disorderly Decade*. Cambridge, MA: Harvard University Press, 2008.
Demshuk, Andrew. "What Was the "Right to the 'Heimat'? West German Expellees and the Many Meanings of 'Heimkehr.'" *Central European History* 45, no. 3 (September 2012): 523–56.
———. *The Lost German East: Forced Migration and the Politics of Memory 1945–1970*. Cambridge: Cambridge University Press, 2012.
Dirks, Walter. *Überlegungen zum Selbstverständnis journalistischer Arbeit*. Freiburg: Katholische Akademie Freiburg, 1984.
Dönhoff, Marion. *Kindheit in Ostpreussen*. Berlin: Siedler, 1988.
———. *Polen und Deutsche: Die schwierige Aussöhnung*. Frankfurt/Main: Lichterfeld Verlag, 1991.
———. *Weit ist der Weg nach Osten: Berichte und Betrachtungen aus fünf Jahrzehnten*. Munich: deutscher taschenbuch verlag, 1993.
Dudek, Antoni. *Bolesław Piasecki: Próba biografii politycznej*. London: Aneks, 1990.
Dudek, Antoni, and Ryszard Gryż. *Komuniści und kościół w Polsce (1945–1989)*. Cracow: Wydawnictwo Znak, 2003.
Eberwein, Wolf-Dieter, and Basil Kerski, eds. *Die deutsch-polnischen Beziehungen 1949–2000*. Opladen: Leske+Budrich, 2001.

Ehmig, Simone Christine. *Generationswechsel im deutschen Journalismus: Zum Einfluss historischer Ereignisse auf das journalistische Selbstverständnis*. Munich: Verlag Karl Alber Freiburg, 2000.

Erb, Gottfried. "Das Memorandum des Bensberger Kreises zur Polenpolitik." In *Ungewöhnliche Normalisierung: Beziehungen der Bundesrepublik Deutschland zu Polen*, edited by Werner Plum, 179–87. Bonn: Verlag Neue Gesellschaft, 1984.

———. "Das Signal, das die deutsche Bischöfe nach Polen gesendet habe reichte uns nicht." In *"Wir vergeben und bitten um Vergebung": Der Briefwechsel der polnischen und deutschen Bischöfe von 1965 und seine Wirkung*, edited by Basil Kerski, Thomas Kycia, and Robert Żurek. Osnabrück: Fibre, 2006.

Fahlenbrach, Katrin. "Protestinszenierungen: Die Studentenbewegung im Spannungfeld von Kultur-Revolution and Medien-Evolution." In *1968: Handbuch zur Kultur- und Mediengeschichte der Studentenbewegung*, edited by Martin Klimke and Joachim Schaloth, 11–22. Stuttgart, Weimar: Metzler, 2007.

Faulenbach, Bernd. *Willy Brandt*. Munich: Beck, 2013.

Feinberg, Melissa. *Culture of Lies: The Battle over Truth in Stalinist Eastern Europe*. Oxford: Oxford University Press, 2017.

Feldman, Lily Gardner. *Germany's Foreign Policy of Reconciliation: From Enmity to Amity*. Lanham, MD: Rowman and Littlefield, 2012.

Fitschen, Klaus, et al., eds. *Die Politisierung des Protestantismus: Entwicklungen in der Bundesrepublik Deutschland während der 1960er und 1970er Jahren*. Göttingen: Vandenhoeck & Ruprecht, 2010.

Freeman, Mark, and Priscilla B. Hayner. "Truth-Telling." In *Reconciliation after Violent Conflict: A Handbook*, edited by David Bloomfield, Teresa Barnes, and Luc Haynes. Halmstad: Bulls Tryckeri AB, 2003.

Frei, Norbert. *Adenauer's Germany and the Nazi Past: The Politics of Amnesty and Integration*. Translated by Joel Golb. New York: Columbia University Press, 2002.

Frei, Norbert, and Frank Bösch, eds. *Demokratie und Medialisierung im 20. Jahrhundert*. Göttingen: Wallstein, 2006.

Friedrich, Klaus Peter. "Collaboration in a Land without a Quisling." *Slavic Review* 64, no. 4 (Winter 2005): 711–46.

Friend, Julius W. *The Linchpin: French-German Relations, 1950–1990*. New York: Praeger, 1991.

Friszke, Andrzej. *Oaza na Kopernika: Klub inteligencji katolickiej 1956–1989*. Warszawa: Biblioteka Więzi, 1997.

———. *Opozycja polityczna w PRL 1945–1980*. London: "Aneks," 1994 (Biblioteka Narodowa, Informatorium).

———. *Koło posłów Znak w Sejmie 1957–1976*. Warsaw: Wydawnictwo Sejmowe, 2002.

———. *Anatomia Buntu: Kuroń, Modzelewski i komandosi*. Cracow: Wydawnictwo Znak, 2010.

———."Jerzy Zawieyski, szkic portretu." In Jerzy Zawieyski, *Dzienniki: Tom 1, Wybór z lat 1955–1959*. Warsaw: Ośrodek Karta, Dom Spotkań z Historią, 2011.

Gabriel, Karl. "Zwischen Aufbruch und Absturz in die Moderne: Die katholische Kirche in den 60er Jahren." *Dynamische Zeiten: Die 60er Jahren in den beiden deutschen Gesellschaften*, edited by Axel Schildt, Detlef Siegfried, and Karl Christian Lammers, 528–43. Hamburg: Hans Christians Verlag, 2000.

Garsztecki, Stefan. *Das Deutschlandbild in der offiziellen, der katholischen und der oppositionellen Publizistik Polens 1970–1989*. Marburg: Herder-Institut, 1997.

Garton Ash, Timothy. *In Europe's Name: Germany and the Divided Continent*. New York: Vintage, 1994.

Geisler, Michael E. "The Disposal of Memory: Fascism and the Holocaust on West German Television." *Framing the Past: The Historiography of German Cinema and Television*, edited by Bruce A. Murray and Christopher Wickham, 220–60. Carbondale: Southern Illinois University Press, 1992.

Gibney, Mark, et al., eds. *The Age of Apology: Facing Up to the Past*. Philadelphia: University of Pennsylvania Press, 2012.

Gienow-Hecht, Jessica. *Transmission Impossible: American Journalism as Cultural Diplomacy in Post-War Germany 1945–1955*. Baton Rouge: Louisiana State University Press, 1999.

Glassheim, Eagle. "Ethnic Cleansing, Communism, and Environmental Devastation in Czechoslovakia's Borderlands, 1945–1989." *Journal of Modern History* 78, no. 1 (March 2006): 65–92.

Gloppen, Siri. "Roads to Reconciliation: A Conceptual Framework." *Roads to Reconcilation*, edited by Elin Skaar, Siri Gloppen, and Astri Suhrke. New York: Lexington Books, 2005.

Gloppen, Siri, Elin Skaar, and Astri Suhrke, eds. *Roads to Reconciliation*. New York: Lexington Books, 2005.

Glorius, Birgit. *Transnationale Perspektiven: Eine Studie zur Migration zwischen Polen und Deutschland*. Bielefeld: Transcript, 2007.

Gniazdowski, Mateusz. "Zu den Menschenverlusten, die Polen während des Zweiten Weltkrieges von den Deutschen zugefügt wurden: Eine Geschichte von Forschungen und Schätzungen." In *Historie: Jahrbuch des Zentrums für Historische Forschung Berlin der Polnischen Akademie der Wissenschaften 2007/2008*, 65–92. Berlin, 2008.

Granovetter, Mark. "The Strength of Weak Ties." *American Journal of Sociology* 78, no. 6 (May 1973): 1360–80.

Greschat, Martin. "Protestantismus und Evangelische Kirche in den 60er Jahren." In *Dynamische Zeiten: Die 60er Jahren in den beiden deutschen Gesellschaften*, edited by Axel Schildt, Detlef Siegfried, and Karl Christian Lammers, 544–81. Hamburg: Hans Christians Verlag, 2000.

Gross, Jan. *Fear: Anti-Semitism in Poland after Auschwitz; An Essay in Historiographical Interpretation*. New York: Random House, 2006.

Hachmeister, Lutz, and Friedemann Siering, eds. *Die Herren Journalisten: Die Elite der deutschen Presse nach 1945*. Munich: C.H. Beck Verlag, 2002.

Hackmann, Jörg. "German East or Polish West? Historiographical Discourse on the German-Polish Overlap between Confrontation and Reconciliation, 1772–2000." In *Disputed Territories and Shared Pasts: Overlapping National Histories in Modern Europe*, edited by Tibor Frank and Frank Hadler, 92–124. New York: Palgrave, 2011.

Hahn, Hans Henning, and Heinrich Olschowsky. *Das Jahr 1956 in Ostmitteleuropa*. Berlin: Akademie Verlag GmbH, 1996.
Hahn, Hans Henning, Heidi Hein-Kirchner, and Anna Kochanowska-Nieborak. "Einleitung: Überlegungen zum Verhältnis von Erinnerungskultur, Versöhnung und Versöhnungskitsch." In *Erinnerungskultur und Versöhnungskitsch*, edited by Hans Henning Hahn, Heidi Hein-Kirchner, and Anna Kochanowska-Nieborak, 3–16. Marburg: Herderinstitut, 2008.
Halbwachs, Maurice. *La mémoire collective*. Paris: Presses Universitaires de France, 1950.
Hannig, Nicolai. *Die Religion der Öffentlichkeit: Kirche, Religion und Medien in der Bundesrepublik 1945–1980*. Göttingen: Wallstein, 2010.
Hansen, Lulu Anne. "'Youth off the Rails': Teenage Girls and German Soliders—A Case Study in Denmark 1940–1945." In *Brutality and Desire: War and Sexuality in Europe's 20th Century*, edited by Dagmar Herzog, 135–168. London: Palgrave, 2009.
Haupt, Heinz-Gerhard, and Jürgen Kocka. *Comparative and Transnational Approaches: Central European Approaches and New Perspectives*. New York: Berghahn Books, 2009.
He, Yinan. *The Search for Reconciliation: Sino–Japanese and German–Polish Relations since World War II*. New York: Cambridge University Press, 2009.
Heinemann, Elizabeth. "The Hour of the Woman: Memories of Germany's 'Crisis Years' and West German National Identity." *American Historical Review* 101, no. 2 (April 1996): 354–95.
Hellbeck, Jochen. "'The Diaries of Fritzes and the Letters of Gretchens': Personal Writings from the German–Soviet War and Their Readers." In *Fascination and Enmity: Russia and Germany as Entangled Histories 1940–1945*, edited by Michael David-Fox, Peter Holquist, and Alexander M. Martin, 123–53. Pittsburgh, PA: Pittsburgh University Press, 2012.
Heller, Edith. *Macht, Kirche, Politik: Der Briefwechsel zwischen den polnischen und deutschen Bischöfen in Jahre 1965*. Cologne: Treff-punkt, 1992.
Hennelowa, Józefa. *Bo jestem z Wilna . . . (z Józefą Hennelową rozmawia Roman Graczyk)*. Cracow: Społeczny Instytut Wydawnictwo ZNAK, 2001.
———. "'Die Zeit ist reif für einen neuen Brief der Bischöfe': Gespräch mit Józefa Hennelowa." In *"Wir vergeben und bitten um Vergebung": Der Briefwechsel der polnischen und deutschen Bischöfe von 1965 und seine Wirkung*, edited by Basil Kerski, Thomas Kycia, and Robert Żurek, 197–210. Osnabrück: Fibre, 2006.
Henschel, Christhardt. "Aus der Geschichte lernen? Zweiter Weltkrieg, Wiederstand und der Oppositionsbewegungen in der DDR und der Volksrepublik Polen." *Gegengeschichte: Zweiter Weltkrieg und Holcaust im ostmitteleuropäischen Dissens*, 57–78. Leipzig, 2015.
Herbert, David. *Religion and Civil Society: Rethinking Public Religion in the Contemporary World*. Burlington, VT: Ashgate, 2003.
Herbert, Ulrich, ed. *Wandlungsprozesse in Westdeutschland. Belastung, Integration, Liberalisierung 1945–1980*. Göttingen: Wallstein Verlag, 2002.
Herf, Jeffrey. *Divided Memory: The Nazi Past in the Two Germanies*. Cambridge, MA: Harvard University Press, 1997.

Hermann, Konstantin. *Die DDR und die Solidarność: ausgewählte Aspekte einer Beziehung.* Dresden: Thielem, 2013.
Hild, Helmut. "Was hat die Denkschrift der EKD bewirkt?" In *Feinde werden Freunde: Von den Schwierigkeiten der deutsch-polnischen Nachbarschaft*, edited by Friedbert Pflüger and Winfred Lipscher, 90–103. Bonn: Bouvier, 1993.
Hildermeier, Manfred, Jürgen Kocka, and Christoph Conrad, eds. *Europäische Zivilgesellschaft in Ost und West: Begriff, Geschichte, Chancen.* New York: Campus, 2000.
Hindenburg, Hannfried von. *Demonstrating Reconciliation: State and Society in West German Foreign Policy toward Israel, 1952–1965.* New York: Berghahn Books, 2007.
Hirsch, Marianne. *Family Frames: Photography, Narrative and Postmemory.* Cambridge, MA: Harvard University Press, 1997.
Hodenberg, Christina von. "Die Journalisten und der Aufbruch zur kritischen zur kritischen Öffentlichkeit." In *Wandlungsprozesse in Westdeutschland: Belastung, Integration, Liberalisierung, 1945–1980*, edited by Ulrich Herbert, 278–311. Göttingen: Wallstein Verlag, 2002.
———. *Konsens und Krise: Eine Geschichte der westdeutschen Medienöffentlichkeit, 1945–1973.* Göttingen: Wallstein, 2006
Hoffmann, Stefan Ludwig, Sandrine Kott, Peter Romijn, and Oliver Wievorka. "Introduction." In *Seeking Peace in the Wake of War: Europe 1942–1947*, edited by Stefan Ludwig Hoffmann, Sandrine Kott, Peter Romijn, and Oliver Wievorka, 9–24. Amsterdam: Amsterdam University Press, 2015.
Hofmann, Arne. *The Emergence of Détente in Europe: Brandt, Kennedy and the Formation of Ostpolitik.* New York: Routledge, 2007.
Holzer, Horst. *Massenkommunikation und Demokratie in der Bundesrepublik Deutschland.* Opladen: C.W. Leske Verlag, 1967.
Huener, Jonathan. *Auschwitz, Poland and the Politics of Commemoration, 1945–1979.* Athens: Ohio University Press, 2003.
Iriye, Akira. *Global Community: The Role of International Organizations in the Making of the Contemporary World.* Berkeley: University of California Press, 2002.
Irwin-Zarecka, Iwona. *Neutralizing Memory: The Jew in Contemporary Poland.* New Brunswick, NJ: Transaction, 1989.
Jacobsen, Hans-Adolf, and Mieczysław Tomala, eds. *Wie Polen und Deutsche einander sehen: Beiträge aus beiden Ländern.* Düsseldorf: Droste Verlag, 1973.
———, eds. *Bonn-Warschau, 1945–1990: Analyse und Dokumentation.* Cologne: Verlag Wissenschaft und Politik, 1992.
Janssen, Karl-Heinz. *Die Zeit in der ZEIT: 50 Jahre einer Wochenzeitung.* Hamburg, 1996.
Jarausch, Konrad. *After Hitler: Recivilizing the Germans, 1945–1995.* New York: Oxford University Press, 2006.
Jarausch, Konrad, and Michael Geyer. *Shattered Past: Reconstructing German Histories.* Princeton, NJ: Princeton University Press, 2003.
Jarausch, Konrad, and Thomas Lindenberger, eds. *Conflicted Memories: Europeanizing Contemporary Histories.* New York: Berghahn Books, 2007.
Jarocki, Robert. *Czterdzieści pięć lat w opozycji (O ludziach "Tygodnika Powszechnego").* Cracow: Wydawnictwo Literackie, 1990.

Jarząbek, Wanda. "The Impact of the Events of the Year 1968 and Their Effects on Polish–German Political Relations between 1968 and 2008." In *1968 and the Polish–West German Relations*, edited by Wanda Jarząbek, Piotr Madajczyk, and Joanna Szymoniczek, translated by Mariusz Kukliński, 11–58. Warsaw: Instytut Studiów Politycznych Polskiej Akademii Nauk, 2013.

Jaskułowski, Tytus, and Jan Rowiński, eds. *The Polish October 1956 in World Politics*. Warsaw: Polski Instytut Spraw Międzynarodowych, 2007.

Jaszczuk, Andrzej. *Ewolucja ideowa Bolesława Piaseckiego, 1932–1956*. Warsaw: Wydawnictwo DIG, 2005.

Johnson, Ross. *Radio Free Europe and Radio Liberty: The CIA Years and Beyond*. Washington, DC: Woodrow Wilson Center Press, 2010.

Judson, Pieter. *Guardians of the Nation: Activists on the Language Frontiers of Imperial Austria*. Cambridge, MA: Harvard University Press, 2007.

Judt, Tony. "The Past Is Another Country: Myth and Memory in Post-War Europe." In *Memory and Power in Post-War Europe: Studies in the Presence of the Past*, edited by Jan-Werner Müller, 157–84. Cambridge: Cambridge University Press, 2003.

———. *Post-War: A History of Europe since 1945*. New York: Penguin Press, 2005.

Kalicki, Włodzimierz. *Ostatni jeniec wielkiej wojny: Polacy i Niemcy po 1945 roku*. Warsaw: Wydawnictwo W.A.B, 2002.

Kałwa, Dobrochna. "PRL w polskiej świadomości/pamięci historycznej." In *Pamięc polska pamięc niemiecki. od XIX do XXI wieku*, edited by Krzysztof Mikulski and Zdzisław Noga. Toruń: Wydawnictwo Adam Marszałek, 2006.

Kamusella, Tomasz. *Silesia and Central European Nationalisms: The Emergence of Ethnic Groups in Prussian Silesia and Austrian Silesia 1848–1918*. Purdue: Purdue University Press, 2006.

———. "The Changing Lattice of Languages, Borders, and Identities in Silesia." In *The Palgrave Handbook of Slavic Languages, Identities and Borders*, edited by Tomasz Kamusella, Motoki Nomachi, and Catherine Gibson. Basingstoke: Palgrave Macmillan, 2016.

Kansteiner, Wulf. *In Pursuit of German Memory: History, Television, and Politics after Auschwitz*. Athens: Ohio University Press, 2006.

Katz, Klaus, et al., eds. *Am Puls der Zeit: Die Vorläufer 1924–1955; 50 Jahre WDR*, Bd. 1. Cologne: Verlag Kiepenhauer and Witsch, 2006.

———, eds. *Am Puls der Zeit: Der Sender; Weltweit Nah Dran 1956–1985. 50 Jahre WDR*, Bd. 2. Cologne: Verlag Kiepenhauer and Witsch, 2006.

———, eds. *Am Puls der Zeit: Der Sender im Wettbewerb 1985–2005; 50 Jahre WDR*, Bd. 3. Cologne: Verlag Kiepenhauer and Witsch, 2006.

Kaufman, Debra. "Post-Memory and Post-Holocaust." In *Sociology Confronts the Holocaust: Memories and Identities in Jewish Diasporas*, edited by Judith M. Gerson and Diane L. Wolf, 39–54. Durham, NC: Duke University Press, 2007.

Keck, Margaret E., and Kathryn Sikkink. *Activists beyond Borders: Advocacy Networks in International Politics*. Ithaca, NY: Cornell University Press, 1998.

Kenney, Padraic. "Martyrs and Neighbors: Sources of Reconciliation in Central Europe." *Common Knowledge* 13, no. 1 (2007): 149–69.

Kerski, Basil, and Wolf-Dieter Eberwein, eds. *Die deutsch-polnischen Beziehungen 1949–2000: Eine Werte und Interessengemeinschaft?* Opladen: Leske+Budrich, 2001.

Kerski, Basil, Andrzej Kotula, and Kazimierz Wóycicki, eds. *Zwangsverordnete Freundschaft? Die Beziehungen zwischen der DDR und Polen, 1949–1990.* Osnabrück: Fibre Verlag, 2003.

Kerski, Basil, and Robert Żurek. "Der Briefwechsel zwischen den polnischen und deutschen Bischłfen von 1965: Enstehungsgeschichte, historischer Kontext und unmittelbare Wirkung." In *"Wir vergeben und bitten um Vergebung": Der Briefwechsel der polnischen und deutschen Bischöfe von 1965 und seine Wirkung*, edited by Basil Kerski, Tomas Kycia, and Robert Żurek, 7–53. Osnabrück: Fibre, 2006.

Khagram, Sanjeev, and Peggy Levitt. *The Transnational Studies Reader. Intersections and Innovation.* New York: Routledge, 2008.

Kisielewski, Stefan. *An dieser Stelle Europas.* Translated by Wanda Bronska-Pampuch. Munich: Piper, 1964.

Kisielewski, Stefan. *Dzienniki.* Warsaw: Wydawnictwo Iskry, 2001.

Klaus, Elisabeth. "Macht und Ohnmacht des Publikums. Oder: Wer macht das Publikum?" In *Radiozeiten: Herrschaft, Alltag, Gesellschaft (1924–1960)*, edited by Inge Marssolek and Adalheid von Saldern, 183–205. Potsdam: Verlag für Berlin-Brandenburg, 1999.

Knabe, Hubertus. *Der diskrete Charme der DDR: Stasi und der Westmedien.* 2nd ed. Berlin: Ullstein Verlag, 2003.

Koch, Hans Jürgen, and Hermann Glaser. *Ganz Ohr: Eine Kulturgeschichte des Radios in Deutschland.* Cologne: Böhlau Verlag, 2005.

Kocka, Jürgen. "Zivilgesellschaft als historisches Problem und Versprechen." In *Europäische Zivilgesellschaft in Ost und West: Begriff, Geschichte, Chancen*, edited by Manfred Hildermeier, Jürgen Kocka, and Christoph Conrad, 13–40. New York: Campus Verlag, 2000.

Kogon, Eugen. *Der SS-Staat: Das System der deutschen Konzentrationslager.* Frankfurt/Main: Verlag der Frankfurter Hefte, 1946.

Komska, Yuliya. "Introduction: West Germany's Cold War Radio; A Crucible of the Transatlantic Century." *German Politics and Society* 32, no. 1 (110) (Spring 2014): 1–14.

Köpke, Wilfried. *Geschäftsführung ohne Auftrag: Das Journalismusverständnis von Walter Dirks.* Munich: GRIN Publishing, 2007.

Kopp, Kristin. *Germany's Wild East: Constructing Poland as a Colonial Space.* Ann Arbor: University of Michigan Press, 2012.

Kopp, Kristin, and Joanna Niżynska. "Between Entitlement and Reconciliation: Germany and Poland's Postmemory after 1989." In *Germany, Poland, and Postmemorial Relations: In Search of a Livable Past*, edited by Kristin Kopp and Joanna Niżynska, 1–24. New York: Routledge, 2012.

Koppe, Karlheinz. *Dreimal getauft und Mensch geblieben.* Berlin: Kathrin Rohnstock Medienbüro, 2004.

Kosicki, Piotr H. "*Caritas* across the Iron Curtain: Polish-German Reconciliation and the Bishops' Letter of 1965." *East European Politics and Society* 23, no. 2 (Spring 2009): 213–43.

———. "Introduction." In *Vatican II behind the Iron Curtain*, edited by Piotr Kosicki, 1–26. Washington, DC: The Catholic Press of America, 2016.

———. "Five: Vatican II and Poland." In *Vatican II behind the Iron Curtain*, edited by Piotr Kosicki, 127–98. Washington, DC: The Catholic Press of America, 2016.

———, ed. *Vatican II behind the Iron Curtain*. Washington, DC: The Catholic Press of America, 2016.

Kowalczyk, Andrzej Stanisław. *Giedroyc i "Kultura."* Wrocław: Wydawnictwo Dolnośląskie, 2000.

Kraft, Claudia. "Who Is a Pole and Who Is a German? The Province of Olsztyn in 1945." In *Ethnic Cleansing in Eastern Europe 1944–1948*, edited by Ana Siljak and Philipp Ther, 107–20. Lanham, MD: Rowman and Littlefield, 2001.

Kraśko, Tadeusz. *Wierność: Rozmowy z Jerzym Turowiczem*. Poznań: Kantor Wydawniczy SAWW, 1995.

Kruip, Gudrun. *Das "Welt"-"Bild" des Axel Springer Verlags: Journalismus zwischen westlichen Werten und deutschen Denktraditionen*. Munich: R.Oldenbourg Verlag, 1999.

Kruke, Anja. "Responsivität und Medialisierung: Meinungsforschung für Parteien in den sechziger Jahren." In *Medialisierung und Demokratie im 20. Jahrhundert*, edited by Frank Bösch and Norbert Frei, 145–78. Göttingen: Wallstein Verlag, 2006.

———. *Demoskopie in der Bundesrepublik Deutschland: Meinungsforschung, Parteien und Medien*. Düsseldorf: Droste Verlag, 2007.

Kucharski, Wojciech, and Grzegorz Strauchold, eds. *Wokół Orędzia: kardynał Bolesław Kominek, prekursor pojednania polsko-niemieckiego*. Wrocław: Ośrodek "Pamięć i Przyszłość," 2009.

Kundera, Milan. "The Tragedy of Central Europe." *New York Review of Books* 31, no. 7 (April 1984): 33–38.

Kunicki, Mikołaj. *Between the Brown and the Red: Nationalism, Catholicism, and Communism in 20th Century Poland—The Politics of Bolesław Piasecki*. Athens: Ohio University Press, 2012.

Kurcz, Zbigniew. *Mniejszość polska na Wileńszczyźnie: studium socjologiczne*. Wrocław: Wydawn. Uniwersytetu Wrocławskiego, 2005.

Kurkowska, Martha. "Archiwa pamięci—oral history." *Historyka* 28 (1998): 67–76.

Kuus, Merje. "Ubiquitous Identities and Elusive Subjects: Puzzles from Central Europe." *Transactions of the Institute of British Geographers*, New Series 32, no. 1 (January 2007): 90–101.

Kwiatkowski, Piotr Tadeusz. "The Second World War in the Memory of Contemporary Polish Society." In *Memory and Change in Europe: Eastern Perspectives*, edtied by Malgorzata Pakier and Joanna Wawrzyniak, 231–45. New York: Berghahn Books, 2016.

Laboor, Ernst. *Der Rapacki-Plan und die DDR: Die Entspannungsvision des Polnischen Aussenminster Adam Rapacki und die deutschlandpolitischen Ambitionen der SED-Führung in den fünfziger und sechziger Jahren*. Berlin: Fides, 2003.

Łada, Agnieszka. "Bekannte und unbekannte Gesichter aus dem Fotoalbum: Die politischen Akteure der deutsch-polnische Nachbarschaft." In *Erwachsene*

Nachbarschaft: Die deutsch-polnische Beziehungen 1991 bis 2011, edited by Dieter Bingen, Peter Oliver Loew, Krzysztof Ruchniewicz, and Marek Zybura, 51–61. Wiesbaden: Harrassowitz Verlag, 2011.

Le Gloannec, Anne Marie, ed. *Non-State Actors in International Relations: The Case of Germany*. New York: Manchester University Press, 2007.

Lebow, Richard Ned, Wulf Kansteiner, and Claudio Fogu. *The Politics of Memory in Postwar Europe*. Durham, NC: Duke University Press, 2006.

Lehmann, Reinhold. "Mietek Pszon: On pokazał nam, dlaczego powinniśmy pokochać Polaków i ich kraj." In *Polacy i Niemcy pół wieku później: Księga pamiątkowa dla Mieczysława Pszona*, edited by Wojciech Pięciak. Cracow: Wydawnictwo Znak, 1996.

Lewandowska, Stanisława. *Losy wilnian: zapis rzeczywistości okupacyjnej; ludzie, fakty, wydarzenia 1939–1945*. Warsaw: Wydawnictwo Neriton, 2004.

Liehr, Dorothee. *Von der Aktion gegen der Spiegel zur Spiegel-Affär: zur gesellschaftspolitischen Rolle der Intellektuellen*. New York: P. Lang, 2002.

Liekis, Šarūnas. *1939: The Year That Changed Everything in Lithuania's History*. Amsterdam: Rodopi, 2010.

Lindenberger, Thomas. "Vergangenes Hören und Sehen: Zeitgeschichte und ihre Herausforderung durch die audiovisuellen Medien." *Zeithistorische Forschungen* 1 (2004): 72–85.

Lipscher, Winfried. "Rückkehr in die Heimat?" In *Feinde werden Freunde. Von den schwierigkeiten der deutsch-polnischen Nachbarschaft*, edited by Friedbert Pflüger and Winfried Lipscher, 427–32. Bonn: Bouvier, 1993.

Lissek, Vincens M. "'Łączy nas filozofia, a nawet sztuka kulinarna . . .'" In *Polacy i Niemcy pół wieku później: Księga pamiątkowa dla Mieczysława Pszona*, edited by Wojciech Pięciak, 97–113. Cracow: Wydawnictwo Znak, 1996.

Liulevicius, Vejas. *Warland on the Eastern Front: Culture, National Identity and German Occupation in World War I*. Cambridge: Cambridge University Press, 2005.

———. *The German Myth of the East: 1800 to the Present*. Oxford: Oxford University Press, 2009.

Long, William J., and Peter Breckle. *War and Reconciliation: Reason and Emotion in Conflict Resolution*. Cambridge, MA: The MIT Press, 2003.

Łos-Nowak, Teresa. *Plan Rapackiego a bezpieczeństwo Europejskie*. Wrocław: Wydawn. Uniwersytetu Wrocławskiego, 1991.

Lotz, Christian. *Die deutung des Verlusts: Erinnerungspolitische Kontroversen im geteilten Deutschland um Flucht, Vertreibung und die Ostgebiete (1948–1972)*. Cologne, Weimar, Vienna: Böhlau, 2007.

Machcewicz, Paweł. *Rebellious Satellite: Poland, 1956*. Washington, DC: Woodrow Wilson Center Press; Stanford, CA: Stanford University Press, 2009.

Madajczyk, Piotr. *Na drodze do pojednania: Wokół orędzia biskupów polskich do biskupów niemieckich z 1965 r*. Warsaw: Wydawnictwo Naukowe PPN, 1994.

———. "Experience and Memory: The Second World War in Poland." In *Experience and Memory: The Second World War in Europe*, edited by Jörg Echternkampf and Stefan Martens, 70–85. New York: Berghahn Books, 2010.

———. "The Impact of the Events of 1968 on the Forming of the Image of Poland and the Poles in Public Opinion in the Federal Republic of Germany." In *1968 and the Polish–West German Relations*, edited by Wanda Jarząbek, Piotr Madajczyk, and Joanna Szymoniczek, translated by Mariusz Kukliński, 59–128. Warsaw: Instytut Studiów Politycznych Polskiej Akademii Nauk, 2013.

Magirius, Friedrich. "'Znaki Pokuty' — próba bilansu." In *Polacy i Niemcy pół wieku później: Księga pamiątkowa dla Mieczysława Pszona*, edited by Wojciech Pięciak, 43–50. Cracow: Wydawnictwo Znak, 1996.

Maier, Charles. *The Unmasterable Past: Holocaust, History, and German Memory*. Cambridge, MA: Harvard University Press, 1988.

Major, Patrick. *The Death of KPD: Communism and Anti-communism in West Germany, 1945–1956*. Oxford: Oxford University Press, 1998.

Manetti, Christina. "Sign of the Times: The Znak Circle and Catholic Intellectual Engagement in Communist Poland, 1945–1976." PhD diss., University of Washington, 1998.

Mansfeld, Michael, and Jürgen Neven-du Mont. *Denk' ich an Deutschland: Ein Kommentar in Bild und Wort*. Munich: Kurt Desch, 1956.

Marczuk, Paulina Karina. "The Origins of the Polish–German Reconciliation, 1965–1966." *Arhivele Totalitarismului* 1–2 (2017): 171–80.

Markiewicz, Władysław. "Erziehung zur Verständigung: Die deutsch-polnischen Schulbuchempfehlungen." In *Feinde werden Freunde: Von den Schwierigkeiten der deutsch-polnischen Nachbarschaft*, edited by Friedbert Pflüger and Winfried Lipscher, 182–92. Bonn: Bouvier, 1993.

Marrus, Michael R. "Papal Apologies of John Paul II." In *The Age of Apology: Facing Up to the Past*, edited by Mark Gibney et al., 259–70. Philadelphia: University of Pennsylvania Press, 2008.

Marshall, Barbara. *Willy Brandt: Eine politische Biographie*. Bonn: Bouvier, 1993.

Marszolek, Inge. "Unforgotten Landscapes." *German Politics and Society* 32, no. 1 (110) (Spring 2014): 60–73.

Marszolek, Inge, and Adalheid von Saldern. "Massmedien im Kontext von Herrschaft, Alltag und Gesellschaft: Eine Herausforderung an die Geschichtsschreibung." In *Radiozeiten: Herrschaft, Alltag, Gesellschaft (1924–1960)*, edited by Inge Marssolek and Adalheid von Saldern, 11–39. Potsdam: Verlag für Berlin-
Brandenburg, 1999.

Mazower, Mark. "Changing Trends in the Historiography of Postwar Europe, East and West." *International Labor and Working-Class History* 58 (Fall 2000): 275–82.

Mazowiecki, Tadeusz. "Von der Gegenwart zur neuen Nachbarschaft." In *Feinde werden Freunde:. Von den Schwierigkeiten der deutsch-polnischen Nachbarschaft*, edited by Friedbert Pflüger and Winfried Lipscher, 433–52. Bonn: Bouvier, 1993.

Meckel, Markus. "1990–2010. 20 Jahre deutsch-polnische Beziehungen: Ein persöhnlicher Ruckblick, Bilanz und Perspektiven." In *Festansprache zur Eröffnung der Tagung "20 Jahre deutsch-polnische Nachbarschaft. Eine Bilanz"; Erwachsene Nachbarschaft: Die deutsch-polnische Beziehungen 1991 bis 2011*, edited by Dieter Bingen, Peter Oliver Loew, Krzysztof Ruchniewicz, and Marek Zybura, 17–28. Wiesbaden: Harrassowitz Verlag, 2011.

Megargee, Geoffrey. "A Blind Eye and Dirty Hands: The Sources of Wehrmacht Criminality in the Campaign against the Soviet Union." In *The Germans and the East*, edited by Charles Ingrao and Franz A. J. Szabo, 310–27. West Lafayette, IN: Purdue University Press, 2008.

Mehlhorn, Ludwig. "Die Polenpolitik der DDR." In *Feinde werden Freunde: Von den Schwierigkeiten der deutsch-polnischen Nachbarschaft*, edited byFriedbert Pflüger and Winfried Lipscher, 223–29. Bonn: Bouvier, 1993.

———. "Szara eminencja." In *Polacy i Niemcy pół wieku później: Księga pamiątkowa dla Mieczysława Pszona*, edited by edited by Wojciech Pięciak. Cracow: Wydawnictwo Znak, 1996.

Meng, Michael. *Shattered Spaces: Encountering Jewish Ruins in Postwar Poland and Germany*. Cambridge, MA: Harvard University Press, 2011.

Merseburger, Peter. *Rudolf Augstein: Biographie*. Munich: Droste, 2007.

Micewski, Andrzej. *Cardinal Wyszyński: A Biography*. Translated by William R. Brand and Katarzyna Mroczkowska-Brand. San Diego: Harcourt Brace Jovanovich, 1984

———. *Stefan Kardinal Wyszyński, Primas von Polen: Eine Biographie*. Mainz: Grünewald, 1990.

Michlic, Joanna. "The Path of Bringing the Dark to Light: Memory of the Holocaust in Eastern Europe." In *Memory and Change in Europe: Eastern Perspectives*, edited by Malgorzata Pakier and Joanna Wawrzyniak, 115–30. New York: Berghahn Books, 2016.

Michnik, Adam. "On Détente: An Interview with Adam Michnik." In *The New Detente: Rethinking East–West Relations*, edited by Mary Kaldor, Gerard Holden, and Richard A. Falk, 117–130. New York: Verso, 1989.

———. *The Church and the Left*. Translated by David Ost. Chicago: University of Chicago Press, 1993.

Miziniak, Wacław. "Polityka Informacyjna." In *Polacy wobec Niemców: Z dziejów politycznej Polski 1945–1989*, edited by Anna Wolff-Powęska, 142–60. Poznań: Instytut Zachodni, 1993.

Moeller, Robert. *War Stories: The Search for a Usable Past*. Berkeley: University of California Press, 2001.

Montei, Amanda. "Performing Reconciliation: Transnational Advocacy in Rwanda." *PAJ: A Journal of Performance and Art* 33, no. 2 (May 2011): 80–90.

Müller, Jan-Werner. *Another Country: German Intellectuals, Unification and National Identity*. New Haven, CT: Yale University Press, 2000.

———, ed. *Memory and Power in Postwar Europe: Studies in the Presence of the Past*. Cambridge: Cambridge University Press, 2001.

———. "Introduction: The Power of Memory, the Memory of Power and the Power over Memory." In *Memory and Power in Post-War Europe: Studies in the Presence of the Past*, edited by Jan-Werner Müller, 1–38. Cambridge: Cambridge University Press, 2003.

Münch, Ingo von, ed. *Dokumente des geteilten Deutschlands*. Stuttgart: Alfred Kröner Verlag, 1968.

Münkel, Daniela. "Als 'deutscher Kennedy' zum Sieg? Willy Brandt, die USA und die Medien." *Zeithistorische forschungen* 1 (2004): 172–94.

Murphy, Colleen. *A Moral Theory of Political Reconciliation*. Cambridge: Cambridge University Press, 2012.
Nalewajko-Kulikov, Joanna, and Magdalena Ruta. "Yiddish Culture in Poland after the Holocaust." In *Jewish Presence in Absence: The Aftermath of the Holocaust in Poland 1944–2010*, edited by Feliks Tych and Monika Adamczyk-Garbowska, 353–394. Jerusalem: Yad Vashem, 2014.
Nawratowicz, Barbara. *Piwnica pod Baranami: Początki i rozwój (1956–1963)*. Cracow: Petrus 2010.
Nord, Philip. "Conclusion." In *Seeking Peace in the Wake of War: Europe 1943–1947*, edited by Stefan-Ludwig Hoffman, Sandrine Kott, Peter Romijn, and Olivier Wievorka. Amsterdam: Amsterdam University Press, 2015.
Nowak, Andrzej. "Political Correctness and the Memories Constructed for 'Eastern Europe.'" In *Memory and Change in Europe: Eastern Perspectives*, edited by Małgorzata Pakier and Joanna Wawrzyniak, 38–58. New York: Berghahn Books, 2016.
Nowak-Jeziorański, Jan. *Polska z bliska*. Cracow: Społeczny Instytut Wydawniczy ZNAK, 2005.
Ochmann, Cornelius. "Neue Ostpolitik der EU. Das Beziehungsgeflecht Deutschland – Polen – Russland – Ukraine." In *Erwachsene Nachbarschaft. Die deutsch-polnische Beziehungen 1991 bis 2011*, edited by Dieter Bingen, Peter Oliver Loew, Krzysztof Ruchniewicz and Marek Zybura, 67–70. Wiesbaden: Harrassowitz, 2011.
Olczak-Ronikier, Joanna. *W ogrodzie pamięci*. Cracow: Wydawnictwo Znak, 2001.
Oppenheimer, Andrew. "Air Wars and Empire: Gandhi and the Search for a Usable Past in Postwar Germany." *Central European History* 45 (2012): 669–96.
Orłowski, Hubert. *"Polnische Wirtschaft": Zum deutschen Polendiskurs im Neuzeit*. Wiesbaden: Harrassowitz, 1996.
Osa, Maryjane. *Solidarity and Contention: Networks of Polish Opposition*. Minneapolis: University of Minnesota Press, 2003.
Ost, David. *Solidarity and the Politics of Anti-Politics: Opposition and Reform in Poland since 1968*. Philadelphia: Temple University Press, 1990.
Pailer, Wolfgang. *Stanisław Stomma: Nestor der polnisch-deutschen Aussöhnung*. Bonn: Bouvier, 1995.
Pakier, Małgorzata, and Joanna Wawrzyniak. "Memory and Change in Eastern Europe: How Special?" *Memory and Change in Europe: Eastern Perspectives*, edited by Małgorzata Pakier and Joanna Wawrzyniak, 1–22. New York: Berghahn Books, 2016.
———. *Memory and Change in Europe: Eastern Perspectives*. New York: Berghahn Books, 2016.
Pappi, Franz Urban. "Boundary Specification and Structural Models of Elite Systems: Social Circles Revisited." *Social Networks* 6 (1984): 79–95.
Pearson, Benjamin C. "Faith and Democracy: Political Transformations at the German Protestant Kirchentag 1949–1969." Dissertation, University of North Carolina–Chapel Hill, 2007.
Pendas, Devin. *The Frankfurt Auschwitz Trial, 1963–1965: Genocide, History and the Limits of the Law*. Cambridge: Cambridge University Press, 2006.

Persak, Krzysztof. "Kontrwywiad i dziennikarze." *Biuletyn Instytutu Pamięci Narodowej* 11, no. 46 (November 2004): 48–61.
Pflüger, Friedbert. "Grenze und Partnerschaft: Die deutsch-polnische Verträge von 1990/1991." In *Feinde werden Freunde: Von den Schwierigkeiten der deutsch-polnischen Nachbarschaft*, edited by Friedbert Pflüger and Winfried Lipscher, 11–28. Bonn: Bouvier, 1993.
Pflüger, Friedbert, and Winfried Lipscher, eds. *Feinde werden Freunde: Von den Schwierigkeiten der deutsch-polnischen Nachbarschaft*. Bonn: Bouvier, 1993.
Pięciak, Wojciech, ed. *Polacy i niemcy pół wieku później: Księga pamiątkowa dla Mieczysława Pszona*. Cracow: Wydawnictwo Znak, 1996.
Plum, Werner, ed. *Ungewöhnliche Normalisierung: Der Beziehungen der Bundesrepublik Deutschland zu Polen*. Bonn: Verlag Neue Gesellschaft GmbH, 1984.
Pokorna-Ignatowicz, Katarzyna. *Telewizja w systemie politycznym i medialnym PRL: Między polityką a widzem*. Cracow: Wydawn. Uniwersytetu Jagiellońskiego, 2003.
Polak, Barbara. "Wszystko pod kontrolą: o inwigilacji zachodnich korespondentów z Krzysztofem Bobińskim, Bernardem Margueritte I Krzysztofem Persakiem rozmawia Barbara Polak." *Biuletyn Instytutu Pamięci Narodowej* 11, no. 46 (November 2004): 18–36.
Polak-Springer, Peter. "Landscapes of Revisionism: Building and the Contestation of Space in an Industrial Polish-German Borderland, 1922–1945." *Central European History* 45 (2012): 485–522.
———. *Recovered Territory: A German–Polish Conflict over Land and Culture 1919–1989*. New York: Berghahn Books, 2015.
Porter, Brian. *When Nationalism Began to Hate: Imagining Modern Politics in Nineteenth Century Poland*. New York: Oxford University Press, 2000.
Porter-Szücs, Brian. *Faith and Fatherland: Catholicism, Modernity, and Poland*. New York: Oxford University Press, 2011.
Porter-Szücs, Brian, and Bruce A. Berglund, eds. *Christianity and Modernity in Eastern Europe*. New York: CEU Press, 2013.
Pürer, Heinz, and Johannes Raabe. *Medien in Deutschland. Band I. Presse*. Konstanz: UVK Medien, 1996.
Pustoła-Kozłowska, Ewa, and Jacek Pustoła. *Hotel Bristol*. Warsaw: Państwowe Wydawnictwo Naukowe, 1985.
Rakowski, Mieczysław F. *Dzienniki polityczne 1958–1962*. Warsaw: Wydawnictwo ISKRY, 1998.
———. *Dzienniki polityczne 1963–1966*. Warsaw: Wydawnictwo ISKRY, 1999.
Ranke, Andrzej. *Stosunki polsko-niemieckie w polskiej publicystyce katolickiej w latach 1945–1989*. Toruń: Europejskie Centrum Edykacyjne, 2004.
Reuber, Angela. "Deutschland- und Ostpolitik im Fernsehen. Die Sendungen der Ost-West-Redaktion des Westdeutschen Rundfunks 1966-1969." Master's thesis, Universität zu Köln, Philosophisches Fakultät, Historisches Seminar, 2003.
Riedel, Heide. *Lieber Rundfunk . . . 75 Jahre Hörergeschichte(n)*. Berlin: Vistas, 1999.
Risse-Kappen, Thomas. *Bringing Transnational Relations Back In: Non-State Actors, Domestic Structures and International Institutions*. Cambridge: Cambridge University Press, 1995.

Rommerskirchen, Eva, ed. *Deutsche und Polen: Annäherungen — Zbliżenia, 1945–1995*. Düsseldorf: Droste, 1996.
Rosenberg, Tima. *The Haunted Lands: Facing Europe's Ghosts after Communism*. New York: Random House, 1995.
Rother, Bernd "Zwischen Solidarität und Friedenssicherung: Willy Brandt und Polen in den 1980er Jahren." In *Nie mehr eine Politik über Polen hinweg: Willy Brandt und Polen*, edited by Friedhelm Boll and Krzysztof Ruchniewicz, 220–64. Bonn: J.H.W. Dietz, 2010.
Ruchniewicz, Krszysztof, and Jürgen Zinnecker. "Einleitung." In *Zwischen Zwangsarbeit, Holocaust und Vertreibung: Polnische, jüdische und deutsche Kindheiten im besetzten Polen*, edited by Krzysztof Ruchniewicz and Jürgen Zinnecker, 11–18. Munich: Juventa Verlag, 2007.
Ruchniewicz, Krzysztof. "Die knifflige Vergangenheit: Geschichtspolitik, innen-politische Instrumentalisierung und grosse Debatten in den deutsch-polnischen Beziehungen." In *Erwachsene Nachbarschaft: Die deutsch-polnische Beziehungen 1991 bis 2011*, edited by Dieter Bingen, Peter Oliver Loew, Krzysztof Ruchniewicz, and Marek Zybura, 128–48. Wiesbaden: Harrassowitz Verlag, 2011.
Ruchniewicz, Krzysztof, and Marek Zybura, eds. *Mein Polen: Deutsche Polenfreunde in Porträts*. Dresden: Thelem, 2005.
Ruff, Mark. *The Wayward Flock: Catholic Youth in Postwar West Germany, 1945–1955*. Chapel Hill: University of North Carolina Press, 2005.
Santa-Barbara, Joanna. "Reconciliation." In *Handbook of Peace and Conflict Studies*, edited by Charles Webel and Johan Galtung, 173–186. New York: Routledge, 2007.
Särchen, Günter, and Brigitte Särchen. "Adres: Mietek Pszon, Kraków." In *Polacy i Niemcy pół wieku później: Księga pamiątkowa dla Mieczysława Pszona*, edited by Wojciech Pięciak. Cracow: Wydawnictwo Znak, 1996.
Sauerland, Karol. "Polen und Juden innerhalb der polnischen Erinnerungskultur." In *Perspektiven einer Europäischen Erinnerungsgemeinschaft: Nationale Narrative und Transnationale dynamiken seit 1989*, edited by Wolfgang Stephan Kissel and Ulrike Liebert, 59–70. Münster: LIT Verlag, 2010.
Sawisz, Anna, and Barbara Szacka. *Czas przeszły i pamięć społeczna: przemiany świadomości historycznej inteligencji polskiej 1965–1988*. Warsaw: Uniwersytet Warsawski, Instytut Socjologii, 1990
Schaefer, Berndt. "The GDR, the FRG and the Polish October 1956." In *The Polish October 1956 in World Politics*, edited by Jan Rowiński, 197–216. Warsaw: Polski Instytut Spraw Międzynarodowych, 2007.
Schelsky, Helmut. *Die skeptische Generation: Eine Soziologie der deutschen Jugend*. Cologne, Düsseldorf: Eugen Diederichs Verlag, 1957.
Scheurle, Christoph. *Die deutschen Kanzler im Fernsehen: Theatrale Darstellungsstrategien von Politikern im Schlüsselmedium der Nachkriegsgeschichte*. Bielefeld: Transcript, 2009.
Schildt, Axel, Detlef Siegfried, and Karl Christian Lammers, eds. *Dynamische Zeiten: Die 60er Jahren in den beiden deutschen Gesellschaften*. Hamburg: Christians, 2000.

Schlosser, Nicholas. *Battling for the Airwaves: The Radio Propaganda War against East Germany.* Champaign: Illinois University Press, 2015.

Schmid, Carlo. "Politische Reisen: Polen 1958." In *Feinde werden Freunde: Von den Schwierigkeiten der deutsch-polnischen Nachbarschaft,* edited by Friedbert Pflüger and Winfried Lipscher, 29–39. Bonn: Bouvier, 1993.

Schneider, Christoph. *Der Warschauer Kniefall.* Konstanz: UKV Verlagsgesellschaft GmbH, 2006.

——. "Der Kniefall von Warschau: Spontane Geste—bewusste Inszenierung?" (Hrsg.). In *Das Jahrhundert der Bilder: 1949 bis heute,* edited by Gerhard Paul, 410–417. Göttingen: Vandenhoeck & Ruprecht, 2008.

Schrafstetter, Susanna. "The Long Shadow of the Past: History, Memory and the Debate over West Germany's Nuclear Status, 1954–69." *History and Memory* 16, no. 1 (Spring/Summer 2005): 118–45.

Schwarz, Hans-Peter, ed. *Akten zur auswärtigen Politik der Bundesrepublik Deutschlands, 1964.* Munich: R. Oldenbourg, 1989.

——, ed. *Akten zur auswärtigen Politik der Bundesrepublik Deutschlands, 1965.* Munich: R. Oldenbourg, 1989.

Schwelling, Birgit, ed. *Reconciliation, Civil Society and the Politics of Memory.* Bielefeld: Transcript-Verlag, 2012.

Service, Hugo. "Reinterpreting the Expulsions of Germans from Poland, 1945–9." *Journal of Contemporary History* 27, no. 3 (July 2012): 528–50.

Serwatka, Tomasz. *Kardynał Bolesław Kominek (1903–1974): Duszpasterz i polityk, zarys biograficzny.* Wrocław: Wydawnictwo "Lena," 2013.

Seung-Lee, Woo. *Das Fernsehen im geteilten Deutschland (1952–1989): Ideologische Konkurrenz und programmliche Koperation.* Potsdam: Verlag für Potsdam Brandenburg, 2003.

Seidler, Manfried. "Das Polenmemorandum des Bensberger Kreises: Wirkung in Deutschland und Polen." In *Feinde werden Freunde: Von den Schwierigkeiten der deutsch-polnischen Nachbarschaft,* edited by Friedbert Pflüger and Winfried Lipscher, 103–12. Bonn: Bouvier, 1993.

Shore, Marci. *Caviar and Ashes: A Warsaw Generation's Life and Death in Marxism.* New Haven, CT: Yale University Press, 2006.

Skibowski, Klaus Otto. *Wolken über weitem Land: Eine Familiengeschichte aus Masuren.* Munich: Langen-Müller Verlag, 2006.

Śliwinski, Błażej, ed. *Mazowsze, Pomorze, Prusy, Gdańskie Studia z Dziejów Średniowiecza nr 7.* Gdańsk: Oficina Ferberiana, 2000.

Smith-Scott, Giles. *The Politics of Apolitical Culture: The Congress for Cultural Freedom, the CIA and Post-War American Hegemony.* New York: Routledge, 2002.

Snyder, Timothy. *The Reconstruction of Nations: Poland, Ukraine, Lithuania and Belarus, 1569–1999.* New Haven, CT: Yale University Press, 2003.

Śpiewak, Paweł. *Pamięć po komunizmie.* Gdańsk: Wydawn. Słowo/obraz terytoria, 2005.

Sroka, Marek. "'Nations Will Not Survive without Their Cultural Heritage': Karol Estreicher, Polish Cultural Restitution Plans and the Recovery of Polish Cultural Property from the American Zone of Occupation." *Polish Review* 57, no. 3 (2012): 3–28.

Stach, Stephan. "Dissidentes Gedenken: Der Umgang mit Holocaustgedenktagen in der Volksrepublik Polen und der DDR." In *Gegengeschichte: Zweiter Weltkrieg und Holocaust im Ostmitteleuropäischen Dissens*, edited by Stephan Stach and Peter Hallama, 207–36. Leipzig: Leipziger Universitätsverlag, 2015.

Stach, Stephan, and Peter Hallama. "Einleitung: Gegengeschichte—Zweiter Weltkrieg und Holocaust im ostmitteleuropäischen Dissens." In *Gegengeschichte: Zweiter Weltkrieg und Holocaust im Ostmitteleuropäischen Dissens*, edited by Stephan Stach and Peter Hallama, 9–28. Leipzig: Leipziger Universitätsverlag, 2015.

———, eds. *Gegengeschichte: Zweiter Weltkrieg und Holocaust im Ostmitteleuropäischen Dissens*. Leipzig: Leipziger Universitätsverlag, 2015.

Stefancic, David. "The Rapacki-Plan: A Case Study of European Diplomacy." *East European Quarterly* 21, no. 4 (Winter 1987): 401.

Stehle, Hansjakob. "Vorwort." Stefan Kisielewski. *An dieser Stelle Europas*. Translated by Wanda Bronska-Pampuch. Munich: Piper, 1964.

———. *Deutschlands Osten-Polens Westen? Eine Dokumentation*. Frankfurt/Main: Samuel Fischer Bücherei, 1965.

———. *The Independent Satellite: Society and Politics in Poland since 1945*. Translated by D. J. S. Thompson. New York: Praeger, 1965.

———. *Nachbar Polen*. Frankfurt a.M: S. Fischer Verlag, 1963 (erweiterte Auflage 1968).

———. *Nachbarn im Osten: Herausforderung zu einer neuen Politik*. Frankfurt/Main: Samuel Fischer, 1971.

———. *Die Ostpolitik des Vatikans, 1917–1975*. Munich, Zurich: Piper, 1975.

———. *Eastern Politics of the Vatican, 1917–1979*. Translated by Sandra Smith. Athens: Ohio University Press, 1981.

———. "Seit 1960: Der mühsame katholische Dialog über die Grenze." In *Ungewöhnliche Normalisierung: Beziehungen der Bundesrepublik Deutschland zu Polen*, edited by Werner Plum, 155–178. Bonn: Neue Gesellschaft, 1984.

———. "Człowiek z właściwościami—od Reicha do Ranickiego: Reflekcje przyjaciela." *Polacy i Niemcy pół wieku później: Księga pamiątkowa Mieczysława Pszona*, edited by edited by Wojciech Pięciak, 167–80. Cracow: Wydawnictwo Znak, 1996.

Stempin, Arkadiusz. *Das Maximilian-Kolbe-Werk: Wegbereiter der deutsch-polnischen Aussöhnung 1960–1989*. Paderborn: Schöningh, 2006.

Stokłosa, Katarzyna. *Polen und die deutsche Ostpolitik 1945–1990*. Göttingen: Vandenhoeck und Ruprecht, 2011.

Stola, Dariusz. "Fighting against the Shadows: The Anti-Zionist Campaign of 1968." In *Anti-Semitism and Its Opponents in Modern Poland*, edited by Robert Blobaum, 286–87. Ithaca, NY: Cornell University Press, 2005.

Stomma, Stanisław. *Pościg za nadzieją*. Paris: Éditions du Dialogue, 1991.

———. "Pater Muckermann—ein Vorläufer der Versöhnung in Wilna." In *Feinde werden Freunde: Von den Schwierigkeiten der deutsch-polnischen Nachbarschaft*, edited by Friedbert Pflüger and Winfried Lipscher, 130–44. Bonn: Bouvier, 1993.

———. "Christliche Ethik gilt auch in den internationalen Beziehungen." *"Wir vergeben und bitten um Vergebung": Der Briefwechsel der polnischen und deutschen Bischöfe von 1965*, edited by Basil Kerski, Thomas Kycia, Robert Żurek, 81–95. Osnabrück: Fibre, 2006.

Stonor Saunders, Frances. *The Cultural Cold War: CIA and the World of Arts and Letters*. New York: The New Press, 2001.

Strauchold, Grzegorz. *Autochtoni, polscy, niemieccy—od nacjonalizmu do komunizmu 1945–1949*. Toruń: Adam Marszalek, 2001.

Stuiber, Heinz-Werner. *Medien in Deutschland. Band II. Rundfunk*. Konstanz: UVK Medien, 1996.

Subtelny, Orest. "Expulsion, Resettlement, Civic Strife: The Fate of Poland's Ukrainians 1944–1947." In *Redrawing Nations: Ethnic Cleansing in East Central Europe 1945–1948*, edited by Philipp Ther and Ana Siljak, 155–72. Lanham, MD: Rowman and Littlefield, 2001.

Suri, Jeremi. "Non-governmental Organizations and Non-state Actors." In *Palgrave Advances in International History*, edited by Patrick Finney, 223–245. New York: Palgrave McMillan, 2005.

———. *Power and Protest: Global Revolution and the Rise of Détente*. Cambridge, MA: Harvard University Press, 2003.

Süss, Dietmar. "The Air War, the Public and the Cycles of Memory." In *Experience and Memory: The Second World War in Europe*, edited by Jörg Echternkampf and Stefan Martens, 180–97. New York: Berghahn Books, 2010.

Süssmuth, Rita. "Gute Nachbarschaft gründet sich auf Versöhnung und Partnerschaft." In *Feinde werden Freunde: Von den Schwierigkeiten der deutsch-polnischen Nachbarschaft*, edited by Friedbert Pflüger and Winfried Lipscher, 1–10. Bonn: Bouvier, 1993.

Sywottek, Arnold. "Nationale Politik als Symbolpolitik: Die westdeutsche Deutschland- und Aussenpolitik in gesellschaftsgeschichtlicher Perspektive." In *Dynamische Zeiten: Die 60er Jahren in den beiden deutschen Gesellschaften*, edited by Axel Schildt, Detlef Siegfried, and Karl Christian Lammers, 342–361. Hamburg: Hans Christians Verlag, 2000.

Szymańska, Agnieszka. "Information, Meinung, Macht, Manipulation: Die Rolle der Medien in den deutsch-polnischen Beziehungen." In *Erwachsene Nachbarschaft: Die deutsch-polnische Beziehungen 1991 bis 2011*, edited by Dieter Bingen, Peter Oliver Loew, Krzysztof Ruchniewicz, and Marek Zybura, 409–25. Wiesbaden: Harrassowitz Verlag, 2011.

Szymoniczek, Joanna. "Polish Public Opinion towards Germany and the Events of the Year 1968 Therein." In *1968 and the Polish–West German Relations*, edited by Wanda Jarząbek, Piotr Madajczyk, and Joanna Szymoniczek, translated by Mariusz Kukliński, 129–56. Warsaw: Instytut Studiów Politycznych Polskiej Akademii Nauk, 2013.

Ther, Philipp. "Beyond the Nation: The Relational Basis of a Comparative History of Germany and Europe." *Central European History* 36, no. 1 (March 2003): 45–73.

Ther, Philipp. "Comparisons, Cultural Transfers and the Study of Networks: Towards a Transnational History of Europe." In *Comparative and Transnational*

History: Central European Approaches and New Perspectives, edited by Heinz-Gerhardt Haupt and Jürgen Kocka, 204–25. New York: Berghahn Books, 2009.

Ther, Philipp, and Holm Sundhaussen, eds. *Regionale Bewegungen und Regionalismen in europäischen Zwischenräumen seit der Mitte der 19. Jahrhunderts*. Marburg: Herder Institut, 2003.

Thum, Gregor. *Breslau: Die fremde Stadt*. Berlin: Siedler, 2003.

———. "Ethnic Cleansing in Eastern Europe after 1945." *Contemporary European History* 19, no. 1 (February 2010): 75–81.

Tilse, Mark. *Transnationalism in the Prussian East: From National Conflict to Synthesis, 1871–1914*. New York: Palgrave McMillan, 2011.

Tomala, Mieczysław. *Patrząc na Niemcy: Od wrogości do porozumienia*. Warsaw: Polska Fundacja Spraw Międzynarodowych, 1997.

———. *Deutschland, von Polen gesehen: zu den deutsch-polnischen Beziehungen, 1945–1990*. Marburg: Schüren Verlag GmbH, 2000.

Traba, Robert. *Przeszłość w teraźniejszości: Polskie spory o historię na początku XXI wieku*. Poznań: Wydawnictwo Poznańskie, 2009.

———. "'Region,' 'Regionalismus,' 'Identität' und 'Identifikation' Bemerkungen zur Begrifflichkeit und ihrer Wissenschaftlichen Rezeption nach 1989." In *Region, Staat, Europa: Regionale Identitäten unter den Bedingungen von Diktatur und Demokratie in Mittel- und Osteuropa*, edited by Matthias Weber and Burkhard Olschowsky, 33–42. Munich: Oldenburg Verlag, 2014.

———. *The Past in the Present: The Construction of Polish History*. Translated by Alex Shannon. Munich: Peter Lang, 2015.

Turowicz, Jerzy. "Przedmowa." In *Polacy i Niemcy pół wieku później: Księga pamiątkowa dla Mieczysława Pszona*, edited by edited by Wojciech Pięciak. Cracow: Wydawnictwo Znak, 1996.

Turowski, Konstanty. *"Odrodzenie": Historia Stowarzyszenia Katolickiej Młodziezy Akademickiej*. Warsaw: Ośrodek Dokumentacji i Studiów Społecznych, 1987.

Tych, Feliks. "The 'March '68' Antisemitic Campaign: Onset, Development, and Consequences." In *Jewish Presence in Absence: The Aftermath of the Holocaust in Poland 1944-2010*, edited by Feliks Tych and Monika Adamczyk-Garbowska, translated by Grzegorz Dąbowski and Jessica Taylor-Kucia, 451–72. Jerusalem: Yad Vashem, 2014.

Tyszkiewicz, Barbara. "Naiwny i heroiczyny: Jerzy Zawieyski jako mediator między kardynałem Wyszyńskim a Władysławem Gomułką." *Zeszyty Historyczne* 156 (2006), 40–102.

Urban, Thomas. *Der Verlust: Die Vertreibung der Deutschen und Polen im 20. Jahrhundert*. Munich: Verlag C.H. Beck, 2004.

Urbanek, Mariusz. *Kisiel (A to Polska właśnie)*. Wrocław: Wydawnictwo Dolnośląskie, 1997.

Uricchio, William. "Television as History: Representations of German Television Broadcasting, 1935–1944." In *Framing the Past: The Historiography of German Cinema and Television*, edited by Bruce A. Murray and Christopher J. Wickham, 167–96. Carbondale: Southern Illinois University Press, 1992.

Vedby Rasmussen, Mikkel. *The West, Civil Society and the Construction of Peace*. New York: Palgrave McMillan, 2003.

Vogel, Meike. "Der 2. Juni 1967 als Kommunikationsereignis: Fernsehen zwischen Medienritualen und Zeitkritik." In *Medialisierung und Demokratie*, edited by Frank Bösch and Norbert Frei, 207–242. Göttingen: Wallstein Verlag, 2006.

von Arnim, Tim. *"Und dann werde ich das grösste Zeitungshaus Europas bauen": Der Unternehmer Axel Springer*. Frankfurt/Main: Campus, 2012.

Von Weizsäcker, Richard. "Rede beim Staatsbesuch des Präsidenten der Republik Polen am 30.3.1992." In *Feinde werden Freunde: Von den Schwierigkeiten der deutsch-polnischen Nachbarschaft*, edited by Friedbert Pflüger and Winfried Lipscher, 289–93. Bonn: Bouvier, 1993.

Walicki, Andrzej. "The Three Traditions in Polish Patriotism." In *Polish Paradoxes*, edited by Stanisław Gomułka and Antony Polonsky, 21–32. New York: Routledge, 1990.

Wawrzyniak, Joanna. *Veterans, Victims, and Memory: The Politics of the Second World War in Communist Poland*. Translated Simon Lewis. Frankfurt/Main: Peter Lang, 2015.

Weber, Matthias. "Germans in Eastern Europe as a Polish-German Lieux de Mémoire." In *Memory and Change in Europe: Eastern Perspectives*, edited by Małgorzata Pakier and Joanna Wawrzyniak, 264–82. New York: Berghahn Books, 2016.

Weber, Matthias, and Burkhard Olschowsky. "Einführung: Regionen des östlichen Europas im 20. Jahrhundert als Thema des Europäischen Netzwerks Erinnerung und Solidarität." In *Region, Staat, Europa: Regionale Identitäten unter den Bedingungen von Diktatur und Demokratie in Mittel- und Osteuropa*, edited by Matthias Weber and Burkhard Olschowsky, 9–32. Munich: Oldenburg Verlag, 2014.

Weber, Pierre Frédéric. "Das 'Weimarer Dreieck' Vom Gründungsoptimismus zur neuen Sinnsuche." In *Erwachsene Nachbarschaft: Die deutsch-polnische Beziehungen 1991 bis 2011*, edited by Dieter Bingen, Peter Oliver Loew, Krzysztof Ruchniewicz, and Marek Zybura, 77–91. Wiesbaden: Harrassowitz Verlag, 2011.

Weigel, George. *The Final Revolution: The Resistance Church and the Collapse of Communism*. New York: Oxford University Press, 2012.

Weiss, Konrad. "Ojczyzna—Polska, ojczyzna—Niemcy, ojczyzna—Europa." In *Polacy i Niemcy pół wieku później: Księga pamiątkowa dla Mieczysława Pszona*, edited by Wojciech Pięciak. Cracow: Wydawnictwo Znak, 1996.

———. *Lothar Kreyssig: Prophet der Versöhnung*. Gerlingen: Bleicher Verlag, 1998.

———. "'Polen hatte eine Vorbildfunktion. Gespräch mit Konrad Weiss." In *Wir vergeben und bitten um Vergebung: Der Briefwechsel der polnischen und deutschen Bischöfe von 1965*, edited by Basil Kerski, Thomas Kycia, and Robert Żurek. Osnabrück: Fibre, 2006.

Weiss, Mathias. "Öffentlichkeit als Therapie: Die Medien und Informationspolitik der Regierung Adenauer zwischen Propaganda und kritischer Aufklärung." In *Medialisierung und Demokratie im 20. Jahrhundert*, edited by Frank Bösch and Norbert Frei, 73–120. Göttingen: Wallstein, 2006.

Werblan, Andrzej. "The Polish October of 1956—Legends and Reality." In *The Polish October 1956 in World Politics*, edited by Jan Rowiński, 13–42. Warsaw: Polski Instytut Spraw Międzynarodowych, 2007.

Werner, Michael, and Bénédicte Zimmerman. "Beyond Comparison: Histoire Croisée and the Challenge of Reflexivity." *History and Theory* 45 (2006): 30–50.
Wilke, Jürgen, ed. *Mediengeschichte der Bundesrepublik Deutschland*. Cologne, Weimar, Vienna: Böhlau Verlag, 1999.
Wilke, Jürgen. "Leitmedien und Zielgruppenorgane." In *Mediengeschichte der Bundesrepublik Deutschland*, edited by Jürgen Wilke, 302–29. Cologne, Weimar, Vienna: Böhlau, 1999.
Wojdon, Joanna, and Jakub Tyszkiewicz. "The Image of Tadeusz Kościuszko in Postwar Polish Education." *Polish Review* 59, no. 3 (2014): 81–94.
Wolff, Stefan. *Disputed Territories: The Transnational Dynamics of Ethnic Conflict Settlement*. New York: Berghahn Books, 2003.
Wolff-Powęska, Anna. "Poszukiwanie dróg dialogu: Świeckie elity katolickie wobec Niemiec." In *Polacy wobec Niemców: Z dziejów kultury politycznej Polski 1945–1989*, edited by Anna Wolff-Powęska, 365–394. Poznań: Instytut Zachodni, 1993.
———, ed. *Polacy wobec Niemców: Z dziejów kultury politycznej Polski 1945–1989*. Poznań: Instytut Zachodni, 1993.
———. "Zur Aktualität von Dialog und Versöhnung im polnisch-deutschen Verhältnis." In *Versöhnung und Politik: Polnisch-deutsche Versöhnungsinitiativen der 1960er-Jahre und die Entspannungspolitik*, edited by Friedhelm Böll, Wiesław Wysocki, and Klaus Ziemer, 388–402. Bonn: Dietz, 2009.
Wolff-Powęska, Anna, and Dieter Bingen, eds. *Nachbarn auf Distanz: Polen und Deutsche 1998-2004*. Wiesbaden: Harrassowitz, 2005.
Wolffsohn, Thomas, and Michael Brechenmacher. *Denkmalssturz? Brandts Kniefall*. Munich: Olzog Verlag GmbH, 2005.
Wóycicka, Zofia. *Arrested Mourning: Memory of the Nazi Camps in Poland 1944–1950*. Translated by Jasper Tilbury. Frankfurt/ Main: Peter Lang, 2013.
Wulf, René. *The Undivided Sky: The Holocaust on East and West German Radio in the 1960s*. London: Palgrave McMillan, 2010.
Wyszyński, Stefan. "Fragmenty kazania wygłoszonego w Warszawie w kościele Najczystszego Serca Marii 19 grudnia 1965 r. dotyczące 'Orędzia' biskupów polskich do biskupów niemieckich." In *Orędzie biskupów polskich do biskupów niemieckich: Materiały i dokumenty*. Warsaw: Wydawnictwo Polonia, 1966.
Zahra, Tara. *Kidnapped Souls: National Indifference and the Battle for Difference in a Bohemian Borderland, 1900–1948*. Ithaca, NY: Cornell University Press, 2008.
Żakowski, Jacek. *Pół wieku pod włos czyli życie codzienne "TYGODNIKA POWSZECHNEGO" w czasach heroicznych*. Cracow: Społeczny Instytut Wydawniczy ZNAK, 1999.
Zaremba, Marcin. *Komunizm, legitymizacja, nacjonalizm: nacjonalistyczna legitymizacja władzy komunistycznej w Polsce*. Warsaw: Wyd. Trio, 2001.
———. "The 'War Syndrome': World War II and Polish Society." In *Seeking Peace in the Wake of War: Europe 1943–1947*, edited by Stefan-Ludwig Hoffman, Sandrine Kott, Peter Romijn, and Olivier Wievorka, 27–62. Amsterdam: Amsterdam University Press, 2015.
Zelizer, Barbie. *Visual Culture and the Holocaust*. New Brunswick, NJ: Rutgers University Press, 2001.

Ziemann, Benjamin. "Öffentlichkeit in der Kirche: Medien und Partizipation in der Katholische Kirche der Bundesrepublik, 1963–1972." In *Medialisierung und Demokratie im 20.Jahrhundert*, edited by Frank Bösch and Norbert Frei, 179–206. Göttingen: Wallstein Verlag, 2007.

Ziemer, Klaus. "Kirche." In *Deutsche und Polen*, edited by Andreas Lawaty and Hubert Orłowski. Munich: Verlag C.H. Beck, 2003.

Zimmerman, Peter. "Vergangenheitsbewältigung: Das 'Dritte Reich' in Dokumentarfilmen und Fernsehdokumentation der BRD." In *Der geteilte Himmel: Arbeit, Alltag und Geschichte im ost- und westdeutschen Film*, edited by Peter Zimmerman and Gebhard Moldenhauer, 57–75. Konstanz: UVK Medien, 2000.

Zitzewitz, Hasso von. *Das deutsche Polenbild in der Geschichte: Entstehung—Einflusse—Auswirkungen*. Cologne, Weimar, Vienna: Böhlau Verlag, 1991.

Żurek, Robert. *Zwischen Nationalismus und Versöhnung: Die Kirchen und die deutsch-polnischen Beziehungen 1945–1956*. Cologne: Böhlau, 2005.

Index

Adenauer, Konrad, 25, 29, 33, 43, 44, 54, 60, 66, 70, 82, 87, 123, 107, 108
Adenauer era, 44, 119, 127n83, 131
Aktion Sühnezeichen, 3, 10, 14, 129, 162, 163, 167, 184, 185, 189, 194
Andrzejewski, Jerzy, 98, 106n84
Ansprenger, Franz, 66
Anticommunism, 43, 95, 69
Anti-Semitism, 14, 33, 50n58, 113, 154, 155, 157, 158, 159, 169, 191, 192. *See also* anti-Zionism
Anti-Zionism, 17, 154, 155, 157, 169, 173
Anti-Zionist purge of 1968, 17, 147, 156, 157, 158, 162, 168, 173, 191, 192, 203
Apologies (conflict resolution), 4, 166, 181
Arbeitsgemeinschaft der öffentlich-rechtlichen Rundfunkanstalten der Bundesrepublik Deutschland (ARD), 86, 88, 103n27, 108, 132, 167
ARD (television channel), 108
Auschwitz, 93, 96, 97, 189, 191, 199. *See also* Second Auschwitz trials

Bahr, Egon, 157, 175n16, 200n69
Bartoszewski, Władysław, 10, 33, 84, 162, 182, 183, 185, 186, 187, 190, 197n31
    and imprisonment, 182
    and Jewish–Polish relations, 190, 197n31
    and post-communism, 185, 186, 187
    and Solidarity, 182
    and war years, 84, 162

Barzel, Rainer, 94, 188
Becker, Hellmut, 130
Beckmann, Joachim, 130
Beitz, Berthold, 45, 46, 93, 103n30, 165
Bensberger Circle, 10, 11, 14, 26, 144, 145, 147, 162, 163, 167, 182, 185, 186, 188, 191, 194
Bensberger Memorandum, 11, 29, 144, 145, 146, 147, 148, 162, 163, 180, 191
Berlin Wall, 111, 123, 130, 132
Besson, Waldemar, 92, 93, 104n51
Bierut, Bolesław, 35, 36
Bilateral Agreements (1970), 162, 167, 161, 164, 165, 166, 191
Bismarck, Klaus von, 10, 11, 14, 15, 25, 26, 28, 30, 31, 82, 83, 84, 85, 86, 87, 88, 89, 92, 93, 94, 97, 98, 100, 118, 121, 122, 130, 132, 133, 159, 165, 166, 167
    and expulsions, 28, 30, 180
    and French–German relations, 30
    and Ostpolitik, 159, 165, 166, 167
    and Poland trips 1964 and 1965, 88, 89, 90, 92, 93, 94, 95, 97, 98
    and the Second World War, 25, 26
    and Stefan Kisielewski, 82, 84, 85
    and Tübingen Memorandum, 130, 132, 133
    and WDR, 31, 83, 84, 85, 86, 87, 99, 118
    youth and childhood, 10, 11, 14, 25, 26
Bismarck, Otto von, 10, 138
Bismarck, Philipp von, 15
Bismarck, Ruth-Alice von, 91, 94

Bonn, 45, 60, 65, 66, 70, 71, 90, 120, 130, 131, 133, 146, 157, 164, 169, 175n16, 194, 206
Borderlands, 6, 10, 11, 38, 70, 75, 87, 99, 99, 111, 114, 118, 136, 137, 145, 147, 167, 183, 189, 190, 191, 195, 204. *See also* Breslau; Gdańsk; Masuria; Prussia; Silesia; Vilnius; Wrocław
  eastern borderlands, 190, 191
  Polish-Lithuanian borderlands, 11, 38, 70, 75, 87, 99
Borowski, Tadeusz, 98, 106n84
Botta, Paul, 66, 71, 73, 84, 100
Brandt, Willy, 123, 127n83, 132, 154, 155, 156, 159, 160, 161, 164, 165, 166, 167, 168, 169, 170, 171, 173, 187, 188, 190, 197n29, 202
Breckhoff, Olrik, 167
Brentano, Heinrich von, 65, 79n55
Breslau, 11, 27, 31, 86, 87, 107, 111, 112, 113, 114, 115, 116, 117, 143. *See also* Wrocław
British Broadcasting Corporation (BBC), 84, 86, 102n18

Cappella Coloniensis, 97, 98, 105n80
Catholic Journalists' Association conference 1958 (Vienna), 63, 64, 79n50
Catholic News Agency (KNA), 65, 201
Center Against Expulsions, 201
Central Committee of Catholics (West Germany), 65, 164, 185
Choromański, Zygmunt, 141
Christian Democratic Union (CDU), 42, 46, 54, 59, 65, 82, 115, 123, 132, 171, 180, 184, 187, 188
Civil society, 1, 2, 4, 7, 8, 14, 17, 37, 42, 47, 82, 92, 93, 129, 139, 195, 202, 205, 206
Cologne, 10, 12, 25, 67, 83, 97, 98, 113, 115, 144
Conflict resolution, 1, 4, 7, 166, 174, 206. *See also* reconciliation
Consensus journalism, 33, 85
Cracow, 10, 13, 33, 34, 35, 38, 57, 61, 63, 64, 84, 97, 89, 90, 92, 94, 96, 103, 138, 139, 172, 180, 181
Czech invasion (1968), 154, 156, 159, 161, 162, 203. *See also* Prague Spring

Das Dritte Reich (documentary), 92, 93, 121, 122, 204
Deutsche National-Zeitung, 113, 117
Deutsche Ostdienst (DOD), 113, 119
Deutsche Presse-Agentur (DPA), 55, 62, 72, 131, 147
Deutschlands Osten-Polens Westen? (documentary), 118, 119, 120, 121, 137
Dirks, Walter, 14, 28, 29, 30, 32, 66, 100, 136, 138, 139, 143, 144, 145, 146, 182
  and Bensberger Memorandum, 144, 145, 146
  and Bismarck, Klaus v., 30
  and French–German relations, 30
  youth and childhood, 14
  and Zimmerer, Ludwig, 32
Division of Germany, 3, 29, 32, 40, 43, 70, 96, 101, 145
Dmowski, Roman, 13, 37, 50n64, 174n3
Dokumente, 31, 66, 84
Dönhoff, Marion, 10, 11, 14, 28, 32, 55, 73, 93, 131, 165, 182
  and expulsions, 28, 32, 165
  youth and childhood, 10, 11, 14
Döpfner, Julius, 139, 142, 144, 146, 164
Drang nach Osten, 67
Drück, Helmut, 83
Dubček, Alexander, 154
Dziś i jutro, 36

East Berlin, 39, 59, 156
Endecja, 13, 14, 50n64. *See also* Dmowski, Roman
Erb, Gottfried, 144, 146, 153n83, 182
Erhard, Ludwig, 82, 87, 123
Erler, Fritz, 115
Estreicher, Karol, 94, 104n57
Ethnic cleansing, 35, 27, 168, 188. *See also* expulsions; removals; population transfers
EU expansion/enlargement, 5, 183, 207
European integration, 5, 17, 183, 184, 185, 187, 189, 195
European Union (EU), 183, 184, 186, 187, 197n27, 202, 207
Europeanization, 179
Expellees, 28, 29, 30, 32, 34, 63, 91, 92, 93, 110, 111, 112, 114, 115, 116, 117, 119, 120, 123, 124, 131, 133, 134, 135,

140, 147, 164, 174, 183, 188, 195 201, 204
   and Bensberger Memorandum, 147
   as participants in Polish–German relations, 28, 29, 34, 91, 92, 93, 183, 188, 195
   in politics and media, 29, 30, 32, 63, 110, 114, 115, 116, 117, 119, 120, 123, 134
   portrayed by the media, 32, 111, 112, 114, 115, 117
   and Protestant Expellee Memorandum, 134, 135
   and Tübingen Memorandum, 131, 133
Expulsions, 43, 68, 69, 75, 112, 134, 188

Fiedler, Rudolf, 85
Forced friendship with GDR, 185, 193
Die Frankfurter Allgemeine Zeitung (FAZ), 10, 29, 32, 42, 55, 56, 57, 62, 72, 112, 131, 142, 156, 188
Frankfurter Hefte, 29, 31, 32, 66, 84, 139, 153n83, 172, 182
Frankfurter Rundschau, 119, 131, 139, 140
Frankowski, Jan, 36, 81n90
Frederick the Great, 138
Free Democratic Party (FDP), 123, 132, 160, 171, 173
French–German relations, 30, 31, 84, 154, 181

Gdańsk, 44, 118, 166, 181
Gembardt, Ulrich, 73, 83, 95, 169
German Catholic bishops' response to the Polish bishops (1966), 129, 139, 140, 143
German Democratic Republic (GDR), 29, 32, 59, 60, 96, 117, 134, 154, 161, 189, 193
German Empire, 8, 9
German invasion of Poland (1939), 9, 25, 33, 53, 118, 170
Gierek, Edward, 166, 168, 181
Glaube und Vernunft, 31
Gomułka, Władysław, 9, 10, 17, 34, 36, 37, 41, 42, 43, 45, 46, 52n107, 54, 57, 58, 60, 63, 64, 90, 137, 138, 143, 154, 155, 157, 158, 160, 161, 162, 165, 166, 168, 169, 172, 173, 205
Grass, Günther, 165

Great Coalition/Grand Coalition, 123, 154
Guillame, Günter, 180

Hallstein Doctrine, 43, 45, 46, 54
Hartmann, Hans, 82, 84
Hasselblatt, Sven, 55
Heisenberg, Werner, 130
Hengsbach, Franz, 139, 140
Hennelowa, Józefa, 34, 128
Hessischer Rundfunk, 83, 108, 119
Hitler, Adolf, 9, 27, 40, 68, 69, 99, 107, 115, 118, 122, 138
Hlond, August, 35
Holocaust, 9, 25, 33, 75, 98, 122, 181, 191
Höss, Werner, 119
Hotel Bristol, 53, 55, 56
Howe, Günther, 130
Huber, Heinz, 92

Israel and Poland, 155, 158, 160, 190

Jaksch, Wenzel, 119
Jarchlino/Jarchlin, 91
Jaruzelski, Wojciech, 182
Jasna Góra, 142, 148
Jewish culture, 110, 168, 172, 190, 191
Jewish memory, 9, 69, 97, 165, 166, 189, 190, 191
Jewish minority in Poland, 2, 3, 4, 6
John Paul II, Pope, 10, 128, 138, 149n2, 180, 181. *See also* Wojtyła, Karol

Kamińska, Ida, 168
Kammer für öffentliche Verantwortung (EKD), 134
Kerneck, Heinz, 86, 87, 88, 89
Khrushchev, Nikita, 36, 54
Kiesinger, Kurt Georg, 123, 156
Kisielewski, Lidia, 90
Kisielewski, Stefan, 10, 11, 13, 33, 37, 38, 41, 59, 61, 67, 68, 69, 70, 71, 72, 73, 74, 76, 86, 90, 103n41, 160, 161
   and neopositivism, 41
   and Stehle, Hansjakob, 59, 61
   and West Germany, 67, 68, 69, 70, 71, 72, 73, 74
   youth and childhood, 13, 33
   and the Znak Circle, 37, 38, 41
Kliszko, Zenon, 157

Klub Inteligencji Katolickiej (KIK), 35, 37, 64, 162, 193
Kneefall, Willy Brandt (1970), 165, 166, 177n68
Kogon, Eugen, 29, 48n21, 66, 100, 108, 144, 146, 182
Kohl, Helmut, 15, 180, 182
Kołakowski, Leszek, 155
Kominek, Bolesław, 10, 11, 136, 137, 138, 139, 141, 142, 143, 148, 163, 164, 204, 205
Kommunistische Partei Deutschlands (KPD), 95
Koppe, Karlheinz, 26, 28, 31, 45, 144, 162, 163, 180, 188, 189
  and Bensberger Circle, 163
  and Wrocław, 188, 189
  youth and childhood, 28, 31
KOR (Workers' Defense Committee), 181
Kościuszko, Tadeusz, 38, 50
Kowalikowa, Janina, 88
Krasicki, Ignacy, 138
Kreyssig, Lothar, 167, 198. *See also* Aktion Sühnezeichen
Kultura, 10

Landsmannschaft Schlesien, 131, 113
Landsmannschaften, 29, 112, 113, 114, 120
Leber, Georg, 164
Lehmann, Reinhold, 190
Lenz, Siegfried, 165
License era, 28, 29
Linnerz, Heinz, 66
Lipscher, Winfried, 11, 162, 163, 180, 185
Lithuania, 1, 9, 11, 33, 34, 100, 190, 191, 192
Lithuanian Poles, 11
"Little Stabilization," 46, 52n107, 54, 157
Lübke, Heinrich, 94

Mansfeld, Michael, 27
Markiewicz, Władysław, 194
Marsch-Potocka, Renate, 55, 62, 74, 81n102, 180
Martial law in Poland (1981), 182
Masuria, 11, 43, 44
Mazowiecki, Tadeusz, 10, 14, 37, 90, 182, 185, 187, 189, 194
  and PAX, 14
Mende, Erich, 94

Meyers, Franz, 95
Michnik, Adam, 141, 155, 171, 173, 174
Miłosz, Czesław, 99, 100, 199n55
Moczar, Mieczysław, 157, 158
Molotov-Ribbentrop Pact, 145, 161
Morawska, Anna, 172, 173, 176n42, 180
Morawski, Dominik, 90
Mortkowicz-Olczakowa, Hanna, 61, 78n39, 89
Mrożek, Sławomir, 62, 98
Mueller-Graaf, Carl Hermann, 64
Müller, Bastian, 99
Mumm von Schwarzenstein, Bernd, 89, 103n30
Munich, 12, 27, 62, 73, 180, 208n9

Nacken, Angela, 55, 62, 169, 170, 180, 208n9
Nannen, Henri, 10, 55, 165
Nationalism, 7, 13, 14, 50n58, 50n64, 67, 99, 100, 115, 136
  ethnic nationalism, 13, 14, 188
Nazi era, 14, 15, 67, 92, 104n45. *See also* Third Reich
Nazi Germany, 9, 15, 29
Neopositivism, 38, 41, 43, 59, 75, 173, 203
Neue Zeitung, 83
Neven-du Mont, Carl August, 12, 27, 28
Neven-du Mont, Christian, 27, 62
Neven-du Mont, Elisabeth, 26
Neven-du Mont, Jürgen, 12, 24, 25, 26, 27, 28, 32, 61, 62, 63, 87, 88, 89, 107, 108, 109, 111, 112, 113, 114, 115, 116, 117, 143, 181, 188
  and Bismarck, Klaus v., 88, 89
  and documentaries, 63, 87, 88, 107, 108, 109, 110–115
  and Poland, 62
  and Polish Catholic bishops' letter, 143
  youth and childhood, 12, 24, 25, 26, 27, 28
  and Zimmerer, Ludwig, 61, 62, 89
"New Germans," 66, 75
"New Left," 141, 155, 174n8
Norddeutscher Rundfunk (NDR), 10, 42, 55, 61, 62, 66, 83, 84, 87, 108, 111, 116
North Atlantic Treaty Organization (NATO), 17, 130, 183, 184

Oder-Neisse Line, 9, 16, 28, 29, 65, 69, 79n58, 85, 87, 92, 123, 132, 133, 136, 139, 140, 142, 154, 162, 164, 171, 189, 192, 193, 204
Odrodzenie, 12, 13, 24
Olczak-Ronikier, Joanna, 61, 182
Operation Barbarossa, 25
Ost West Gemeinschafts-Redaktion (WDR/NDR), 83, 85, 117
Ostkirchenausschuss der EKD, 133, 135
Ostpolitik, 2, 6, 16, 17, 78n35, 82, 84, 155, 156, 157, 158, 159, 160, 162, 166, 167, 168, 169, 170, 171, 173, 180, 182, 201, 202, 203

Panorama, 108, 112, 124n7
Paul VI, Pope, 145
Pax Christi, 145, 144, 153n83, 182
PAX Movement (Polish), 14, 36, 42, 43, 50n58, 56, 72, 81n90, 162, 163, 172, 182, 186
Peace, 1, 2, 3, 4, 5, 6, 7, 8, 14, 15, 29, 30, 40, 41, 42, 43, 45, 46, 60, 70, 72, 75, 76, 110, 134, 136, 143, 144, 159, 162, 164, 167, 181, 188, 202, 204, 207
    and GDR, 3
    and Ostpolitik, 159, 162, 164, 167
    peace treaties, 2, 6, 29, 164, 165, 179
    and religious memoranda, 134, 136, 143, 144
Pflüger, Friedbert, 184
Piasecki, Bolesław, 14, 49, 50, 36, 42, 49n58, 56, 162. *See also* PAX Movement
Picht, Georg, 130
Pieniężna, Wanda, 37
Piłsuski, Józef, 9, 13, 37, 50n64
Piwowarczyk, Jan, 34
Podkowiński, Marian, 80n72, 133
Polak-Katolik, 13, 139, 204
Poland weeks, 86, 87, 97, 98
Polen in Breslau (documentary), 86, 107, 111, 112, 113, 116, 117, 118
Polish Catholic Bishops' letter of reconciliation to the German Catholic Bishops (1965), 16, 19, 128, 129, 135, 140, 142, 143, 145, 146, 147, 148, 184, 185, 186, 203, 204, 205
Polish Novena, 128, 142

Polish October, 16, 25, 36, 41, 42, 43, 44, 45, 46, 54, 63, 64, 75, 86, 121, 155
Polish People's Party (PPR), 9, 10, 34, 35, 36, 38, 39, 58, 64, 90, 97, 111, 140, 154, 155, 156, 157, 158, 159, 160, 173, 181, 188, 191, 192
Polnische Wirtschaft, 58, 63, 75
Polskie Radio i Telewizja, 42, 86, 88, 89, 99, 100
Pomerania, 11, 15, 30, 45, 88, 91
population transfers, 69, 188
Potsdam Conference, 27, 188
Poznań, 34, 36, 42, 64, 97
Prague Spring, 17, 147, 154, 155, 156, 159
Preussische Treuhand, 201, 202
Proske, Rüdiger, 108
Protestant Expellee Memorandum (1965), 10, 16, 129, 134, 135, 136, 138, 139, 140, 143, 163
Prussia, 9, 11, 28, 138, 145
Pszon, Mieczysław, 10, 14, 33, 185, 190, 191, 199n53

Radio Bremen, 88
Radio Free Europe (RFE), 56, 84, 109, 121, 125, 160
Radio in the American Sector (RIAS), 84
Raiser, Ludwig, 130, 134
Rakowski, Mieczysław, 61, 80n72, 188, 198
Rapacki, Adam, 45, 155
Rapacki Plan, 45, 46, 54, 59, 109
Rapprochement, 95, 121, 171, 191
Recht auf Heimat, 29, 30, 133
Reconciliation, 1, 2, 3, 4, 5, 6, 7, 8, 10, 12, 16, 17, 30, 46, 71, 75, 83, 128, 129, 135, 139, 143, 144, 145, 146, 147, 148, 154, 155, 160, 161, 162, 163, 165, 171, 172, 173, 174, 178n95, 179, 183, 184, 185, 186, 188, 189, 191, 192, 193, 194, 195, 201, 202, 203, 205, 206, 207
    in the 1990s, 17, 179, 183, 184, 185, 186, 187, 188, 189, 193, 194
    definition and scholarship, 1–8
    and memory, 194, 195
    and Ostpolitik, 155, 160–165, 171, 172, 173, 174, 181, 203, 206, 207
    reconciliation kitsch, 179, 201
    and religious memoranda, 128, 129, 143–148, 185–186, 191, 192
    truth-telling, 195

Reich-Ranicki, Marcel, 62, 78n46, 191, 199n55
removals, 27, 168
Rheinischer Merkur, 41, 44, 56, 59, 117, 135, 149
Riedel, Clemens, 115
Rome, 12, 36, 126n54, 137, 138, 139, 141, 164, 180
Ruge, Gerd, 92, 104n46, 127n80
Rühle, Jürgen, 102n3, 117
Russian Empire, 8, 9, 38, 50n68

Sanacja, 9
Sapieha, Adam, 35
Schellhaus, Erich, 113
Der Schlesier, 113
Schmid, Carlo, 193
Schmidt, Helmut, 175n15, 180
Schröder, Gerhard (minister, CDU), 94, 103n30
Schröder, Gerhard (television executive), 89, 90, 116
Second Auschwitz trials (1963), 96
Second Vatican Council (1962–1965), 12, 130, 141, 145, 152n52
Seidler, Manfred, 144, 153n83, 167, 194
Sejm, 4, 9, 54, 57, 64, 65
Sender Freies Berlin, 83, 117, 154, 169
Silesia, 9, 11, 27, 31, 110, 112, 113, 114, 115, 117, 120, 136
Sind wir Revanchisten? (documentary), 111, 112, 113, 114, 115, 116, 117, 119
"The Situation of the Expellees and the Relations of the German People to Its Eastern Neighbor," 134
Skeptical generation, 15, 23
Skibowski, Klaus Otto, 25, 26, 28, 43, 44, 45, 53, 63, 65, 188, 197n31, 199n69
  and Stomma, Stanisław, 44, 45, 53, 63, 65
  youth and chldhood, 25, 26, 28, 188
Słowo Powszechne, 36, 121, 162
Social Democratic Party of Germany (SPD), 82, 115, 119, 123, 132, 154, 157, 160, 164, 171, 173, 182, 193
Solidarity/Solidarność, 181, 182
Soviet Union, 9, 13, 25, 27, 29, 32, 33, 34, 36, 38, 39, 40, 41, 42, 45, 54, 58, 70, 71, 72, 85, 100, 108, 132, 139, 142, 145, 147, 155, 156, 157, 161, 162, 169, 181, 190, 102, 201, 202, 205
The Soviet Zone, 27, 31, 32, 85, 101, 194
Der Spiegel, 10, 36, 42, 55, 87, 113, 117
Spiegel Affair, 87, 113, 117
Stability, 6–8, 16–17, 75, 135, 168, 174
  and Cold War order, 40
  and consensus journalism, 33
  and multiculturalism, 37, 69, 110
"Stability before liberty," 168
Stehle, Hansjakob, 12, 26, 29, 32, 42, 44, 45, 55, 56, 57, 58, 59, 60, 62, 63, 71, 72, 73, 74, 77n11, 79, 86, 94, 95, 96, 109, 118, 119, 120, 126n54, 136, 137, 138, 139, 142, 143, 149, 157, 158, 164, 168, 169, 180, 191
  career, 29, 32, 42, 118, 126n54
  and Gomułka, Władysław, 58, 157, 158, 168
  and Poland, 42, 44, 45, 55, 56, 57, 58, 60, 62, 63, 72, 77n11, 169, 191
  and Polish Catholic Church, 59, 136, 137, 138, 139, 142, 143, 149, 164
  and radio, 94–96
  and television, 109, 118, 119, 120, 180
  war experience, 26
  youth and childhood, 12
  and Znak Circle, 59, 73, 74, 86
Steinbach, Erika, 201, 202
Steinmayr, Jochen, 55
Stern, 10, 55, 118, 165
Stern-TV, 120
Stomma, Elwira (Ela), 34, 65, 90
Stomma, Stanisław, 1, 8, 11, 12, 13, 33, 34, 35, 36, 37, 38, 39, 40, 41, 43, 44, 57, 59, 60, 61, 64, 65, 66, 70, 72, 73, 90, 160, 162, 163, 166, 167, 182, 183, 185, 186, 192, 193, 194, 205, 207
  and Bensberger Circle, 163
  and Bismarck, Klaus v., 90
  and East Germans, 193, 194
  and Ostpolitik, 162, 166, 167
  and Polish Catholic bishops' letter, 185, 186
  and Polish politics, 181, 183, 185, 207
  and Polish Purge (1968), 160, 191, 192
  and *Tygodnik Powszechny*, 35

and West Germany, 40, 43, 44, 57, 64, 65, 66, 72, 163
youth and childhood, 8, 11, 12, 13, 33, 34, 192, 193
and Zimmerer, Ludwig, 61, 73
and Znak Circle, 37, 38, 39
Stoph, Willi, 161
Strauss, Franz Josef, 87
Süddeutsche Zeitung, 55, 131, 150, 165
Süddeutscher Rundfunk, 92, 99, 132, 169
Südwestfunk, 98, 122
Süssmuth, Rita, 184
Szymborska, Wisława, 201

Der Tag, 31, 42
Tern, Jürgen, 156
Third Reich, 9, 15, 25, 66, 122, 159, 172. *See also* Nazi era
Times, 62, 133
Tito, Josip Broz, 42
Transnationalism, 2, 6, 7, 8, 17, 46, 202
Treaty of Good Neighbourship and Friendly Cooperation (1990), 2, 4, 5, 6, 29, 207
Trybuna Ludu, 61, 117, 121, 133
Tübingen Memorandum, 70, 86, 93, 129, 130, 131, 132, 133, 134, 140, 146, 192
Turowicz, Anna, 13
Turowicz, Jerzy, 10, 11, 12, 33, 34, 37, 41, 61, 84, 92, 141, 162, 190
    and Bismarck, Klaus v., 92
    and Botta, Paul, 84
    interwar era and war, 33, 34
    and Jewish memory, 190
    and peace, 41
    and Polish Catholic bishops' letter, 141
    and purge, 162
    youth and childhood, 10, 11, 12
    and Zimmerer, Ludwig, 61
    and Znak Circle, 37
Two Plus Four Agreement of 1990, 2
Tygodnik Powszechny, 9, 10, 11, 12, 14, 34, 35, 36, 37, 40, 43, 44, 49n55, 54, 64, 66, 67, 70, 71, 72, 128, 136, 163, 166, 172, 190, 193, 207
Tygodnik Warszawski, 35
Tyrmand, Leopold, 66, 67, 80n69

Ukraine, 6, 9, 25, 110, 168, 188, 191, 199n57
Ulbricht, Walter, 70, 156, 161

Vatican II, 130, 141. *See also* Second Vatican Council
Vergangenheitsbewältigung, 57, 76, 82, 121, 204
Versailles Treaty, 9, 13
Vienna, 11, 63, 64, 65, 118, 157, 183
Vilnius (Wilno, Wilna), 9, 11, 13, 33, 34, 190, 192, 193
Von Hase, Karl-Günther, 116

Wałęsa, Lech, 181
Wandel durch Annäherung, 160
Warsaw, 1, 12, 19, 24, 29, 33, 34, 37, 42, 43, 44, 45, 53, 54, 55, 56, 57, 58, 59, 60, 61, 62, 63, 64, 65, 70, 74, 76, 83, 84, 88, 89, 90, 93, 94, 97, 98, 110, 111, 117, 119, 122, 124, 133, 138, 141, 155, 157, 158, 162, 164, 166, 168, 171, 180, 181, 182, 183, 186, 194, 206
Warsaw Ghetto, 166, 168
Warsaw Uprising (1944), 24, 33
Wehner, Herbert, 164
Wehrhahn, Hans, 146
Weimar Germany, 9, 14, 83
Weimar Triangle, 187, 198n41
Weiss, Konrad, 189
Weizsäcker, Carl Friedrich von, 130
Weizsäcker, Richard von, 187, 188, 195
Die Welt, 42, 55, 56, 113, 117, 135, 139, 149
West German trade mission to Warsaw, 45, 46, 88, 89, 103n30
Westdeutscher Rundfunk (WDR), 10, 66, 71, 74, 82, 83, 84, 86, 88, 92, 93, 94, 97, 98, 99, 100, 117, 118, 121, 133, 1201, 122, 130, 132, 133, 167, 169, 180
Westphalia, 26, 28
Więź, 9, 14, 35, 36, 37, 54, 72, 172
Wojna, Ryszard, 170
Wojtyła, Karol, 10, 128, 138, 141, 149, 180, 181. *See also* John Paul II, Pope
Wördemann, Franz, 84
World War, First, 1, 8, 192, 207
World War, Second, 1, 2, 6, 9, 11, 16, 17, 24, 33, 37, 44, 45, 53, 57, 58, 63, 68, 69,

72, 75, 76, 90, 92, 93, 95, 101, 121, 122, 136, 148, 154, 158, 169, 170, 194, 204
Wrocław, 10, 11, 33, 43, 45, 63, 107, 109, 110, 112, 122, 124, 136, 163, 206. *See also* Breslau
Wyszyński, Stefan, 36, 37, 38, 41, 42, 44, 53, 57, 59, 64, 136, 137, 138, 141, 142, 143, 147, 148, 158, 162, 163, 164, 186, 198n35, 204, 205

Za i przeciw, 64, 72
Zawieyski, Jerzy, 10, 11, 33, 37, 57, 59, 140, 149n2, 159, 160
    interwar era and war, 11, 33
    and Znak Circle, 37, 57, 59, 140, 149n2, 159, 160
ZBoWiD, 157
Die Zeit, 10, 28, 55, 91, 94, 112, 118, 131, 135, 136, 156, 157, 158, 166, 182, 188
Zimmerer, Ludwig, 12, 26, 31, 32, 42, 44, 55, 56, 60, 61, 62, 73, 77, 87, 88, 89, 90, 91, 92, 93, 96, 97, 98, 104n52, 158, 159, 168, 169, 170, 171, 182, 203
    and Bismarck, Klaus v., 77, 88, 89, 90, 92, 93
    and Dirks, Walter, 32
    and Ostpolitik, 168, 169, 170, 171, 182
    and the purge, 158, 159
    and Stehle, Hansjakob, 12, 56
    youth and childhood, 12, 26, 31, 32
    and the Znak Circle, 61, 73
Znak (journal), 9, 35, 36, 37, 43, 54, 72, 172, 182, 207
Znak Circle, 9, 10, 29, 37, 38, 43, 44, 54, 57, 59, 61, 64, 65, 72, 73, 74, 75, 89, 90, 92, 132, 140, 141, 146, 147, 158, 159, 160, 161, 162, 172, 173, 181, 182, 185, 191, 198n35, 203, 205, 206
Zweites Deutsches Fernsehen (ZDF), 108
Zwischen Ost und West: Polen 1961 (documentary), 56, 110, 111
Życie Warszawy, 94, 121, 140, 170, 178n56

www.ingramcontent.com/pod-product-compliance
Lightning Source LLC
Chambersburg PA
CBHW070121110526
44587CB00017BA/2879